S0-BJN-055

WITHDRAWN

WITHDRAWN

LIBERTINES AND RADICALS IN EARLY MODERN LONDON

A 'Deluge of Libertinism' swept through England in the turbulent seventeenth century: class and gender relations went into deep crisis, and sexually explicit literature took the blame. Bridging periods often kept apart, *Libertines and Radicals* analyses English sexual culture between the Civil Wars and the death of Charles II in unprecedented detail. James Grantham Turner examines a broad range of Civil War and Restoration texts, from sex-crime records to Milton's epics and Rochester's 'mannerly obscene' lyrics. Turner places special emphasis on women's writing and on pornographic texts like *The Wandring Whore* and *The Parliament of Women*, flavoured with cockney humour or 'Puritan' indignation. Throughout, Turner reads satirical texts, whether political or pornographic, as an attempt to neutralize women's efforts to establish their own institutions and their own voice. This exhaustive study will be of interest to cultural historians as well as literary scholars.

JAMES GRANTHAM TURNER is Professor of English at the University of California at Berkeley. He is the author of *The Politics of Landscape: Rural Scenery and Society in English Poetry, 1630–1660* (1979) and *One Flesh: Paradisal Marriage and Sexual Relations in the Age of Milton* (1987) and editor of *Sexuality and Gender in Early Modern Europe: Institutions, Texts, Images* (Cambridge, 1993).

LIBERTINES AND RADICALS IN EARLY MODERN LONDON

Sexuality, Politics, and Literary Culture, 1630–1685

JAMES GRANTHAM TURNER

CAMBRIDGE
UNIVERSITY PRESS

PUBLISHED BY THE PRESS SYNDICATE OF THE UNIVERSITY OF CAMBRIDGE
The Pitt Building, Trumpington Street, Cambridge, United Kingdom

CAMBRIDGE UNIVERSITY PRESS
The Edinburgh Building, Cambridge CB2 2RU, UK
40 West 20th Street, New York NY 10011-4211, USA
477 Williamstown Road, Port Melbourne, VIC 3207, Australia
Ruiz de Alarcón 13, 28014 Madrid, Spain
Dock House, The Waterfront, Cape Town 8001, South Africa

http://www.cambridge.org

© James Grantham Turner 2002

This book is in copyright. Subject to statutory exception
and to the provisions of relevant collective licensing agreements,
no reproduction of any part may take place without
the written permission of Cambridge University Press.

First published 2002

Printed in the United Kingdom at the University Press, Cambridge

Typeface Baskerville Monotype 11/12.5 pt.   *System* LaTeX 2ε   [TB]

A catalogue record for this book is available from the British Library.

Library of Congress Cataloguing in Publication data
Turner, James, 1947 –
Libertines and radicals in early modern London: sexuality, politics, and literary culture,
1630–1685 / James Grantham Turner.
p.   cm.
Includes bibliographical references and index.
ISBN 0 521 78279 1
1. English literature – Early modern, 1500–1700 – History and criticism.   2. Politics
and literature – Great Britain – History – 17th century.   3. English literature –
England – London – History and criticism.   4. Women and literature – Great Britain –
History – 17th century.   5. Libertinism – England – London – History – 17th century.
6. Radicalism – England – London – History – 17th century.   7. London (England) –
Intellectual life – 17th century.   8. Libertinism in literature.   9. Radicalism in literature.
10. Sex in literature.   I. Title.
PR438.P65 T87 2001
820.9′358 – dc21   2001025959

ISBN 0 521 78279 1 hardback

Non si può mantener superiore chi non si sa far bestia

We cannot keep ourselves superior if we don't know how to make ourselves into beasts.

(Giordano Bruno)

Contents

vii

Illustrations

viii

Preface

'POPULAR LIBERTINISM', 'LUXURIOUS CITIES', AND
THE DISCOURSE OF PROSTITUTION

For the poet and novelist Jane Barker, writing in the early 1680s, gender-relations seemed to be in deep trouble – and she lays the blame firmly on literature. Changes in fiction wreak havoc on the social fabric. The novel, promoting 'Interest and loose Gallantry', triumphs over the romance, loyal to 'Heroick Love'; modish readers dislike narratives that 'confine the Subject to such strict Rules of Virtue and Honour'. For Barker, such shifts in taste create 'an Inlet to that Deluge of Libertinism which has overflow'd the Age', with direct and disastrous consequences in 'many unhappy Marriages and unkind Separations'.[1] John Milton made the same diagnosis of modern corruption in *Paradise Lost*, pointedly contrasting the 'Wedded Love' of Paradise with 'the bought smile / Of Harlots', with 'Casual fruition', with upper-class 'Court Amours' and the riotous debauchery of the Sons of Belial (IV.775–7, I.497–502). This 'Deluge of Libertinism' – a concept at the juncture of literature and social practice – defines my own 'subject' too: the discourses and rituals that constituted illicit, transgressive sexuality in the early modern period.

'Deluge' seems an appropriate metaphor for what seemed a universal liquefaction, a dissolving or sweeping away of norms and boundaries, a chaos in which, as Barker puts it, 'Interest and loose Gallantry' replace 'Heroick Love'. In this new world moistened and loosened by libertinism, generic preferences have immediate consequences in actual behaviour: marriages collapse because romance is neglected. When the fashionable 'Sparks' and libertines of Restoration England complain about 'confining the Subject to such strict Rules' of morality, we inevitably hear a double meaning: both the literary topic and the individual are confined by romance and liberated – so the implication runs – by the new 'free' sexual discourse. Like many critics of the period I challenge the liberationist claim of libertinism, since its doctrine of sexual freedom is always complicated by the politics of class and gender. But I do take seriously the theory shared by Jane Barker and her libertine opponents: that in the troubled area of sexuality texts provoke actions, that literary effects are inextricably linked to questions of attitude and behaviour, which in turn take on the nature of an erotic artefact. Hence the subject calls for the interaction of what Barker might call books and manners, or in academic terms a synthesis of literary and social history.

The word 'libertine' in early modern Europe could denote a challenge to orthodox religion, an attempt to construct an authentic self on the basis of the passions, a loosening of family bonds and respect for maternal authority, or a deliberate celebration of what Barker called 'loose Gallantry'; these separate strands of meaning are often woven together in a single work. The Fifth Monarchist Thomas Venner, executed for armed rebellion in 1661, is labelled 'Seducer and Captain of the Libertines' (fig. 9 below). Many commentators felt that the revolutionary puritanism of the 1640s and 1650s (radical in the religious or political sense) had much in common with the libertinism of the 1660s and 1670s (radical in its social attitude and contempt for conventional morality): one 'Tunbridge lampoon', for example, laments that the 'Free conversation' made possible by the resort has been destroyed by two equal but opposite forms of extremism, 'crusht betweene / The starch't fanaticke and wild Libertine'.[2] In fiction, the 'London Jilt' traces her own 'Libertinism' to boarding school, where she learned upper-class accomplishments rather than traditional female skills, and the 'London Bully', similarly corrupted at Westminster, explains that his 'Libertine Humor' prevented him from weeping when his parents die. In studies of Restoration England 'libertinism' generally denotes the kind of sexual behaviour manifested by the Court Wits of Charles II and the seducer-heroes of drama, buttressed by an attempt to apply philosophical principles to 'free' or extramarital sexuality; by the end of the century, Edward Ward can refer unambiguously to the 'Fashionable Libertine' who defines his entire purpose in life as 'a hot pursuit of Vice without any Cessation' (chapter 4, section 4 below). But libertinism was not so much a philosophy as a set of performances, and its defining 'properties' (as I suggest in an earlier article) are better understood as theatrical props than as precise attributes. Attacks on Restoration comedy recognize its seductive attempt to shift élite male sexuality from the realm of ethics to the realm of style and manner: one contemporary of Jane Barker claims that 'Some of our Late Comedies have given the greatest Countenance to Libertinism that can be, by

setting forth the extravagant Debauches of the Age as the True Character of a Gentleman, . . . set[ting] off Whoring with all the Delicacy of
Expression and most obliging Character they could invent.'[3] *Libertines and
Radicals* substantiates this complaint and explores the class-confusion it
laments, showing how the two cultures of sexual transgression intermingle and define one another: the gross material substratum of 'whoring',
reconstituted in court records and 'porno-political' pamphlets, meets
the upper-class gallantry that 'gives the greatest Countenance to
Libertinism'.

As the moralist's hint about 'Delicacy of Expression' suggests, 'libertine' (like the French *libertin*) could be used in a light and neutral way,
referring to all kinds of playful transgressions set loose from the sense of
religious and sexual scandal. Shakespeare associates the 'puff'd and reck-
lesse Libertine' with the young man's sexual adventures (*Hamlet* I.ii.49),
but calls the air itself a 'charter'd Libertine' – a dense phrase that
places libertinism simultaneously within and outside the institution. The
'chartered' is at once free and bound by an official utterance, at once
licensed and *licentious*: when the charismatic king speaks, 'The Ayre, a charter'd Libertine, is still' (*Henry V* I.i.48). As a stylistic description *libertine*
denotes letters written without a 'subject', dramas that break away from
the Unities, loose translations and imitations that catch the spirit rather
than the letter, indeed any improvised and impudent text; John Evelyn
uses the term 'Libertine Libells' for the mocking whore's petitions of
1668 (chapter 5 below), even though they protest *against* the sexual freedom and political influence of Charles II's mistress. (The parallel words
in French could refer to the little mischiefs permitted when a carnival
atmosphere breaks out at home, or they could define a more disturbing
pleasure; the commander of the French army in the Rhineland explains
that he could not prevent his soldiers from indulging in the 'libertinage'
of burning down every town they captured.)[4] Applied to sexuality, then,
'libertinism' could evoke all these contradictory extremes – reckless hedonism, pleasurable freedom, 'hot pursuit', carnivalesque indulgence,
unruly conflagration, obliterating deluge.

The particular focus of this book is defined by another phrase of
Evelyn's, the 'popular Libertinism' that he finds rampant in the streets of
London. Speaking through the persona of a French visitor, he finds this
lower-stratum libertinism in the rough behaviour of the crowds (blamed
on 'parity' and 'Insulary manners'), and in the adoption of plebeian tavern culture by the children of the dispossessed élite.[5] (Chapter 4 will set
Evelyn's account of their ritualized sex and violence into the context of

pornographic publication and aristocratic 'riot'.) Significantly, he made these observations not in the unbridled Restoration but during the closing years of the 'Puritan' Interregnum. Taking my cue from Evelyn's 'popular Libertinism' and from Milton's depiction of the Sons of Belial, I study transgressive behaviours and texts in the decades of Civil War and revolution (chapters 2 and 3) rather than concentrating on the Restoration in isolation. Milton in fact defines my historical and social trajectory: his comments on the ribald 'brood of Belial' in 1644 (cited as the epigraph to chapter 2) place them in the lower dregs of society, but by the time he published his denunciations of the 'Sons of Belial' in *Paradise Lost* (the epigraph to chapter 5) they have migrated to the 'Courts and Palaces' of 'luxurious Cities'. 'Vagabond lust' (in Milton's memorable phrase) saunters across the boundaries that separate the undeserving poor from the dissolute aristocrat.

Libertines and Radicals in Early Modern London provides a detailed analysis of English sexual culture from the Civil Wars to the death of Charles II (*c.* 1640–85), interpreting a broad range of representations from lampoons and pamphlets to Utopian political theories, from street defamations to Whitehall comedies, from aristocratic 'riots' to popular expressive rituals like the charivari or 'rough music'. I focus on the seething subcultures of the capital city – on what a recent collection of essays calls 'material London' – but I treat the metropolis and its liberties or 'zones of misrule' as a permeable space, open to shaming-rituals imported from the villages and illicit texts translated from the wickedness of Europe. Drawing on Italian and French libertine literature (disseminated in English publications like *The Wandring Whore* and *The Whores Rhetorick*), I use the Italianate figure of the *'puttana errante'* and the 'honourable courtesan' to trace analogies between high and low libertinism, picaresque bawdy and gentlemanly transgression. The core subject is 'pornography' in the literal sense, the sexually explicit discourse of prostitution and its application to social institutions and political events; for this I coin the faux-Renaissance term *pornographia*, to distance it from modern debates and to emphasize its etymological roots in the lower-class 'whore' and her 'graphic' or punitive marking (chapter 1 below). The abject *pornē* and the sublime *cortegiana honesta* or royal mistress – more like the ancient Greek hetaira – between them define all sexual transgression, gendered female even when the wild libertines are ostensibly male.[6]

Chapter 1, which serves as an introduction, establishes the main paradigms that run through the book, drawing parallels between

English legal and fictional texts and those Continental sources that for English readers defined the splendours and miseries of the courtesan. I show the importance of the disorderly substratum – the ribalds or Sons of Belial who defy 'Christian discipline' and turn the authorities into figures of fun – and the intimate connection of sex, violence, carnival play, and political anxiety in narratives of 'whoring' uncannily similar in Rome, Paris, and London. Successive chapters explore the carnivalesque dimension of the social upheavals of 1640–60, anticipated in the riots and charivaris of earlier decades; the fusion of political and sexual themes in both anti-Puritan and anti-royalist satire; the correspondences between scurrilous pamphlet representations of the 'parliament of women' and more serious interventions in the public sphere, like women's petitions and contributions to the literature of the ideal commonwealth; the revival of pornographic publication at the Restoration, and the growing sense that the twin extremes of society, the court and the brothel, mirrored each other disturbingly; the expropriation of lewd and riotous behaviour by the newly empowered aristocracy, and its resumption in popular insurrections protesting against 'the great bawdy-house at White hall'. Chapter 6, moving finally into high literary culture, pursues the spectacle of cultivated rudeness in Wycherley, Rochester, Behn, and their contemporaries – an aristocratic simulation of 'popular Libertinism' in words and gestures, praised by Rochester as 'mannerly Obscene', which radically influenced literary conceptions of decorum and wit. A brief Epilogue defines the 'terminal condition' of *pornographia* at the close of Charles II's priapic reign, bringing all the subthemes of the book – sexuality, politics, and literary culture – to a conclusion with the extraordinary book-length *Parliament of Women* of 1684. My goal throughout is to reveal common 'porno-political' preoccupations across widely different decades, and to embed illicit sexual discourse in the material life and rituals of the metropolis, relating them to the ambivalent mixture of festivity and violence expressed in charivari, carnival, and apprentice riots. Throughout, I read pornographic satire as a deliberate attempt to confront and neutralize women's efforts to establish their own institutions – an attempt that frequently unravels, either by paying an unintended tribute to women's achievement, or by feminizing the norms that supposedly serve as a touchstone.

The post-Foucauldian decades have seen a surge of interest in the 'discourse of sexuality' and its poor relation 'pornography' – once dismissed as an insignificant bore. This interest is shared by social historians seeking light on the family and the sexual underworld, by feminists exposing the politics of masculinity or defining 'performative' alternatives to orthodox gender roles, by theorists trying to confirm or deny Foucault's 'history of sexuality', and by literary scholars wanting to put 'the body' back into their reading. The essays in Lynn Hunt's *Invention of Pornography*, or the many studies of gendered abuse and 'porno-political' propaganda in the English revolution, show how earnestly historians now look to the sexual subculture to solve political questions – particularly, why rulers and institutions lose their aura of authority. *Libertines and Radicals* contributes to this new discipline by embedding *pornographia* and 'pornotropic' satire in the specific historic context of disorderly 'popular Libertinism' at either end of the social spectrum. The 'new cultural studies' ask us to treat literature not as 'a strictly aesthetic object' but as 'a culturally operative text'.[7] I aim to encompass both these possibilities, reading texts and gestures simultaneously as imaginative artefacts and consequential documents, Utopian fantasies and ideological weapons. I treat the text (however trashy) as a signifying practice in its own right, and not as an example of discourse-in-general or as raw material from which historical truth must be extracted.

Even in Hunt's *Invention*, historians tend to assume that 'pornography' becomes meaningful to the extent that it reveals ulterior political ends or documents the emergence of 'modernity'; where psychoanalytic criticism discovers sexual meanings buried within more acceptable topics, they do the reverse, scrutinizing the ostensibly sexual text to throw light on political culture or the formation of identity (its power to 'confine the Subject', in Barker's words). I want to realize this political dimension without abrading the literal. Like *queer* in recent theoretical usage, the insulting designation *whore* mutated from noun to verb and in the process extended its sphere of operation; if a woman can be 'prostituted', so can a man, a cause, and a nation. Genital metaphors stand everywhere for prowess or failure in office: Charles I tries to copulate with Parliament, Oliver Cromwell 'prostitutes' and 'ravishes' the Goddess Victory, 'commonwealth' means common whore, Charles II cannot tell the difference between his sceptre and his 'Prick', which 'foams and swears it will be absolute'. But I am unwilling to reduce sexuality to a mere epiphenomenon or allegory of power. At the risk of stating the obvious, *pornographia* is 'about' power and representation but it is still 'about' lust in action, genital conquest and its discontents, fear of female domination, loss of control in passion. I am particularly interested in the slipperiness of sexual discourse at the point where 'pornographic' arousal and political satire merge: as one Civil War satirist observes of a rampant commonwealth woman, "tis a very hard matter to know whether she be a *Lady* or *Leviathan*'. Reviving seventeenth-century usage, I explore the *lubric* instability of designation and the *satyric* fusion of priapism and indignation. Sex figures politics, but (at least since St Augustine equated erection with rebellion) sex has its own politics of domination and dissolution. Another member of the female parliament, expressing her faux-feminist anger in pseudo-Biblical language, describes herself 'pierced to my very Bowels, when I have lain stretched forth under the Pressure of Male-insurrection'.[8]

In the process of setting this 'insurrection' of the flesh into its cultural context, I draw upon well-known authors such as Pepys, Milton, Marvell, Butler, Evelyn, Wycherley, Rochester, Dryden, and Hobbes (who makes a surprise appearance as a feminist theorist), the records of disorderly sexual mockery preserved by Church courts and state prosecutors, and a crawling mass of clandestine and popular obscene writing. The reader will find no separate chapter on 'women writers', but instead my account of *pornographia* is integrated with critiques of masculine 'free' sexuality and 'debauched' wit by female authors like Lucy Hutchinson, Aphra Behn, Jane Barker, and Margaret Cavendish – who also features as a Utopian writer. In social terms, my authors range from duchesses to shadowy Grub Street hacks. But common themes run throughout this disparate material: the conjunction of religious and sexual rebellion under the shadow of the Puritan revolution, the craving for theatricality and display, the fascination with the prostitute as an analogy for state affairs, the paradoxical relationship between upper-class libertinism and the ideals of worldly politeness, which generated a psychological strain that sometimes erupted into outright violence. I expand the close reading of texts into a kind of cultural geography, showing how London evolved occasions, institutions, and localities where normal ethics could be provisionally suspended – zones of misrule like Billingsgate, Bartholomew Fair, the river, the theatre, the genteel brothel, the city park, and (most controversially) the Court itself. (Charles II and his flamboyant mistresses play a central role in the post-Restoration chapters, translating to a national scale the problems of status-confusion and moral ambiguity already posed by the *honesta cortegiana* of the Italian Renaissance.) I thus establish the full spectrum of what Peter Stallybrass and Allon White call 'discursive sites . . . where ideology and fantasy conjoin', each with its 'distinctive associations between location, class and the body', and its distinctive 'complicity of disgust and desire'.[9] These 'institutions' of discourse and behaviour could be interpreted as a wholly male phenomenon, but I pose the further question: what changes in the role of women might be provoking this deluge of sexual representation? Female political and cultural institutions form not merely one theme of male sexual fantasy, but its motive and core, as the titles of pornography reveal: *The Whores Rhetorick, L'Escole des filles, The Poor Whores' Petition, Venus in the Cloister, The Parliament of Women*. These works attempt to sexualize the very idea of autonomous social or political action by women; to undo the ridicule, I set them in a context of women's real impact on the political culture of Interregnum England, the conflict over Restoration absolutism, and the formation of polite society.

Despite its low-libertine focus, this book grew quite easily from my earlier study of paradisal sexuality in the Judaeo-Christian tradition. I show there that 'libertines', spiritual and otherwise, haunted orthodox interpretations of Adam and Eve's relationship. St Paul applied the sacred words 'they shall be one flesh' *both* to the erotic union of Christ with the Church *and* to coupling with 'an harlot', using them for brutally literal *pornographia* as well as to represent larger powers.[10] Milton evokes 'Court Amours' and upper-class prostitution in the very centre of the nuptial bower. God's command to 'increase and multiply' gave rise to infinite bawdy jokes, as did Paul's egalitarian rule that neither the husband not the wife must ever refuse sexual 'due benevolence'. And the Great Whore from the Book of Revelation persists as the most vivid embodiment of corruption.

I am happy to acknowledge several intellectual and personal debts. David Foxon's *Libertine Literature in England* and Roger Thompson's *Unfit for Modest Ears* provided an essential resource for locating primary material. Michel Foucault's *Volonté de savoir*, when it first appeared, demolished the naive dichotomy of liberation-versus-repression (already besieged by feminism) and raised the challenge of reconstructing the entire 'discourse of sexuality' for a specific period, even though most of Foucault's hypotheses failed to hold up. The history of sexuality has been ravaged by an epidemic of premature generalization, particularly in studies based on literature, though the balance of claim and evidence has been restored by a new generation of theoretically aware and archivally grounded social historians.[11] Margaret Rosenthal's biography of Veronica Franco gave me a window on courtesan culture, recovering Franco's own voice but also revealing how the ambiguous figure of the *cortegiana honesta* brings out the anxieties of her male contemporaries, the symbolic charge of the 'female' in areas of public life denied to flesh-and-blood women, the 'parasitical rapport' between the misogynist attacker and the object of his satire. My thinking about the transgressively 'public' woman, the shameful-and-yet-honoured courtesan who throws categorical hierarchies into confusion, was sharpened by Julia Kristeva's concept of the abject, as it is suggestively sketched in both *Histoires d'amour* and *Pouvoirs de l'horreur*: 'what disturbs identity, system, order. What does not respect borders, positions, rules. The in-between, the ambiguous, the composite.' In the context of Eros, abjection forms one end of a spectrum or 'gamut' that leads to the sublime, and in a sense *is* sublime since both ends of this scale can be played together ('the supreme guarantee against boredom'); following this connection, the later, post-Restoration chapters turn to the inversionary transgressions of the bored classes, the faux-popular libertinism of the 'savage noble'.[12] Though my emphasis and chronology are different, I also draw here on a long tradition of critiquing the philosophical bases of libertinism and the contradictions in its doctrine of freedom, beginning in the 1950s with Dale Underwood and Thomas Fujimura and culminating in Warren Chernaik's *Sexual Freedom in Restoration Literature*.

The grand 'theory fathers' of the nineteenth and twentieth centuries, on the other hand, appear only in brief, inverted reflections. Except for his notion of the excluded-yet-present female in the male sex joke, Freud offers little help in interpreting the carnivalesque sexuality of this period: Auden commemorated Freud for discovering 'Eros, builder of cities', whereas I show the city building Eros. Bakhtin's conception of the grotesque lower stratum has been adopted only when it does not obscure the violent, authoritarian side of carnival, its 'chartered' mixture of riot and repression. Marxist historiography influenced my choice of subject – particularly Christopher Hill's synthesis of Milton's divorce tracts and Ranter sexuality in *The World Turned Upside Down* – but Marx himself features only as the author of a few crucial aphorisms: amidst the rotting monarchies of 1848 it seemed that history repeated itself twice, once as tragedy and a second time as farce; reading innumerable pornographic fabrications of female agency, endless *Poor Whore's Petitions* and *Parliaments of Women*, I conclude that world-changing ideas make their *first* appearance as farce.

This research has been helped over the years by grants from the John Simon Guggenheim Foundation, the American Council of Learned Societies, and the National Endowment for the Humanities (including fellowships at the Newberry and Folger Libraries), and by a President's Research Fellowship in the Humanities from the University of

California. I would like to thank the staffs of the Bodleian Library, Oxford; the British Library, the Guildhall Library, the British Museum, Department of Prints and Drawings, and the Victoria and Albert Museum Library, London; the Herzog August Bibliothek, Wolfenbüttel; the Bibliothèque nationale, Paris; the Huntington Library, San Marino; the Clark Library, Los Angeles; the Kinsey Institute Library, Indiana University; the Library of Congress and the Folger Shakespeare Memorial Library, Washington, DC (especially Betsy Walsh for printed books and Laetitia Yeandle for manuscripts); the University of Chicago; and above all the Newberry Library, Chicago. I should also acknowledge a series of remarkable research assistants, some of them now tenured professors: Catherine Patterson, Richard Barney, Wendy Motooka, Robert Wicks, and Mary Pollard Murray.

Many individuals have contributed ideas and criticisms at some point, including Dympna Callaghan, Elizabeth Cohen, Alison Conway, Josie Dixon, Margaret Doody (an early encourager of the project), Martha Feldman, David Loewenstein, Nancy Maguire, John Marino, Alan Nelson, Martha Pollak, and Laura Rosenthal. I would particularly like to thank those who have read sustained portions of the text and given helpful comments: James Winn, Joanna Picciotto, Warren Chernaik, and Roy Porter.

A few passages have been published in earlier articles or delivered as conference papers, though they have been thoroughly revised. For this opportunity to work up some of my examples in preliminary form, I would like to acknowledge the late Jean Hagstrum, Robert Maccubbin, Ann Bermingham and John Brewer, Lawrence Klein, Warren Chernaik and Martin Dzelzainis, the History of Consciousness Program of the University of California Santa Cruz, and the editors of *Review* and *Studies in Eighteenth-Century Culture*. Specific debts will be acknowledged in the relevant notes. For permission to publish illustrations I am grateful to the Metropolitan Museum of Art, New York, to the Lilly Library, Indiana University, to the British Museum, to the Bibliothèque nationale de France, and to the Musée Lorrain, Nancy.

Abbreviations and frequently cited works

Achinstein	Sharon Achinstein, 'Women on Top in the Pamphlet Literature of the English Revolution', *Women's Studies* 24, special issue, *Gender, Literature, and the English Revolution*, ed. Sharon Achinstein (1994), 131–63
Aretino	Pietro Aretino's *Ragionamenti* are cited by dialogue number and page from *Sei giornate*, ed. Guido Davico Bonino (Turin, 1975), followed [in brackets] by the corresponding page in Raymond Rosenthal's translation, *Aretino's Dialogues* (New York, 1971), reissued with Epilogue by Margaret Rosenthal (New York, 1995). (*Ragionamento della Nanna e della Antonia* [1534] is designated as 'I' and *Dialogo nel quale la Nanna . . . insegna a la Pippa* [1536] as 'II', with small roman numerals for the dialogues internal to each.) Aretino's sonnets on the *Modi* exist in several versions; I cite them by number from the Appendix of Bette Talvacchia, *Taking Positions: On the Erotic in Renaissance Culture* (Princeton, 1999). His letters will be cited from *Lettere*, ed. Francesco Erspamer, vol. I (Parma, 1995).
Behn	Aphra Behn, *Works*, ed. Janet Todd (Columbus, OH). Vol. I, *Poetry* (1992); vol. II, *Love-Letters between a Nobleman and His Sister* (1993); vol. V, *The Plays, 1671–1677* (1996); vol. VI, *The Plays, 1678–1682* (1996). Plays will give act and scene before the page number
Butler, *Hudibras*	Cited by part, canto, and line (sometimes also with page numbers) from Samuel Butler, *Hudibras*, ed. John Wilders (Oxford, 1967)

Cavendish, *Letters*	Margaret (Lucas) Cavendish, Marchioness and later Duchess of Newcastle, *CCXI Sociable Letters* (1664)
Orations	*Orations of Divers Sorts, Accommodated to Divers Places* (1662)
Chernaik	Warren Chernaik, *Sexual Freedom in Restoration Literature* (Cambridge, 1995)
CPW	*See* Milton
CW	*See* Wycherley
Dryden	*The Works of John Dryden*, ed. Edward Niles Hooker, H. T. Swedenberg, et al. (Berkeley and Los Angeles, 1956–). The California edn
Etherege	Plays cited by act, scene, and page number in Sir George Etherege, *Dramatic Works*, ed. H. F. B. Brett-Smith (Oxford, 1927)
Friedman	*See* Wycherley
Greaves, *Deliver Us*	Richard L. Greaves, *Deliver Us from Evil: the Radical Underground in Britain, 1660–1663* (New York and Oxford, 1986)
Enemies	*Enemies under His Feet: Radicals and Nonconformists in Britain, 1664–1677* (Stanford, CA, 1990)
Higgins	Patricia Higgins, 'The Reactions of Women, with Special Reference to Women Petitioners', in Brian Manning (ed.), *Politics, Religion and the English Civil War* (1973), 179–222
Ingram, *Courts*	Martin Ingram, *Church Courts, Sex and Marriage in England, 1570–1640* (Cambridge, 1987)
'Rhymes'	'Ridings, Rough Music and Mocking Rhymes in Early Modern England', in Barry Reay (ed.), *Popular Culture in Seventeenth-Century England* (1985), 166–97
'Ridings'	'Ridings, Rough Music, and the "Reform of Popular Culture" in Early Modern England', *Past and Present* 105 (November 1984), 79–113
Jonson	Cited by page number (with act, scene, etc. where needed) from *Ben Jonson*, ed. C. H. Herford, Percy Simpson, and Evelyn Simpson (Oxford, 1925–63)
Manley, *London*	Lawrence Manley, *Literature and Culture in Early Modern London* (Cambridge and New York, 1995)

Marvell	*The Poems and Letters of Andrew Marvell*, ed. H. M. Margoliouth, 3rd edn, rev. Pierre Legouis with E. E. Duncan-Jones (Oxford, 1971)
Milton	Poems will be cited by title and line, using the standard abbreviations *PL* for *Paradise Lost*, *PR* for *Paradise Regained*, and *SA* for *Samson Agonistes*
Columbia	*Works*, ed. F. A. Patterson et al. (New York, 1931–8). The Columbia edn
CPW	*The Complete Prose Works*, ed. Don M. Wolfe et al. (New Haven, 1953–82). The Yale edn
Newcastle	*See* Cavendish
PD	*See* Wycherley
Pepys	Cited by entry date (or page for material in the notes) from *The Diary of Samuel Pepys*, ed. Robert Latham and William Matthews, 11 vols. (Berkeley, 1970–83)
PL	*See* Milton
POAS	*Poems on Affairs of State: Augustan Satirical Verse, 1660–1714*, ed. George deF. Lord et al. (1963–75)
PR	*See* Milton
RCH	David Farley-Hills (ed.), *Rochester: the Critical Heritage* (1972)
Rochester	John Wilmot, Earl of Rochester, *Works*, ed. Harold Love (Oxford, 1999). Includes works unreliably attributed to Rochester. *See also RCH, Sodom*
Letters	*The Letters of John Wilmot, Earl of Rochester*, ed. Jeremy Treglown (Oxford, 1980)
SA	*See* Milton
Sodom	Anonymous burlesque verse drama (*c.* 1672–8), cited from Rochester, *Works*, ed. Harold Love (Oxford, 1999). Included in Love's 'Appendix Roffensis' of works once attributed to Rochester but unlikely to be by him
Thomason	To avoid confusion with similar titles, I sometimes add the shelf-mark (and hand-written date where relevant) for pamphlets in the George Thomason collection of the British Library, London
Thompson	Roger Thompson, *Unfit for Modest Ears: a Study of Pornographic, Obscene and Bawdy Works Written or Published in England in the Second Half of the Seventeenth Century* (1979)

Underdown   David Underdown, *Revel, Riot, and Rebellion: Popular Politics and Culture in England, 1603–1660* (Oxford, 1985)

'Language'   'The Language of Popular Politics in the English Revolution', in Alvin Vos (ed.), *Place and Displacement in the Renaissance: Essays from the 25th Annual CEMERS Conference* (Binghamton, 1995)

Wandring Whore   Serial publication by John Garfield, supposed author, and others, cited by part number and page. *The Wandring Whore: a Dialogue between Magdalena a Crafty Bawd, Julietta an Exquisite Whore, Francion a Lascivious Gallant, and Gusman a Pimping Hector* appeared some time in late 1660. Thomason dates *The Wandring Whore Continued... Num.* 2 on 5 Dec. 1660, and two more (numbered) parts that month (12, 19), plus *The Fifth and Last Part of the Wandring Whore... By Peter Aretine* (March 1661), which is then repudiated in *The Sixth Part of the Wandring-Whore Revived* (1663), evidently from a different publisher.

Wilson   John Harold Wilson (ed.), *Court Satires of the Restoration* (Columbus, OH, 1976)

Wycherley   Plays will be cited by act, scene, and page from *Plays*, ed. Arthur Friedman (Oxford, 1979). *The Country-Wife* is abbreviated *CW* and *The Plain-Dealer, PD*

Works   *Complete Works*, ed. Montague Summers (1924)

Pornographia *and the markings of prostitution: an introduction*

Mrs Ellen Gwyn being at the duke's playhouse was affronted by
a person who came into the pitt and called her whore; whom Mr
Herbert, the earl of Pembrokes brother, vindicating, there were
many swords drawn, and a great hubbub in the house.

(Narcissus Luttrell)[1]

This is most brave
That I, the son of a dear father murder'd
Prompted to my revenge by heaven and hell,
Must (like a whore) unpack my heart with words
And fall a-cursing like a very drab.

(*Hamlet* II.ii.578–82)

What does it mean to call somebody a whore, or, more precisely, to
write prostitution across a person or institution? The etymology of the
modern word 'pornography' encapsulates these questions. Many of the
discourses that we will study in this book – including bawdy tales, lawsuits
protesting against sexual defamation, political satires, prosecutions for
disorderly behaviour, and crusading journalism, as well as direct depictions of sexual practice – exploit the ambiguous relationship between two
elements that would eventually combine: *pornē* (signifying the prostitute
openly revealed and reviled) and *graphē* (the expressive mark or engraved
sign, verbal as well as visual). Everything depends on who is making that
mark and who controls its interpretation. Is it writing about, upon, or by
the alleged prostitute? Does *pornē* refer narrowly to sex for hire, or to any
sexual act that transgresses the marital norm or violates the taboo against
direct depiction? with boys or women? active or passive? celebrating or
abhorring the arousal it represents and elicits? These texts often pit a
woman's autographism or self-representation against efforts by the nar-
rator/defamer to pry open or cut into her respectable exterior, to reveal
the expected story of sexual exposure and conquest – the 'pornographic'
moment in the modern sense. Some anticipate the eighteenth-century

coinage of the would-be scientific term *pornographe*, part-way between the modern meaning and its etymological roots: ostensibly moralistic works such as John Garfield's *Wandring Whore* (analysed in chapter 4 below), like Restif de la Bretonne's *Pornographe*, offer a collective portrait of urban vice brought to light by a private citizen who blends into the murky demimonde and extracts its most salacious truths.

I begin, then, by conceiving pornography as an act of *designation* or *marking*, at once accusation, distinction, signage, and signature. At its crudest it means uttering and affixing the single word *whore*, as in the fight over Nell Gwyn cited in my first epigraph. This simple act had complex results, for even though Gwyn gave herself witty titles like 'Protestant Whore' her honour was immediately 'vindicated' by sword-wielding aristocrats when someone else dared to flourish the term. But that chivalrous sword, like its counterpart the pen, could also turn upon the woman it protects, engraving her with a stroke that would mark on the exterior the cryptic truth about female sexuality. The 'graphic' element in my imaginary term *pornographia* carried associations of punishment and publication, writing on the body and expository display of its achievements. Cruel as it seems to us, the connection between corporal punishment and artistic expression would have been familiar to anyone who read Plautus or Ben Jonson. When the clever slave in Plautus's *Pseudolus* invites his master to 'conscribe' his entire back with the whip, 'just as letters are written into a book with a calamus', he is punning on what an admirer has just called him – a real *graphicum*, a prize exhibit worthy to be posted or written up, 'graphic' in the most vivid sense. Jonson, himself threatened with facial mutilation for his seditious writing, frequently imagined satirical invectives as 'prints' or 'publike brands' stamped into the offender's face, 'cut' like a portrait engraving or 'told in red letters', while at the same time he identifies this desire for revenge as a 'feminine humour' or 'scolding rage'. The same 'graphic' mechanism, I will argue throughout this book, defines the sexually errant female. It runs the social gamut, from the abject spectacle of the whore attacked in the street to the polite compliment that the Earl of Rochester pays to the Court beauty, inviting her royal audience to 'See my Credentials written in my Face.'[2]

We cannot assume, however, that the courtesan remained the passive object of these male (re)marks. *Pornographia* equally implies the manipulation of signs *by* the prostitute or mistress, fashioning herself a higher status, defining herself as a refined libertine above mercenary considerations, above the rough subculture of the brothel and the street. In Italian literature, where most 'pornographic' motifs originate, this active, self-crafting capacity is most fully elaborated in Ferrante Pallavicino's *La retorica delle puttane* ('The Whores' Rhetoric'); as its title implies, this mock-didactic satire instructs the common 'whore' in the expressive arts of high culture – rhetoric, gesture, decor, music, architecture – to create a façade both literal and figurative. In contrast to the brutally colloquial *puttana*, the term 'courtesan' or *cortegiana* could denote this higher cultural aspiration, especially when combined with *honesta* – which meant honourable, respect-worthy, acceptable to the élite, rather than 'honest' in the modern sense. The etymological affinity with *cortegiano* or 'courtier' could be invoked with various degrees of irony, as in *The Whores Rhetorick* (1683), a loose English adaptation of Pallavicino by an author styling himself 'Philo-Puttanus': 'acting *alla Cortegiana*' means precisely 'cringing, fawning, supplanting, and undermining'; 'the wise *Italians* by *Cortegiano* and *Cortegiana* . . . intimate that a Whore ought to be furnished with all the Courtly qualities' (33). This chapter will therefore introduce the crux that runs through virtually all representations of sexuality outside the sanction of marriage: the abject associations of the common prostitute constantly conflict with the glamour and prestige of the *cortegiana honesta* or the royal mistress.

Given this inversionary affinity of high and low, the courtesan becomes a perfect vehicle for political commentary, a funhouse mirror of social corruption or cataclysm, at once trivializing and perpetuating its trauma. Hence my preoccupation with the 'porno-political' throughout this book. Just as the Sack of Rome shows up relentlessly in the most violent episodes of proto-pornography like Pietro Aretino's *Ragionamenti*, so the English Civil War is belittled, reenacted, and diagnosed in contemporary prostitute-narratives and obscene lampoons: a life of reckless copulation becomes 'Nature's Good Old Cause'; when two lovers 'tilt and thrust' simultaneously in Phillis's '*Cunt and Arse*', the mock-heroic narrator announces that we must 'Now for Civil *Wars* prepare, / Rais'd by fierce intestine bustle.' The body-word 'intestine', already applied to civil conflict, is now reliteralized 'in the *Bowels* of the fair'.[3]

England did not develop in isolation, and though future chapters concentrate on London I will here, if only briefly, cite parallels from Continental Renaissance sources that anticipated or influenced Stuart culture. 'Pornographic' texts (in both the modern sense and the historically restricted sense that I am proposing here) circulated widely in England, especially the two notorious dialogues that Pepys mentions in his diary, the French *Escole des filles* and the Italian work attributed to Aretino, *La puttana errante* – the 'Wandering' or 'Errant Whore'. Alongside these bawdy narratives and their English equivalents I will read legal cases from England, France, and Italy so similar that they suggest a plebeian sexual culture common to otherwise very different countries. Since my goal is to show 'cultural operation' I find it essential to go beyond mere textuality, studying actions and actionable words, rituals of abuse or celebration, episodes of disorderly conduct and obscene libel that ended up in court. Sexual practices are notoriously difficult to reconstruct, of course, and most purported descriptions of reality come mediated through scandalous texts with their own sensational or judicial agenda. Nevertheless, narratives that lead to successful prosecutions should be given special weight, as representations endorsed by social power, texts with 'consequence' in every sense.

My second epigraph raises a further question: what does it mean to *identify* with the whore? Suddenly self-conscious of his fervent curses against Claudius, Hamlet in a single convulsive moment repudiates *and recognizes* his own whorishness. And the flash of identity passes through the tongue rather than the genitals; the Prince defines the whore by a quality of language, a kind of *pornoglossia*, coarse and unbridled but yielding direct access to the heart (hence analogous to the art of the soliloquy itself). When the Renaissance courtesan published her own poems this association of active sexuality and intensified language migrated upwards into literary history, and it flourishes in the age of frank and worldly writers like Aphra Behn. Sometimes facetiously and sometimes in earnest, the Logos is conceived as a material product of Eros, corrupted and yet stimulated by whoring. 'Wit' derives from 'Cunt', ribald talk resembles cunnilingus, literary inspiration becomes a sexually transmitted disease. We must explore not just the representation of the whore (and her equally scandalous male companions), but the prostitution of representation.

1 . *CORTEGIANA HONESTA* OR *PUTTANA ERRANTE*?

Nobody in early modern England used the term *pornographia* – the word appears only once in ancient Greek, and its modern cognates do not emerge until the late eighteenth century – but everybody participated in it. Thousands of working women took their neighbours to court for it, defending the honour of their person and their household against the graphic designation 'whore'. As I define it, *pornographia* is an act as well as a text, a performative gesture of such resonance that a single word, uttered against the king's mistress Nell Gwyn in the highly charged space of the playhouse pit, triggered a furious swordfight among the earls. The elements of my new-old term would have been recognized by the literate, moreover. Aretino's *Ragionamenti*, the quintessential Renaissance account of the whore's life and opinions, circulated under the title *Pornodidascalus*, and the English translator of an important treatise on sexual medicine defines his learned sources as '*Pornodidascalians*'.[4] The concept of *graphē* as punitive 'writing' boils up in dramatizations of sexual rage from Shakespeare's Othello (who sees Desdemona as a 'fair paper to write Whore upon') to Pinchwife in Wycherley's *Country-Wife*, who promises Margery that he will 'write Whore with this Penknife in your Face' (chapter 6, section 1 below). The notion of the prostitute as the *subject* or *agent* of sexual writing could be derived from the vivid portrait of the wicked seductress in the Biblical book of Proverbs; when John Dunton confronts an American woman who came to his bookshop for *L'Escole des filles*, he sneers that "'tis not with her Eyes only she draws in Customers, but with her feet also, for she writes Characters of wantonness as she walks'.[5]

Whore is a fighting word, a cutting remark. But what does it cut through? Firstly, of course, it breaks down the exterior shell of honour and good fame that every citizen needed to maintain her social standing. As defamation trials show, the accusation 'whore' served as a universal indicator of guilt, the clearest possible evidence that no 'credit', in court or in the shops, should be extended to this person.[6] Ascribing sexual infamy thus broke down the categorical distinction between kinds of crime. More important still, 'whore' also cuts through the entire process of classifying women, assigning social status according to their sexuality. It brings into conflict two incompatible modes of categorizing, which we can call the *binary* and the *graduated*.

The binary system notoriously allows only two categories of woman, polarized and exclusive: the chaste and the whore. *Any* sexual act outside marriage put her instantly and irrevocably into the abject category, which also constitutes a call to action: the woman of honour must be 'vindicated' against the accuser, by lawsuits, fist-fights, shaming rituals, or aristocratic swordplay; the 'whore' must be 'kicked out of doors' (as Rochester put it), pelted with filth, 'pointed at for something monstrous' (in Aphra Behn's words), whipped and paraded in a cart. On the other hand, society in practice recognized an infinite series of steps, overlappings, and distinctions within the realm of sexual possibility. The ruler's mistress, whose bastards were often acknowledged with noble titles and state pensions, occupied a vastly different position from the rambling street prostitute, who in turn differed from the wealthy citizen's kept 'Miss' (in some cases later married) or the pleasure-seeking wife who scorned any suggestion of financial reward. Even within the brothels, historians recognize large material differences between 'those who rented themselves out as private mistresses forming long-term liaisons, . . . those whose earnings were tied to the volume of clients they handled, and the more casual prostitutes at the lower end of the market' (as Ian Archer concludes from an exhaustive study of London Bridewell records).[7] This archival finding is confirmed by texts as divergent as the 1535 *Tariffa delle puttane di Venegia* (where prices vary a hundredfold) and the comedies of Thomas Killigrew or Aphra Behn, where the great courtesan Angellica Bianca openly advertises her colossal monthly fee, announcing both her availability and her cultural capital by displaying her portrait commissioned from Van Dyck.

'Whore' and its equivalents signify *both* the Universal Unchaste *and* the lowest rung in this status-graduation, lacking cultural accomplishment, the protection of a powerful client, or the possibility of financial security. This 'low' vocabulary strikes up two semantic oppositions at once – defining itself versus the respectable matron on one side and the higher-status courtesan on the other. The *pornē*, a common prostitute or someone who lived and thought like one, was counter-distinguished from the *hetaira*, who formed an educated and relatively liberated class, an exception to the general Greek contempt for women. The protagonists of explicitly sexual discourse evolve, during the period studied in this book, from the raunchy *puttane* of Aretino and *The Wandring Whore* to the aristocratic married women of Nicolas Chorier's neo-Latin *Aloisiae Sigeae Satyra Sotadica*, the most 'pornographic' text of the seventeenth century according to the modern use of the term. Chorier's 'erudite' libertines could be called 'hetaira' but not 'pornē', and when a young acolyte calls the private villas of their orgies 'honorable brothels' (*honestae lupanares*) she is haughtily rebuked.[8] Since the etymology of 'pornography' links it to class degradation, these high-libertine texts are more accurately characterized as 'Dialogues of the Hetaira' (the title of a well-known work by Lucian). In Italy, the distinctions between cultivated *cortegiana*, plain *meretrice*, and vulgar *puttana* roughly correspond to the estates of society, and further gradations could be obtained by tonal inflection and by oxymoronic combinations like *cortegiana honesta* or *puttana errante*.

Do these qualifications mitigate the infamy or deepen it? As *cortegiana* dropped down the social scale, losing its connection with courtliness, *honesta* could be added to mark out a privileged exception, but the term could equally convey bitter satire against unwarranted respectability. A *Catalogo* published in Venice in 1575 might list its subjects as *le principale e più honorate cortigiane di Venezia*, but it clearly degrades them by publishing their address, bawd's name, and price (including Veronica Franco at a derisory 2 scudi). When Claude Le Petit, the most virulent of the French *libertins* in the mid seventeenth century, addresses an obscene sonnet to the 'Courtisanes d'honneur' inviting them to use his manuscript as a dildo, he means to expose the secret desires of the upper-class *précieuses* who dominated salon culture.[9] *La puttana errante*, the title given first to a mock-chivalric poem and then to a highly influential pseudo-Aretine prose dialogue, identifies the prostitute simultaneously as a picaresque or 'wandering' vagabond – the lowest kind of '*arrant* whore', detached from any fixed location or property – and as a female knight-*errant*, whose sexual exploits match the martial prowess of Ariosto's Bradamante or Spenser's Britomart.

All these fine distinctions were in any case fragile and unstable, since at any moment the graduated model could be replaced by the binary, according to which every sexually active woman is a mere whore and the great courtesan all the more culpable because she pretends to rise above that criminal, abject status. Verbal, legal, and physical attacks could be sprung without warning, and the *cortegiana honesta* was particularly vulnerable; she represented the anomalous middle term that binary thinking cannot tolerate, the unchaste-but-still-honourable woman whose avowed 'free' sexuality has not (yet) plunged her into the gutter.

In several Italian city-states legislation tried to level the distinction between *cortegiane* and *meretrice*, using the words as if they were interchangeable synonyms and imposing the same penalties on both – barring them from church, forbidding aristocratic clients to save them from prosecution, forcing them to wear the yellow veil. (In London, a similar levelling-effect was procured by empowering Bridewell to punish 'vagabondes, strumpets, or single women gotten with childe'.) Even courtesans with the highest cultural credentials, like the poets Tullia d'Aragona and Veronica Franco, found themselves subject to legal persecution, though Tullia escaped the veil when Cosimo de Medici personally endorsed her appeal 'pardon her because she is a poetess'. Satirical *pornographia* pursues the same legislative goals: Veronica Franco, who elevated her own sexual skills by representing them as 'opere amorose' or works of art, is attacked as 'Ver unica puttana'; Tullia d'Aragona's poetic ambition is brutally mocked in the Venetian *Tariffa delle puttane*, where (despite her massive price) she 'washes chitterlings' in the 'Helicon' of her own urine. (In contrast, the 'little people' who charge only a few pence and merely 'earn their bread with their rear ends' are treated more

mildly.) In a dialogue ascribed to Aretino the dour Zoppino, invited by a
friend to speak freely and to use the vulgar words 'puttane, cazzo, potta,
culo, fottere', retorts that '*puttane*, or *cortegiane* as you like to call them, are
a terrible thing' – levelling the all-important verbal distinction just as the
law was trying to do.[10]

The same author, in fact, could uphold and demolish the special status
of the 'honest whore'. Aretino himself sometimes endorses the courtesan's claim to have created a refined art of pleasure, sometimes drags
this ambition down by emphasizing, in the grossest street language, the
violence of the sex-act and the cunning avarice of the *arte puttanesca*.
He commends Angela La Zaffetta for her ability to 'put the mask of
onestà over the lascivious', but encourages a disciple to write a hideous
poem about her gang-rape by thirty-one men. Tullia d'Aragona's successful performance in a philosophical dialogue inspires a dizzy rapture
of paradox, simultaneously lifting her above the most respectable women
and marking her with the brand of *impudicizia*: 'after receiving such an
honour her shamelessness can properly be envied by the most modest
and the most fortunate women'.[11] (The author of that dialogue himself
went on to write a vicious diatribe proving that '*Cortegiana* means nothing but *meretrice*.') The ambiguous 'splendour and misery' ascribed to the
courtesan no doubt reflects the male author's ambivalence about sexuality itself, which in Montaigne's great essay 'On Some Verses of Virgil'
seems at one moment a kind of excretion, shameful and ridiculous, and
the next moment the supreme goal of life, a transcendent pleasure which
must be preserved and extended by turning it into an elaborate art (*Essais*
III.v). Jacobean drama ensured that this fascinating ambiguity flourished
in England: Dekker's *The Honest Whore* eulogizes the strumpet's freedom (Part II, IV.i); Marston's *The Dutch Courtezan* translates directly from
Montaigne's praise of sex-as-art, calling the courtesan the 'Ambrosia of
Delight' (v.i).

The simple designation *whore*, then, cuts through this aura of paradoxical qualification and nails the errant woman in the coffin of abjection.
In lower-class *pornographia* – the lampoon pinned on the door, the oral
defamation taken down in court – we can see this disambiguation at
work. Stripping away accretions like 'honest' and euphemisms like
'courtesan', the bald word is doubled with synonyms like 'buttock'
that associate prostitution with gross materiality, and multiplied into
Rabelaisian strings of epithets that reinforce the link to other kinds of
transgression, presumed to be interchangeable with sexual adventure

once it has reached the lowest stratum: 'thou art a whore and an arrant whore and a common carted whore and thou art my husbands whore' . . . 'thow hackney queane thou hackney jade comon ridden jade codpeece whore codpeece quean thow monster thow, putt off thy long pettycote put on a pair of britches!' Venetian and English assailants alike enact the monstrosity of the enemy or rival by creating verbal monsters of their own, as it were turning mere assertion into *de-monstration*. In both cultures, too, the creature is further alienated-and-contained by tying her to the most shameful locations in town, the addresses most notorious for poverty as well as cheap prostitution: Veronica Franco is accused of living in the worst slum of Venice; the London neighbour is told that 'Turnbull Streete is more fitt for her to live in than amongst honest people.'[12]

The 'whore' confronted (and constituted) by these ritualized insults anticipates the 'abject' as conceived by Kristeva, at once definitively *low* and fluidly unclassifiable, disturbing 'identity, system, order' and flowing over 'borders, positions, rules' (Preface, above). The 'whore' is incontinent, leaky in every sense, unruly because outside the marital or parental control of one man, ribald, coarse, lacking the restraints required by the increasingly self-conscious Civilizing Process, loose-mouthed as well as open-flapped. Hamlet feels shame, my second epigraph reminds us, because he 'must like a whore unpack my heart with words'. Attempts to discipline the 'scold' often blur the distinction between the termagant and the whore, however different they might seem in their surface appeal.[13] And the common prostitute is further tainted – if rendered more fungible – by her association with money. Centuries before Marxism, the whore stood for the human face of the Commodity, and vice versa.

The exchange of sex for coins, literally thrown into the vagina in *The Wandring Whore* (chapter 4 below), defines her as a wage labourer, neither 'liberal' nor 'free' even though she is free with her favours. Within the hierarchy of sex work, the fee-for-service women who owned no share in the business performed what was often described as 'drudgery' or 'slavery', while the strolling 'buttock', who solicited in the open street, found herself associated with other kinds of mobile and full-throated vendor – the oyster-wench, the Billingsgate fish-seller, or the Parisian *poissarde*. (The more odorous and perishable the food the more it analogizes depraved sexuality, the 'Salt Commodity' that can be bought as easily as an oyster.) In pornography associated with Bartholomew Fair, the closest thing London had to a carnival, the whores call on customers to try 'the best buttock-beef in England', so that the same word serves for the woman, the part she offers, and the meal she resembles.[14] Pursuing the cycle of consumption still further into the urban lower stratum, prostitutes are identified with the 'common shore' or sewer and with the cinder-women who recycled fuel from the ashheaps. Rochester could airily refer to lower-class sexual opportunities with the generic 'oyster-cinder-beggar-common-whore', and the same conflation occurs in political *pornographia*: the women petitioners to Parliament in Civil War England are belittled as 'Whores, Bawdes, Oyster-women, [and] Irish women' (chapter 3 below), and in a later crisis Nell Gwyn's contaminating power over the king is exaggerated by calling her a cinder-woman, a herring-crier, or a 'wench of orange and oyster'.[15]

Public fascination with these public women turned them into urban entertainments, heroines of abjection, ironically romanticized with names like Fuckadilla (one of the royal mistresses in the burlesque drama *Sodom*) or her better-known cognate Cinderella. The whore and the fishwife both elicited a kind of celebrity, finding themselves (in)famous as local characters, hawked in public in the form of popular prints (fig. 1). The best-known prostitute-cum-procuress of the Restoration, Mrs Cresswell, appears in an astonishing array of texts from *The Wandring Whore*, *The Poor Whores Petition*, *The English Rogue*, and *The Whores Rhetorick* to *Venice Preserved* and *Absalom and Achitophel* (chapters 4–7 below), eventually receiving the honour of a (facetious) funeral sermon and an entry in the *DNB*. Small wonder then that she can be assimilated into the 'Cries of London' and transformed into a specimen of the engraver's porno-graphic art, her commodified image paired with the 'London Courtezan' she cries up (figs. 2a–b).

2. RULING-CLASS COURTESANS: THE REIGN OF STATUS-CONFUSION

Pornographia aims to drive a wedge between sexuality and honour, between the infamy of prostitution and the material benefits of high status: political power through alliance with patrons and courtiers, economic power to display wealth and taste in design, didactic power to train or 'form' élite youth, expressive power in music, poetry, and 'rhetoric'. But if the intention is to demolish this anomalous high–low hybrid, the result is often to realize her ambiguity more graphically. The 'honourable courtesan' and her descendents fluctuate across many conceptual thresholds. She operates below the level of civil society and above it. For the misogynist she typifies all women, and yet – as Aretino proposed and

Figure 1. François Chauveau, *A Fish Market* (1652), etching

The Whores Rhetorick repeated – 'A Whore is a Whore, but a Whore is not a Woman.'[16] Opposed to marriage by definition, she nevertheless offers a contract that differs from marriage only by greater openness about the cash-for-sex nexus. She is expunged from the world and yet the very image of worldliness, a sordid criminal and yet the quintessential businesswoman, the emblem for all kinds of commerce and the prototype of the freelance, the entrepreneurial, the untenured.

London Curtezan
La Putain de Londres
Cortegiana di Londra

M Lauron delin :

P Tempest excud :
Cum Privilegio

Figure 2a. After Marcellus Laroon the Elder, 'London Curtezan', *The Cryes of the City of London*, 3rd edn, ed. Pierce Tempest (1688), engraving

Madam Crefwell
Vne Maquerelle
Vecchia rufiana

M. auron delin:

P. Tempest exc:
Cum privilegio

52

Figure 2b. After Marcellus Laroon the Elder, 'Madam Creswell', *The Cryes of the City of London*, 6th edn, ed. Henry Overton (?1711), plate 52, engraving

I am particularly interested, then, in the ambiguous figure who throws categorical hierarchies into confusion, who embodies the possibility of transgression *without* infamy or whoredom *with* honour, the 'shameless' courtesan-philosopher whose cultural prowess gains her even more 'honour' than respectable women could achieve (as Aretino claimed of Tullia d'Aragona only half-ironically), or the brilliant seductress whose liaison with the king gets her a duchy. Transgressively 'public' women provoke an unstable mixture of erotic worship and indignation in the respectable imagination, and consequently serve as figures for dubious authority in other spheres – living embodiments of passion ruling reason, tail ruling head, women ruling men. *Pornographia* in the literal sense readily mutates into the 'porno-political', which uses images of the 'regnant whore' (and her ritual punishment) to delegitimize actual or emergent institutions – women's political movements, the Cromwellian oligarchy, the Restoration Court. The logic of this association will unfold throughout this book. The central chapters explore parliaments of women, whores' petitions, and depictions of the brothel as a government 'Office', while later chapters draw on lampoons and satires less like modern 'pornography' than tabloid journalism, embroiling named celebrities in a prurient fascination masquerading as vigilante exposure. In Court culture the personal is always political, and private parts open into public issues.

Phrases like 'courtisanes d'honneur', used with varying degrees of irony, carry anti-prostitute satire into the upper echelons of society, at the opposite end from the raucous, plebeian bawdy-house. Women were officially excluded from the political nation, and upper-class women (unlike the female proletariat) played only a marginal part in the economic nation. But they had one precious asset in a culture rapidly evolving from old-fashioned godliness and courtliness to a self-consciously refined *politesse*: membership, even leadership, in the social nation, 'the World'. Freedom of manner, seductive flair, and expertise in the finer points of love were the keys to success in this world – and the occasion for instant expulsion, since the debutante who actually yielded to a lover would be 'ruined' and ostracized. The mistresses of the royal family form a striking exception, since their avowed 'wanton and free' sexuality installed them at the centre of the fashionable world rather than in the demimonde or the gutter; they benefitted from an exceptionally forceful and impudent style or from a lover whose social status was so high that it transferred impunity as it were by touch. But such anomalies or paradigm clashes generated a considerable strain, as we will find when reading the gross and violent satires directed against the mistresses of Charles II.

The 'greater whore' stood simultaneously beyond the pale and inside the charmed circle, enjoying cultural influence and protection from prosecution thanks to the influence of powerful courtiers. (Venice passed a law to prevent this, and even in Elizabethan London a surprising number of brothels escaped the intermittent purges because of the intervention of aristocrats.)[17] During the Restoration, particularly, the stylish hegemony of the royal mistresses influenced the entire 'World' and made it fashionable to seem erotic. Renaissance moralists and their pornographic imitators denounced or celebrated the courtesan for her ability to assume a chaste and honourable façade, but by the time of Wycherley's *Country-Wife* the reverse prevails: thanks to the modish bedroom look now requisite in 'civil' society, Horner complains, upper-class women cultivate a sexy availability-effect that in no way corresponds to their inward disposition. The inverse of Aretino's Zaffetta, they pull the mask of lasciviousness over *honestà*. As another dramatist puts it, modesty

> is of late so out of fashion grown,
> She that is honest scarcely dares it own,
> But does, howe'er her mind affected is,
> Put on the brisk gay carriage of a Miss.

Even conventional conduct-books advised women to adopt a 'free' discourse and a 'carriage delightful and agreeable, and flowing with a seeming carelessness'. Less flexible interpreters assume a direct relation between equivocal style and open prostitution: 'Brisk and Airy (which our dull Grandmothers would have call'd Wanton and Impudent) is long since become the Character of a Well-bred woman; to be a Miss, was both a pleasant and thriving Undertaking.'[18]

Did the culturally privileged royal 'Misses' have honour, or did they not? Were her noble friends right to draw their swords for Nell Gwyn, making her *de facto* a fine lady defended by her chevaliers, even though she herself accepted the title 'whore' and openly joked about the string of lovers who culminated in 'Charles the Third'? This is exactly the question brought to a sharp point by the mistresses of Charles II, heaped with wealth and favour while they lived in open breach of the laws of Church and state, which forbade adultery and fornication in the name of the king. The grandest of those mistresses, like Barbara Villiers, Duchess of Cleveland, or Louise de Kérouaille, Duchess of Portsmouth, claimed an élite status beyond the reach of infamy – though verbal attacks on them increased in inverse proportion to their impunity. Humbler mistresses like the actress Nell Gwyn became the flashpoint for every kind of ambiguity, situated on the contested boundary between high and low libertinism, between the privileged *cortegiana* and the abject *puttana*. The swordfight in the theatre – recorded by Narcissus Luttrell under the category 'State Affairs' – could be considered a border incident. Half in, half out of that inner circle, she makes its sharp edges visible: Gwyn was considered important enough for slurs against her to be violently avenged, prestigious enough to receive dedications from playwrights like Aphra Behn, elevated enough for the Earl of Rochester to include her in his list of royal mistresses obsessed with their own 'honour', whose 'humble taile' belies their 'Heroick head'; and yet King Charles gave her no title and 'never treated her with the decencies of a mistress, but rather with the lewdness of a prostitute' (chapter 6 below). Election to the royal bed (a kind of aristocracy by contagion) gave her sufficient kudos for an earl's brother to 'vindicate' her honour in blood, yet her common origins and rampant strumpet-like demeanour made it at least thinkable to call her 'whore' in public. Indeed, in one famous anecdote, when threatened by a furious mob protesting against the influence of King Charles's French mistress – a kind of absolutism by contagion, but this time flowing from the female to the male – she openly avows the dreaded word and adds another oxymoron to the repertoire: 'Pray, good people, be civil; I am the protestant whore.'[19]

As Behn's warm dedication to Nell Gwyn suggests, accretion of status made the upper-class courtesan strangely fascinating to women authors who would have indignantly repudiated any *literal* suggestion of affinity between them. Margaret Cavendish, Duchess of Newcastle, an old-fashioned *virtuosa* who complains bitterly about the ascendency of 'Wanton and Free Women', nevertheless savours the 'Attractive Power' of the great *hetaira* Aspasia, who taught 'Rhetorick' to respectable wives, and grudgingly admires the courtesan's 'Superior Art of Allurements, . . . Pleasant Speech, and Harmonious Voice, as also the Arts of Musick, Dancing, Dressing, and the like', which give her an 'Artificial Perfection' that 'makes its Triumphs in many Hearts, like as in many Nations'. 'Courtesans are often assisted by the Powerful' in law-suits and petitions for government favour – areas where Cavendish herself felt conspicuously inadequate.[20] In *The Rover* Behn compares her own authorship to the pictorial self-advertisement of the great Italian courtesan, a passing fancy that Janet Todd expands into a paradigm of feminist literary history in *The Sign of Angellica*. The glamour of transgression is registered even more forcefully in Behn's comedy *The Feign'd Curtezans*. To exploit the aura of sexual freedom without actually breaking down the binary polarization of chastity and whoredom, Behn invents two sisters trying to escape confinement, one timidly virtuous and one more spirited, who decide to play the role of the 'Curtezan' – impudently declared to be 'a Noble title' with 'more *Votaries than Religion*'. As Warren Chernaik points out, this carnivalesque simulation of the high-courtesan life, with its 'thousand satisfactions' and its luxurious 'Merchandize of Love', comes to an abrupt end when a suitor offers to turn one of them instantly into what she represents (193–4). Evidently a single thrust would be enough.

Behn's *Love-Letters between a Nobleman and His Sister* dramatizes the entire range of possibilities for negotiating sexual licence within the aristocracy, from absolute binarism to the romantic cult of sublime transgression. Ferrante Pallavicino, bitterly criticizing the deceptive high-class prostitute in *La retorica delle puttane*, protests that his satire does not apply to the rare 'puttana honorata' who gives delight without 'interest', and the English whore-biography likewise makes an exception for the female hedonist who refuses to link her own pleasure to 'mercenary' gain – despising such materialism as 'a mean mechanick Chamber-maid trick'. (Scornful repudiation of the 'mercenary' became *de rigeur* in Restoration narratives of socially ambitious prostitution.) In Behn's novel, the lordly Philander claims that he would *not* be jealous of his wife Mertilla if she were to avow her *grande passion* for the Duke of Monmouth, that he would 'adore' the woman who follows her heart and 'generously owns the Whore', remaining true to her aristocratic nature; what he cannot forgive is the 'Jilting' and 'dissimulation' that makes her resemble the *common* whore.[21]

Untrustworthy as he is, Philander correctly identifies the problem as one of class more than sex, and his solution is to create another oxymoronic phrase poised between insult and admiration, the 'generous Whore'. In contrast, Mertilla creates a powerful and unambiguous picture of abjection when she warns her sister Silvia about the dangers of eloping with Philander (though her extreme severity can be explained by the fact that the dangerous lover is her own husband). Silvia will go straight from the condition of the most privileged aristocracy to 'the infamy of being a Prostitute', which inevitably means that she will be 'loath'd, undone and infamous as hell, despis'd, scorn'd and abandoned by all, lampoon'd, perhaps diseas'd'. The victim of the Restoration Court lampoon 'must obscure thy self in some remote corner of the world, where honesty and honour never are heard of: No thou canst not shew thy face, but 'twill be pointed at for something monstrous' (II.74–5). This vision is in many ways confirmed by the subsequent story, as Philander does indeed abandon Silvia once she becomes pregnant. But she is never wholly exposed or 'pointed at for something monstrous' (unless Behn's novel itself constitutes this de-monstration). Mertilla's prediction of infamy anticipates the indignant lampoon or 'poem on affairs of state', which in turn replicates the swelling fury of the crowd protesting against Charles's indulgence of Nell Gwyn:

> Ev'ry day they do the Monster see,
> They let ten thousand curses fall on thee:
> Aloud in public streets they use thee thus,
> And none dare quell 'em, they're so numerous.
>
> (*POAS* I.426)

Like the angry neighbour crying 'thou monster thou', Mertilla drops her 'abandoned' sister-rival into the lower stratum, hands her over to the punitive mob.

The 'pornographic' devolves into the political whenever power is perceived to depend too much on personal charisma and clandestine, unaccountable favour, and this was particularly true after the Restoration of a hedonistic culture and a seducer-king; 'in the courtier subculture to which Rochester belonged', Claude Rawson suggests, 'sex and politics were interconnected as if by definition'.[22] Sexual defamation was a universal solvent of reputation and an effective way to denigrate false empire ever since the Book of Revelation allegorized Nero's Rome as the great whore, but the flamboyant sexuality of the restored monarchy made this image literal. The transformation of the royal mistress into what Andrew Marvell called the 'new Whore of State' (chapters 2 and 5 below) came all the more easily because the relation between monarch and Parliament was already gendered, and the king's authority phallicized: Milton mocks Charles I's claim to perform 'masculine coition' on the Commons, and seditious gossip alleged that Charles II 'did bugger this Parliament much like the buggering of an old woman'.[23] Thanks to the archival labours of Richard Greaves, we know that the most outrageous gossip about royal sexuality circulated, not only on the fringes of the Court, but in the radical underground. Satires on corruption and arbitrary government frequently use the vehicle of the omnipotent courtesan, whose sexual domination of the ruler bends his judgement and inclines him to a kind of reckless, passionate absolutism in both the king's bodies, physical and politic: 'Out Flyes his Pintle for the Royall Cause / Prick foams and swears he will be absolute' (chapter 5, section 3 below).

Rochester's notorious lampoon asserts that Charles II's 'sceptre and his prick' are not only the same length but equally manipulable by whoever lays her hand on them (85–6). Scandalous rumours circulated about the papacy of Innocent X, supposedly in the thrall of Olimpia Maldachini, and even before the Civil War sexual gossip had fuelled the opposition to James I (with his 'catamite' favourites) and Charles I (cuckolded by a French Catholic queen who made the royal heirs bastards).[24] But the virulence of these sexual lampoons increased during Charles II's reign, in direct proportion to his defiance of Parliament and the (very real) influence of the French Catholic Duchess of Portsmouth, *maîtresse en titre*. This is the climate in which Nell Gwyn wins over the crowd by stressing that she is the *Protestant* whore.

The open flaunting of illicit sexuality by the privileged classes, the unreproved debauchery of what Milton calls the 'Sons of Belial', provoked anxious fascination, romantic celebration, and full-voiced denunciation. When Milton hails the 'wedded Love' of Adam and Eve before the fall, he pointedly contrasts it with the modern corruption of 'Court Amours'; more provocatively still, he equates upper-class libertinism with 'the bought smile/Of Harlots' – naming the open secret that, under Charles II, the upper and lower strata had merged into a single realm (*PL* IV.750, 765–7). In a more plebeian mode, some voices in the great riots of 1668 threatened to attack 'the great bawdy-house at Whitehall' (chapter 5 below). Court culture itself dressed up its own sexuality in a powerful myth of amorous sublimity, 'great' passion, 'generous lust', the civilizing power of Love. But even its most eloquent laureate recorded the strain: Dryden may proclaim in *Alexander's Feast* that 'only the brave deserve the fair', and in *Cymon and Iphigenia* that Love transforms even the grossest male – yet one ends in a burning city and the other in rape.

What effect, what pressure did this royal whoredom exert on the body politic? The best barometer is Samuel Pepys, who was utterly devastated by the most eminent royal mistress, Barbara, Countess of Castlemaine (later Duchess of Cleveland), 'though I know well enough she is a whore'. His ambivalence appears most graphically in his account of a conversation with the Court official Sir Thomas Crew, troubled with vapours and fits of dizziness. Crew's pornographic tale –

that the King doth mind nothing but pleasures and hates the very sight or thoughts of business. That my Lady Castlemayne rules him; who he says hath all the tricks of Aretin that are to be practised to give pleasure – in which he is too able, having a large—; but that which is the unhappiness is that, as the Italian proverb says, *Cazzo dritto non vuolt consiglio* –

comes from a disordered head, and deranges the listener too. It is hard
to tell where the gossiping courtier leaves off and the diarist begins
his commentary. The vision of Charles and Lady Castlemaine disturbs
the flow of the text by forcing a long dash, one way of expressing the
secret that must be told and not told; immediately afterwards, Pepys
again writes-and-conceals the royal organ by switching into the robust
Italian of Aretino and *La puttana errante* (a work that Pepys expertly compares to *L'Escole des filles* in a famous passage describing his response to
that lewd book). The conjunction of the fabulous 'whore' and the 'erect
Prick that wants no counsel' forces Pepys's world to split in two, just as
he himself splits into the aroused masturbator and the 'sober man' as he
reads *L'Escole des filles* 'for information sake'. Charles's priapism makes
him ignore 'the Sober counsellors' who advise him responsibly and listen
only to the mob of libertines and courtesans who surround him. But this
sexual gang have their own politics and their own *consiglio*; by calling
them 'the other part, which are his counsellors of pleasure', Pepys forms
them into a kind of carnivalesque counter-government.[25]

We shall see throughout this book that the supposedly free sexuality of
the courtesan and the adulteress was universally translated into institutional power. The porno-political theme generates innumerable satires
on the parliament or commonwealth of women, imaginary societies in
which female organization is entirely devoted to the insatiable demand
for sex. I show in chapter 3 that this trope goes back to Renaissance
fantasies of Amazonia – to the 'Realm of Women' in Ariosto, where
men are kept only for ploughing and copulation, or 'Virago-land' in
Joseph Hall's *Mundus Alter et Idem*, where women likewise rule the roost.
I will show, too, that political *pornographia* responds somewhat hysterically to serious Utopian discourses by women and to the gendering of
oppositional discourse ('Raising of Tumults is the more Masculine, and
Printing and Dispersing Seditious books, is the Feminine part of every
Rebellion'). Even the most hard-core texts participate in this politiciza-
tion, questioning the fundamentals of social order but at the same time
neutralizing that critique by defining women's interests as exclusively
sexual. Chorier's aristocratic sex queens reconstitute the Roman 'senate
of women', and in Pepys's favourite *Escole des filles*, produced in France
while England was generating *Leviathan* and the *New Parliament of Women*,
the more experienced speaker declares 'I cannot think leachery a sin;
I am sure if Women govern'd the World and the Church as men do, you
would soon find they would account Fucking so lawful as it should not
be accounted a Misdemeanor.' (This passage in the English translation

seemed scandalous enough for the prosecution to transcribe it into the indictment, when the publisher was arrested in 1688.) Margaret Cavendish
evidently agreed, putting this dialogue into the mouth of two discontented virgins: 'Certainly, if we had that breeding [that men enjoy], and
did govern, we should govern the world better than it is . . . for it cannot
be govern'd worse than it is.'[26]

It would be naive to assume, then, that the troubled categorizing of
women had no effect on male self-definition. *Pornographia* 'marked' men
too. Prostitutes transferred their taint, physically, socially, and sometimes
legally. Consorting with low-class whores made you a whoremonger, an
outlaw, one of that disreputable if entertaining band of scapegoats whom
Italian civic authorities called *ribaldi* and whom Milton called 'the brood
of Belial, the draffe of men, to whom no liberty is pleasing but unbridl'd
and vagabond lust without pale or partition'.[27] I will frequently draw on
Milton's phrase 'vagabond lust' as I trace the parallel history of male and
female infamy, since it shows the looseness of the *puttana errante* flowing
through the 'pales and partitions' that separate the sexes and the classes;
the whoremonger 'wanders' into the ruffian subculture, and even his
lust turns 'vagabond'. The genitals constituted the Low Countries of
the microcosm, the lumpenproletariat of the body, and consequently all
'Libertinism' – in John Evelyn's phrase – was potentially 'popular' as
well as criminal. Despite the double standard, male customers were intermittently prosecuted in *Measure for Measure*-style purges. A reputation
for sexual prowess did not necessarily enhance manhood in early modern England, and association with the fashionable hooliganism of the
Restoration, which inevitably involved stylized attacks on women, could
spoil a man's chances in the marriage market; men accused of rape normally tried to deny the shameful fact rather than boast that penetration
was consensual.[28] 'Rogue' and 'whore' were symmetrical if not equally
grave defamations, and one can invoke the other in ways that collapse
several distinctions at once: when Thomas Otway imagines two soldiers
fighting, one of them responds to the insult 'rogue' by asserting 'Sirrah
you are a Whore, an errant Bitch-Whore, I'll use you like a Whore, I'll
kiss you, you Jade, I'll Ravish you, you Buttock.'

Like *queer* more recently, *whore* and *prostitute* became verbs as well as
nouns, and could signify something done to a man as well as to a woman.
The contaminating power ascribed to the prostitute might simply derive
from a fear of venereal disease, but this normally doubles as a figure for
other kinds of invasive agency. Rochester's witty parallel between whores

and men of wit – alike because their patrons first 'enjoy' them and then 'kick them out of doors' – extends to the aftermath of enjoyment too: 'a threatening doubt remains' in both cases, since the satirist's sting lingers on like the burning of syphilis (58). Nor was it only damaged libertines who projected sinister powers onto the sexual female. Milton's *Samson Agonistes* shows with alarming clarity just what a 'deceitful Concubine' was thought to do to a man, even when (in Milton though not in the Bible) she is his wife. In a fit of self-disgust Samson declares that his emotional bondage to Dalila made him 'ignoble, / Unmanly, ignominious, infamous'. Far worse than his literal servitude, this was 'True slavery', all the more dangerous because it awakened some cross-gendered faculty *in himself*; it was not so much the Philistine woman than 'foul effeminacy' itself that 'held me yok't / Her Bond-slave'. In the eighteenth century, Randolph Trumbach has argued, the prostitute may have served as an essential marker of heteronormative masculinity, but in the seventeenth century she evoked effeminacy and bondage. Sexual enslavement is often expressed in economic terms, as alienated labour; in a famous passage of *The Doctrine and Discipline of Divorce*, Milton groans at the thought of the husband 'grinding in the mill of an undelighted and servile copulation', and even supposedly sex-positive writers complain of the 'drudgery' of stud work.[29]

One feature of the (imaginary) courtesan loomed even larger than her power to pollute: her reversal of the supposedly innate qualities that assigned activity to the male and passivity to the female. Modern liberals might see the prostitute as an objectified victim, hunted, consumed, and discarded by men, but early modern *pornographes* saw agency rampant. Every fornicatrix is assumed to be potentially a dominatrix, an Amazon, a virago – reminding us that in the Aristotelean system the active principle conferred power to rule and to initiate action, being equivalent to the 'efficient cause'. As Thomas Coryate assumes in his famous description of the Venetian 'Cortezan', this causative power was linguistic as much as sexual: she is not only a great singer but 'a good Rhetorician and a most elegant discourser, so that if she cannot move thee with [vocal music] shee will assay thy constancy with her Rhetoricall tongue'. In Hamlet's terms she could not only 'unpack' her own heart with words, but extract others. The harlot traditionally 'allureth and entyceth many yonge men to their utter ruyne and decay,' and they are often imagined 'calling' their wares like street vendors, as we have seen. In celebrations as well as condemnations of the sexual underworld, the 'whore paramount' is assumed to *make* young men hunt after her, to *create* the desires she assuages. The seductress is assumed to have gained the upper hand, to have become a 'codpiece queen' riding men with a 'snaffle' or bridle – which explains the strange blurring of boundaries, in popular rituals like the charivari or Skimmington ride, between the whore and the husband-beater, the passive male and the cuckold (chapter 2 below).[30]

Agency-reversal even defines the dynamic of arousal and consummation. In Donne's first satire the 'fondling' London humorist, addicted to 'plump muddy whore and prostitute boy', finds himself 'Violently ravish'd to his lechery' when he glimpses his Love at a window. In the heat of his epistolary passion, Behn's Philander declares *himself* the 'ruin'd' party, the helpless slave of his emotions, even though Silvia will clearly be the one 'undone'. The unpredictability of the genital mechanism itself takes agency away from the would-be phallocrat; in Behn's poem 'The Disappointment' it is the swain embarrassed by sudden impotence who is 'o'er-Ravished' and 'debauch'd', not the nymph he had hoped to conquer. Even in hard-core texts like Chorier's *Satyra Sotadica*, where we might expect the phallus to reign unchallenged, the vagina is dramatized as a hungry creature that 'eats the prick raw' and inspires outbursts of mock-consternation like 'Give me back the one I lent you, you bad girl! The one you've given me isn't mine! I don't recognize it!'[31] Chorier assigns a moulding and consuming force to female sexuality, but he also assumes that the priapist wants women to make him 'recognize' himself. Legal records show that similar powers were indeed projected onto the courtesan. She was frequently associated with the kind of corporeal magic that created invincible desire in men, breaking down their self-control by infiltrating menstrual blood or a specially inscribed communion wafer into their diet. Other cases show her 'forming' her male acolyte and telling him who he is, placing him in the social world. Her sexual expertise extended to refinements associated with upper-class voluptuarism, so she can initiate the raw male into élite pleasures or refuse to grant him that privilege, reflecting back his own class-identity in a reduced mirror. Hence the indignant retort of the Roman prostitute to an aggressive client from the upper-servant class, who had asked to sodomize her: 'that was not the behaviour of a gentleman, but rather of a papier maché gentleman', a hollow simulation made of recycled scraps or *carte stracce*.[32]

This capacity to ratify or cancel male identity, to confer or deny honour, can only increase with the social advancement of the upper-class courtesan or royal mistress, to whom even Margaret Cavendish had attributed 'Magick Power'. This power is partly imaginary and partly

material: the influential mistress could indeed instigate attacks to 'vindicate' her honour, protect courtiers out of power and writers in danger,
promote plays, create fashions, guarantee friendly access to royal favour,
and procure plum positions even in the Church – the source of obscene
jokes about the 'Bishopricks' enjoyed by the Duchess of Cleveland (chapter 5 below). The *cortegiana honesta*, herself a living oxymoron, mediates
between competing models of masculinity and reverses the 'marking'
process of *pornographia*. She insists on actively distributing the favours of
a *grande dame* rather than passively receiving the ignominy of a common
'prostitute'. In Dryden's *All for Love*, a virtual catalogue of the powers
ascribed to the emergent category of 'mistress', the Roman general fears
that Cleopatra will emasculate Antony, entice him away from the military
ethos, and 'ruin' him entirely (a neat antithesis to the wanton rakes 'ruin-
ing' young ladies); she herself, in contrast, encourages his battle-prowess
with the chivalric gift of a 'Ruby bracelet set with bleeding hearts' and
promises to crown his Mars-like victory with a night of love during which
she will 'mark you red with many an eager kiss' – a vivid *hetairography* that
leaves the heroic body as 'red' as any militarist could require.[33]

3. UNRULY WOMEN AND THE CULTURE OF FESTIVE VIOLENCE

We can now begin to account for the violence that surrounds the prostitute world, all too evident in the legal records as well as in the more
aggressive genres of literature. There seems to be no intrinsic reason why
shopping for temporary sexual liaisons should result in knife wounds,
showers of filth, insulting graffiti, broken windows, mass assault, and
rape. But so it happened. This phenomenon can be located at the convergence of three powerful forces: the competition for honour among
women themselves; masculine fear of incontinent female agency, converted into a graphic counterattack on women who might 'mark them
red' as Cleopatra marked Antony; and society's disciplinary desire for order and visible hierarchy, such that the different grades of woman could
be 'read' on the surface either in their dress (yellow veil, scarlet letter) or
in their flesh. The impulse is to render alien or excessive woman *graphicae*,
just as criminals could be identified instantly by the brands imprinted on
their faces. As Laura Gowing concludes from London defamation trials,
the threat to 'slitt your nose and marke you for a whore', like the insults
'flat-nosed whore' and 'your nose turns up like a drabb's tayle', expresses
the wish that prostitutes be recognizable through their physiognomy, dis-
tinguishable from chaste women by something gaping and obscene in

DEL SOZZO AMANTE IN SECONDAR LE BRAME,

OTTOBRE

SORE

CH'ESCA DA LA PRIGIONE E GIA DECISO,
MENTRE TAL'VN DE SYOI PIV FIDI AMICI
PER DE INO DE SVO AMOR LE SFRECIA IL VIS

Figure 3. Giuseppe Maria Mitelli, *La vita infelice della meretrice* (1692), etching (detail)

their features – a distinction that Nature should have already wrought, but which the thug's attack can easily arrange.[34] 'See my Credentials written in my Face . . .'

Cutting the face remained the cruellest of these revenges and the one closest to *graphē* as engraving or inscription. When the graphic artist Giuseppe Maria Mitelli depicts this assault as a normal episode in the life-cycle of the *meretrice* (fig. 3) he uses a light slashing line almost as rapid as the cut it represents, and dramatizes the paradox at the heart of these rituals of humiliation: though the attack is supposed to manifest the woman's guilt and the vigilante's righteousness, in Mitelli's etching it is the assailant who looks more furtive, raising doubts about whose face is more shamed.[35] This disfiguring punishment, which 'marks' the victim permanently as a whore but at the same time guarantees that she can never again exercise that profession, was so common in Renaissance Rome that Aretino's Nanna commissions the artist Maestro Andrea to paint a false wound on her cheek, spurring revenge against a hated customer. The ghoulish equivalent of face and artefact was reinforced when the courtesan Antea, subject of Parmigianino's transcendently beautiful portrait, was herself assaulted and maimed this way. Plebeian women would attack each other by threatening the face, Parliamentary soldiers dispersed women petitioners by cutting off their leaders' noses (chapter 3 below), and in the highest echelons courtiers would use the same kind of violence to eliminate an unpopular or too-powerful mistress. In a particularly lurid episode of *The English Rogue*, an estranged lover cuts off the husband's ear, tried to do the same to the wife's nose, then pulls out a poem in which he declares himself free of his former sexual idolatry: 'Down must the *Dagon* of thy face I vow.'[36] Facial mutilation occurs in quarrels between men too, but the occasion often turns out to be a loose tongue betraying the secrets of a loose woman or transferring the taint of whoredom. When Charles II ordered a troop of guards to slash the nose of the MP Sir John Coventry (chapter 6 below), the true cause was his disparaging remarks in Parliament about the king's 'pleasure' with actresses like Nell Gwyn – a paradigm for every other kind of arbitrary prerogative. Charles's savage attack, like other punishments meted out to those who spread prurient gossip or joked about the royal mistresses, 'vindicated' Gwyn's dubious honour in the style of a 'Hector' or 'bravo', a street bully or a prostitute's bodyguard, at once quashing and confirming the association with whore culture.

Even the most privileged courtesan lived in constant fear of physical assault, and even when they did not permanently scar the victim these attacks often 'de-face' her in revolting ways. In a case discovered by Elizabeth Cohen, one Roman courtesan hires a man to thrust a paper package of excrement into her rival's face, and this offensive action became common enough to earn its own category in legal discourse and to feature in revenge narratives across Europe. Grimmelshausen's Courasche, the picaresque figure later translated into Brecht's 'Mother Courage', performs the same disgusting trick on a rival whom she calls 'the most celebrated *Putana*' (using the Italian loan-word to drive home the alienation-effect). And in Restoration London the actress Rebecca Marshall was put in her place by precisely the same means. Determined to resist the threats and scurrilous accusations of aristocratic back-stage visitors who treated the theatre as a brothel, Marshall filed several petitions for royal protection. In response one hostile courtier hired an anonymous 'Ruffian' to perform an attack almost identical to Courasche's: when challenged as a pickpocket the assailant 'turned his face and seemed to slink away', then wheeled around, picked up excrement, and smeared it on the actress's face and hair.[37] As in Mitelli's face-cutting vignette the intended shame seems to redound back on the furtive perpetrator; to attack a putative whore this way makes him a bully, a common thug or street 'Hector', and thus the inseparable companion of the whore herself.

In more sophisticated versions of this 'smearing', a shameful image or text is attached to the person or the dwelling. Rabelais's Panurge, as well as sticking horns on husbands and sexual fluids on women he wants to humiliate, pins phallic amulets to their clothing (II.xvi, xxii). Contemporary court records show similar exercises of ingenuity – fastening horns to create cuckoldy monsters, attaching lampoons, obscene pictures, or fabric models of the genitals (chapter 2 below). Other assaults bring the shameful part into view more literally, 'tumbling' women on their heads, lifting their skirts, covering their overproud genitals with homely substances like beer or butter (chapters 2, 6). Most common of all are what Cohen has identified as 'house-scorning' rituals, where the pornographic mark is transferred to the symbolic body of the building. These attacks, sometimes reinforced by obscene songs, could express the male aggression of the disappointed Romeo or the humiliated social climber, but are frequently instigated by women themselves; in one case the assailant took part in the raid herself, in male disguise.[38] The goal is to brand the female occupant as a whore, and the ensuing lawsuit aims to restitute her honour and undo the public shame. Interestingly, some of these cases are brought by women who clearly identify themselves as courtesans – like Aurelia, the rejector of the 'papier maché gentleman' – but who still fight to preserve their civic honour, to resist the equation of prostitution with the most abject outlaw status, and so to reject the binary system that would throw all sexually unconventional women into the gutter, making them literally *puttane errante*.

Sexualized attacks on bawdy houses are already familiar in ancient Roman ritual abuse, and survive at least into the eighteenth century. When Catullus threatens to rape an entire roomful of his rivals, what he means is 'I'll write over the whole façade of your tavern with penises'; instead of the literal phallus humiliating the mouth (*irrumare*), the 'forehead' or *frons* of the building will be sullied with graphic representations.[39] The same expressive device still flourished in seventeenth-century Rome, where various other house-marking gestures (throwing excrement, blood, ink, stones, or animal horns, breaking down doors and windows) are taken to court and explicitly forbidden by law 'even if the victims are prostitutes or courtesans or Jews' – the three categories of scapegoat most liable to being smeared with impunity. Like the excremental assault on the face, many of these house-scorning gestures migrate across national boundaries and form a kind of gestural lingua franca: throwing or fastening horns on the house, for example, shows up in Roman legal codes and in London defamation suits, which also record fantastic verbal images of the cuckold's horns getting stuck in doorways and breaking holes in neighbours' walls. In France, as Jacques Rossiaud and Natalie Davis have shown, violent attacks on the houses of suspected women featured in the repertoire of the 'youth fraternities' or 'abbeys of misrule', organized gangs of adolescent males – and occasionally females – whose ritual abuse of deviants sometimes ended in mass rape. In England, the same unstable mixture of vigilantism and youth riot was licensed in the Shrove Tuesday demonstrations of the London apprentices, who broke in the doors and windows of brothels, mauled their inhabitants, and in some cases demolished the entire house. After the Restoration this calendrical festival of violence evolved in two directions, into the alarming bawdy-house riots of 1668 (chapter 5 below) and into the 'frolics' of the upper-class Sons of Belial (chapter 6), as epitomized by Rochester's 'Disabled Debauchee':

> I'll tell of Whores attack'd, their Lords at home,
> Bauds Quarters beaten up, and Fortress won:
> Windows demolish'd, Watches overcome;
> And handsome Ills, by my contrivance, done. (45)

At a time when glass panes were relatively new and expensive, the broken window became the ubiquitous symbol of cracked reputation, inflicted by the aristocratic hooligan, the middling apprentice, and the plebeian neighbour; according to one accusation that ended up in court, the splendidly named Emma Bacchus even broke her *own* windows to advertise her place as a 'whore house'.[40] The window-smashing mob is still feared by the inhabitants of the genteel brothel where Richardson's Lovelace keeps Clarissa.

Pornographia thus applies to the 'house' of prostitution in every sense – the physical fabric, the social institution, the symbolic body. Raids on the home are closely associated with literal disfiguring: loud banging or smearing excrement on the door represents the foul mouth of the alleged transgressor, broken windows (or shutters before the advent of glazing) undo the seductive power of the eye, and the façade itself, spattered with foul liquids or scrawled with horns and phalluses, stands in for the social and physical countenance. As Cohen points out, 'both bodies and houses are enclosures which honor decrees must be protected from illegitimate penetration by outsiders', and contemporary humour even referred to the vagina as a *casa*.[41] Throughout this book we will trace the interchange between sexual body and urban locale, building, household, street, institute, office – even royal palace, as ruling-class libertinism turns the House of Stuart into a 'great bawdy-house'. The increasing wealth and prestige of the 'mistress', exacerbating the status-confusion provoked by the *cortegiana honesta*, focussed even more resentment on her 'house'. Already in Pallavicino's *Retorica delle puttane* the modern courtesan maintains (literally and metaphorically) a façade of the utmost respectability, a simulacrum of quality that the text attempts to 'demolish' by aggressive exposure. As we shall see in chapter 6, house-scorning flourished in Restoration London even as the codes of politeness began to reduce the general level of personal violence: the rebuilt and expanding metropolis, where fashionable status was expressed in well-glazed and architecturally uniform new streets and squares, rang to the sound of breaking glass. The paradox of the home-owning whore is nicely encapsulated in the opening scene of Etherege's *Man of Mode*, where the plump, bawdy Orange-Woman, a figure straight out of Rabelais or *Bartholomew Fair*, turns out to own the lodging-house where the dazzling heroine Harriet is staying. Property brings propriety, as she herself reminds the rake-hero Dorimant when she sets limits to his ritual abuse: 'say your pleasure of me, but take heed how you affront my House' (I.i.192).

'House-scorning' and other attacks on the successful but deviant woman take on the protective colouring of festivity – carnivalesque, ritualized, and therefore exempt from the usual strictures and interpretations. 'Pleasure' and 'affront', in Etherege's terms, were interchangeable. Sexual acts claim to be punishments, executions of justice mutate into bawdy theatre, tolerated 'misrule' slips into priapic disorder – and vice versa. Protests *against* prostitution become indistinguishable from a failed attempt to insinuate oneself *into* the world of illicit sex. Rossiaud makes it clear that the house-attacks and gang-rapes of the *confréries de jeunesse* should not be understood as random explosions of sexual energy, any more than rape in the twentieth century; they acted out a distinct ideology and imposed a deliberate social identity on women, forcing them into the underclass under the guise of 'moral' punishment. In Roman lawsuits as well as English drama, the vigilante attack often expresses the sexually charged fury of the rejected suitor; by a kind of inverse semiotics, he marks the 'whore house' because its occupant refuses to act the whore, or yells 'procuress' at a woman who refused to procure her sister.[42] Whether he meets virtuous resistance or the selectivity exercised by the better class of courtesan, the response is the same: mark her as the commonest whore, powerless to refuse anybody. *Pornographia* evolves into what we might call the *pornotropic*, its purpose being to turn the victim *into* a prostitute rather than to bring out her existing condition.

Sex, violence, judgement, and festivity intermingle with Protean ease. Solemn divorce proceedings in the House of Lords turn into ribald entertainment when Charles II pronounces them 'better than going to a Play', and conversely libertine celebrations of sexual pleasure evoke its punishment: in Donne's elegies a flash of white sheet suggests penitence as well as intimacy, and in Carew's 'A Rapture' the vision of sexual Elysium dissolves when he ends by calling his lover 'Whore'.[43] Lampoons against royal mistresses like Nell Gwyn, sometimes no more than the sexual gossip of an adolescent in-group, can spill over into the jeering of what Tim Harris calls the 'police crowd', adapting old shaming rituals to the *bagarre* of urban politics. Traditional carnivals balance on the knife-edge between civil war and sexual anarchy, as Emmanuel Le Roy Ladurie shows in a vivid French case where the festive 'King of Youth' initiates a peasants' revolt and the gentry cite the ladies' fear of gang-rape to justify killing him. Udine had its 'Cruel Carnival', while in London the 'Evil May Day' and bawdy-house riots boiled over into violence perceived as undermining the state itself, even though their leaders claimed to be upholding ancient custom.[44] We will see this paradox acted out repeatedly in the following chapters, in the charivari and in pseudo-vigilante pornography like *The Wandring Whore*: riotous disorders, lewd exposés, and even sexual assaults could claim to be enacting traditional social justice, while the official sentences of the courts often echoed popular shaming rituals and provoked exactly the bawdy, irreverent response they were meant to stamp out.

The very fact that the English Church court – the main body that disciplined sexual behaviour and the source of the richest archival stories – was universally known as the 'bawdy court' indicates the perceived relation between illicit sex and its punishment. Cuckoldry and adultery constituted at once the most serious and the most hilarious transgression, so that all attempts to regulate them could dissolve into shameless laughter – itself a kind of illicitly procured pleasure, as the word 'bawdy' implies. The constable who enforced order is also the chief figure of fun, considered fair game for blows and crude jests. Numerous travel writings and rogue narratives suggest that spectators flocked to Bridewell to enjoy the sight of prostitutes' breasts under the lash. When King Lear

denounces the 'rascal beadle' for secretly desiring the whore he disciplines, he stops short of suggesting that the whipping itself might be an
expression of his lust, but by the Restoration punitive rage and carnivalesque enjoyment had fused into a voyeuristic and even sadistic response.
Punishment abutted on entertainment just as Bridewell stood close to
the Duke's Theatre, a fact that Wycherley points out to his audience with
some glee; their proximity in his own mind is revealed in his remarkable
image of sexual 'drudgery', when copulation itself starts to resemble the
punishment inflicted on fornicators in Bridewell ('each dull Husband
beats / The Hemp of Wedlock in the Wedding Sheets'). Official penalties exploit this ambiguity and encourage popular mockery when they
feel confident that the shame will focus on the malefactor: the blasphemous preacher must ride backwards like the cuckold in charivari; the
brothel-keeper must be carted to the accompaniment of rough music,
'all the way basons to be rung before her'.[45]

We shall see in chapter 2 that revellers arrested for indecent disorders
put up two opposite kinds of defence, sometimes simultaneously: they
were enforcing traditional values by some 'ancient administration of justice', or they were letting off steam on an equally traditional holiday. In
both cases they claim that their behaviour was customarily 'chartered'
for a particular date or place. The ambiguity was deep-seated: scholars to this day remain unable to decide whether carnival represents a
celebratory liberation of the lower stratum *à la* Bakhtin or a repressive
containment that reinforces the frame by temporarily suspending it, as
Umberto Eco argues; early modern authorities were similarly puzzled,
and their paradigm-confusion had real consequences. Annual holidays
produced not only drunken riots but attacks on women – faces cut over
Christmas, bawdy-houses smashed on Mardi Gras, rape at Midsummer –
though they also *licensed* women to take bawdy initiatives.[46]

In the great metropolis of London, moreover, the suspended account-
ability of carnival time extended into space. Certain zones of the city
denote perpetual, semi-tolerated misrule: Turnbull Street or Whetstones
Park signified full-time prostitution, Smithfield meant coarse entertainment and Grub Street poetry, St James's Park sustained aristocratic
promiscuity, Billingsgate and the Thames permitted fluent obscenity
from the fishwives and watermen *and from their customers*, temporarily released from decorum. These fishy, runny areas constituted a kind of
alternative sexual city, what one pornographic satirist called 'Erotopolis' and another '*London* separate from *London*'. The 'liberties' of the city
could literally be free-floating. Edward Ward's *Rambling Rakes or London*

Libertines describes the Folly, a 'floating Seraglio' or pleasure-boat moored on the Thames, whose inhabitants are 'as lewd as *Sodomites*' and whose entertainments are 'far more hideous than the ruff Musick at *Ludgate*', conducted 'with as much *Decorum* as the *Cripplegate* Pioneers on my Lord Mayors day'. The point of Ward's work is to identify and reconstruct the pockets of festive misrule in London, connecting them by cross-reference in an equally loose narrative scheme; the whole pamphlet, as its title suggests, is a 'ramble'. But London 'free' discourse mixed graphic discipline with its priapic licence, as Ward shows when he reconstructs a typical bantering-match between a Thames waterman and his lady passengers: 'Have a care of your Cheeks, you Whores; we shall have you branded next sessions, that the World may see your trade in your Faces.'[47]

My paradigmatic example of ambiguous licence is the 'riding' or anti-procession, displaying those who transgress the laws of gender in a public ritual at once humiliating and triumphant. The dominant wife and timid husband – inevitably branded a cuckold – were forced to ride backwards on a wretched horse; the indicted whore was dragged behind a cart and whipped, to the same accompaniment of rough music; the loudmouthed scold, before being 'cucked' or ducked in the pond, was dragged in a festively adorned iron bridle like a dancing bear, or paraded on a chair or privy-seat, a kind of parodic throne that recalled the pre-Reformation cult of the Virgin. (The interchangeability of these anti-processions can be glimpsed in *The Taming of the Shrew* when Kate's old suitor wonders whether to 'court' her or 'cart' her (1.i.55).) The excessive woman and in-adequate man (often impersonated by neighbours in a kind of burlesque) are 'pointed at for something monstrous', but they also flaunt that excess and animate the disorderly creativity of the crowd, who wave horns, hoist up underwear, invent lewd lampoons, and act out what the mismatched couple do in bed. The carnivalesque shaming ritual may be licensed up to a point, but it always threatened to overflow the bounds of decorum (which is why it is best documented in legal records). Charivari could be feared as an outpouring rather than a disciplining of vagabond lust, since it stirred up the dregs, the 'brood of Belial', the ribalds who played such an enthusiastic part in European cruel carnivals: time and again we hear from the hooting chorus of street boys – or 'Boys and Girls' according to Marvell – who ridicule the whore, the cuckold, and the female protester with bawdy abuse. The riding could be experienced as a sexual event in its own right, inflamed by what Ben Jonson called 'car-nivale concupiscence' and what another seventeenth-century wit called

'Carnelevation', a kind of erection of the flesh that gave the festival its name.[48]

Reversing this association, copulation itself is frequently compared to public festivities of sportive humiliation, stylized violence, and flamboyant display of what should remain private. Aretino describes a group orgy organized as a joust, and this mock-chivalric imagery flourishes in English pamphlets like *The Wandring Whore* and *The Hue and Cry after Beauty and Virtue*, where vigilante violence and carnival concupiscence merge into a single rage, the degree zero of *pornographia*: 'Every *Apprentice* Codpiece almost itches / To run a-tilt at those polluted Bitches; . . . Brand them like *Cain*, let *Whores* wear *Whorish* marks!' The Sack of Rome is figured as the rape or punishment of a pornographized *Roma lasciva* – most vividly in images taken directly from Giulio Romano's sexually explicit *Modi* – while the gang-rapes described in Aretino's *Ragionamenti* explicitly recall the ritual atrocities committed during the Sack.[49] Sex becomes 'scouring' – a term that denoted the festive-violent assault on a tavern as well as the dirty work of cleaning – or 'roasting the Bartholomew pig', or 'Fescennine games', referring to the traditional Roman festival of licensed obscenity; this euphemism is used by the 'Puritan' Milton as well as the 'pornographic' Chorier. Underlying all these abject and sublime images of sex as public spectacle is a kind of genital mock-heroic, most fully organized in the poem that coined the title *Puttana errante*. Here the 'wandering' whore mutates into a female knight 'errant', with the full panoply of a warrior-heroine out of Ariosto: she marches to increasingly outrageous sexual exploits under a 'banner' of flying penises and strange positions, her weapons being the 'arse naked' and *la potta spalancata*, the cunt displayed (or literally 'splayed out'). These exploits end with a full triumphal procession into the devastated city of Rome, where she both exemplifies and allegorizes the sexual predation of the invading army.[50]

That the mock-procession signifies both the denigration of female agency and the triumph of the genitals is already captured in Renaissance graphic art. The meeting of Phallus Couchant and Cunt Displayed is fully realized in an extraordinary drawing attributed to Francesco Salviati, disseminated in several engravings (fig. 4).[51] In an etching attributed to Parmigianino (fig. 5) Priapus assumes the position that heralds would call Rampant, ridden in a strange nocturnal procession that is half witches' sabbath and half charivari. The grotesque but powerful rider, of indeterminate sex, wields the distaff that feeble husbands were forced to carry in the charivari, but the diabolical attendants suggest a sorceress and the owls perhaps identify her as the carnival figure Mother Folly,

Figure 4. After a drawing attributed to Francesco Salviati, *Triumph of the Phallus*, etching

Figure 5. Attributed to Francesco Parmigianino, *Phallic Sabbath*, etching

tamer of unruly males. Obscure as it is, this image emblematizes the associations of rampant arousal that energized even those mock-processions that ostensibly attacked the unleashed sexuality of the dominant woman. It certainly does not glamorize sex, and cannot be called 'erotic' in the soft sense; indeed, its *diablerie* could be interpreted as a protest or exposé of illicit priapism in an unholy alliance with witchcraft. But the etching also *constitutes* an illicit sexual act, an indecent exposure flamboyantly violating every canon of modesty, making the phallus vastly and comically visible. Riding rituals may censure but they do not censor; demonstration reveals shame, (di)splaying the *pudenda* in every sense.

Renaissance phallicism opened a vein of imagery that still flows in Restoration satire. Etherege describes his drinking partners scratching 'couchant cunt and rampant prick' on sooty tavern candlesticks. Samuel Butler's famous account of the charivaresque Skimmington ride (chapter 2, section 3 below) includes the distaff and spindle, the mock-heraldic '*Petticoat* displaid and Rampant', and the flaunted phallus, wielded by the 'triumphant' wife in the form of a 'Bull's pizzle'. (Hogarth's illustration adds a witch, as we see in fig. 7 below.) And one of the best-known lampoons of the period, 'Signor Dildo' (later attributed to Rochester), invents a life-sized running penis with the Italian title Count Cazzo, beset by a disorderly 'rabble' of English pricks and Court mistresses when he visits Whitehall.[52]

It comes as no surprise, then, that the focus of charivari shifted so fluidly. Where did humiliation stop and celebration begin? Who was the butt and who the ringmaster, or more often mistress? 'Riding' had positive as well as negative connotations, and the charivari against the upside-down couple assigns the wife a role like that of 'Phyllis Riding Aristotle' in popular engravings: in Butler's excruciating rhyme, the Petticoat Rampant is indeed the appropriate standard for a woman described as 'Amazon triumphant'. Riding *backwards*, an almost universal symbol of ignominy, could be imposed on a surprising variety of transgressors – not only the submissive husband but the over-confident wife-beater (the speciality of Mother Folly in Dijon), the adulterous priest, the over-zealous Quaker, or the reactionary 'Abhorrer of Petitions and Parliaments'; he who 'abhors' one kind of political procession finds himself stuck in another.[53] Even this abject role could be played with gusto and converted into a gesture of ribald defiance – for example, by lifting up the animal's tail and turning the *pudenda* back on the audience – just as the humiliating exposure of women could become the classic mooning gesture: rather than being helplessly stripped or 'tumbled' by a male gang, the proud woman hoists up her *own* skirts, either to shame the enemy (like Caterina Sforza in Machiavelli's *Prince*) or to illuminate her surroundings, like the villager who

> went and laid upon the ground
> And tucked her coats about her round,
> And because she is so brave and fine,
> She tucked up her heels and said she would show the moonshine.

Even the most misogynist ridings, like the ducking of the scold, could be perceived as triumphs. Marvell recalls a woman who, every time she emerged from the water, unabashedly continued to make the hand-gesture that declared her adversary a 'Lousy Rascal and Cuckold'. 'The *Cucking Stoole*', one antiquarian remarked, 'gives the tongue liberty 'twixt every dipp.'[54]

4. UNPACKING THEIR HEARTS WITH WORDS

'Liberty of the tongue' proved to be the most alarming and the most appealing feature of whore culture. The prostitute's speech-acts broke through deference and modesty, solicited strange men, initiated encounters, 'called' her wares like Billingsgate herring. The flurry of ribaldry and festive-violent ritual that surrounds her generates a reciprocal discourse that contaminates (and amuses) the male customer too: a typical social handbook imagines new visitors to Town 'bantering the *Whores*, and what's more probable, the *Whores* bantering of them'. Whorish speech in men struck Samuel Butler as itself a form of sexual perversion:

A Ribald . . . is an unclean Beast that chews the Cud; for after he has satisfied his Lust, he brings it up again into his Mouth to a second Enjoyment, and plays an After-game of Letchery with his Tongue much worse than that which the *Cunnilingi* used among the old Romans.

In a similar vein, the Elizabethan statesman Lord Burghley genders discourse itself as a scandalous female: 'Qu. What strumpet of all other is the most common prostitute in the World? A. *Lingua*, that common-Whore, for she lies with all men.'[55]

Burghley's playful riddle recalls Hamlet's fiercer equation of language and prostitution, his intellectual's fury at finding that he 'must like a whore unpack my heart with words'. Though Hamlet refers only to the cursing of the most vulgar 'drab', he still concedes her the power to 'un-pack' interior feelings (or the lack of them) like a literary critic. Higher in the social scale, the Renaissance courtesan produces a refined form of conversation for which (Montaigne complains) she charges as much as for the 'whole business' of sex, and the influential mistress deploys an even more valuable kind of speech when she intervenes with powerful patrons or promotes a literary career: even Ferrante Pallavicino, resentful author of a 'Whore's Rhetoric', benefitted from it when a well-placed courtesan had him released from prison. Hamlet defines (and adopts) the 'low-libertine' fluency of the oyster-wench, but analogies soon developed between the upper courtesan and the most culturally developed language, the most ornamental and sensuous poetry (or 'Rhetoric' as Pallavicino and Coryate put it). For George Herbert, the 'sweet phrases, lovely metaphors' of devotional verse can only be conceived as redeemed Magdalenes, denizens 'of stews and brothels' whom he has washed with his tears and brought to church. Jonson similarly promised to 'raise the despis'd head of *poetrie*', whom the degenerate age has 'adulterated', but the career he proposes for her is more worldly: she will emerge 'worthy to be imbraced and kist [by] all the great and master-*spirits* of our world'.[56]

The 'Magick Power' of courtesans consisted in their ability to compose themselves in every sense, to transform gesture and speech into artefacts and fix them in writing, turning *pornographia* into *autographia*. (Quite literally, inscribed hosts and written 'goodwill cards' played a significant role in the sexual spells that Venetian prostitutes were accused of casting.) Coryate attests to the seductive power of the 'Rhetoricall tongue' and 'that heart-tempting harmony of her voice'. High courtesans like Tullia d'Aragona and unclassifiable goddesses like Gaspara Stampa – 'sirens' in several senses – attained high standards in vocal and instrumental music, particularly in reciting their own poems to *arie* that supported the words. As Martha Feldman points out, such status as the courtesan enjoyed depended on her cultural performance, on a Protean adaptability shared with her namesake the *cortegiano*, and her critical instrument was the voice, in conversation, song, and poetic composition; correspondingly, vocal articulation came to be sexualized, by hints that all sopranos must be courtesans, or by images of poetry and music as the *ruffiana dolcissima* or 'sweetest bawd' who entices the soul towards unknown pleasure.[57] Tullia d'Aragona escaped the public shame of prostitution 'per poetessa', on account of being a poet, while Veronica Franco reclaimed the courtesan's right to control the representation of her own sexuality, creating 'opere amorose' in literary and corporeal form. Royal mistresses became literary patrons, and freely mingled their sexual and cultural 'favours' – as we shall see in the tangled relationship of Wycherley and the Duchess of Cleveland (chapter 6 below). These associations were precisely reversed when professional women authors were disparaged as mere whores. Wycherley himself, accused of being a 'he-whore' for his services to Cleveland, wrote a laboured poem 'To the Sappho of the Age, suppos'd to Ly-In of a Love-Distemper, or a Play,' slandering Behn by equating her authorship with pregnancy and venereal disease; what else can she expect when 'Men enjoy your Parts for Half a Crown'?[58]

Like Falstaff, the *cortegiana honesta* was 'not only witty in herself, but the cause that wit is in other men'. Lustfulness is next to lustiness, and this vibrancy can be transferred from body to discourse – a transference figured in bluntly sexual terms. The Earl of Dorset declares that 'cunt' drives every literary endeavour, and the Rochesterian gentleman-poet claims to have 'never Rhym'd but for my Pintles sake'; in Rochester's own obscene poetics, the penis becomes a sort of pen just as the vulva speaks in the mouth and the mind itself becomes a 'Whore'. In a politer version of the same trope, the mistresses of London boast that they provide the poet with all his 'Humours, and smart Repartees, for garnishing his next Play'; indeed, 'without us the Theatres would be empty' – meaning empty of ideas as well as audience.[59] Wycherley may have demoted Behn's wit to a kind of gonorrhea (masking his own writerly dependence on the illicit sex-world), but other versions of this parallel between inspiration and disease mitigate the insult by their sheer exuberance, playing fantastic variations on the symmetry of pen and penis, copulation and conversation. In *The Whores Rhetorick*, for example, the author Philo-Puttanus praises the literary influence of the 'University of London Courtesans' with an almost Swiftian surge of invention:

> You have at this instant got the Maiden-head of my officious scribling Instrument, as you have some years since the Virginity of another Quill. The Ink of this is black and smutty, but that of the other was of a more innocent and pleasing colour; though after having been improved by your conversation, it changed once its native Simplicity for the variety of all the colours in the Rainbow ... A little of that sharpness you inspire into your Lovers Urine, would give my periods a grateful relish: and a small proportion of that Mercury you procure for the Salivation of your faithful Servants would sublimate my fancy beyond the feculent dregs of matter ... May every line be as poignant as an embrace of yours, and each Sentence, like you, carry a sting in its tail. (ff. A3-v, A6-v)

Tom Brown, writing in the persona of the 'virgin actress' Anne Bracegirdle, recalls that Aphra Behn could turn a raw young student into 'an establish'd Poet' by means of 'a buttered bun'; 'bedding with a Poetess' transmits literary inspiration, like other kinds of 'Contagion', through the

exchange of erotopoetic juices. A dour moralist like Nathaniel Ingelo uses
the same metaphor of venereal infusion to *denounce* imagination, when
it 'transgresses the limits' of decorum and 'returns abus'd with hurtfull
delight, and instead of being us'd decently, is unworthily prostituted'.
(As Margaret Doody observes, 'Fancy is here oddly gendered; like a
school*boy* straying out of school into unlawful play, sneaking off to prostitutes at midnight, Fancy is yet also a *whore*, feminine and effeminate,
"prostituted".')[60] This 'hurtful delight' could be deplored or endorsed.
Just as 'queering' now denotes a brilliant, energizing, critical distortion
of received truth, so 'prostituting' or whoring connoted zest, salty wit,
forbidden inventiveness, a worldly kind of intelligence incapable of being
duped by established morality.

Rochester's own parallel between whores and wits extends to the roots
of authorship itself. As in *The Whores Rhetorick*, they share an economy
of diseased body fluids that 'sharpens' the satiric expression. In *A Satyr
against Mankind*, for example, he wittily spins out the similarities that link
'Women and men of Witt' as 'dangerous tools': men normally 'kick them
out of doors' after enjoying prostitutes, but 'The Pleasure past, a threat-
ning doubt remains, / That frights th'enjoyer with succeeding pains'
(58). In mercurially rapid alternation, Rochester occupies the position
of the kicker and the kicked, the fearful priapist smarting from syphilis
and the active wit-as-whore or whore-as-wit, who arouses the patron
and burns him with the virus of 'satyr'. Elsewhere, Rochester invents
a hysterically jealous male persona who calls his ex-mistress 'a *Whore*
in understanding' even though it is he who 'like a whore unpacks his
heart with words', and a female author who hesitates to write because
'Whore is scarce a more reproachfull name / Than Poetesse' (79, 64).
Rochester's pedestrian followers turn this formula into simple denunciation; the misogynistic satirist Robert Gould, for example, quotes the
'Punk and Poesie' equation to condemn female authorship *per se*, after the
feminist critic Sarah Fyge had shrewdly remarked that he 'would adulterate all Womankind, / Not only with your Pen'.[61] But Rochester himself
relishes it. The man of pleasure who 'never rhymed but for his pintle's
sake', or the lewd satirist who writes on a menstrual cloth and 'dipps his
Pen in Flowers' (37), becomes not merely a creature constituted by the
genitalia and therefore ideologically 'female', but a particular kind of
female defined by vice, scandal, and extremity – a whore in understanding. Through his female mouthpiece Rochester admits that transgression itself is the chief spur to writing, 'Pleas'd with the Contradiction and
the Sin' (64).

Public sexuality induced not only flashes of wit but entire narratives. The severe aristocrat Mertilla in Behn's *Love-Letters* unwittingly turns her sister's 'monstrous' self-prostitution into a provocative if covert advertisement for the novelist herself: 'a hundred ages may not produce a story so lewdly infamous and loose as thine' (II.74). As Alison Conway suggests, the projected career of the high courtesan 'sounds like a formula for good fiction-writing', and the more 'lewdly infamous' the tighter its hold on the reader.[62] This helps to explain the extraordinary recurrence of similar whore stories across time and space: the wit of the errant mistress herself – escaping detection or devising some humiliating trick for a rival or customer – spurs the emulation of the story-teller, who authenticates it by finding new details and new reasons to believe it first-hand. Stories from Boccaccio show up as eye-witness accounts in *The London-Bawd*. The trick that prompts Courasche's revenge – the wily *puttana* slips her a drug that causes embarrassing bowel movements – is told in the sixteenth-century *Tariffa delle puttane di Venegia* and again in Restoration London, where Nell Gwyn reputedly disables a rival this way. The tale of Robert Carnegie, who supposedly contracted the pox from a common prostitute in order to infect his own wife and her royal lover, circulated in Court like the disease itself (chapter 4, n. 54 below), but the identical story had been told about François I of France. The 'pornographic' narrative migrates between fictional and truth-telling contexts, bawdy tale and bawdy court, suggesting a close symbiosis between the tricks and insults circulated in the scandalous text and those recorded as fact in legal prosecutions. One London defamation case hinges on just such a comic tale, though its consequences are tragic (the husband dies of shame and the widow's chances of remarriage are blasted): in a modern variant of the old Boccaccian bed-trick, a City wife claims to be attending the Puritan sermons in St Antholin's church while she secretly works in a brothel; the husband disguises himself as a gallant and encounters her in this illicit realm. Though this real-life case lay in the archive until Laura Gowing unearthed it, the double-trickster story itself, complete with its anti-Puritan setting and its local urban details, resurfaces in low-libertine fiction like *The London-Bawd*.[63] Narratives migrate or 'wander' like the picaresque heroine herself.

What kinds of literature, then, did the courtesan culture sustain? From the lower stratum came hybrid narratives combining criminal and sexual 'tricks', from rudimentary Elizabethan whore-dialogues to the 1660s *Wandring Whore* pamphlets and the largely plagiarized *London-Bawd*.

(Dialogue-form was suggested both by Continental models like Aretino and by the native flyting tradition, still alive in a slanging-match between Billingsgate and Turnbull Street that Pepys collected among his 'Penny Merriments'.) Disorderly 'ridings' and calendrical festivals generated such an abundance and variety of lewd lampoons that Martin Ingram considers them a 'separate genre' of ritualized mockery ('Rhymes', 178); these low-libertine performances already constituted a kind of charivari on paper, and so could be incorporated all the more easily into the ceremony of abjection. This was 'licentious' discourse in a double sense, poised between 'chartered' or licensed indecorum and the sort of obscenity that undermined Christian discipline and corrupted the king's subjects.[64] As the political conflict intensified, so did the vogue for sexually charged 'parliaments of women' (chapter 3 below); this genre, initiated by Erasmus but rising to a double peak in the 1640s and the 1680s, clearly articulates a fear of women's loose tongues as well as a feeling that politics have been feminized by extending the franchise. Specific 'hot zones' of London even spawned their own texts, as we gather from the composite title *Newes from the New Exchange, or the Commonwealth of Ladies* (1650). John Taylor the 'Water-Poet' converted the traditional licence of the Thames boatman into a literary career, pouring out an astonishing mix of bawdy jests, royalist propaganda, and social commentary on whores and apprentices. Low festive markets like Bartholomew Fair not only *inspired* literary representations (the best known being Jonson's play of that name) but actually produced printed 'fairings', keeping alive the licentious atmosphere. In the 1640s these souvenir pamphlets identify the carnivalesque Fair as a 'fucking exchange' or as a nest of radicalism, in the 1660s they play variants on the Wandering Whore motif, and in the 1690s, as the air filled with financial revolution, they become facetious catalogues of women for sale, like John Dunton's *An Auction of Whores, or the Bawds Bill of Sale for Bartholomew Fair* (1691) or Richard Ames's *Catalogue of Jilts, Cracks, Prostitutes* on display 'every Night in the Cloysters in Smithfield . . . during the time of the Fair'. The respectable visitor could take home items like

Mrs. *Eliz.* (alias *Betty*) S----*ds*, formerly a Retailer of Oranges at the Playhouse; the very Quintessence of Leudness, who brags she has been tilted at by as many Lances, as there are Men in the Confederate Army: her price is 5*s.* and a Clap she gives into the bargain.[65]

Aretino's mock-chivalric jousting image has been updated for a polite and commercial age.

Disciplinary efforts by the middling classes likewise produce textual *pornographia*, and even the outrageous *Wandring Whore* announces its goal as 'publishing to destroy' the prostitutes it lists. The loose-tongued Water-Poet carries an aura of festivity with him, but so does the earnest constable and the social reformer who emulates the constable's beat in literary form. Theatrical displays of punishment in Bridewell yield theatrical scenes on stage (notably in Dekker's *Honest Whore*) and suggest an entire volume of flogging verse, John Heath's *The House of Correction, or Certayne Satyricall Epigrams* (1619).

Humphrey Mill's book-length poems *A Nights Search, Discovering the Nature and Condition of All Sorts of Night-Walkers* (1640) and *The Second Part of the Nights Search* (1646) continue this publish-and-destroy mission on epic scale. As the title implies, Mill's 'Muse' and 'Genius' prowl through the streets at night 'apprehending' whores and procuresses, capturing them in a variety of verse narratives and dialogues – and in the process giving detailed instructions in how to find them. In this relentless *pornographe*, Restif de la Bretonne meets Dogberry. Mill's vigilante search takes a 'humorous' form, however, when he replicates the festive-violent shaming ritual, describing (and emulating) the 'kettle Musique' that rings out as the ambitious bawd, who aspires to ride in a carriage, is instead carted and 'crown'd / With Carret-tops' and chamber pots. The commendatory poems by gentlemen and lawyers play with amused condescension on the author's name (a more efficient 'Mill' than Bridewell) and on his office, as if he both represented and replaced the plodding constable. But they also take a significantly defensive tone. Like Milton defending the radical divorce tracts against the 'brood of Belial', one supporter attacks those '*Beefe-braines*' who judge Mill 'guilty as the worst of men', and another feels the need to protest that 'your booke's no bawdy-house, but a Bridewell'. We shall see in chapter 4 that fictional 'wandering whores' did indeed recommend *The Nights Search* as a training manual, and *The London-Bawd* greedily plagiarizes it. Mill himself prefaces his work with Defoesque disclaimers – 'My Muse hath kept her selfe from infection, notwithstanding the many temptations, occasions, provocations that she hath met withall in her search' – and devotes several sections to those wicked poets who lend their gift to lascivious causes, defining himself by opposition. Lewd counter-reading almost prevails in the penultimate dialogue, where the high-spirited Bawd, Pandar, Whore, and Pimp promise to lampoon the author (after lighting their pipes with his book) and analyse his motives for writing: Mill must have been rejected by his whore or barred from his usual haunts by the pox, otherwise how could he know so much and yet object so strongly?[66]

Humphrey Mill's vision of the lascivious poet proved quite prophetic. Outsiders and insiders alike perceived a kind of creeping pornotropism that transformed the whole of Restoration literature into an epiphenomenon of whoring. Nathaniel Ingelo disparaged the novel because its 'chief Design' is 'to put fleshly Lust into long Stories', and Jane Barker blames it for the 'Deluge of Libertinism', likewise defining the entire genre in terms of its sexual effect.[67] Swift's *Tale of a Tub*, in 1697, defined 'the noblest branch of *modern* wit or invention' as the art of 'deducing similitudes, allusions, and applications, very surprising, agreeable, and apposite, from the *pudenda* of either sex, together with *their proper use*' (section VI) – a habit that the *Tale* itself does nothing to dispel.

Moralists and libertines alike thus agreed with Rochester and Etherege that wit derived from the genitalia. Much of what we call Restoration comedy – particularly in the 'sex-craze' of the 1670s – is generated by the salacious wit of the rake-hero and the flirtatious heroine; Horner in Wycherley's *Country-Wife* explicitly derives his own inventiveness from the ingenious dissembling of the ladies, who adopt the fashionable look of the courtesan without actually making themselves available. Behn flirted with the idea that, for women authors, inventing sexual positions or 'making joys' in bed is exactly the same as 'making plays' for the theatre (chapter 6, section 3 below). Licentious and seductive wit became the mark of a gentleman, and class assurance the mark of literary excellence. Dryden's *Essay of Dramatick Poesie* repudiates the coarseness of popular drollery and canonizes Beaumont and Fletcher because they 'imitated the conversation of Gentlemen much better' than the rustic Shakespeare, especially capturing their 'wilde debaucheries and quickness of wit in reparties' (XVII.35, 56). Debauchery, wit, and aristocratic *élan* are qualities that he evidently considers inseparable. Even when he turns away from Restoration libertine values, Dryden still equates the literary and sexual character of his own culture: the virgin purity of Anne Killigrew will counteract the bawdiness of all other poets, redeeming 'this lubrique and adult'rate age'.

Embracing and elevating 'wild debauchery' required new theories of decorum and a new kind of critical reading. This was already grasped in the late sixteenth century by Giordano Bruno, who influenced English Court culture through his *Spaccio della bestia trionfante*. How should later generations receive obscene classics like Aretino's *Ragionamenti* ? In the second dialogue of the *Spaccio* Bruno proposes a stance of amused, exalted appreciation that finds a kind of divinity in ribaldry. The adept Saulino is surprised to hear, from Sophia or Divine Wisdom herself, that the Gods' public library contains the *Priapea*, popular romance, scurrilous poetry, and most notably 'la Pippa, la Nanna, l'Antonia' – that is, the notorious *Ragionamenti* that initiate the pornographic genre. Sophia insists over Saulino's protests that the true philosopher finds these texts 'weighty and serious', since there is no reading-matter that the Gods exclude, provided it has some 'saltiness'; *sale* in this Aretine context must mean salaciousness as well as Attic wit. The divine mode of judgement (as opposed to that of the 'common' reader for whom these things are sinful) involves the aesthetic appreciation of a creative mind at play: the élite reader, like the gods themselves, 'takes pleasure in the multiform representation of all things, and in the multiform fruits of all kinds of genius'. When Saulino earnestly presses Sophia to exclude books written by 'infamous, dishonorable, and dissolute' authors, she praises their 'educational' value as 'fruits of cognition' in the highest philosophical language: the scurrilous writings of *ribaldi* such as Aretino teach

how laughter is set in motion, how disgust, pleasure, nausea; and in all there is wisdom and providence, and in everything there is everything, and where one contrary exists there the other exists to the utmost, each generating the other to the utmost.

This account of the 'extraordinary' reading process confirms the cosmological conception of divinity that runs throughout the *Spaccio*, rising and falling between the extremes in a metamorphic cycle. Though the old, immoral deities are being expelled from heaven, Capricorn is retained because he teaches an important lesson, that the gods must infuse themselves into animal Nature in order to maintain their transcendence: 'non si può mantener superiore chi non si sa far bestia'; 'we cannot keep ourselves superior if we don't know how to make ourselves into beasts'.[68]

High-libertine culture acted out this paradoxical principle to the full. Rochester and his contemporaries sought a kind of sublimity in abjection, by recasting 'wild debauchery' as *pose* or *attitude*, detached and aestheticized. They differentiated themselves from the world of 'popular Libertinism', plebeian whores, 'rough' charivaris, coarse lampoons, rascal beadles, brawling 'Hectors', and riotous apprentices, but – as we shall see in the closing chapters of this book – they did so precisely by expropriating that carnivalesque lower stratum to assert aristocratic privilege, to 'maintain themselves superior' in Bruno's terms. In this world upside down the *cortegiano* merges with the *cortegiana*, as predicted in *The Whores Rhetorick*. We have traced their affinity in Bruno, theorizing the legacy of Italian Renaissance *pornographia*, and in *Hamlet*, where the Prince feels compelled to 'unpack his heart with words' like a cursing whore, and we can find it even in the Court culture that preceded the 'Puritan' upheaval and subsequent Restoration. The extremes of high and low, the South Bank brothel and the Whitehall Banqueting House, share a common theatricality and a common impulse to transmute the body into 'Protean entertainment'. In Thomas Carew's masque *Coelum Brittanicum* – directly modelled on Bruno's *Bestia Trionfante* and thus a crucial link in the transmission of literary ideas between Italy and England – the comic character Momus declares himself the parallel of 'old *Peter Aretine*', and his scurrilous infusion of bawdy *double entendre* contaminates and destabilizes the official doctrine of the entertainment, the reformation of a once-libertine Olympus, inspired by the virtuous marriage of Charles I and Henrietta Maria. Jove is said to renounce his former lewdness with a solemn 'oath on *Junos* Breviary, religiously kissing the two-leav'd book', but the solemnity *and* the moral reform dissolve as soon as we realize what he is kissing: 'two-leaved book' was underworld slang for the vulva, the ultimate fusion of textuality and sexuality.[69] Even before the Civil Wars, then, the heritage of Aretine *pornographia* permits a transgression-effect that became ubiquitous in the Restoration, the vivid flaunting of the sexual and verbal lower stratum in the most exalted society, even in the royal presence itself.

CHAPTER 2

Ceremonies of abjection: sex, politics, and the disorderly subculture

The brood of Belial, the draffe of men, to whom no liberty is pleasing but unbridl'd and vagabond lust without pale or partition, will laugh broad perhaps . . .

(John Milton, *The Doctrine and Discipline of Divorce*)

The Conqueror's *Standard-bearer* rid,
And bore aloft before the *Champion*
A *Petticoat* displaid and Rampant;
Near whom the *Amazon* triumphant
Bestrid her *Beast*, and on the *Rump* on't
Sate *Face* to *Tayl*, and *Bum* to *Bum*,
The *Warrior* whilome overcome. . . .
'Tis but a *Riding*, us'd of Course,
When the *Gray Mare's the better Horse*.
When o're the Breeches greedy *Women*
Fight, to extend their vast *Dominion*,
And in the cause Impatient *Grizel*
Has drubd her Husband, with *Bulls pizzel*.

(Samuel Butler, *Hudibras*)

In England as in Italy, 'low-libertine' performances and representations grow from a common soil: a culture of what David Underdown calls 'expressive violence', sometimes contained within sanctioned rituals, sometimes boiling over into transgressive acts and speeches prosecuted (and therefore recorded) in the courts.[1] (The alternative term 'male popular culture' begs several questions, since 'unruly' women participated quite fully in these rituals of festive violence, and since the gentry often approved and sometimes emulated them.) What Evelyn called 'popular Libertinism' produces a range of theatrical, emblematic, and textual 'postures', charades of sexual violence that seem to reenact current political and religious conflicts in the grotesque body. We have seen in chapter 1 the striking affinity, or unholy alliance, of 'pornographic' writing and legal documents from Italy, France, and England that record (or perhaps invent) sex-related crimes, defamations, physical and verbal attacks on women during carnivals and similar occasions of misrule. The common purpose, most lucidly expressed in assaults on the houses or the faces of women judged to be prostitutes, is to incise an indelible mark or break open the façade – an all-too-literal *pornographia* that inscribes the insult 'whore' into the flesh or the dwelling-place, evicting and branding the *puttana errante*.

Since 'pornographia' is here defined as an action as much as a text, this chapter will establish the language of *gesture*, sometimes violent and sometimes prurient, that surrounded illicit or 'disorderly' sexuality in mid-seventeenth-century England. It draws upon the extraordinary wealth of stories – virtually a new genre of oral drama and written lampoon – that historians have recently mined from the archives of the Church courts and local sessions. As my epigraphs suggest, the main focus will fall on the ritualized or carnivalesque expression of this ostensibly comic violence, produced by the ribald subculture of the 'Sons of Belial' who formed a ubiquitous chorus in every village and city street. I will pay particular attention to the legal and literary representation of the charivari or 'Skimmington ride', described in texts by Cavendish, Butler, and Marvell that emulate its riotous energy. We shall see in section 2 that the violent 'marking' of the prostitute, cuckolding wife, or disorderly woman can be transferred to more general kinds of protest against illegitimate or excessive authority; this study of the political use of sexualized shaming-rituals during the English Civil Wars will serve to prepare for chapter 3, on pornographic satire and political theory during that tumultuous period. To encapsulate the inextricable fusion of priapic display, ritualized entertainment, and anti-establishment protest I shall frequently use the portmanteau-word 'Carnelevation', a clever hybrid of carnival and erection coined to describe what the Antinomian, religious 'Ranters' had in common with the debauched, secular 'Hectors'.[2] But charivari – defined by Margaret Doody as any 'mixture of the celebratory and the violent, enacted by a crowd' – cannot be contained within a single model of political opposition or phallocentric conservatism; in Doody's terms, though it 'has self-conscious criticism of sexuality as an intellectual motive, [charivari] has the sexual energy itself as a motive force', and its literary version 'often entails the strong presence of a feminine being'.[3] As Butler puts it (in a shameless mixed metaphor that resembles the Skimmington itself), when the grey mare is the better horse she literally wields the phallus, the disciplining whip made from a bull's pizzle.

1. 'VAGABOND LUST': CHARIVARI AND FESTIVE VIOLENCE

I have already established in chapter 1 the deep ambiguity of purpose and effect in festive-violent *pornographia*, the metamorphic shifts of focus from ridicule to celebration and from discipline to orgiastic release of energy. The various 'riding' and 'tumbling' rituals, like their literary counterparts, ostensibly enforce traditional sexual politics by cashiering the dominant wife or too-successful courtesan, but easily transfer their animus to established authority and enjoy a kind of roguish solidarity with the loose woman. In all kinds of ritualized disorder, and in many different cultures, the ribalds *act out* the official world as they act up. Often they assume a counter-institutional house style – 'abbeys' of prostitutes and their youthful customers or assailants, 'colleges' of thieves and whores – and even the most spontaneous-seeming frolics parody the ceremonies that regulate passion.[4]

The antics of those low enough in the social scale to be prosecuted in the English Church courts were irreducibly semiotic and rhetorical, shot through with representation and play-acting. Sexual assaults involved *both* the prurient-aggressive exposure of the whore *and* the mockery of authority, deflecting into genital farce the resentment caused by compulsory Anglican worship. Villagers would expose themselves with the words 'draw near and take this holy sacrament to your comfort', fling up a neighbour's skirts to 'show her nakedness to many' (and so declare her a public woman), or set her on her head to be 'bishoped' or confirmed, parodically inverting her body to anoint the sex rather than the head. These liturgic travesties include a drunken mock-sermon (advocating marital violence) and a mock-birthing and baptism, starring a farm labourer reputedly sodomized by the unpopular bailiff.[5] This grotesque travesty of the female birthing ritual, performed by men but stage-managed and costumed by women, evidently 'straightened' the sexual life of the village by acting out its inversions; identical ceremonies supposedly took place in the London 'Molly houses', but such pseudo-reportage must be interpreted as an urban extension of this mocking ritual rather than direct evidence for an emergent homosexual subculture.

Church court prosecution records show rural Englishmen improvising sexual versions of the rough festivities that flourished throughout Europe – baiting animals, storming a wooden castle – and replicating the sexual tricks of Rabelais's Panurge and the mock-chivalric 'jousting' orgies of Aretino's *Ragionamenti*. (Since direct literary influence can be ruled out in these cases, the satyric text and the unruly act must derive

from common roots in early modern tavern culture.) One male gang in
Somerset captured a female victim and pretended to be dogs baiting a
bear, then paraded like soldiers with a torn scrap of her clothing as a
flag; another spread-eagled a woman and acted the part of knights breaking down the walls of 'Grimcunt Castle'. In both cases they assaulted
her symbolically, throwing beer over her genitals in an ale-house simulation of gang-rape that on other occasions degenerated into the real
thing. Festive reenactments of warfare were so deeply engrained in ritual
culture that the Parliamentarians, sworn enemies of traditional 'sports',
organized a carnivalesque battle of Roundheads and Cavaliers for May
Day 1645.[6] But this 'edifying' version of stylized aggression could not ex-
tirpate its older association with sex-as-war. This performative continuity
helps to explain the resurgence of military imagery in obscene literature
after the death of Cromwell: in *The Practical Part of Love* (1660), Lucia the
inn-keeper's daughter 'stifly held out her Maiden-Castle', but 'the scaling
Ladders were erected, and the Guns planted ready to make a breach'
(3); in *The Sixth Part of the Wandring Whore* (1663) a pimp laments that
street-trading prostitutes cannot 'persuade a Gallant to enter their Forts'
despite the white flags or 'Colours' they hang out (4); in *Holborn-Drollery,
or the Fair Chloret Surprised in the Sheets* (1673), the libertine poet celebrates
the storming of 'Smock-Castle' (58).

Defamatory rituals such as the charivari or Skimmington ride seem particularly intent on creating an encyclopaedic array or *Gesamtkunstwerk*
of sexual derision and display. As the centre-piece of this performance
unruly bachelors or officious neighbours would nail emblematic horns
on houses and churches to mock the ill-matched couple, and create visual hybrids or living chimeras by fastening horns to mares and geese;
these improvised symbols amplify the visual language of the 'world
upside down' – often associated with the hen-pecking and cuckolding that provoked the Skimmington – developed in misericords and
marginal illustrations and most fully elaborated in Rabelais. The victims
themselves, or an effigy or scapegoat neighbour, would be arranged
to form a pattern of inversion, pelted with excrement and garbage,
cross-dressed, seated backwards or '*Bum to Bum*' on their improvised
mount. (Many details of the famous account in Butler's *Hudibras*, cited
in my epigraph, are confirmed by the non-literary commentary and
court records used by Underdown and Ingram for their definitive reconstructions.) Though purporting to regulate excessive or incongruous
sexuality, these processions would often turn punitive 'publication' into a

priapic display; outraged observers noticed simulated copulation or even (after the Restoration) two males in 'a sodomitical kind of conjunction' – a performance strikingly similar to the 'postures of lust and buggery' enacted by Sedley and Dorset in their celebrated Cock Tavern riot (chapter 4, section 3 below).[7]

The Skimmington procession involved its inventors in something like a low-cultural travesty of grand opera or Renaissance pageantry, drawing on all the arts. It included not only the 'rough music' of pots and pans common to all charivari, but the lifting up of anti-triumphal 'standards' made of women's underwear and animal horns, and prosecution-documents also record the display of icons such as 'a picture of a woman's privities'.[8] Butler's travestic presentation of the 'riding' as an antique Triumph conveys something of its heady excitement and pride in perverse inventiveness. Hogarth's illustrations to Butler (fig. 6) show the battle-standard of horns and smocks rampant, the riders flinging foul matter into the crowd rather than at the errant couple, and the husband forced to ride backwards and ply the distaff, prominently displayed as it was in the 'Phallic Sabbath' procession (fig. 5 above). Reinforcing the mock-triumphalism, Hogarth parodies Annibale Carracci's *Triumph of Bacchus* in the Galleria Farnese; bringing out the double association of mirth and female disorder, in one version he adds a witch (fig. 7) and in another an onlooking couple (fig. 6, upper left) whose state of undress identifies them as lovers excited by the spectacle – presumably the lusty apprentice and the tailor's wife, who makes the sign of the horn. Despite its ostensibly misogynistic purpose, women contributed to this unacknowledged branch of folk art by lending their clothes and helping to stage transvestite riots, by fabricating models of the vulva to present to neighbours they wished to shame, and apparently by acting the role of 'Amazon triumphant'. In Butler as in Hogarth, the supposed victim plays her part with evident gusto.

The multiple intersections of the visual and the discursive may be illustrated in one of the more elaborate May Games of Jacobean England, recorded because its victim prosecuted the ringleaders in Star Chamber. One float in a Wells pageant of 1607 allegorized an unpopular Puritan constable as a 'Satyr', visualizing the accusations of adultery that had already been launched against him in verbal lampoons and formally 'presented' in an accusation before the bishop. Viewers could see the illicit-yet-censorious couple in the satyr himself – who held a picture of a 'spotted calf,' the Biblical term that his alleged mistress had used to denounce the idolatrous Maypole – and in another float of a giant and

Figure 6. William Hogarth, *Hudibras Encounters the Skimmington*, large-format illustration to Samuel Butler's *Hudibras* (1726), etching and engraving (detail)

Figure 7. William Hogarth, *Hudibras and the Skimmington*, small-format illustration to
Hudibras (1726), etching and engraving (detail)

giantess preceded by a naked Cupid; according to the verse descriptions
inspired by this pageant, they simultaneously acted 'in lustie manner'
and 'looked Precise'. Tableaux and texts together form a rebus on the
two reformers linked by sexual scandal – happily named Mrs Yard and
Mr Hole – and this pun was then elaborated in further charivaresque
demonstrations. These involved transvestite allegories, a 'horned horse',
and a portable fairground 'Holing Game' incorporating portraits of the
two Puritans, perforated so that spectators could try their skills with the

ball.[9] This satyric depiction of the satyr, and this 'holing game' that literally broaches the precise exteriors of Hole and Yard, presumably generated intense verbal humour and bawdy excitement – cheering on sexual rampancy as much as exposing hypocrisy – and certainly provoked more poems that were captured as evidence. Such exuberant performances of anti-Puritan sentiment fuelled a more general suspicion of festive spectacle and spectatorship among the godly, voiced in explicitly pornotropic terms: one Wiltshire curate, shocked by Midsummer feasting, maintained 'that all women and maids that were singers and dancers were whores, and as many as did look upon them no better than they' (Underdown, 59).

Alongside their visual emblems and representations, then, festive shaming-rituals generated texts both oral and written. Already in Italy, legal records of attacks on prostitutes show that verse lampoons entered into these verbal battles over female honour – anonymous subliterary counterparts to *La puttana errante* or *La Zaffetta* (chapter 1, n. 11 above). In the English charivari, errant couples were hounded with the stylized hunting-cry 'à whore, à whore!' To judge by court actions for defamation, obliquely mentioning an insecure husband's horns was tantamount to flinging a real pair into his house. One Somerset woman fashioned a model of the vulva out of black cloth, presenting it as 'a token' to the neighbour whose genitals her husband had boasted of fondling; this fabric sculpture evidently served the same dishonouring purpose as the verbal insults for which women so often took each other to court (constituting the majority of all defenders *and* accusers in defamation cases, especially in London).[10] Creative insults included an entire play about a neighbour's adultery, performed on a temporary stage in the defamer's back yard. Rude libels and lampoons, often rhyming on obscene words, accompanied most eruptive rituals and cast a sexual slur on the hero-victim (bridegroom, proud woman, meek husband, zealous officer, political rival); many of these verses survive because of legal actions against their authors or distributors. These compositions originally formed part of the visual display: the ridiculous tackle of the horned horse involved a paper of obscene verses, or quasi-official summons to 'Cuckold's Court', fastened to its tail, and the maypole likewise came to function as a place to post rude libels, like the statue of Pasquino in Rome or Pissing Conduit in London. Once crystallized in a text, however, the spirit of 'satyric' mockery or carnivalesque display could also survive the specific occasion and proliferate in other sites and other media. The anti-Hole poems (verbally decent but filled with bawdy innuendo) circulated throughout the small cathedral town of Wells, giving merriment even to the dean's wife; one ringleader sent the manuscripts to London, making a bid for publication and national distribution.[11]

The flourishing of libertine verse in the Restoration, brought to a gamy height by Rochester and his peers, had thus been prepared in the 'festive-violent' lower stratum, where obscene text and riotous gesture became equivalent, and transgressive verbal expression was 'licensed' by a ritual-performative context. The social gulf between London Wits and Somerset yeomen might seem insuperable, but the Wells case suggests that some channels of communication lay open between the capital and the provinces. The centralized legal system allowed the outraged Hole to take his mockers to Star Chamber, and the centralized publishing industry inspired those mockers to disseminate their Holing Game as a printed broadside, part of a 'street literature' distributed nationwide and consumed by young readers of all classes.[12] Rural shaming verses frequently rework themes from the printed ballad. Country readers wrote to London for the latest lampoon (not for the scandal but to 'see the varietie of wittes'), and a few of these urban verses, as obscene as any Restoration text, survive in manuscript from the Jacobean period; one proclaims the sexual excesses of specific Court ladies in the voice of the unemployed 'Westminster Whore' – 'We pore Whores may go hang in dispaire; / Wee're undone by the Maydes of Honour' – and lament having to fall back on the ubiquitous 'Dildo'. To judge from prosecution records, oral and written scandal-texts reflect awareness of this interchange of rural and urban, Court and village: one Wiltshire woman accused her 'whore bitch' neighbour of having 'showed her arse before the king'; one libel from Bath brands its victim as a 'whore' worse than any come 'from Court'.[13]

In any case, town and country shared some common features at the level of 'popular Libertinism'. The language of sexual insult was identical in both places, and defamation cases seem even thicker in the densely crowded metropolis, where 'boys' form a ubiquitous chorus of derision: Mary Walker for example, accosted in the Strand so suggestively that 'all the boyes in the streat [did] wonder at me', took her revenge in three ways whose inconsistency did not seem to have impeded her – by hurling accusations of adultery at him and naming his 'whore', by ordering her apprentice to hang a pair of horns on the insulter's door (an urban as well as a rural trope), and by taking him to court for defamation. London had its own zones of misrule and festivals of 'licensed' excess, moreover. In 1562, for example, the

butchers and fishmongers set up a horn-covered Maypole at a point
on the South Bank already famous as 'Cuckold's Haven', and 'made
great cheer'; this totem remained in place for over fifty years, defining
the spot as a permanent Horn Fair and occasioning further carnivalesque discourse by figures like John Taylor.[14] Many of these urban
festive customs survive the Puritan reforms, or were consciously revived as a way of inducing loyalty to 'Merry England' and the restored
monarchy: 'rough music' in the prisons and on the street, customary
liberties like the verbal obscenity of Billingsgate fishwives and Thames
watermen, apprentices' riots on Shrove Tuesday or May Day (chapter 5
below). (Stylized and 'licensed' versions of this discourse, part pornographic jest and part vigilante patrol-work, sustain the work of Taylor
the Water-Poet and Mill the rhyming constable.) Bartholomew Fair above
all, delimited in time and place and regulated by its own justice system,
remained a fertile source of indecorous gesture, lewd publication, sensuous indulgence, cross-class mingling, and theatricalized riot; virtually
every motif in Jonson's play can be matched in street-literature, including the whores' complaint that upper-class promiscuity has ruined their
trade.[15]

The rural and urban élite participated in their riotous subcultures
both literally – by mingling with the promiscuous, carnivalized crowd
at events that could be interpreted as entertainment rather than
insurrection – and symbolically, by literary or artistic appropriation.
The Skimmington ride provides the decorative theme for the great
hall at Montacute and significant episodes in Margaret Cavendish's
Orations and Butler's *Hudibras*, as well as that paradigmatic scene in *Last
Instructions to a Painter* where Marvell claims to be modelling his entire
project on the instructive mockery of the charivari (section 3 below).[16]
The whole range of gang behaviour towards the 'whore', from lampoons to window-breaking and 'tumbling' assault, can be matched in
the frolics of the Restoration aristocracy (chapter 6 below). Bartholomew
Fair was visited by courtiers as well as country yokels, just as in France
Henri IV visited the Foire St Germain and bought 'six little pictures
of the "figures of Aretino"', which he 'showed laughing' to other male
courtiers. Jonson's great comedy can be seen as another example of this
expropriation, while its bold metatheatrical prelude provides a less benign model of élite intervention in the carnival. The old stage-keeper
complains that Jonson has failed to catch the true spirit of the Fair,
by failing to include upper-class violence against prostitutes: to make
his play authentic, 'a *Punque* set under upon her head, with her Sterne

upward,' should have been 'sous'd by my wity young masters o' the *Innes o' Court.*' In the Commonwealth and Restoration, Bartholomew Fair continued to provide opportunities for the carnivalesque fusion of high and low culture; 'Lady Holland's Mob', a riotous crowd instigated by their noble patroness herself and bearing her effigy in triumph rather than mockery, would declare the Fair open the night before it officially began.[17]

Even serious-minded moralists like Evelyn and Milton register the presence of the festive-libertine subculture, mentally recreating its responses in order to define their own ideals by contrast. Defending his revolutionary divorce tracts against the charge of 'Libertinism' and voluptuarism, Milton acknowledges that

> the brood of Belial, the draffe of men, to whom no liberty is pleasing but unbridl'd and vagabond lust without pale or partition, will laugh broad perhaps, to see so great a strength of Scripture mustering up in favour, as they suppose, of their debausheries; they will know better, when they shall hence learne, that honest liberty is the greatest foe to dishonest license.[18]

Milton places this festive-aggressive chorus both within and outside high culture; they may be the 'draffe' or dregs of society, but they will 'perhaps' read his learned treatise and extract dangerously subversive ideas from it, under the guise of carnivalesque laughter. His divorce writings were indeed mentioned in a familiar and jocular spirit by the bawdy pamphleteers of the London underworld; in one malicious gossip-sheet, 'Mercurius Philalethes' asks whether certain adulterous neighbours 'have not studied the Doctrine of Polygamy and Divorce together'. Milton himself participated in this comic discourse by writing 'Sotadic' diatribes and rough sonnets about the divorce-tract scandal. His contemptuous reference to marriage as a pair of 'clogs', in a privately circulated manuscript poem, anticipates Restoration lampoons on wives as 'The clog of all Pleasure, the luggage of Life'.[19] The very terms of his original attack combine echoes of two converging traditions, English underclass ribaldry and Italian 'pornography': 'vagabond lust' is precisely what drives *la puttana errante*.

Milton's characterization of the ubiquitous 'brood of Belial' raises an important question: what, if any, is the *purpose* of the signifying practices that I group here under the term 'festive-violent' or 'low-libertine' representation? The lewd chorus will 'laugh broad' in anarchic merriment, but Milton assumes that their mirth has a distinct goal beyond mere trivialization – a programmatic justification of their 'debaucheries', a systematic deconstruction of the distinction between 'licence' and 'liberty', a levelling of all the 'pales and partitions' that separate marital rapture from 'vagabond lust'. Where convenient, however, participants in festive violence would emphasize their 'broad laughter' as an end in itself, denying purposiveness altogether. Ringleaders arrested for disorderly conduct passed off Skimmingtons as harmless 'sports' or traditional merriments 'without any hurt done', even though they clearly aim to damage their victims' 'credit' and regulate sexual behaviour by mocking those couples who deviate from the norm.[20] The violent frolics recalled by the old stage-keeper in *Bartholomew Fair*, again, denote pure theatrical merriment tinged with nostalgia for the bygone 'humors' of the Fair, yet they seem strongly motivated by the same punitive impulses that created the grotesquely '(di)splayed' body of Italian satire. The Wits' gesture of inversion ('a punk set under upon her head, with her stern upward') expresses the misogynistic desire to cancel the upright posture and bare the sex. The 'sousing' of the whore – in these London revels as in rural disturbances – replicates the 'pumping' of thieves and the 'ducking' of scolds (to wash off the filth thrown over them or to 'cool' their overheated sex); the participants flood away the community's own impurity, but also vicariously pump their fluids into her. Florio made the connection explicit in his dictionary, explaining the Italian *trentuno* – the gang-rape by thirty-one men, gloatingly recreated in Aretino's *Ragionamenti* and the poetry of his followers – as the exact counterpart of an English 'pumping of a common whore'.[21]

When mocking ritual boiled over into riot, then, its proponents could put up a double defence against charges of immorality, libel, and public disorder. Either they define their transgression as a 'chartered' or 'licensed' merriment without programme or designation, an exercise of 'sportive wit', 'a harmless pastime ... not only lawful but in some sort necessary'. Or else, like Swift defending his *Tale of a Tub*, they claim a traditionalist moral purpose, an enforcement of 'community values' that justifies the anarchic, excitable form of expression.[22] Mockeries like the Skimmington drove home a conservative and misogynist ideology, particularly targetting strong and sexually expressive women, but their anti-sexual purpose was often belied by lewd diction, transvestism, 'obscenity and filthiness acted publicly', genital exposure, and sadistic quasi-rape; as Ingram points out, 'mocking rhymes and the like involved a prurient or even pornographic element which suggests that they sometimes served as a proxy form of sexual indulgence rather than a clear-cut condemnation of it'.[23] Contemporaries defined this conjunction of prurience and festivity by coinages like 'Carnelevation'. Nevertheless, moralistic and disciplinary claims could be made even for unequivocally genital behaviour, such as the gang-rapes perpetrated by sexually aggressive adolescent subcultures throughout Western Europe, apparently tolerated by the authorities as long as they affected only the lower orders and maintained social barriers. In Aretino's circle literary commemoration (and reinstigation) serves the regulatory purpose of destroying social ambition by levelling the *cortegiana onesta* to the *puttana errante*, and in the French cases researched by Rossiaud this vigilantesque motive is even more explicit: youth gangs 'would smear their victims in advance by calling them whores, so that they could present themselves as dispensers of justice, acting on behalf of some moral code'.[24]

The 'pornotropic' shaming ritual, like the 'pornographic' narrative, thus embodies what Ingram calls a 'peculiar mixture of the penal and the festive', and this mixture could be reproportioned to suit the occasion ('Ridings', 96). Festive misrule sometimes purports to enforce the laws against immorality, and sometimes proclaims a Rabelaisian or Bakhtinian gaiety, according to the source of the challenge. Godly authorities (including Milton) treat irruptive mockery as an onslaught against the 'pales and partitions' of social order, anticipating Kristeva's definition of the abject as 'what does not respect borders, positions, rules'; rioters and their sympathizers assert the reverse, anticipating Umberto Eco and the containment theory of carnival. When deviant sexuality or 'vagabond lust' plays a central role – as the object of punitive scorn or the main ingredient of explosive 'Carnelevation' – it doubles this slippery, indeterminable quality, creating what a seventeenth-century wit might have called a 'lubric' effect. The same paradox or referential instability runs through the English charivari and the Italian urtexts of pornography: do these discourses and gestures represent punishment or celebration? indecent exposure or moralistic exposée? a critique of 'dishonest' sexuality, or an instance of it?

The sexual culture of what Milton calls the 'brood of Belial' should thus be understood as a synthesis of 'disorderly' behaviour and 'loose' text, a ritualized theatrics that provides the context, occasion and analogue for discourse. Its ostensible purpose is to castigate female agency as sexual excess, to designate or pillory the termagant wife and submissive husband, according to the pornotropic logic that makes them automatically 'whore' and 'cuckold'. Text and gesture alike forge the association between shame and sex-made-public, attempting to obliterate the status-confusion provoked by the successful courtesan, the assertive and pleasure-loving wife, and later the royal mistress. This involves fixing foul words and signs onto the body (in some cases literally), forcing it into inverted postures that confirm traditional hierarchies of high and low, exposing ignominious nakedness rather than defiant or resplendent nudity, emphasizing the 'bottom' in every sense. (One rural lampoon repeatedly assures an exhibitionist neighbour that 'her breech is not the moonshine'.)[25] Despite these protestations, however, the regulatory goal remains elusive and 'slippery'. The charivari – like all other attempts to harness transgressive sexual representation for political purposes – remains ambiguously poised between the release of prurient energy and the control of deviance through mockery.

This work of abjection might suggest a homogenous culture of histrionic masculinism, bent on adjusting gender relations through violent theatrical display. But women too joined in these stigmatizing parties, belonged to the 'abbeys of youth', led riots against oppressive conditions that affected the food supply, helped male neighbours with their transvestite disguise, instigated verbal defamations and house-scorning raids, and achieved a kind of authorship as 'makers of rhymes and lewd songs', inglorious but certainly not mute. Before and after the Restoration, the squire's wife herself sometimes prompted or acted in shaming rituals like the Skimmington ride. Nor can the rioters' motivation be explained by sexual politics alone. On one occasion, female protesters turn the ambiguity of carnival into the argument that because 'women were lawlesse, and not subject to the lawes of the realme as others are', they are licensed to demonstrate against abuses like enclosure.[26] Male participants are likewise driven by larger issues of community politics, acting out the whole range of contradictions and rivalries that divide their society – youth versus age, bachelors against married men, village against town, apprentice against master, decency against lewdness – using gender as a stalking-horse. They take every opportunity to dress as women, to occupy the 'lawless' position vicariously. Several observers note their marginality and insecurity in the masculine role; as Swift observed, the inadequate husband was mocked by 'Those Men who wore the Breeches least', and his 'riding' was organized by adolescent apprentices. Ingram traces the 'explosive laughter' of these male rioters to a recognition of masculine limitation, 'a cathartic release of tensions built up by "everyman's" experience of the day-to-day conflicts between the dictates of the patriarchal ideal and the infinite variety of husband/wife relationships'.[27]

It seems especially appropriate, then, that carnivalesque uprisings against deviant sexuality should be associated with over-masculine women and pubescent males – or, more precisely, should provide these type-characters as disguises that allow the participation of all ages. Apart from the Skimmington, the most prevalent form of this ritualized disorder was the Shrove Tuesday storming of brothels by apprentice-boys. John Taylor's mock-encomium of the bawd allows us to grasp the multiple simulations involved, and the disturbing conjunction of priapism and aggression unleashed by an action that supposedly restrains the illicit. To demonstrate the bawd's virtues of patience and courtesy, Taylor recounts how

On former Shrove-Tuesdayes, when the unruly Rabble did falsely take upon them the name of *London* Prentices, then two or three thousand of those boothaling pillaging Rascalls, would march madly to the habitations of the most infamous *Bawds*, where they would robustiously venter, breaking open Doores, battring downe Wals, tearing downe tyles, pulling downe windowes, rending Trunkes, Chestes, Cupboords, Tables, and Bedsteads in pieces; ripping and embowelling Bolsters and Featherbeds, ravishing her mayds or stale virgins, spoyling all they stole not, and stealing what they liked, beating the grave *Bawd*, and all her female vermine, most unmanly and unmannerly.[28]

Carnival violence easily becomes 'carnival concupiscence' or 'Carnelevation', exploiting the sanction given to the apprentices and blurring the boundaries between protest and housebreaking, gang-rape and the 'disembowelling' of pillows and mattresses. The bawd limits herself to polite entreaties and refuses to take her assailants to law, presumably because she knows that the magistrates will side with the supposed apprentices. Taylor sums up their semi-authorized mix of vagabond lust and vigilante fury in one oxymoronic phrase: 'uncivill civill hostilitie'.

2 . POLITICAL CARNIVAL AND WOMEN'S CULTURE

Sexuality and female transgression thus formed the core and catalyst of actions like the charivari and Skimmington; as Ingram points out, no parades were organized to shame sons who disobeyed their fathers. But social agitation on the subject of gender could never be detached from issues of government, and the lewdness of the accompanying text forced it into the ambiguous zone between jollity and sedition; as Sir Francis Bacon framed the crucial distinction, in a royal proclamation of 1620, 'convenient freedom of speech' should be encouraged but 'licentious' and 'lavish' discourse severely forbidden. Charivari frequently generated a surplus of signification, spilling over into more seditious areas and gaining what Ingram calls an increasingly 'political flavour'. Until King's Bench unequivocally declared the Skimmington a riot rather than a festive custom, in 1676, subversive messages could be conveyed in slippery, 'lubric' disguise – exploiting the double meaning of 'lawless' articulated by female protesters.[29]

Sexually charged carnival (masquerading as innocent merriment) was used to protest abuses of power in all the theatres of authority that could be conceived in gendered terms. Charivaris, horn-displays, 'satyrical' tableaux, and lampoons attacked Puritan spoilsports, rivals for local office, incompetent justices, enclosers, strip-miners, oppressive bailiffs, lackeys of the Crown, and absentee landlords – a tradition that resurfaced in Jacobite Skimmingtons against George I as a 'damned cuckoldy rogue'. In one tight-knit community studied by the historian Richard Cust, horn imagery and rude lampoons target a bailiff who could not go about his business because crowds of children chanted a poem about him, provoke a Star Chamber suit against a rival for a place on the bench, and fuel an extended campaign against the squire's 'patriarchal control', including allegations about the sexual escapades of his wife and daughter with the servants, and poems about his son's impotence (*and his frolics with London whores*); in each case, the point was to destroy 'credit' and thus authority to administer. Critics charged that such lewd parodies of insurrection would 'utterly subvert all manner of order and government' (referring to an improvised 'jury of whoremongers' who put local notables on trial).[30] Defenders, as we have seen, would sometimes hide behind traditional liberties and sometimes claim to be carrying out the work of the authorities.

Evasive as it sounds, this conservative line of defence was quite plausible; official sanctions and promulgations did indeed emulate popular spectacle in both its celebrative and punitive aspect. English customs continue the punishments common in many Italian cities, described in unabashedly festive terms by eyewitnesses: in the Ferrarese ceremony of the *scopa* or 'sweeping', for example, the adulteress ran naked through the town, beaten by 'boys' and pelted with rotten vegetables by the courtiers – one of whom reported to Isabella d'Este that 'the merriment was as great as can be, and great the noise when the poor lady's fleshly charms came into view'.[31] (*Mostra delle carne* plus unbridled violence generates *la festa grandissima*, a combination that the English would call 'Carnelevation'.)

Anti-enclosure rioters dressed as 'Lady Skimmington' were forced to stand in the pillory in their female costume, reversing the direction of the mockery.[32] Branding and other facial mutilations resemble the disfiguring violence unleashed on prostitutes. Carting and whipping recreate the abusive procession, while pillory and stocks 'display' the victim to encourage showers of eggs and filth. Skimmington riders flaunted underwear on poles, Shrove Tuesday rioters slashed up feather beds, and the Church courts ordered penitents to wear a white sheet in public; each of these actions turns the place and trappings of intimacy inside out. (The penitential association of bed-linen, which recurs throughout seventeenth-century libertine writing, already dominates Donne's attempt to imagine 'his mistress going to bed' as a wholly pleasurable event.)[33] The male customer of a whore may be forced to 'ride the wooden horse' and then be ducked like a scold. Star Chamber would frequently condemn malefactors to ride backwards, the posture of the cuckold in Skimmington rides (and a symbol of ignominious reversal that seems to have been imposed on scapegoats throughout early modern Europe); in one case they even deliberated upon whether a horse or an ass would draw the greater crowd of hooting boys. In the village of Enborne, a widow found guilty of sexual 'incontinence' could only regain her economic rights if she rode backwards and recited a lewd rhyme, declaring 'Here I am, / Riding upon a Black Ram, / Like a Whore as I am.'[34] The authorities demand this act of *autopornographia* in order to purge the offence itself and undo the designation of whore, but the poem and the 'riding' mark her indelibly.

This official expropriation of festive-violent carnival continued irrespective of régime. James Nayler, the insurrectionary Quaker suspected of succumbing to the influence of his female disciples, had to ride backwards en route to his public disfiguration; though the Commons debated Nayler's punishment at great length, this carnivalesque provision was accepted without discussion.[35] Four years later Parliament showed a similar awareness of popular festivity when it voted to restore the monarchy on May Day 1660, in synchrony with the erection of maypoles and the outbreak of rituals that 'resembled a protracted May-Day celebration'. Once restored, Charles II introduced obscene 'rump' imagery into his Coronation Arch, initiated new holidays, and expanded Bartholomew Fair from three days to two weeks; simultaneously he chose St Bartholomew's Day, already notorious for the butchery of the Huguenots in 1572, to begin his draconian ejection of Puritan ministers, while his judges designated Smithfield for the execution of dissidents.

Grasping this logic, the visionary Solomon Eccles protested 'a savage raid on a Quaker conventicle' by walking naked through Bartholomew Fair, wearing his famous fire-and-brimstone hat and crying 'remember Sodom'. As we shall see in the later chapters of this book, elements of the old festive bawdy crept back into anti-Stuart sentiment despite Charles's efforts to monopolize the Dionysiac: a rhyming lampoon fastened to Lady Castlemaine's door proclaims that the only reason she has not been 'ducked' is that 'she is by Caesar------'; Pepys records that her scandalous life in the royal bed is already cried out by 'every boy in the street' – the perennial chorus of ribalds and corner boys of any age.[36]

Throughout the various 'great rebellions' that marked the 1640s, both sides exploited this carnivalesque element in popular politics. To an observer in 1643 the Skimmington ride seemed ready to 'escalate into sedition', and alarmists throughout the period of conflict characterized the opposition as a carnival out of control. The Lenten figure of the 'Puritan' steps straight out of such a scenario, as does Milton's allusion to the royalists as 'Suburb-roysters' or 'the ragged Infantrie of Stewes and Brothels'. Contemporaries draw frequent parallels with the revolt of Masaniello in Naples, which erupted out of the ritualized mischief of organized youth groups, and emphasize the elements of carnivalesque violence and sexual display: the storming of a paper castle; a mock-battle turning serious; women's brigades marching under their own officers, armed with halberds and roasting-spits; the castration of collaborators accused of 'treason to the people'; the charismatic leader 'dropping his trousers in public'; his corpse flung into the open sewer. In his lewd and outspoken newsbook *The Man in the Moon*, John Crouch expropriates popular ceremonies of mockery for the royalist underground. The Lord Mayor's procession becomes a classic parade of City cuckolds, with a triumphal display of horns in Cheapside. And Lord General Thomas Fairfax, whose withdrawal from politics seems to have been influenced by the anti-regicide convictions of his wife, becomes the classic hen-pecked and over-domesticated husband; Crouch's nickname for the general, 'Tom Ladle', plays on the derivation of the word 'Skimmington' from the massive skimming-ladle used in cheesemaking, an exclusively female activity. Crouch even invents (or perhaps records) a Skimmington ride staged by stallholders in Smithfield against Lord and Lady Fairfax, one year after the execution of Charles I (which Anne Fairfax had vociferously denounced from the gallery of the Commons). In this case, royalist counter-culture coincides with the pornotropic sanctions imposed by state power: as the soldiers moved to silence Lady Fairfax, who appeared in a vizard-mask, they cried out 'Down with the whores!'[37]

Links between insurrection and shaming ritual thus went deeper than mere propaganda, giving dramatic form and energy first to popular protest (on both sides), and later to official repression. The apprentices who drove Laud from Lambeth Palace – an organized version of the hooting boys unleashed against malefactors and deviants – reportedly carried the latest libel in their hands. Viscount Conway, responding to this intensely political uprising, captures its genre and its ambiguity of purpose by declaring 'I beleave the prentices will make but a Shrove Tuesday busines of it.' Conversely, after the Presbyterians had committed a violent action in 1647, denounced by Stephen Marshall as a 'horrid rape' of Parliament, they tried to excuse it as a mere apprentice riot.[38] As in the Sack of Rome, the iconoclastic forays of the Parliamentary army often became a prurient, spectacle-hungry riot, in one case accompanied by the 'ceremonial riding and ducking of a whore'. Early in the Civil War, at a rally organized by the Cavaliers, a butcher's wife 'came running with her lap full of ram's horns to throw at them', and later attempts to destroy Quaker meetings also used this time-honoured gesture of lewd repudiation. The Antinominian 'Ranters' embraced and simulated the disorderly performative subculture, but in many cases popular festive violence turned against the sectarians: the Diggers were attacked by a crowd of men in female dress as well as by 'ignorant bawling women' themselves, pornotropically described by Winstanley as 'the ammunition sluts that follow the *Norman* camp'; anti-Quaker demonstrations, as Underdown has found, 'often contained elements of charivari ritual'. As with earlier enclosure riots, official punishment of Quakers staged its own cruel carnival, launching a kind of Skimmington ride for Nayler, and humiliating women preachers with the cucking-stool or the scold's bridle.[39]

This disorderly reinforcement of hierarchic order had already been launched against the Levellers, and their indignant descriptions of police raids reveal the continued political utility of ceremonial abjection, sexual innuendo, and pornotropic abuse. Agents of the Stationers' Company ran through Elizabeth Lilburne's house and stole linen prepared for her imminent childbirth, evoking the festive-penitential display of white sheets and smocks. The Cromwellian officer sent to arrest Richard Overton behaved like an apprentice storming a brothel or a gang leader preparing a mass rape, hurling accusations of adultery, whoredom, and cuckoldry at everyone in the house, and proclaiming 'in the Court and Street, amongst the souldiers and neighbours, that *it was a Bawdy-house, and that all the women that lived in it were whores*'. Overton even allows himself a grim pun on 'sheets', having hidden his seditious books in the bed being rifled for signs of adultery. His wife Mary received the worst of this 'porno-political' treatment when the House of Lords, 'for ever to obliterate the honour of her *modesty, civility,* and *chastity*', committed her to Bridewell, that public sewer or 'common Centre and receptacle of bauds, whores, and strumpets, more fit for their wanton retrograde Ladies, than for one who never yet could be taxed of immodesty'. She is literally dragged through the dirt, accompanied by highly theatrical shouts of '*Strumpet* and vild *Whore*, thereby to possesse the people that she was no woman of honest and godly Conversation'; never again will she be able to 'passe the streets upon her necessary occasions any more without contumely and derision, scoffing, hissing, and poynting at her, with such or the like saying, as see, see, *there goes a Strumpet that was dragged through the streetes to Bridewell*'. The Puritan establishment unleashes its own lewd spectacle, which Overton assumes will be irrefutably effective and endlessly replicated in the neighbours' responses. It harnesses the tainting power of charivari to destroy the image of the 'honest household' on which the Levellers depended for legitimacy, and to redefine public space as a dangerous pornosphere, 'a common shore and sinke' rather than a zone where women like Mary Overton can go about their proper business.[40]

Mary Overton's abject or pornotropic treatment – and her vociferous appeal against it – reminds us that the Civil War and the period of radicalization created multiple opportunities for women's intervention in public activity. In the political, religious, and military arenas these innovations compelled alarm and admiration, creating both heroic and mock-heroic possibilities for representing the *virago* or assertive woman, the principal target of charivari. During the war itself women on both sides launched donation campaigns to raise troops, commanded country houses under siege, organized supply-trains, built fortifications, and even bore arms; metaphors that women had used to describe their devotions ('I have according to my duetie brought my poore basket of stones to the strengthening of the wals of that Jerusalem') now became more literal and concrete.[41]

Before the outbreak of hostilities, royalist townspeople like Taylor the Water-Poet used sexual mockery to allay their fears for the city's destruction, reviving ancient jokes about City wives who 'know well enough already the danger of Courtiers and Cavaliers, and therefore dare meete the roughest Gamester of them all in any posture whatsoever'. After London had been fortified with the help of women's brigades who marched in military order and 'Labour'd like *Pioners* in *Trenches*', satirists and eulogists alike evoked this more activist model of women's power to force the enemy to 'stand'. A clergyman-poet on the Parliamentary side, James Strong, celebrated women's contributions to the defence of Lyme in a heroic poem, but then found himself the victim of a kind of literary Skimmington ride; his manuscript fell into the hands of royalist enemies who published it under the travestic title *Joanereidos*, with mock-commendatory poems and satirical annotations full of bawdy *double entendre*. This hooting gathered momentum in the thirty years between the Civil War and the reprint of 1674, where additional poems extol 'the Masculine-Feminine Poem of Mr. *James Strong*, Poet Hermaphrodite'. As with the molly and the cuckold, Strong's alleged identification with or deference to women causes his sexuality to be dragged into the open, belittling his feminism and his artisanal origins by reducing him to an 'Implement' of women's desires; prefatory poems praise his 'experimental' skill in removing obstructions from the womb and fighting 'at Poniard point / (The Western Women know it)'. The subjects of his celebration are downgraded by evoking lower-class women's experiences (assisting at the birth of 'Monster-children', teaching infants from a horn-book, bidding for oysters and herring at Billingsgate with 'tongues more loud than bellowing Drums', being flogged by the constable), yet even this mockery fails to undo the sense of achievement. Where Strong writes 'The weaker vessels are the stronger grown', the would-be misogynist editors come up with the same proverb that Butler uses to explain the Skimmington ride: 'The gray Mare is the better Horse.'[42]

Away from the battle front, women initiated a number of independent political actions, drawing on popular stocks of fighting words and ritualized gestures. The best known of these public demonstrations are the massive mobilizations of women to petition Parliament during the 1640s, which generated a bawdy counter-literature still flourishing in the Restoration (chapter 3, section 2, chapter 5, section 2 below). But even their smaller-scale interventions suggest that women had evolved a festive-aggressive culture of their own, ready to break out on both sides of the political divide. Its rituals of affirmation (with undertones of militant coercion) include the 1642 anti-enclosure protest in which women marched with their own 'pipe' and afterwards celebrated with 'ale and cakes', fortification-building processions led by 'drum and ensign', peace demonstrations (in 1643) by women uniformly dressed in white silk ribbons, and the highly organized May Day ceremonies that welcomed the newly restored Charles II: 'a hundred maids in white marched behind their own drummer'; a 'crowd of young women' took over the ceremonies, issued orders forbidding any father or employer to detain girls from the dancing, threatened fines, fell in behind their own elected 'captain', and caroused to the king's health.[43] Women's rituals of abuse (with undertones of celebratory freedom in their 'Billingsgate' language and 'unbridled' behaviour) include those shaming-gestures that bound the sexual and the political together at community level – flinging horns, flaunting skirts, making lewd songs, 'showing her arse before the king'.

3. CAVENDISH, BUTLER, MARVELL

To some privileged observers, the raucous masculine form of charivari attacked precisely the autonomy of women's culture, the advance of women into public life, and their specific contribution to religion and politics in the Civil War. Margaret Cavendish, soon to be Duchess of Newcastle, clearly makes this connection in her book of imaginary public speeches, *Orations of Divers Sorts* (1662). As Cavendish herself explains, these orations follow each other in a narrative sequence: thus a speech proposing reforms in the Skimmington ride immediately leads to 'An Oration against the Liberty of Women'. This in turn provokes so much anger in the female citizens of this market town, even after a gallant but lightweight counter-argument by another man, that they form their own deliberative assembly. (The author's preface uses the politically loaded term 'Private Conventicles', even though these gatherings are presented sympathetically and without a trace of anti-Puritan burlesque.) Then follows an entire section of 'Female Orations', starting with the celebrated diatribe that Virginia Woolf cites in *A Room of One's Own*: a militant feminist calls for 'a Combination amongst our Sex' and complains that male destruction of their freedom of association forces women to 'Live like Bats or Owls, Labour like Beasts, and Dye like Worms'. Cavendish's remarks on the Skimmington, and their position on the threshold of this display of women's eloquence, reveal her peculiar mixture of traditionalism and radicalism. She presumably endorsed the royalist association of customary rituals most vividly expressed by her husband, who in 1660 urged his former pupil Charles II to reintroduce 'all the olde Holyedayes with their Mirth', and yet her orations encourage a vision of women's public action that charivaresque 'Mirth' was intended to quell.[44]

The first speech in Cavendish's sequence, on the mocking ritual, endorses its conservative goal but calls for a more direct recognition of male responsibility; instead of the innocent *neighbour* being dragged out and humiliated, 'the Foolish Husband of such a Wife Rampant should Ride in Disgrace, Scorn, and Pain, by Reason he Suffers himself to be Degraded of his Masculine Authority' (*Orations*, 221). Building a bridge from disorderly misogyny to her next theme, female discursive community, Cavendish now invents a more direct portrait of masculinity under threat: 'I shall not be Silent, although I were sure to be Tortured with their Railing Tongues, and to be Exclamed in all their Femal Societies, which Societies ought to be Dissolved, allowing no Publick Meetings to that Sex, no not Child-bed Gossipings, for Woman Corrupt and Spoil each other' (222). The effeminization of public life, crumbling the distinction between courtesans and courtiers, flows naturally from this growth in the female 'Publick' sphere. Cavendish's impersonation of male hysteria moves easily from this vision of mass prurience to the universal assertion that 'Liberty makes all Women Wild and Wanton' (223).

Writing from a very different gender and class position, Samuel Butler signals his agreement with this identification of the Skimmington's true target by giving Hudibras an eloquent attack on the custom. When they first encounter the carnivalesque procession, however, both Hudibras and Ralpho are 'transported' and speechless for many lines, while the narrator himself describes it with a weird poetic coherence that makes the musical and triumphal references more than mere travesty; as Doody observes, the 'conglomerate and detailed misrule' of Butler's charivari 'apparently satisfies its actors in its successful creation of total dissonance', and imparts a similar pleasure to the reader. Celebration edges out victimization as the description proceeds, reinforced by the 'rough music' of the outrageous verse. The quasi-military Cornet 'proudly' hoists his 'Smock display'd' and the standard-bearer follows with 'A *Petticoat* displaid and Rampant' (the same heraldic construction as the wandering whore's *potta spalancata*, giving the whole parade the air of a genital triumph). Other riders 'busily' fling excrement, eggs, and brewers' waste into the crowd (not at the miscreant couple), as if to turn the shameless shaming ritual inside out and focus its derision on outsiders like Hudibras. The wife herself shares this aggressive pride, and evidently becomes the principal actor of the mockery rather than its abject victim. In theory the Skimmington humiliates the assertive woman, but Butler makes it *her* triumph. Like many of the boisterously sexual women recorded in the legal records, this '*Amazon* triumphant', 'Proud *Virago-Minx*', or 'insulting *Female Brave*' always takes the active role and the active verb: she 'sate' her husband in the reverse position on the horse's tail, 'made him' spin from a distaff, and turns around to 'Chastize' him when he fails (the moment depicted in fig. 6, though Hogarth substitutes the eponymous skimming-ladle for the bull-penis whip); she 'Carries' him like a victorious Roman general dragging his '*Slave*'. The opposite of '*Patient Grizel*' – the submissive heroine whose memory was kept alive in the puppet-plays of Bartholomew Fair – she belabours both her husband and the rhyme with the symbolically appropriate '*Bulls pizzel*'.[45]

When Hudibras and Ralpho recover their voices, they puzzle over the significance of this spectacle but never quite contain it. Legal records show that the Skimmington presented an acute interpretive puzzle for those who participated and for those who adjudicated: was it supposed to end in violent chastisement or innocent merriment? was it an illegal riot or an official custom? did it express royalist or radical sentiment? who was its primary target, the husband or the wife? did it concern sexuality or insubordination? Butler's characters ask similar questions. The knight is torn between his denunciation of pagan idolatry and his 'judicious wonder' at its fidelity to the ancient triumphs that scholars had only recently reconstructed. The squire drops his usual 'Puritan' jargon and adopts the Sancho Panza role of voicing what Butler intends as common sense, explaining the Skimmington as a protest against 'greedy *Women*' who 'Fight, to extend their vast *Dominion*' and 'ride their *Husbands*, like *Night-mares*' (though he admits that this only happens 'When the *Gray Mare's the better Horse*').[46]

Butler himself evidently agreed that the principal object of this abjection-ceremony was the restoration of traditional gender hierarchy. His prose character of 'The Henpect Man' reenacts the Skimmington in its metaphors of inversion and monstrosity: the dominated male 'is a Kind of preposterous Animal, that being curbed in goes with his Tail forwards'; 'under her arbitrary Government . . . He and she make up a Kind of Hermaphrodite, a Monster.' In the Skimmington episode of *Hudibras*, where these associations become literal, Butler's own narrative voice tries to impose this misogynist reading (and mitigate its unintended tributes) by comparing the androgynous wife to the popular mythical figure of Pope Joan and to '*Nero's Sporus*', the emperor's boy-lover – as if all disturbances of patriarchal hierarchy hastened the collapse of

heterosexuality.[47] In the latter part of Hudibras's speech, he responds
to Ralpho's 'Gray Mare' interpretation by amplifying the predictable
Puritan invective against pagan idolatry – reminiscent of Zeal-of-the-
Land Busy's assault on Bartholomew Fair – with a long and detailed
praise of women. Butler's vivid representation opens up all kinds of possibilities, which he then tries to shut down by confining interpretation to
traditional lines, anti-feminist and anti-Puritan.

Though Hudibras's goal is to gain the widow by performing deeds
of knight-errantry, he offers no conventional gallantry or generic list of
female worthies; instead, he defends (and thereby conflates) two specific kinds of active women – 'scolds' and militant supporters of the
Good Old Cause. The Skimmington offends him, not only because
it displays the Whore of Babylon astride her Horned Beast, and encourages men to 'run a-whoring' after 'self-Inventions', but because it
intends

> To scandalize that *Sex*, for scoulding,
> To whom the *Saints* are so beholding.[48]

Butler then pours out a litany of civil-war grievances against revolutionary women, in the guise of a panegyric. Female 'Apostles' set off the
conflict with their preaching, collected and melted down their silver for
the war-chest, gave moral and physical support to seditious preachers
(rubbing them down and feeding them suggestive '*Marrow-puddings*'). The
list becomes more and more specific as Hudibras gathers momentum.
Autonomous bands of women

> March'd, rank and file, with *Drum* and *Ensign*
> T'entrench the *City*, for defence in;
> Rais'd *Rampiers*, with their own soft hands,
> To put the enemy to stands.

(This hoary *double entendre* reverberates throughout the pamphlet literature, as we shall see.) Collective effort had levelled social differences,
when everyone 'From *Ladies* down to *Oyster-wenches*' helped to dig the
earthworks around London. Worse still, working women had organized
themselves into political action committees to raise funds for a cavalry
regiment, and took an active role in assessing their manpower: 'do they
not as *Tryers* sit, / To judg what *Officers* are fit?' At this moment the im-
passioned Hudibras ceases to be the spectator of the Skimmington ride,
and becomes its target-object. The rotten egg that interrupts his eulogy,
revealing the text as a kind of pillory, serves to release Butler from the
spell of an oration that threatens to compromise the poem's belittling

purpose, an unintentionally impressive catalogue of women's political achievement.[49]

Where Butler tries to confirm the Restoration settlement by making the Skimmington distinctly royalist and traditionalist, Marvell plays a double game; as he praises and emulates the Skimmington ride, he expropriates it for high culture but at the same time rescues it for oppositional politics. For him, the ancient shaming ritual launched by 'the just Street' works better than corrupt modern justice, while the 'Boys and Girls in Troops' who 'run hooting by' form a better jury because they cannot be 'concerned' for their own interest (lines 381–8). In a sense the entire text of Marvell's *Last Instructions* should be regarded as an expansion of the lampoon and the Skimmington ride, not only in its inventive obscenity but in its form – a mock-triumphal parade of emasculated leaders and sexual transgressors whose dirty linen is held up for prurient-indignant arousal. Leah Marcus characterizes both Marvell and charivari as 'merry, celebratory, grotesque, potentially violent, and tending ultimately toward reform'.[50] But that 'tendency' has nothing inevitable or straightforward about it. In Butler the sexual politics of the Skimmington (egg-splattering opposition to female assertiveness) supposedly concur with the anti-Puritan sentiment of the whole poem, but inadvertently remind us of the strengths of radical women; in Marvell the courtiers' expropriation of the riot as pure entertainment reveals their decadent irresponsibility, but his critique rests on traditional misogyny.

The Court actually visited the Greenwich riding that Marvell describes with such relish in *Last Instructions*, but if their intention was to 'relax' during the disastrous Dutch War (line 393) Marvell's festive-aggressive interpretation would have spoiled their holiday. Pepys's diary for 10 June 1667 inscribes the political implications of this event by oblique association: as the Dutch penetrate deep into English waters, he agonizes over the inability of the nation's leaders to maintain 'a good posture and credit', lamenting that everything now goes 'backwardly' – and immediately afterwards reports seeing the crowd going to watch the riding of 'the constable of the town whose wife beat him'. Marvell makes the connection explicit. The old humiliation ritual becomes a metaphor for naval defeat – the Dutch 'ride' their neighbour just as in the street ceremony – and a metapoetic emblem for what Marvell and his painter-friend are trying to achieve by reformist satire; the Skimmington 'taught Youth by Spectacle Innocent', and the 'quick *Effigy*' of his poem will do the same.[51] A typical ambiguity of phrasing complicates this statement of intent, however, just as the disorderly tumult of charivari compromises its claim to enforce order (by equally 'innocent' spectacles). To cure the nation's faults Marvell promises to 'feign / By making them ridiculous to restrain' (391–2), allowing us to read 'restraint' – his ostensible goal – as another object of feigning.

We should conclude, then, that what *Last Instructions* borrows from the lower-stratum Skimmington is neither its 'innocence' nor its antiquity – which serve as a convenient disclaimer – but its anarchic obscenity. After his lewd portraits of female influence, Marvell assails his enemies as cuckolds directly (151–4), and his subsequent pun on the cowardly 'Knight of the Horn' and his 'posture strange' (162–5) confirms the slur, turning the whole episode – the parliamentary procession of Court adherents – into a riding. 'Posture' here signifies the grotesque body as emblem of the disordered body politic, and 'Horn' reminds us of its ubiquitous sexual meaning; the phrase prompts us to look for Aretine tableaux of perverse copulation – in keeping with the aggressive display of 'prodigious tools' promised in the opening lines – as well as mockeries of impotence and cuckoldry. A similar play on the king's 'Procurers' (170) extends this charivaresque aggression to the bawd, echoing earlier radical attacks on the 'pimp of tyranny'. Beneath the ponderous elegance of the heroic couplet lurks the unruly bachelor or 'boy in the street', jeering at the duchesses as disorderly whores, exposing genitalia, nailing up horns, and reenacting the feebleness of the Court party as a parade of cuckolds. Interregnum satires (as we shall see in the next chapter) use popular shaming rituals to associate female dominion with the most abject kind of whore; by the Restoration, however, concern has shifted to the absolutism and corruption supposedly emanating from the royal mistresses. Marvell explicitly defines his subject as the 'Whore of State', and his Skimmington-like mockery reduces government to the trope to which we now turn, the 'parliament of women'.

CHAPTER 3

'The posture of a free state': political pornography and the 'commonwealth of women', 1640–1660

> By an opinion which I hope is but an erronious one in men, we are shut out of all power and Authority by reason we are never imployed either in civil nor marshall affaires; our counsels are despised and laught at, the best of our actions are trodden down with scorn, by the over-weaning conceit men have of themselves.
>
> (Margaret Cavendish, Marchioness of Newcastle)

> Our fellow-creatures shan't be deifi'd.
> I'll now a rebel be, and so pull down
> The Distaff-Hierarchy, or females fancy'd Crown.
> In these unbridled times, who would not strive
> To free his neck from all prerogative?
>
> (John Phillips)

The satire that proliferates in the 'English revolution' focusses for good reason on the targets of ritualized sexual mockery. The constitutional crises that erupted in 1640, altered but not concluded by the Stuart Restoration in 1660, did indeed interweave the political and the sexual at every level, sometimes metaphorically and sometimes directly – when confronting the initiatives of women, or when gauging the influence of the king's personal life upon the country. Thus the ultra-royalist Margaret Cavendish comes to realize that women are excluded from power by masculine 'conceit', while Lucy Hutchinson, resolute radical and 'Puritan', endorses masculinism without a shred of Cavendish's irony when she blames the nation's disasters on Charles I's 'effeminate' domination by Henrietta Maria: woe to the kingdom 'where the hands that are made only for distaffs affect the management of sceptres'.[1] (Cromwell maintains this family romance when he symbolically emasculates the Rump parliament, first denouncing the 'whoremongers' among them and then taking away their 'bauble'.) Gender-hierarchy clearly served as a synecdoche for social order in general, and by the same logic sexual deviance provided a near-universal metaphor for political and

74

religious abomination: each faction applied guilt by association to its enemies, using familiar tropes like the 'whoredoms' of Babylon, the syphilitic courtier, the zealot seething with repressed lust, the rampant Cavalier, the orgiastic Ranter, the republican whoremonger who reduces 'Freedom' and 'liberty' to passwords for entering brothels.[2] The Restoration only amplified this gallery of stereotypes, adding the priapic but impotent monarch whose 'sceptre' remains in the hands of unscrupulous lovers. Though Milton takes a high moral tone against the roistering 'Sons of Belial', he imitates their sexual mockery of authority when he imagines Charles I proposing 'copulation with his Mother' – the parliament that *Eikon Basilike* had gendered female – but failing to achieve 'Masculine coition' with her (*CPW* III.467).

I locate this 'porno-political' writing at the intersection of two forms of expression, the representations of the status-confusing courtesan inherited from Italian *pornographia* (identified in chapter 1), and the native 'ceremonies of abjection' described in chapter 2. In each case transgressive sexuality and prostitution serve as the general equivalent for politics – that is, for public actions mediated through public oratory but really determined by private passions. 'Politically flavoured' Skimmington rides (chapter 2, section 2 above) protest abuses of authority using as paradigm the dominant and sexually promiscuous wife; conversely, charivaresque pamphlets lash and pelt the transgressor as if she were a common 'strumpet'. Charles becomes the effeminate husband unable to prevent his wife from playing the whore (and Amazon), Cromwell the village ribald ready to take his place, the brutally phallic 'town bull'. In the *Parliament of Women* satires (section 3 below) this triangle is completed when Lady Cromwell and other grandees' wives alter state policies to serve their own insatiable appetites. When the concern shifts to the petitions of Leveller women, popular journalism adapts the carnivalesque humiliation-rituals previously unleashed against Parliamentary viragos and royalist cuckolds. The petitioning 'Ladyes-errants' – in reality '*Kate* of the kitchin and *Tym* the turnspit' – are exhorted to 'muster up your Pettycoates and white Approns, and like gallant *Lacedemonians* or bold Amazons advance your Banners once more'.[3] These were the mock-heroic 'standards' of underwear hoisted in the Skimmington to confront and embarrass the woman who had made her sex or her authority 'public'. In this version, however, the petitioners 'advance their Banners' themselves. Like Butler's 'Amazon' dominating the procession that supposedly disciplines her and regarding the 'petticoat displayed' as her triumph rather than her shame, these 'ladies errant' reincarnate the *puttana errante* of Renaissance Italy (chapter 1, n. 50 above). She too invaded the public square with the confidence of an Amazonian knight errant, brandishing as her chivalric emblem *la potta spalancata*, the Cunt Displayed.

In conditions of crisis, the division between sexual and national politics dwindles away, and figurative correspondences become literal. The corrupted state is a whore in Marvell as in the Apocalypse, but the Restoration satirist can point to Lady Castlemaine as its embodiment. The fall of a great city is a rape and the incompetent leader is a eunuch, but in the Sack of Rome these metaphors mutate into reality as the invading soldiers *act them out*. The London 'Gentlewomen and Tradesmens-Wives' petition speaks with terror of the 'savage uses and unheard-of rapes, exercised upon our Sex in *Ireland*, and have we not just cause to feare that they wil prove the forerunners of our ruine?' Cavendish, in a letter written during rioting in Antwerp, describes the panic induced in her maids (and herself) by the rumour 'that the Souldiers have liberty to Abuse all the Women'.[4] Even after the Civil Wars this close and literal association remained in place. The Adultery Act of 1650 defines transgressive sexuality as an intimate concern of the commonwealth – as if, having simultaneously broken the hereditary monarchy and the 'families of love' at the sectarian fringe, the new régime needed to reaffirm the identity of marriage and the state. In postwar discourse the association of misrule with the dominant woman and the passive male, formerly confined to fantasies like Joseph Hall's Isle of Hermaphrodites (section 3 below), takes concrete form in Cavendish's satire against 'effeminate' rulers, Lucy Hutchinson's blame of the 'uxorious' Charles I and the 'catamites' at his father's court, and Samuel Butler's identification of the termagant wife in the Skimmington ride with Nero's eunuch-lover Sporus.

Issues of gender and politics converge when the agents of social change are female, and even the historian who warns us not to 'depict the war as a milestone in the liberation of women' finds 'renewed signs of female resistance to male dominance' in this period.[5] Hostile images do not form in a void, but precisely in *reaction* to a historical change in women's agency; those critics who interpret them *merely* as projections of male anxiety miss some of their literal and topical signification. We have seen in chapter 2 some evidence of women's political culture in the part-military, part-festive demonstrations they organized for construction, celebration, and protest. We saw, too, how these rituals of assertion set the agenda for literary reconstructions of the charivari. The upheavals of 1640–60 in Britain, like the Fronde in France, did indeed create new opportunities for women – in public speaking, religious and political activism, estate management, and warfare – which in turn generated new texts *pro* and *contra*, new tropes of sublimity and abjection. The texts that justify these 'actions of public appearance' themselves evoke a frisson of voyeurism: as the 'Gentlewomen and Tradesmens-Wives' point out, 'it may be thought strange and unbeseeming our sex to shew our selves by way of Petition . . .' (*True Copie*, 6). The courtesan, the mistress of appearances in Aretino, had most recently been reconceived by Ferrante Pallavicino as a professor of 'Rhetorick', public discourse *par excellence*. It comes as no surprise, then, that satyric invention should work hard to sexualize the performative force of women's public language in parodic sermons, petitions, and 'parliamentary' deliberations.

Chapter 3 will explore the 'discourse of sexuality' that springs up around these vocal interventions in the public sphere. I start with preaching and other innovative demonstrations of the Spirit – poured out on sisters as well as brothers, according to the prophet Joel – that hostile witnesses denounced as 'strumpet-like'. Sectarian women, particularly Quakers, developed not only a practice but a theoretical defence of their preaching (later summed up in Margaret Fell's *Womens Speaking Justified*), and similarly self-conscious 'justifications' supported the women's petitions studied in the following section. From petitioning Parliament or devising new constitutions, it is a logical step to women establishing their own 'commonwealth'; pornotropic satire faithfully follows this logic. I focus especially on points of contact between low-libertine ribaldry and serious commentary on politics, gender, and sexuality – Hobbes's theory of the origins of power, Utopian fantasies of Amazonian rule, French-dominated eulogies of the *femme forte*. Alongside the army of anonymous pamphleteers I set Madeleine de Scudéry and the Queen of Sweden, Joseph and John Hall, the poets Denham and Milton (uncle and tutor of the John Phillips whose pungent attack on female 'prerogative' I cite as an epigraph above). The chapter turns finally to Margaret Cavendish's notoriously Protean discourse, where brutally anti-feminist homilies jostle with calls for 'Combinations amongst Our Sex, that we may unite in Prudent Counsels, to make ourselves as Free, Happy and Famous as Men' (*Orations*, 225) – a serious plea for collective discursive institutions equivalent to 'parliaments of women'. Without satirical intention, Cavendish's Utopian fictions and orations conjure up a feminism in which the militant heroine takes on features of the courtesan without losing her Amazonic virtue, gaining 'Strength and Wit' – as men already do – by making themselves conversant in taverns and brothels as well as courts and colleges. It is precisely this agency that pornotropic satire seeks to expunge.

I. 'STRUMPET-LIKE POSTURES', OR WOMEN'S SPEAKING VILIFIED

The pornotropic alliance of shaming ritual and political satire came easily to all sides in the conflict. Milton adopts the derisive tone of an unruly bachelor to mock the impotence of Charles I. Among more traditional 'Puritans', fornication and whoredom signified not political efficacy but idolatry and tyranny, according to Old Testament usage; this provided a broad target for establishment satirists like Richard Brathwaite, who imagines one descendent of Zeal-of-the-Land Busy denouncing Bartholomew Fair because 'The very *Booths* are *Brothells* of iniquity.' Authentic uses of this prostitutional vocabulary, metaphorical equivalents for discontent and outrage, surface among radicals and conservatives, in America as well as England: the New England enthusiast Ichabod Wiswall brands his local churches as 'Stews', and the Maryland servingman George Alsop denounces the Cromwellians as 'lustful *Sodomites*', yearning 'to satisfie each dark unsatiate will'. Within a few years of the Restoration, however, the same poet uses 'vagabond lust' and gender-inversion to describe his own seduction by Apollo, ironically celebrating the publication of his book in the imagery of illicit plebeian sexuality – violent penetration 'on a Bench', impregnation, abandonment, bearing a bastard ('black as Ink'), beating hemp, and running from the beadles.[6]

Royalist propaganda counters the ascendency of Parliament, and exploits the gathering crisis that would bring Cromwell to power, in a series of pamphlet-plays that travesty political events by transferring them to the gynaecological realm. In *A New Marriage between Mr King and Mrs Parliament* (1648), the Army tries to forbid the banns on the grounds that Mrs Parliament is 'a woman of a light carriage, inconstant, and likely to be fruitlesse, by reason she is troubled with the consumption in her Members, the bloody issue, and falling-sickness, about the time of our approach' (4); this accusation of 'light carriage' combines medical diagnosis with the familiar designation-as-whore. Carrying the trope to its next logical step, the parodic birthing-ritual that occasionally substituted for the Skimmington ride, Mercurius Melancholicus's *Mistris Parliament Brought to Bed of a Monstrous Childe of Reformation* (1648) conjures up a vivid child-bed scene. The nurse encourages Mrs Parliament to vomit up evil matter, Mrs London the respectable midwife refuses to deal with an illegitimate birth, and Mrs Truth draws up a confession for the labouring mother to sign; all these gossips, rather than supporting Parliament, denounce her fall from upper-class gentlewoman to common whore,

> now to be despised by every sauce-boxe boy and loose fellow, [who] make Rimes . . . and sing-songs of her, making of her a Whore, and no better than the arrantest Strumpet that ever went upon two shooes, telling her, that she hath imprisoned her Husband, and prostituted her body to a very *Eunuch*, that had nothing to help him self withall.

The narrator clearly participates in this exposure of impotence and 'arrant' whoredom (virtually translating 'la puttana errante'), and continues by dragging her through the lower depths in a trajectory that makes her sound like Grimmelshausen's Courasche: she 'since hath followed the *Camp*, and become an Amunition-W[hore], and turn'd up her tayle to every lowly *Ill-dependent* Rascall in the *Army*; Sir *Thomas* himself, and king *Cromwall* too, a very Town-Bull, and committed flat fornication with *Broom-men*, *Tinkers*, and *Channell-rakers*.'[7] In order to make its point, however, this pamphlet-drama must take on precisely the 'loose' and saucy tone it associates with the horrors it attacks, a paradox probably endemic to all shaming rituals. As Lois Potter points out, associating these pamphlets with charivaris and carnivals, *Mistress Parliament* presents itself as a fairground booth that can be entered for 'but three halfpence'. The voice of traditionalist outrage merges with the hoots of lampooning boys, pig-women, tinkers, and channel-rakers. The author's appeal to the reader becomes a leering invitation ('The *Sight* will please ye'), just as his handling of Babylonic imagery expands its prurient detail ('the glorious Queene [is] become so base a whore, to prostitute under every hedge, to open her quiver to every arrow, to act every new invented sin . . .').[8] Lewd and disorderly representation produces an image as deformed as the '*Monstrous Childe of Reformation*' it pillories, exposing the etymological root that underlies the 'remonstrance' and the 'demonstration'.

Such 'transferred' or allegorical meanings merge easily into the literal. In a culture still dominated by patriarchal ideology, the family served not only as 'metaphor for the state' but as 'the basis for political and social order' (as Susan Amussen puts it). By the same 'inextricably intertwined' logic, illicit sex remained tied to the family norms it both violated and confirmed, and so betokened – even exemplified – departures from traditional political order. Hence it could seem equally symptomatic of the new rebellion and the new absolutism. Furthermore, sexual arousal itself constituted a rebellion within the body; as St Augustine explained, God made the erectile mechanism uncontrollable after the fall as a direct expression, not a mere parallel, of the primal disobedience in Eden. By the same logic, childbirth was conceived as a violent insurrection against the body, raising 'commotions and seditions in that whole Region'. *Mistress Parliament* merely reverses tenor and vehicle in this deeply engrained metaphor, which is shared by radicals, libertines, and traditionalists. Independents and sectarians, seeking to transform society by a spiritual renewal that mitigates or reverses the fall, confirm the conservative equation of 'rebellion' with disorderly sex by redefining or defying marriage. Milton (to take the best-known example) placed divorce on the radical agenda, drawing not only the jeers of the 'brood of Belial' but the fulminations of the godly, who attacked him as a pornographer and a 'libertine'. In the course of his arguments for rethinking marriage and divorce, he simultaneously justifies and belittles sectarian enthusiasm by tracing it to the sexual frustration caused by indissoluble marital problems; Milton's serious diagnosis confirms precisely the linkage of independence and sexuality that underlay ribald anti-Puritan satire.[9]

Even allowing for the excesses of the pornotropic imagination, heterodox marital arrangements undoubtedly flourished during the 'great rebellion'. The impressionable Presbyterian Thomas Edwards records many examples of sexual experimentation in *Gangraena* (1646), including one supposedly inspired by Milton's divorce tracts: in one case a man refuses to accept a clergy wedding, alleging radical religious principles, but then denies the marriage and abandons his victim; in another case, the preacher Mrs Attaway investigates Milton's new doctrine and then sets up house with an equally inspired apostle.[10] One Antinomian commune took the name 'My One Flesh', expropriating the scriptural words that sanctioned marriage, and individual Ranters proclaimed their ability to copulate freely without sin – prompting the satirist to equate them with those riotous street gangs that always included 'a whore or so' in their revels, 'for creature-comfort, as they call it, or as the *Hectors* for *Carnelevation*'. Two Quaker missionaries, Katharine Evans and Sarah Cheevers, used words from Genesis and the Marriage Service to sanctify their own woman-to-woman bond. Several Ranter women, like Mary Adams or Mary Gadbury, named the Holy Ghost as the father of their illegitimate child, thus presenting the authorities with a paradigm-dilemma: should they be revered as prophets or prosecuted for vagabond lust? The magistracy chose the sadistic-spectacular model normally reserved for the wandering whore, consigning Gadbury to repeated whippings in Bridewell – a punishment 'too light for such a lewd woman' – and provoking Adams to commit suicide in prison after similar treatment. As with another Antinomian, Anne Hutchinson in Massachusetts, hostile pamphlets lingered obscenely on the details of her deformed infant, an emblem of heresy in the flesh, literally bodying forth the identity of 'intellectual aberration and sexual promiscuity' (as Mitchell Breitwieser puts it). If the *Mistress Parliament* pamphlets allegorize the 'monstrousness' of reformation by harnessing memories of Anne Hutchinson, the metaphor returns to reality in these anti-Ranter actions and representations, monstrous exhibitions of monstrosity through which the English revolution sought to regain control over its own fringes and discipline female religious autonomy.[11]

Against constant opposition from the ribald and the godly, then, women took active roles in prophesying, preaching within the gathered churches, setting up their own meetings, enforcing a more radical theology by storming church services and railing at the established preacher with a free tongue ('I care not a pin or a fart' for the Archbishop of Canterbury). These outpourings of the Spirit inspired multiple and inconsistent responses. Anna Trapnel and Elizabeth Poole (both women of the artisan class) found their visions taken seriously by high officers of state, perhaps because their imagery had been made familiar and therefore graspable by rehearsal in the comic mode; Poole compared king and Parliament to a married couple whose relationship is strained but not wholly dissolved by masculine violence, and Trapnel saw Cromwell as a bull about to gore her. Within a brief period, however, Poole was ostracized and denounced as a woman who 'went about seducing', and Trapnel was prosecuted as a vagabond. (To sober her judges, Trapnel reminded them that during the Civil Wars 'I sold my plate and my rings, and gave the money to the public use; you did not call me vagabond then.') The Congregationalist Vice-Chancellor of Oxford, otherwise famous for his tolerance, applied the full 'wandering whore' treatment to two Quaker women who began to preach to the students, ordering them jailed and flogged.[12] Elsewhere, we have seen, they were ducked or bridled, the traditional humiliation for a scold.

Female sermons attracted large crowds of supporters as well as hecklers – perhaps drawn by what one critic called the 'narrative or discoursing manner' that distinguished women's preaching – and in turn generated many bawdy-punitive satires and unruly lampoons, predictably identifying women's discursive initiative with the lower stratum of prostitution and fish-wifery. In one 1641 comedy, for example, the rogue's wife claims to have 'read *Aretine*, both in print and in Picture', when she was 'house Lecturer' in a brothel. The pamphlet *A Discoverie of Six Women Preachers* (also from 1641) reveals the need to translate this alarming new verbal power into the kind of sexual burlesque that designates a common whore. One of these preachers is made to break off for an assignation in the disreputable Salisbury Court theatre, and they are all invited to improve their learning in those institutions that discipline the lewd and the deranged: 'Thus I have declared some of the female Academyes, but where their University is I cannot tell, but I suppose that Bedlam or Bridewell would be two convenient places for them.' They transgress the limits of class and gender, aspiring to 'Rhetorick' and arguing 'that husbands being such as crossed their wives wils might lawfully be forsaken' – exactly the doctrine that Poole would propose, eight years later, as the model for a bloodless divorce between king and Parliament. An earlier lampoon on another group of six Puritan women jokes about their fondness for 'standing' while 'good Mr Prick' preaches to them; one pamphlet on the 'female Academyes' of 1641 suggests that the six speakers seek their own public expression because 'their husbands cannot sufficiently preach to them at home'.[13] One exception to this pornotropic treatment is Margaret Cavendish's story of an acquaintance who 'become[s] a Preaching Sister'. Though Cavendish despises 'female Flocks' who 'gossip Scripture', and opposes every detail of their sanctified religion, her disapproval is tempered by a sense of familiarity and a continued willingness to listen and discuss. When she and an élite 'Company' attend a conventicle they withhold comment on the 'Sister's' sermon and disperse the meeting 'without Noise or Disturbance'; a male friend impersonates a true believer, but gradually drives his audience away by introducing unwelcome orthodox ideas into his sermon. Rather than complaining that a woman has become excessively vocal or energized by a zeal that resembles sexual arousal, Cavendish concludes that her 'Sighing and Winding' manner, her reliance on inspiration and rejection of true 'Eloquence', renders her *insufficiently powerful*.[14]

Thomas Edwards's thunderous denunciations of sectarian women, symptoms of the heretical 'gangrene' infecting England, steer closer to the underlying assumptions of bawdy satire than to the Anglican condescension of Cavendish. Like the low-libertine pamphleteer, he focusses on the convergence of verbal agency and sexual action. (Edwards was particularly sensitive to the new female articulacy because his first published tract had been refuted by the prophetess Lady Eleanor Davies and mauled by the preacher Katherine Chidley.)[15] An officer in Fairfax's army encourages a sister to preach, then proves the lawfulness of copulating with him while her husband is away or asleep. The lace-woman Mrs Attaway – at first given the disintegrative name 'Atomy' – draws thousands of spectators to her public lectures and exerts a comparable fascination over Edwards's text, featuring in each of his three successive volumes: in an astonishingly detailed and novelistic account of a meeting she improvises a sermon, leads a question-and-answer session, encourages a gentlewoman who fails to speak, and debates with another woman who challenges her warrant to preach or do 'Exercises' outside the single-sex meetings where this is usual; later two 'Gentlemen' eye-witnesses attend for 'novelty' and tease her on the subject of Milton's divorce theory, evidently hoping to draw her into a sexual confession; in the shocking finale, she leaves her husband to set up a new relationship with the sanctified William Jenney, mapping out their future in a 'great parchment role'. As Sharon Achinstein notes, Edwards's informants seem unclear whether their 'horror' derives from Mrs Atomy's forceful coherence or from the confused multivocality that springs up all around her. Porno-political satire reiterated the theme of the preaching lace-woman, whose sermons arouse a male disciple so much that he 'Desir'd a private Application / Unto the point in Agitation'.[16]

In July 1652, in the dramatic location of Whitehall Chapel, a particularly vivid incident illustrated the hermeneutic as well as social confusion induced by the public actions of radical women. As Peter Sterry preached on the Resurrection a woman stripped naked to the waist, causing great disturbance. Presumably this was an early example of the Quaker ritual 'going naked for a sign', but what did it signify and how did it relate to the occasion? Did the Whitehall setting prompt her to protest against the carnality of Charles I's picture collection, whose many 'naked Venuses' were then being auctioned off? Did she *act out* the Resurrection in the spirit of the Adamites, with an antinomian gesture of Edenic freedom? Satires against this religious nudism had for a long time exploited its orgiastic appearance, and popular woodcuts even showed Adamites and Ranters with tiny matchstick erections (in one of them an officer with a pole stands ready to knock down these signs of 'resurrection' or 'Carnelevation').[17] Should the Whitehall performance have been interpreted *literally*, and *sexually*, as a Dionysian release of libido or the self-advertisement of a courtesan? Was it an eruption of festive-violent

bawdy against Puritan authority, like the gestures explored in chapter 2 –
throwing horns or 'showing her arse'? Or was it an allegory of Naked
Truth?

One indignant eyewitness, David Brown, rehearses these issues in a
pamphlet appropriately titled *The Naked Woman*. The preacher himself explains that he struggled to grasp the event ('monstrousness...
incredible...enormous Scandall') and then settled for the simplest
paradigm, insanity; Brown, however, insists that he should have arrested
and interrogated the woman to discover her 'reasons and intentions'
(and force her to name her accomplices). In a sense he does consider
her 'capable of rational political action', as Achinstein argues, but his
condemnatory language never suggests that he saw her 'absurd act' as 'a
sincere and coherent gesture of protest' by 'a fully autonomous, rational
creature'. Instead, what passes before Brown's eyes is the entire disorderly subculture embodied in a single person, simultaneously flaunting
her scandalous sexuality and 'outfacing Authority'. Despite her 'sober'
speech, the Scottish zealot has no trouble constructing her enigmatic
gesture as a lewd 'posture', combining associations of courtesan display,
unruly mirth, and popular shaming ritual that we might consider logically incompatible. As he explains to the chaplain, the naked woman
'came in a most Strumpet-like posture, mocking you', indeed, 'such a
posture which is a shame to expresse, ... a vile disgrace, provocation,
contempt, yea and (as it were) a defyance to God'. Brown makes it not
merely a '*Sodom*-like action', redolent of the whorehouse or the incestuous
coupling of animals, but a theatrical event that revives the horrors of the
playhouse and the 'whorish masks' once performed in that very place,
the palace of Whitehall. Once launched, however, this porno-histrionic
theme takes over the 'Puritan' discourse that denounces it. Brown lures
the reader with a 'Prologue' and announces that Sterry was 'interrupted
on his stage, from acting his own part, whereby all his Auditors for a
time became spectators of the other impudent act'. The 'Strumpet-like
posture' turns the preacher himself into a 'spectacle' of erotic fixation;
Brown berates him both for 'your silent beholding her, even like other
spectators, whereof many lookt far more on you, than her,' and for missing his cue (by failing to show 'any sign of grief or detestation'). The only
solution for this 'lascivious and licentious carriage' – 'no lesse grievous
to the Godly, than ridiculous to the wicked' – is to counter lewd theatricality with another kind of institution, consigning the strumpet to
Bridewell.[18]

Throughout the libertine satire of the period, mocking fantasies of female rule equate the unbridling of speech and behaviour with revolutionary freedom. Libidinous Fifth Monarchists declare

> We will not be Wives
> And tye up our Lives
> To Villanous slavery.

The bawdy *Newes from the New Exchange, or the Commonwealth of Ladies*, a product of the year that followed the execution of Charles I, shows women clamouring for 'their owne *freedoms*' now that men have won theirs, voting themselves 'the *Supreme Authority* both at home and abroad', and forming 'an *Academy*' that exactly mirrors the disorderly conviviality of the Sons of Belial – a '*Club*' devoted to smoking, swearing, drinking obscene toasts to the genitals, and polymorphic copulation. (The hermaphroditic Lady Hungerford 'over-rid and excarnated no lesse than three of her women' and four gentlemen-ushers.) The protagonists of *Now or Never, or a New Parliament of Women* (1656), angry chargers breaking away from restraint, insist that 'we have bit so much of the bridle, that now we do intend to throw off the Rein of their Government, and rule our selves'. When male speakers borrow this analogy between sexual and political liberation, however, a different version of the 'Politicks of Queen *Venus*' emerges:

> Our fellow-creatures shan't be deifi'd.
> I'll now a rebel be, and so pull down
> The Distaff-Hierarchy, or females fancy'd Crown.
> In these unbridled times, who would not strive
> To free his neck from all prerogative?[19]

This poem from John Phillips's scurrilous anthology of 'Sportive Wit', burnt by the hangman in 1656, renders explicit the misogyny only implied by the ironic 'Parliament' satires. Despite its affinity with the 'low' subculture of lampoons and shaming rituals, its gendered politics – calling for the violent uncrowning of effeminate royalism – perfectly matches the beliefs of Phillips's uncle and tutor, John Milton. Libertinism exploits the loosening of traditional hierarchies in the Republic, and reasserts male dominance, by attacking those chivalric restraints that had guaranteed at least a semblance of respect for women.

Like most powerful lies, these portraits of sexual 'rebels' conceal an important half-truth. Several convergent factors sharpened the focus on women's public discourse and its relation to sexuality. Women's literacy was rising rapidly, especially in London, and the emergence of sex-in-print triggered fears that women of all classes would learn the kind of libertine expertise formerly confined to prostitutes. As we have seen, radical initiatives in preaching, petitioning, and military service (and their exaggerated representation by alarmist reporters) exacerbated the sort of 'tensions' that inspired rural mockeries – conflicts between the chaste, submissive female required by patriarchal theory and the forceful, artic-ulate women encountered in practice. Indeed, political theory itself sent contradictory messages about women's participation in the *polis*. Sexual transgression by the wife was taken seriously because it concerned 'the commonwealth' rather than merely private morality, and on this basis Parliament legislated the Adultery Act of 1650 (following the draco-nian model already established in America).[20] The family–state analogy gave wives and mothers a ministerial position, and women high in what Phillips called the 'Distaff-Hierarchy' were expected to exercise leader-ship in the public sphere. Sixteenth-century arguments for the public role of 'heroic ladies', by Tasso and others, had already been worked into Robert Cleaver's *Godly Form of Household Government* (1598): 'in divers actions of publike appearance', the husband of a well-born lady should 'hold her his superior.' Arguments deriving from controversy over female *monarchy* move down the social scale, a process that ends with Phillips's use of 'prerogative'. Several feminist theorists, praising women's achieve-ments in their traditional roles, prove from historical examples that they have shown equal ability when given the opportunity to perform in con-ventionally male areas; for some writers, a survey of other cultures shows that the entire structure of female subordination rests on 'custom' and 'consensus' rather than 'Nature'. Opposing voices in this theoretical dis-course, downplaying those 'prerogatives' that women derive from rank, attempt to brand their souls as naturally 'base' and their speech intrinsi-cally 'plebeian'. Such assaults on the 'Distaff-Hierarchy' reveal the same uncrowning or 'underclassing' impulse that turns Cromwellian women into bawdy rioters, or parodies democracy by equating 'females of all de-gree' with the most loutish and plebeian men.[21] Confronted with 'diverse actions of public appearance', defensive misogyny takes refuge in the pornotropic equation: 'public' woman can only mean common whore.

2 . HOBBESIAN THEORY AND THE WOMEN'S PETITIONS

The interrelated issues of women's sexuality, 'Dominion', and public voice exert their pressure even on Hobbes's radical revision of political

theory. The infamous state of Nature – explained as an 'Inference' from
the passions revealed by civil war, and constantly evoked in the laws established to prevent it – applies equally to the relation between the sexes.
When the state does not exist or cannot 'bridle' the appetite for pleasure
and dominance, the only exceptions to total anarchy are 'small Families'
held together by 'naturall lust' (still seen 'in many places of *America*').
What power relations obtain within this microcosm or '*Leviathan* writ
small'? Hobbes holds this truth to be self-evident, that all men are created equal and therefore live in perpetual warfare: without enforceable
laws 'every man has a Right to every thing, even to one anothers body';
fear of invasion or 'pleasure in contemplating their own power' drives
men to assault one another, but no one can prevail because 'Nature hath
made men so equall, in the faculties of body and mind.' 'The weakest
has strength enough to kill the strongest', and nobody has significantly
greater wisdom or prudence than anyone else – except for men of true
'Science' like Hobbes himself.[22]

Precisely the same devastating equality obtains between men and
women. Since the child cannot obey both parents simultaneously, dominion must be assigned to one, but that assignment is wholly arbitrary.
With exhilarating contempt for essentialism, Hobbes demolishes the very
idea of a natural gender-hierarchy:

Whereas some have attributed the Dominion to the Man onely, as being of the
more excellent Sex, they misreckon in it. For there is not always that difference
of strength or prudence between the man and the woman, as that the right can
be determined without War. In Common-wealths, this controversie is decided
by the Civill Law: and for the most part (but not alwayes) the sentence is in
favour of the Father; because for the most part Common-wealths have been
erected by the Fathers, not by the Mothers of families. (20:253)

Hobbes spells out as a serious argument what contemporary pornography like *L'Escole des filles* articulated as the scandalous opinion of a
nymphomaniac (chapter 1, section 1 above) – that the laws confining
female sexuality derive wholly from the accident of male power rather
than from any natural condition, and that left to their own sexual devices
women would establish a primitive gynocracy.

Even in constituted governments the Hobbesian 'War' of the sexes
is barely held in check by legal systems that are themselves purely customary and patently constructed to serve the interests of one side in
that war. In the state of nature, however, power reverts to the woman.
Parental right could be determined by a contract like that drawn up
by the Amazons – for Hobbes an example from 'History' rather than

myth – or a stipulation defining the man as a kind of plaything, 'for society of bed only'. Without such a female-dictated 'Contract', however,

> the Dominion is in the Mother. For in the condition of meer Nature, where there are no Matrimoniall lawes, it cannot be known who is the Father, unlesse it be declared by the Mother: and therefore the right of Dominion over the Child dependeth on her will, and is consequently hers.

Steering close once again to the ribald imaginings of libertine satire, Hobbes assumes that without the 'bridle' women would express their 'natural lust' in complete and carefree promiscuity ('it cannot be known who is the Father'), and would establish dominion over the child – the *only* form of hegemony in the state of nature not founded upon raw violence – by merely expressing their will. The means of this expression are fundamental acts – nurturing the child or exposing it to die – or powerful voice, in 'declarations' of paternity or 'contracts' like those of the Amazons.[23] Hobbes thus imagines women creating a protopolitical language of strong performatives, speech-acts that translate their 'will' into 'dominion'. Given that paternity still depended on the mother's verbal declaration in highly regulated societies, the stage-libertine expressed a more general truth than he realized when he declared that 'In matter of Women, we are all in the State of Nature.'[24]

Of all the political actions initiated by women, mass petitions most vividly embodied male fears about the return of Hobbes's 'natural' woman – an autonomous, Amazonian creature fully equipped for 'War', with the additional capacity to exercise 'Dominion' through the voice. Petitions combine text and action into a collective, self-legitimizing demonstration, a spectacle of 'consensus' refashioning itself and a reminder that arbitrary 'custom' can be rescinded by new arbitration. One of Charles II's first Acts, in 1661, sought to prohibit 'tumultuous petitioning', since the remonstrances of the previous two decades were often accompanied by large ritualized processions and crowd movements to reinforce their presentation. They could acquire the momentum of a moral crusade, addressing cultural and even sexual issues far broader than the original grievance: the Root and Branch petition against episcopacy, for example, complained about the growth of 'whoredoms and adulteries' and the 'swarming of lascivious, idle, and unprofitable books and pamphlets' including *The Parlament of Women*; immediately after the execution of Charles I, a Leveller-influenced petition demanded that brothels and bawds be 'duly punished and not tolerated' as they were under the king. (Failure to prevent immorality, a frequent cause of presentation to Church court, also underlies the habit of parading the 'next neighbour' in Skimmington rides.) The vast majority of petitions were launched by men (or at least apprentice-boys), but petitions by women did play a significant role at moments of crisis in the early 1640s, during the Civil Wars, in the Leveller campaign of 1647–49, in protests against the debt laws in 1651, and again in 1659 when Margaret Fell presented a Quaker petition against tithes.[25] Whatever interpretation historians now give to these interventions by women – whether isolating their feminist potential or recognizing their integral part in political movements – they certainly generated intense publicity at the time, and released enough energy to register a tremor on the sensitive instrument of male defensiveness.

These waves of 'tumultuous petitioning' contributed greatly to the extension of women's activity. Apart from the composition and publication of the document itself, they had to gather signatures, adopt and distribute the marching colours that identify their demonstrations as ceremonial processions (white for peace, sea-green for levelling), and move coherent masses of women by water and land. Under the guise of traditional deference, they articulated not only alternative policies but forthright justifications of their independent action. As early as 1642, the *True Copie of the Petition of the Gentlewomen and Tradesmens-Wives* adds to its title-page *Their Severall Reasons Why Their Sex Ought Thus to Petition*, since 'it may be thought strange and unbeseeming our sex to show ourselves' in this way (6). Obligatory references to female weakness were further belied by the oral and physical vigour of the demonstrations themselves, which besieged the Parliament building, mounted the stairs, broke staffs of office, and confronted increasingly violent efforts to control them. Eye-witnesses record them threatening short-haired MPs as 'Roundheads', banging on the doors, and pushing down the Trained Bands, who then 'shot powder at them; for this they cared not, crying, nothing but powder, and having Brickbats in the yards, threw them very fast at the trained Bands'. To punish the immodesty of women 'not any whit scared or ashamed of their incivilities', horse-troopers ordered them to remove their provocative ribbons, beat them back with the flat of their swords, then slashed at their faces – the classic gesture to shame a whore. At least one woman bled to death after her nose was cut off. Obviously strengthened by their own taste of military experience, the petitioners promised to return with guns, and to demolish all the fortifications their own hands had built.[26]

Though these women's petitions were respectfully praised by figures as different as Milton and Clarendon – and reprinted extensively even by those newsbooks that interspersed them with derisory comments – most contemporary reactions shelter behind the typical equation of female agency with comically 'plebeian' sexuality. The entry of women into the political arena demanded a gendered language, which could range in tone from gallant to pornographic. Gerolamo Agostini, the Venetian secretary, creates a kind of chivalric-sentimental epic: women resort to petitioning 'in the hope that their sex may meet a more courteous hearing and a more pitiful heart'; they form a heroic tableau 'with their children in their arms, to soften the hardest hearts and implore peace', and are then scattered by the brutal Parliamentarians with 'more than a hundred injured, mostly women'. English observers tended towards the bottom end of this spectrum. Political invective frequently sought to associate hated policies with gender and class transgression. A male opponent becomes 'an Oyster-woman at Billinsgate', royalist newsletters are written by 'Pimps, Players, Poets and Oyster Women', cowardly Levellers 'deale like Billingsgate wenches with nothing but words'. Private diarists, facetious journalists, and official propagandists apply the same terms to the spectacle of women marching en masse in white silk ribbons: 'Oyster wives, and other dirty and tattered sluts . . . cried for Peace'; 'some say 500 of them were whores', or 'for the most part, Whores, Bawdes, Oyster-women, Kitchenstuffe women, Beggar women, and the very scum of the Suburbs, besides abundance of Irish women'.[27]

Every kind of animosity could thus be projected into this spectacle of women on parade. Where the modern historian sees an extension of women's political culture – noting affinities with the women-led enclosure and fen riots of 1641–42 – contemporaries saw Irishwomen, prostitutes, comic viragos, and royalist secret agents. The first women's petitions were indeed hard to classify: one combines traditional female fears (of 'savage uses and unheard of rapes') with fierce criticism of the Catholic queen, while another combines Puritan moral demands (to punish 'licentious and scandalous Pamphlets') with support for Henrietta Maria – couched, however, in economic rather than strictly political terms, since her patronage of luxury trade kept them in business. Rumour strives to fit the new phenomenon to existing patterns of riot, blaming 'Men of the Rabble in Womens Clothes', or the royalist ladies who allegedly supplied the ribbon, or the machinations of the Earl of Holland, leader of the peace faction within the Parliamentary élite. (Holland was indeed executed in 1649 for starting a royalist uprising, and in the 1650s his daughter-in-law encouraged clandestine theatre and created the carnivalesque 'Lady Holland's Mob'.) One private letter (sent to amuse Brilliana, Lady Harley) casts Pym as the husband in the Skimmington, actually 'beaten' by the petitioners, and in the title-page of the parodic *Resolution of the Women of London to the Parliament* (1642) the husband sent to the front by a militant wife wears horns. Adding a mock-heroic touch that simultaneously elevates and debases the petitioners' social rank, one eye-witness sees among the prisoners led off to Bridewell 'a most deformed Medusa, or Hecuba, with an old rusty blade by her side'. Though no other cutting edge appeared among the women, *The Parliament Scout* turns instinctively to armament-metaphor when he concludes that 'swords in womens hands doe desperate things; this is begotten in the distractions of Civill War'. Grammatical slippage reenacts the category-confusion induced by militant women: swords act independently of their handlers, and collective phenomena beget a monstrous child.[28]

When female militancy surged in the late 1640s, as 'lusty lasses of the levelling party' came to the defence of Mary Overton and John Lilburne, hostile accounts once again mingle mock-heroics and lower-stratum travesty, with a tinge of anti-Puritan satire. The Cromwellian authorities sought to prostitute Overton by forcing her into Bridewell, as we have seen in chapter 2 above; correspondingly, in the newsbooks the petitioners become not just 'Amazones' and 'Queenes' but 'the Meek-hearted Congregation of *Oyster-wives*, the Civill-Sisterhood of *Oranges* and *Lemmons*'. By an unsurprising irony, as Leveller women's participation in demonstrations becomes more ritualized and orderly – in single-sex marches and in processions of the whole community – festive-violent reportage grows more disorderly and far-fetched. Journalism characterized them as 'a company of meddlesome gossops', and official Parliamentary orders proscribed women who 'hang in clusters' and 'clamour about' the building, as if their excessively free voices constituted the kind of insect 'swarming' denounced in the Root and Branch campaign. (In contrast, when the petitioners refer to having 'chattered like Cranes, and mourned like Doves', they ennoble their grievance with Old Testament language.) 'Mercurius Pragmaticus' (a facetious royalist gazetteer impersonated by several authors) associates '*Peticoat Petitioners*' not only with oyster- and orange-wenches but with the carnivalesque army of dairywomen and cooks – 'down go the supream *Dagons* with *Ladles* and *Dish-clouts*' – while at the same time denouncing the Parliamentarians for 'jeer[ing] Woemen with their *Huswifery*, when their business is *Liberty*'. The MPs themselves try to 'redomesticate' and proletarianize them by commanding them back to their household chores, saying 'in effect, that they should go home and spin'; one parliamentary reporter prints out each clause of their petition fairly, but then interlines it with italicized sneers about women demanding 'the breeches' when they should be washing dishes, spinning, and submitting to their husbands (*we shall have things brought to a fine passe, if women come to teach the Parliament how to make Lawes*'). Straining for comic effect dilates conventional anti-Puritan satire, turning the lascivious but supine 'She-saint' into a murderously bawdy activist: '*Holofernes Fairfax* look to thy head, for *Judeth* is a comming, the women are up *in armes*, and vow they will tickle your *Members*.' This dense allusion combines the Biblical heroine – who did indeed use her sexual attraction in the service of a legitimate political cause – with a more diffuse evocation of the militant female mob. Though episodes of dismemberment in riots and battles occurred throughout Europe, Englishmen might especially recall the parodic inversion of physiognomy hinted at in Shakespeare's *1 Henry IV* and spelled out in Holinshed: visiting fallen English soldiers on the battlefield 'the women of Wales cut off their privities, and put one part thereof into the mouthes of everie dead man, in such sort that the cullions hoong down to their chins; and not so contented, they did cut off their noses and thrust them into their tails'.[29]

Even partial supporters like 'Mercurius Pragmaticus' take refuge behind the Hobbesian image of the sexually commanding and physically ruthless Amazon, who threatens to 'commit a Rape upon these Capons' (the inadequate 'Members' cowering inside Parliament). Metaphor heightens and masks the literal violence; first the women's 'Tongues pelted *hail-shot*' against the MPs, then Parliament orders them driven down the stairs by files of musketeers. As 'Pragmaticus' warms to his role as hooting boy or Skimmington rider, his sexual mockery shifts from fumblers and 'cuckolders' to the female agents he supposedly encourages. When he announces that 'Whole *Troopes* of *Amazons* . . . came in their warlike posture taking hold of their *Tayles* in stead of their *Targets*', he transforms them into a band of whores by virtually translating that passage in Venier's *Puttana errante* where the pornographic body is 'displayed' as chivalric armament. (Concomitantly, their male supporters become *ribaldi* or whoremongers, 'good *Lads* who are for *liberty* of *Codpiece*', and Pragmaticus incites them to 'take your *P-----* in your hands presently' and express their militancy in a kind of gang-rape.) In another version, the 'Levelling *sea-greene Sisters*' threaten to '*scale* the wall at *Westminster*, and with boyling *water* scald the Hornets out of their *nests'.*[30] Women's instrumentality must be scattered in two directions – the impossibly grand equipment of siege warfare, and the petty domesticity of pest control – and 'lubric' sexual imagery best achieves this levelling-effect.

To complete the military analogy Pragmaticus brings his female army under the command of Henry Marten, the 'radical gentleman' whose republicanism and support for women's petitions drew constant sexual slurs; Marten will provide the '*Standard*', promising to 'keep his *unshaken*' until the day of the grand attack and then 'mount it amongst them, and display the banner of his *mettle* right valiantly so long as hee can stand'. Royalist satire evidently drew comfort from this comic eroticization of military equipment that had conspicuously failed to 'stand' for them in the literal field. *Mercurius Militaris* takes this familiar mock-chivalric imagery still further, and again unwittingly confers phallic power on the enemy it intends to belittle. In this overcrowded discourse the women petitioners become 'brave Virago's, the Ladyes-errants of the Seagreen Order' (as well as 'devoted Vestals to the new erected *Alcoran*' and 'Amazons' advancing the banners of their own petticoats). Their public action makes them simultaneously grand courtesans and carnival sluts: they display the alluring 'charmes' of fashionable beauty – 'there is exorcisme in your eyes and black-patched faces (brighter than the brothers swords) of sufficient power to make the proudest States-man lower his top-gallant to your Saint-ships' – but they march to impose a Rabelaisian world upside down, insisting that ''tis high time that Kate of the kitchen and Tim the turnspit should rule the rost' (n. 3 above). All the resources of charivaresque mockery are focused on making these saints into common women and cuckold-makers, screwing down their political goals into the conventional figure of the lustful Puritan. The petitioners are urged to 'tell the Parliament that it is liberty they fought for, liberty you come for, and without liberty the spirituall burdens of your bellyes are quite lost, that your humble spirits will never submit to their proud flesh'. But though their potent charms would make the 'proudest' statesman lower his topsail, they in turn are rendered subject to 'proud flesh' once it is fully manifested. These 'kitchen' Amazons will only be satisfied when they make Parliament 'untruss the great Cod-peece-point of Government (which makes the egges of your eyes turne adle at the sight thereof) and shew you the naked truth'.[31]

New pornographic genres crystallize in this murky sea of apprehension and reaction. Libertine mock-petitions respond to the same social

problems and moments of crisis addressed by the women's remonstrances, dispelling their seriousness by translating them into the closed
world of female desire and 'codpiece liberty'. For the most part these
simulations of women's articulacy, like the satires on their preaching
and enthusiasm, combine a conventional disparagement of their ability
to conduct public business with an equally conventional phallocentric
model of sexuality; the petitioners long insatiably for something that will
'stand stiff'. But associations with the Skimmington ride endow politicized women with a kind of Amazonian activism: when the wife in the
Resolution of the Women of London orders her horn-decked husband to 'Go
to the wars', she is seen as sustaining and even initiating the militant
mood. Alternately *The Petition of the Weamen of Middlesex* (8 December
1641) – which seems to have actually predated the earliest women's
petitions – stresses the sensuousness and susceptibility of women, but
makes their desire seem autonomous and independent of the 'Standard'.
What aspect of Catholicism is so alluring that it can 'put wee women
which are the weaker vessels in mind of a Bawdi-house'? Not the stiff-
ness of the Cavalier or the priest but the beauty of young choristers, 'the
melodiousness of the voyces of those well-tuned boys'.[32]

The titles alone map out the concerns of the decade. In January and
February 1643 – when the Venetian ambassador reports the beginnings
of a women's campaign that would appeal to courtesy and compassion,
but five months *before* the actual petitions – there appeared *The Virgins
Complaint for the Losse of Their Sweet-Hearts, by these Present Wars* (the voice of
some 200,000 supposed virgins, frantic with 'green-sicknesse' and forced
to resort to the only men left, 'frosty-bearded *Usurers*', ancient fumblers
and diminutive tailors); *The Humble Petition of Many Thousands of Wives
and Matrons of the City of London . . . for the Cessation and Finall Conclusion
of These Civill Wars*, discrediting the powerful peace movement by associating all 'change' with inordinate desire, all wives with 'Ale-wives,
Oyster-Wives, Fish-wives, Tripe-wives', and all political opposition with
the priapic Cavaliers; and *The Mid-Wives Just Petition . . . Shewing . . . Their
Sufferings in These Distracted Times, for Want of Trading*, setting up their
own 'Standard' of free sexuality now that Queen Henrietta Maria has
set up her own military standard in the North. Early in the following
year *The Widowes Lamentation for the Absence of Their Deare Children and
Suitors*, beginning in tragic tones but gradually modulating into bawdy
comedy, pleads for an end to warfare because young women have to
make do with tailors and renounce their 'daily hopes of obtaining good

and lusty young husbands'. (As well as the predictable satire on female insatiability, these mock-complaints try to expose the homoerotics of war itself, protesting how 'barbarous it is for men, especially young handsome men, to run at one another with their naked weapons'.)[33] The Virgins' and Midwives' complaints were reissued in 1646, and in *The City-Dames Petition, in the Behalfe of the Long Afflicted But Well-Affected Cavaliers* (1647), 'Mary Lecher', 'Hannah Snatchall', 'Priscilla Tooly', and 'Dorothy Swivewell' complain about the exhaustion of their husbands and the shabby state of the men who might replace them. Before 1642 the Cavaliers 'alwaies stood stiffe to the City', but now they must depend on the ugly Puritan 'with a long thing God blesse us by his side as rusty as himself' and only his ears 'erected' (5). The petitioners of *A Remonstrance of the Shee-Citizens of London, and of Many Thousands of Other Free-Borne Women of England* (1647), an exceptionally lewd pamphlet that dwells on the showers of sperm they used to receive from the courtiers, pay tribute to Lilburne as 'that stiffe stander for the subjects Liberties', demanding the right to 'trade a broad in the Country' and to 'utter our warres to our best advantage' (3). In this odd spelling the female Levellers 'trade' simultaneously in utterance, warmongering militancy, and sexual favours.

After the Civil Wars, these mock-petitions respond to the fluctuating power of the Cromwellian régime and the attempt to extend social control across an ever-wider area of London. But what kind of response do they articulate? When *Mercurius Fumigosus* announces in 1654 that 'the Bawdes in the Suburbs are Petitioning against the putting down of the poor *Actors*', does it mock the legitimate presentation of petitions, does it render the authorities ridiculous for dabbling in such low matters, or does it reinforce the very equation between the theatre and prostitution that caused the repression in the first place? In the uncertain year 1659 the genre revives again (*The Ladies Remonstrance*, 'Imprinted at London for Virgin Want; to be sold by John Satisfye'), and popular-festive violence once again edges into the streets to challenge authority. At an important turning-point in the return to royalism, described by one sympathizer as 'beginning the World again', the London apprentice-boys had pelted the once-dreaded army with footballs, turnips, and mocking words. When the *Declaration of the Maids of the City of London* (1659) promises to support the apprentices' fight against 'this Army-fied Parliament' with sexual favours ('we shall live and dye for you, stand to you, and fall with you'), does it really cheer on their carnivalesque violence?[34] Or does this satire in effect side with the authorities, by turning a potentially alarming 'rising' into a lubricious pun?

3 . SATIRICAL AND UTOPIAN 'PARLIAMENTS OF WOMEN'

Low-libertine representations of the commonwealth of ladies or parliament of women launch a two-fronted attack, aiming to sink the credentials of the actual Parliament by gendering it female, and to explode the freedoms and 'prerogatives' of women by equating them with disorderly sexuality. Sometimes the wives of City tradesmen or newly empowered Puritans constitute their own parliament, sometimes the Commons itself changes sex and class; thus Mercurius Melancholicus turns 'Mistris Parliament' into a pregnant whore (section 1 above) and dramatizes the power-struggle between the Civil War victors as a Billingsgate slanging-match between 'Queen Fairfax and Madam Cromwell', reaching into the festive-aggressive lower stratum for the readiest and grossest images of female articulacy. The serious Root and Branch petition actually cites the 1640 *Parlament of Women* as evidence for the 'swarming' of lascivious pamphlets, noting that it 'came out at the dissolving of the last Parliament' and thus establishing that sexual mockeries of representative institutions relate directly to their suppression. (Lucy Hutchinson clearly saw that as Cromwell grew more 'wanton' with power he created 'several sorts of mock Parliaments', but just as arbitrarily 'turned them off again'.) 'Dissolving' satires against women's organizations clearly intended to brand the very possibility 'hilariously unthinkable', in David Underdown's words. But the Duke of Lenox's panicky exclamation when confronted by a militant crowd of petitioners ready to break his staff and storm Westminster – 'Away with these women, wee were best to have a parliament of Women' – suggests that the trope lay very near the surface.[35] It was at least *thinkably* unthinkable.

Lenox's fearful, apotropaic response shows that the theme of the women's assembly, already circulating in ancient Athens and Rome, could be revived at a moment's notice. Like the sexual tableaux of Tiberius that initiated the 'postures' of Giulio Romano, the 'parliament of women' topos derives from a narrative of imperial decadence. The Emperor Heliogabalus had reputedly set up a 'senaculum' of women that gave legal power to the old *conventus matronalis*, though it could only legislate on matters of female dress and precedence; this detail augments the fantastic list of scandals compiled around this emperor, all tending to discredit him as effeminate – that he invented new recipes and styles of dress, that he depilated his body and assumed the female position in intercourse with men, that he was governed by his own mother, and (most shocking of all) that he introduced female relatives into the senate with full power to draft legislation. By association with the genital-political perversions ascribed to Heliogabalus, the 'parliament' itself became the occasion to reconstruct a female discourse of illicit sexuality. Erasmus's popular dialogue *Senatulus*, for example, turns the ancient story inside out, giving voice to the deliberations of a group of women who find Heliogabalus 'a most praiseworthy Emperor' and try to reconstitute his 'little senate of women'. This dialogue probably initiates the strategy of mingling 'feminist' zeal and 'feminine' trivia for diminutive effect. The principal speaker Cornelia denounces the exclusion of women from local government, and links this directly to male definitions of women, restricted to pleasure ('pro delectamentis') or household labour ('they think that we're no more than laundresses and cooks'). But her proposals only enforce these definitions, dwelling with obsessive garrulity on dress codes and determining the status of MPs according to the most traditional criteria – husband's rank and number of children. Against this conservative and matronly voice Erasmus sets the dialogic interruptions of the younger women, whose impudent suggestions bring in an anarchic sexuality that confounds neat categories and strata: should place be given to concubines? the wives of monks? experienced women who pass for virgins? public prostitutes? wives with husbands too feeble to consummate the marriage? This sexual disruption begins as a play of stylistic levels; when Cornelia uses the verb *coitur* in its lofty sense, to mean coming together for a deliberative assembly, a junior member pipes up with a bawdy pun on coitus – forcing us literally to 'hear double', to set the low meaning against the high.[36]

In the mock-Utopian *Mundus Alter et Idem* (c. 1605), Joseph Hall fuses the Erasmian 'female parliament' with other Renaissance tropes of gender-inversion – Ariosto's 'Realm of Women' (who order men to copulate on pain of death) and Thomas Artus's 'Isle of Hermaphrodites', which mocks the homoeroticism of Henri III's court. Using Ariosto's device of the traveller captured by a militant gynocracy, Hall literally maps out the tender apprehensions of men by creating four different regions of gender trouble within the nation of Viraginia: Amazonia, the realm of bearded viragos who only sleep with their husbands for sexual pleasure and otherwise treat them like servants, where kind-hearted women are condemned by the senate to a Skimmington-like public mockery; Aphrodisia, where total sexual freedom for women becomes bondage

for men; the 'Iland of the Hermaphrodites', who compare themselves to
the homosexual 'pedicatores' of Rome (changed in the English translation to '*Pathiques*' or passive sodomites); and the mainland, where women
emigrate to take refuge from the brutality of jealous husbands (and where
the entire female population of England might emigrate if they could).[37]
In the capital Gynaecopolis (translated 'Gossipingoa'), the narrator
'Mercurius Britannicus' is forced to sign a contract that anticipates the
rules of the *précieux* salon or Millamant's provisos, banning interference
in the domestic 'empire' and stipulating a gallant-chivalric language
and attitude (172–3; 66). Here he witnesses a parliament (explicitly related to Erasmus's dialogue) where laws are dissolved every day and
where the members, elected for their 'beauty and eloquence', speak all
at once in an uncontrolled stream. The English translator of Hall's Latin
adds 'as if horne mad', broadening the associative path that leads from
Gynaecopolis to the next location, Aphrodisia. In this oddly lyrical fantasia on the public woman, the citizens of 'Shameless City' live in glass
houses and wear transparent dresses, enjoying a variety of urban entertainments and a continual stream of captives from the neighbouring
land of male libertinism (unsubtly translated as 'Lecheritania'), whose
inhabitants are reportedly so salacious that they enjoy boys, 'putanas',
and mares. These men they entice, bribe, or openly 'force' into stud
service (*vi cogunt turpissime libidini inservire . . . non aliter quam equi*), feeding
them up with special 'Indian roots' and 'philtris potentissimis' (a passage
much amplified in the English).[38] Mercurius is suitably outraged, but his
repudiation is undercut by a certain wistfulness that lingers like the floral
scents and sophisticated perfumes that greet him when he first enters
this country – an episode surely remembered by Milton when Satan approaches Paradise. He expresses relief that his virtue was not put to the
test, and assures us that he is now thankful to Nature for making him so
ugly, or *deformis* (174–5; 69–70).

What kind of 'deformity' does he mean? Significantly, we learn later
that Mercurius escapes from this land of dominatrices because he is
himself a kind of hermaphrodite or Sporus, a beardless 'adolescent'
who could easily hide his sex.[39] The title of *Mundus Alter et Idem*, 'a world
different and the same', draws attention to the play of alterity and identity endemic to the Utopian mode, and Hall's outside observer – though
clearly intended as the voice of masculine common sense and the means
of mocking female power – turns out to be 'different and yet the same'
himself, fitting into the inverted erotic economy of Viraginia. This hint
of 'pathic' sexuality gave Milton the cue for his attack on Joseph Hall

in the 1642 *Apology for Smectymnuus*, where the author (now an eminent bishop) is collapsed into his narrator. Milton had been accused of writing with the expert sensuality of the brothel-goer (at Hall's instigation, he thought), so in revenge he presents the entire Viraginia episode as a kind of paedophilic ravishment: 'What if I had writ as your friend the author of . . . *Mundus alter et idem*, to have bin ravisht like some young *Cephalus* or *Hylas*, by a troope of camping Huswives in *Viraginia?*' 'Conversation among the *Viraginian* trollops', he explains, made Hall complicit with the desires of commanding women and thus permanently incapable of resisting 'the lascivious promptnesse of his own fancy'. Risking the same criticism, Milton chooses to read Aphrodisia as a sensuous idyll rather than an extension of the mocking ritual. To invent the place is to celebrate it, even to perform in it; only a committed libertine, 'as constant at the Bordello as the gally-slave at his Oare', could have imagined 'com[ing] into *Aphrodisia* that pleasant Countrey that gave such a sweet smell to his nostrills among the shamelesse Courtezans of *Desvergonia*'. According to this 'lascivious' reading, the entire book becomes a 'venereous' decoration, suitable only for a bawdy-house.[40]

English mock-parliament pamphlets had already begun building on Milton's assumption that, despite Hall's distinctions, Gynaecopolis and Aphrodisia were really the same place. They amplify the sexual interpretation of the female assembly hinted in Erasmus, parodying what men imagine women say in traditional gatherings like the gossips' feast, and defusing by comic exaggeration whatever legitimate demands women might have been making. *Parliament of Women* titles reappeared with increasing rudeness in 1640, 1647, 1650, and 1656, keeping time with the crises of that institution. In the 1640 pamphlet denounced by the Root and Branch petitioners, women gather to counteract a senate decree permitting polygamy for men; behind the façade of ancient Roman history, the programme of the Short Parliament is being belittled by equating it with transgressive desire. When the protagonists demand even greater permission to keep multiple partners (the number gauged according to the size of their 'vessel') and assign them distinct duties and schedules, the satirist takes aim against the attempt to extend state regulation into private life, as well as against women in general, whose freedoms can only be sexual. He also mocks City pageantry and the civic pride of the guilds, just when London was testing its strength against royal prerogative; each speech is delivered by the wife of a different tradesman, describing his feeble sexual equipment in appropriately mechanical *doubles entendres*. But these preposterous demands also reflect upon the double standard, the polarization of women into wives and mistresses according to the rubrics of pleasure and duty: these newly organized and articulate women demand the right to keep two men, 'one for delight and the other for drudgery'.[41] Like the citizens of Aphrodisia or the Hobbesian 'natural' matriarch, they draw up a contract defining the male as a plaything or a house-cleaner.

Henry Neville's *Parliament of Ladies, or Divers Remarkable Passages of Ladies in Spring-Garden, in Parliament Assembled* (1647), and its sequels, shift the scene to the new zones of fashionable assembly in London, raising the social level of the 'gynaecopolitical' satire in order to yoke together royalist women, Parliamentary leaders, and their arriviste wives. (The Leveller Richard Overton had also attacked the 'wanton retrograde Ladies' of the Cromwellian hierarchy, we recall from chapter 2.) Though much of Neville's satire consists of opaque in-jokes about individual leaders, he salts it with bawdy innuendos that equate political zeal with genital prowess and cultural patronage with sexual experiment: one member appreciates the 'great parts and able performances' of the preacher John Saltmarsh, a pun later applied to 'Bishoprickes'; another wishes to promote a 'play' by Suckling, dead (like the joke) some years before. Among the serious business (anti-Cavalier legislation, sequestration and purgation, garrisons and fortifications) appear issues like the true meaning of 'due benevolence', with a statute ordering men to pay it on a regular basis. One version of *The Parliament of Ladies* ends with the spectacle of Lady 'Swive-all-she-met' Hungerford, the 'Madam with a Dildoe' later accused of exhausting all her lesbian lovers, who 'publickly thrust her selfe into their secrets' and provokes apocalyptic speculation about the return of the primal hermaphrodite ('whereas *Eve* was once taken out of *Adam*, *Adam* was now seen struting out of *Eve*'); another version ends with a crude antecedent of the Restoration Court lampoon, in doggerel couplets ('Digbies Lady takes it ill, / that her Lord grinds not at her mill'). Unlike Margaret Cavendish then, whose 'Female Orations' embrace a broad range of positions and topics, Neville and his imitators envisage the kind of female speaker 'whose *rhetorick* is *Ribaldry*' and 'whose wit is in *Baudery*'.[42]

These gossipy pamphlets – culminating in the 1650 *Newes from the New Exchange*, where the 'commonwealth of ladies' becomes a mirror-image of male debauchery – narrow the focus on sexual 'ribaldry' while simultaneously scattering broad hints about corruption and illegitimacy. Henry Neville, the radical MP who probably authored at least the first

of them, was constantly devising alternative constitutions and ideal commonwealths, and evading the controversy they provoked; his character-
istically slippery *Isle of Pines* (1668), where one man fathers a complete
society on a desert island, has been variously interpreted as a Utopian
robinsonade and a satire on Charles II. The jocular misogyny of the earlier
Parliament satires gave him a passport into a political world he simultaneously despised and yearned to master, and their 'lubric' ambiguity
provided a cover for subversive critique; they seem to hover between
the literal and the metaphorical use of sex and gender. The outrageous,
metaphor-encrusted characters of these prose lampoons express resentment at the activism of aristocratic women on both sides in the Civil
War, as military organizers, negotiators, encouragers of female petitions,
and conduits of information; the Parliamentary ally Lady Carlisle, for
example – once a figure of erotic speculation in the poetry of Suckling
and Carew – is first 'charged in the *Fore-deck* by Master *Hollis*, in the *Poop*
by Master *Pym*, whilst she clapt my Lord of *Holland* under hatches', then
switches to the royalist party and ends up in the Tower, frustrated 'since
the *State* hath cut off all her *pipes* of Intelligence'. But these allegories
collapse back into literalism under pressure from another anxiety, male
fear of insatiable sexual demands. As in Ariosto's kingdom of women,
these Parliamentarians use their legislative power to regulate copulation,
drawing up a libertine Statute of Labourers which obliges men to make
love as often as physically they can, and an ordinance permitting the
wife to sleep with her most senior servant or nearest neighbour when the
husband's 'parts and abilities' fail.[43]

Newes from the New Exchange remarks of one of the 'commonwealth'
women that "'tis a very hard matter to know whether she be a *Lady* or
Leviathan', and this conceptual confusion applies to the whole politico-
pornographic discourse of women's parliament.[44] Some radical agenda
clearly lurks beneath the smut: the 'English revolution' was being fought
on two fronts, a triangular conflict in which republicans and Levellers
opposed both the decadent Cavaliers who lost and the Parliamentary
grandees who won the first Civil War; by smearing all political 'ladies',
Neville tries to collapse both these enemies together. He certainly uses
female activists 'as signs of the disruption of the socio-political and economic assignation of value' (as Susan Wiseman argues), and he may well
intend to 'identify erotic superabundance with megalomania', to recommend by implicit contrast 'the patrician values of classical republicanism', and to mock 'any form of political action which appears to elevate
the "feminine" principle'.[45] But the 'lubric' vehicle runs away with the

political programme. The cause of freedom itself comes under suspicion, downgraded by the low-libertine mockery and outvoiced by the carnival figures it brings to life. This is particularly true in the 1650 *New Exchange*, where the '*Ladies Rampant*' explicitly borrow free-parliament rhetoric to seize '*the Breeches*' and 'settle themselves in the posture of a *Free-State*' (1–2).

Just as 'posture' plays with the pornographic theme of 'Aretino's Postures', so the double title of *Newes from the New Exchange, or the Commonwealth of Ladies* reveals the economic substratum of political agitation. The élite shopping centre known as the New Exchange is identified as a source of 'Newes', a place where scandal meets print culture, and as a gendered figure of 'commonwealth' instability: clearly the public presence of women (as shopkeepers, consumers and passers-by) allows this association between the equivocal-respectable market and the 'female parliament'. The pamphlet may begin with grandiose declarations of women's ancient oppression and newly won freedom, but it ends, like the Venetian *Tariffa delle puttane* and the London *Wandring Whore*, with the ultimate promotion of commodified sexuality – a list of the ladies on sale in the building, as if they were race-horses or luxury goods. The anxieties of the Restoration already lie compressed within this republican satire; the newly liberated 'Exchange' woman, like the royal mistress of the 1660s and the predatory females in Wycherley's comedies, 'is like a *Politique Merchant* in our *Commonwealth*, and (if she be not taken off by Preferment) may chance to spoile the Trade of all *Stallions* in Pension, by teaching the rest of the Ladies how to prize their Commodities' (14–15).

Subsequent Parliament satires only fall deeper into this paradox: any initiative from those unfit to rule must be exploded by equating it with something 'unthinkable', but political events (women's petitions, dissolutions of Parliament, new advances by the effeminate Cavaliers) bring the unthinkable closer to reality; the topos then requires more work to maintain its vilifying power, which in turn involves more verisimilitude in the 'female' speakers, posing more danger that their rhetoric may sound legitimate. Thus in the 1656 *Now or Never, or a New Parliament of Women* the City wives (typical butt of West End comedy) gather in the disreputable zone of Moorfields to hammer out a programme of reform, de-authorizing any genuine demands that women might have been making by mingling moderate proposals (wife-beating legally abolished, women given the right to choose husbands) with what the author evidently considers preposterous. (As in Joseph Hall's Viraginia, men must be fed a special aphrodisiac diet, forbidden to leave their rooms without permission, ordered to make love night and morning without fail, and prescribed an exclusively affectionate vocabulary – in short, treated like private whores or kept mistresses.) This 'New Parliament' combines the forceful language of radical politics – angrily determining to cast off the reins of male government – with the economic realism of the 'complaint for lack of trading'. (It ends with a poem lamenting the mercenary spirit that has corrupted the world of love.) Responding to what they see as a sudden gain in freedom by apprentices and workers, women insist that their situation is even harder; 'deprived of our Liberties, living in the bonds of servitude, and in the Apprentiship of slavery, (not for a term of years, but during life)', they must assemble to expel 'those *Ægyptian* Task-masters (men) who by their subtil policy still insult and domineer over us'. One unintentionally eloquent speech, by a 'Grave Matron', even adds a rudimentary diagnosis of false consciousness: 'the fault of our enslaving hath been our own selves', for acquiescing in gallant courtship before marriage.[46] Obviously this *New Parliament* pamphlet voices a programme of liberation only to imprison the speakers again in male definitions, expressing only the insatiable demand for sex; to use Neville's words, the 'bawdy' strives to undermine the 'rhetoric'. When the secondary or subaltern voice achieves its own critical mass, however, this staged contest of ideologies fails to produce the requisite triumph of masculinity.

The prospect of women speaking their political ambitions, and acting on their theories by assuming power, seemed real enough in the mid seventeenth century. For obvious historical reasons, the most prominent cases came from the aristocracy – which helps to explain the constant proletarianizing tendency of humiliation-ritual and satire. In France, despite the Salic 'law' that banned women from the throne, influential consorts and regents had played a large historical role, and in contemporary celebrations of the *femme forte* the queen of France headed the procession. One dynasty in particular yielded three generations of powerful rulers, Catherine de Médicis (still hated by Protestants as the instigator of the St Bartholomew's Massacre), Marie de Médicis, and the sisters Christine (regent of Piedmont) and Henrietta Maria of England, focus for much of the animus against Charles I's absolutism. Under such a government, legitimized by art of great magnificence, oppositional satire merges the sexual and the political and forces both to the lowest possible level; one vehicle for hostility to Marie's regency, for example, was the *caquets de l'accouchée*, lewd pamphlets that report on the 'cackling' of women gathered for a childbirth. (These were later imitated in English satires against the authority of 'Mistress Parliament'.)[47] The deliberative and self-constitutive assembly of female speakers must be reduced to obscene gossip, bawdy midwifery, and 'swarming' noise; the threat of female rule – from above or below, by queenly decree or mass petition – must be dispersed by exaggerated generalization, expressed-and-negated in the form of a paradox.

The cult of the *femme forte* permeated French and English culture with images of glamorous gynocracy and Amazonic heroism that in some cases bordered on reality. The regency of Anne d'Autriche encouraged not only projects like Pierre Le Moyne's *Galerie des femmes fortes* (dedicated to her) but a proliferation of stage-heroines who articulate, or inspire, gallant statements of female supremacy: 'Women's Sovereignty is all the more appropriate because nature has marked the characters of sovereignty on their faces ... The valiant Victorina rules to this day over the Gauls'; 'the privilege of the Crown and the privilege of the face blend to make a perfect assemblage, mixing Power with Beauty, reconciling sweetness with Majesty'.[48] Until the outbreak of civil war Henrietta Maria and Charles I had projected exactly this 'perfect assemblage' of male and female, legitimizing divine right through erotic beauty, conveying 'le droit de la Couronne' through 'le droit du visage'. This was most effectively captured in the portraiture of Van Dyck and in the *discordia concors* of Denham's *Coopers Hill*: the 'gentle bosome' of Windsor – where the king and queen have literally taken refuge and hence 'where *Mars* with *Venus* dwels, / Beauty with strength' – becomes an 'Embleme' of the royal master

> in whose face I saw
> A friend-like sweetnesse, and a King-like aw;
> Where Majestie and love so mixt appeare,
> Both gently kind, both royally severe.[49]

Such hermaphroditic imagery persisted even after war broke out: Henrietta Maria gave herself the title 'generalissima', leading her troops 'on Horseback without the Effeminacy of a Woman', and the royalist army reconstituted her *in absentia* as their chivalric-Amazonic leader, naming one formidable siege-cannon 'the Queen's Pocket Pistol'. (When the Parliamentarians captured it they changed the name to 'Sweet Lips'.) Richard Flecknoe, inventing an idealized female community that recalls the homoerotic friendship of 'the Queen and her Ladies here formerly', calls it 'a Commonwealth of Amazons'.[50]

Figure 8. Claude Deruet, *Barbe de Saint-Baslemont on Horseback* (1643), oil on canvas

As we have seen in chapter 2, the English Civil War saw many small-scale interventions by women, particularly at sieges, and a corresponding rise in gendered mockery (the fortifiers of London compared to Sporus, the male feminist branded a 'Poet Hermaphrodite'). In the French-speaking world, warfare provided more spectacular and autocratic opportunities to literalize the *femme forte*. In Lorraine, the author and countess Barbe de Saint-Baslemont commanded her own troops during the Thirty Years' War and kept her region safe from marauding armies; the painter Claude Deruet commemorated her androgynous leadership in a magnificently naive equestrian portrait (fig. 8). During the Fronde, several aristocratic women followed this archetype and took military control, most notably the duchesse de Montpensier ('La Grande Mademoiselle'). In England as well as France, postwar retrenchment into more conventionally 'feminine' realms like the salon and the imaginary community shifted the focus from military to cultural hegemony. Thus the 1652 translation of Le Moyne's *Galerie* reenacts the original homage to the regent Anne by imagining the book's 'Heroick Women' crossing to England, 'and finding no Queen here to whom they might render the same obedience, they resolved to address themselves to you' – that is, directly to the ladies (who thus reconstitute the female ruler by collective, emulative readership).[51] A similar assumption – that female-led coteries replace the Court but preserve the gynocratic cultural politics of France – drives Cowley's praise of Katherine Philips for having abolished 'great *Apollo*'s Salick Law'.

This equation of monarchy and female domination, now transformed from compliment to denunciation, prompted John Hall to argue in his 1653 *Paradoxes* 'That *Women* ought to govern States rather than *Men*'. As in other 'gynaecopolitical' satires of the post-regicide years, Hall's aim swivels wildly to bring down a multiplicity of targets – actual and metaphorical female power, radical Utopianism and aristocratic prerogative. He begins by suggesting that those revolutionary thinkers who 'have employed their deepest *resveries* in the *Transformation* of *Common-Wealths*' might simply have overlooked 'this most excellent and considerable piece of reformation'. The reactionary tone of this passage continues in the prefatory matter. The editor makes the sarcastic point that gynocracy would bring England 'greater *settledness* and *certainty* of *Government*, in regard that *Women*, where they once come to *govern*, do it *perpetually*' – simultaneously mocking the instability of English politics and the supposed power-hunger of women – and one commendatory poem claims that paradox is the only true response to the discursive eruptions of the present age: Hall may as well teach women they can govern, now that they have started to preach.[52] Hall himself plays a more complicated game, however. He mingles bland but moderate arguments (from women's '*sweetnesses*', distaste for warfare, loyalty, piety, and motherly care) with increasingly misogynist assumptions; as he counters objections to his thesis, he concurs in granting women every bad quality, so that he can then argue that artifice, pride, false delicacy, inconstancy, and cruelty are the true qualifications of a ruler. Hall's contempt for women thus serves as a vehicle for an anti-royalist polemic that might have offered comfort after the regicide: 'What *King*', he asks in his mock-defence of cruelty, 'ever boggl'd much if a head or two were in his way? ... How many *sotts*, and *naturals*, and *changelings* by virtue of *succession* have mounted the Throne?' (132). Absolutist monarchs may as well be women, when they rely so much on display, seductive grace, 'the *Air* and *command* of their *smiles*' (112); as in contemporary French drama, the 'rights' of the Crown and the face are assumed to converge. In an earlier paradox, 'That Women ought to goe naked', Hall had paid involuntary tribute to the erotic power of appearance, embellishing (and undermining) his argument with lush descriptions that suggest the fascinated gaze of the adolescent.[53] Now he distances and exorcizes that power by projecting it onto the political enemy, the feminized monarch or Cavalier-as-courtesan. As in John Phillips's association of chivalric gynocentrism with 'prerogative' (the second epigraph to this chapter), Hall literalizes the political metaphors of gallant discourse when he casts his gender-slurs on those who govern by 'the majesty or *comeliness* of the person, . . . *Magically* chaining and winning the *People*' and thereby enforcing the equivalence of '*pleasure* and *liberty*' ([1653], 113, 126).

In the half-century that separated Joseph Hall's Gynaecopolis from his younger namesake's gynocratic paradox, women themselves had begun to author Utopias and ideal constitutions. This helps to explain how John Hall could yoke together female rule, feminized monarchism, and the Utopian 'reveries' that sought to transform society. In France, during and after the Fronde, Utopianism emanated from aristocrats like Anne de Montpensier and Madeleine de Scudéry; in England during the period of anti-Stuart revolution, women's writings swelled the chorus of projects, platforms, visionary commonwealths, and treatises reinventing the state from first principles. (These 'reveries', as Hall called them, include not only well-known tracts by Hobbes, Winstanley, Harrington, Hartlib, and Milton, but an *Advancement of Learning* by John Hall himself.) Mary Pope, for example, published her visionary exegesis under the rational-political title *A Treatise of Magistracy* (1647), and defined occasions when women might disobey 'whatsoever governors we are under, whether magistrates, ministers, husbands, fathers, or masters'. One version of 'Mercurius Pragmaticus' moves on from the petitioning Levellers ('lusty *Lasses*' ready to cuckold their husbands) to the visionary proposals handed to Cromwell by an '*old woman*' from Yorkshire, a Utopian document asking the Commons to reform the clergy, simplify the laws, and solve the problem of poverty.[54]

The most comprehensive and carefully argued contribution to women's reform literature – and the least preoccupied with women's issues – came from the Fifth Monarchist exegete Mary Cary (who also published under the name Rande). Her *New and More Exact Mappe or Description of New Jerusalems Glory* (1651) – a volume whose dedication to

the wives of Cromwell and Ireton confirmed the cultural leadership attacked in the Parliament satires – sets out the imminent transformation
of society under the personal reign of Jesus, which had begun in 1645;
as she spells out the material and political advantages soon to be enjoyed
by the Saints, apocalyptic exegesis merges with the Utopian impulse. In
the related *Twelve Humble Proposals*, published the same year that Hall
produced his 'Paradox', Cary dictates social reforms to the Barebones
Parliament and thus establishes her right to address concerns broader
than the 'feminine' issues of marital reform and women's preaching:
going further than the women's petitions, she proposes the elimination
of tithes, a national postal service whose profits would go to the poor, a
salary cap for state officials, and the destruction of all law books.[55] Cary
identifies her gender very clearly in the forematter of *New Jerusalems Glory*,
but the main text avoids discussion of sexual politics (since marriage will
cease to exist) and eschews the rapturous tone that could be construed
as typically female. Nevertheless, Hugh Peters's introduction praises the
author in heavily sexualized terms: 'good wine may be found in this
Cluster: in this dress you shall neither see naked Breasts, black Patches,
nor long Trains; but an heart breathing after the *coming of Christ* and
the *comfort of Saints*' (f. a2). The Biblically sanctioned sensuality of the
'cluster' leads him by Tartuffian association to the breast emerging from
its 'dress', simultaneously an object of sexual display and religious pant-
ing in Peters's binary vision; echoing the 'black-patched' allure of the
Leveller petitioners, anticipating in miniature the erotic gazing and the
'Strumpet-like posture' of the Whitehall nudity scene, he 'reinscribes'
the fashionable courtesan in the act of denying her relevance.[56]

When female Utopianism *does* address the problems of marriage, we
find a surprising affinity between Francophone aristocratic discourse
and the extreme experimentalism supposedly produced by the English
revolution. Carnivalesque insurgents declare 'we will not be wives' and
refuse the 'villainous slavery' of wedlock; the *New Parliament of Women* denounces marriage in the same vocabulary and identifies gallant courtship
as a device to make women consent to their own 'enslaving' (nn. 19, 46
above). In Michel de Pure's novel *La Précieuse*, somewhere between satirical ventriloquism and direct reportage of salon discussion, a group of
advanced women propose startling revisions in the institution of marriage, including abolishing or rotating the authority, stipulating that the
same terms of endearment and courtly respect be used before and
after the wedding, renewing the contract each year, or dissolving the
marriage automatically after the first child is born (the husband keeps

the child while the wife gains her 'liberty' and a substantial fee); the sole male participant in this deliberative assembly, however, proposes the total abolition of marriage in favour of a different kind of freedom, 'la douce liberté de faire des conquestes'. (Royalist mockery of the English Levellers had likewise reduced their programme to 'liberty of codpiece', we recall from section 2.) In the most Utopian part of *Le Grand Cyrus*, the autobiographical tenth book that shifted the focus of French fiction from action to conversation, Sapho-Scudéry herself declares marriage 'un long esclavage' and all men potential 'tyrants' inasmuch as they could become husbands. The duchesse de Montpensier, defining an ideal all-female retreat in correspondence with her friend Françoise de Motteville, identifies marriage as the sole cause of female inferiority and denounces it in rhetoric that combines the Amazonian slave revolt – 'Tirons-nous de l'esclavage!' – with the Utopian desire to create some 'corner of the world where women are their own mistresses'. This critique of marriage need not mean disengagement from the world of political power, however: when Christina, ex-queen of Sweden, declares that since God has created her free she could never submit to the intolerable 'slavery' of a husband ('me donner cet esclavage qui seroit le plus insupportable pour moy que mon imagination peut concevoir'), she is setting forth her qualifications for the elective crown of Poland.[57]

4. MARGARET CAVENDISH: 'COMBINATIONS AMONGST OUR SEX'?

Margaret Cavendish, a true contemporary of La Grande Mademoiselle and Queen Christina, combines French-aristocratic and English-radical models when she incorporates playful fantasy, worldly libertine speculation, and social critique into her Utopian fiction. While Mary Cary Rande was spelling out the details of Christ's kingdom and drawing up her radical policy document, at the other end of the political spectrum Cavendish was composing her own carelessly grand lists of social reforms and her own fantastic-Utopian alternative realms, where the fixities of gender and decorum dissolve. Both in the essay 'The Liberty of Women' and in the romance of Travelia ('Assaulted and Pursued Chastity'), Cavendish like Scudéry imagines alternative sexual cultures that are nevertheless compatible with her cult of militant virtue. In Lacedemonia 'any Man ... might enjoy any Woman he fancied', 'the Young Women and Men dance uncloathed in the publick Theaters', and yet paradoxically both Chastity and female Liberty flourish; in the

Kingdom of Fancy – as in Joseph Hall's 'Shameless City', but without the moral disapproval – the population lives in houses of crystal and 'their women are common to everybody's use', an arrangement that again promotes 'chear and liberty'.[58] Thus Cavendish's ideal and imaginary kingdoms refute the masculine assumption impersonated in her *Orations* (chapter 2, section 3 above), that 'Liberty makes all Women Wild and Wanton.'

Cavendish's Amazonian protagonists, who enjoy equal success in action and discourse, attempt to rescue a heroic image from the catastrophic experience of civil war. They excel in all the military skills: Travelia shoots the Prince who tries to ravish her in a brothel, and later commands a victorious army (though in male disguise); the Empress of the Blazing World obliterates entire cities using advanced techniques of aerial and naval bombardment; Lady Victoria raises an intractable siege and rides in triumph into the capital. Though sometimes interpreted as pure compensatory fantasy, the last of these episodes should be recognized as an *à clef* version of Anne de Montpensier's successful campaigns during the Fronde, when her brilliant grasp of siege-tactics won the cities of Orleans and Paris; the heroine's name may also echo the 'vaillant Victorine' who rules over the Gauls, a transparent allusion to the regent. In one respect, however, Cavendish's heroinism incorporates English rather than French materials. Lady Victoria campaigns together with her husband (a joint command imagined but never achieved by Henrietta Maria) and recruits an army of feminist volunteers who raise sieges, turn the tide of battle, and build fortifications; the energy of protesters and Parliament-defenders could thus be transferred to an idealized memory of royalist victory. Capturing the 'parliament of women' trope from the satirical substratum, Cavendish then imagines an official 'Act' that establishes (though it trivializes by domestication) the freedoms newly won by women.[59]

Despite their *femme forte* exoticism and self-conscious exaggeration, Cavendish's royalist-Amazonian fantasies cannot be isolated from the Civil War phenomenon of women's mobilization and petitioning. Occasions for women to try the power of their voices, we should recall, included not only the collective demonstrations recorded by the newsbooks and lampooned by the mock-petitions, but many individual actions by women against Parliament and innumerable private petitions, for marital separation (initiated far more by women than by men), for mistreatment and wrongful imprisonment (sometimes at the hands of powerful mistresses), and for the restitution of sequestered estates.

Satirical newsbooks equated all kinds of female vocal action – when *The Man in the Moon* declares 'The Parliament have this week been much troubled with Women', he links in one sentence the 'new Prophetesse', the mass petitions of Leveller women, and two wives applying to save their husbands from destitution or execution – and the authorities were always prepared to turn public action into public sexuality: when Lady Fairfax vociferated against the condemnation of Charles I from the gallery of the Commons, for example, the soldiers silenced her by shouting 'Down with the whores!' Cavendish herself entered this vocal public sphere when she attempted to negotiate for her exiled husband's property, but found herself unable to speak a word in that confrontational and 'ungentlemanly' atmosphere. This humiliating failure undoubtedly spurred her to develop the omnipotent inner voice that dictates her literary compositions. As Sophie Tomlinson points out, Cavendish explains her silence not merely in terms of bashfulness, but as a reaction to the *prise de parole* that has already taken place in post-royalist England, where women have already 'become pleaders, attornies, petitioners, and the like'.[60] As she does with other popular manifestations of female agency, like the Italian comediennes that fascinated her in Antwerp, Cavendish consciously transfers the 'petitioner' to the inner stage of her own mind. And she follows the logic of pornotropic association by speculating, with surprising sympathy, about the rhetorical gifts of the courtesan and the 'Magick Power' they give her; as a result of their sexual and representational arts, 'Courtesans are often assisted by the Powerful', especially in their 'petitioning' (*Letters*, 75).

Cavendish's Utopian rules for a new society – 'The Inventory of Judgements Commonwealth, the Author cares not in what World it is established' – form part of her essayistic miscellany *The Worlds Olio* (1655), and they emulate that title by combining apparently incongruous ingredients in a common sauce.[61] Hard-headed Hobbesian precepts for an absolutist state mingle with surprisingly worldly provisos, again revealing her familiarity with the pornosphere:

Item, No Man shall Father a Whores Child, or Children, unless he were sure he were the Father, which few can tell . . .

Item, That no Husband shall keep a Houshold Friend, lest he should make love to his Wife, and he become a Cuckold thereby . . .

Item, No Husband nor Wife, although but a day married, shall kiss each other in publick.

To reconcile pleasure and liberty, straightforward reforms in the rules of marriage ('none shall marry against their own liking or free choice') alternate with libertine mock-regulations; men must change mistresses every six months, beautiful but tongue-tied women with insufficient wit to keep their lovers will be 'accounted no better than a senceless Statue', and husbands will be disgraced for courting a 'Common Whore' as much as if they were cowards or cuckolds. ('But if a Gentleman must or will have a Whore, let him have one of his own making.')[62] The effect of this mélange is to break down the separation of sexual-domestic and political issues, formally reinforcing Cavendish's insistence that gendered criteria apply equally to public and private 'Governments'. Thus kings must abandon the 'Effeminate' taste for collecting precious objects, women must stop adopting the worst masculine features (drunken swaggering and impudent talk), and society must stop valuing 'men that have Effeminate Bodies, . . . loose Limbs, smooth Skins, fair Complexions, fantastical Garbs, affected Phrases, strained Complements', and other marks of the new *politesse* (207, 213, 215). Rather than true men and women coexisting in freedom, the world is now dominated by ladylike tyrants of both sexes. On this matter Cavendish would agree with Lucy Hutchinson and John Hall, though their politics are diametrically opposed. All three link the chaos of gender-confusion directly to political events, as if the salon and the battlefield mirrored one another; the Fronde may have seemed glamorous and liberating to Cavendish, and the female petitioners suggestive, but fundamentally 'Civil Wars corrupt good Manners', destroying the Utopian project of reconciling chastity with 'the Liberty of Women' (75).

Cavendish's multifarious writings give voice to the full, contradictory range of possibilities raised by women's entry into political discourse and action. Like Christina of Sweden, she alternates withering assertions of female defectiveness with the recognition that institutional 'slavery' creates that weakness.[63] Much of the time she seems no friend of the rationalist feminism then forming in intellectual circles. Her speech on the Skimmington ride, as we saw in chapter 2, proposes reforming the shaming ritual to define the gender-hierarchy more sharply and to punish more directly the husband who allows his 'Masculine Authority' to lapse. Cavendish's *Sociable Letters* frequently deride 'Effeminacy' and praise women who condone their husbands' philandering or insist that 'Debauched' men make the best husbands, even though her first book of poems had *welcomed* this 'Age when the effeminate spirits rule' because it gave greater advantages to women writers and prophets.[64] Her passionate outpourings of contempt for women sometimes reduce them to the abject 'natural' condition described by Hobbes; his famous parody of the Golden Age, listing all the conveniences absent in the state of nature ('no Culture of the Earth, no Navigation, no commodious Building'), pales beside the rolling catalogue of male inventions and female incapacities in the preface to Cavendish's *Olio*:

Women have no strength nor light of Understanding, but what is given them from Men; this is the reason we are not Mathematicians, . . . Navigators, Architects, . . . Skilfull Souldiers, Politick Statists . . . Our Governments would be weak, had we not Masculine spirits and Counsellors to advise us; and for our strength, we should make but feeble Mariners, . . . neither would there be such Commerce of Nations as there is, nor would there be so much Gold and Silver and other Mineralls fetcht out of the Bowells of the Earth if there were none but Effeminate hands to use the Pick-axe and Spade; nor so many Cities built . . .

All this rhetorical force is mustered to disprove women's fitness for rule, as if Hall's 'paradox' had become a proposal serious enough to be refuted. Within a few lines, however, the political thesis has shifted as if to match the energy of the performance; Cavendish now welcomes the improvements achieved by women's education and reinterprets their refinement not as weakness but as evidence of angelic superiority.[65] In her essay 'Noble Minds in Strong Bodies', which calls for a regimen of exercise that will allow women to 'practice the Fortitude of Men' (*Olio*, 215), weakness itself is understood as a product of restriction – a Wollstonecraftian principle reiterated in the most feminist of the 'Female Orations', as we shall see below. And in another preface, addressed 'To the Two Universities' and published in the same year as the *Olio*, Cavendish unequivocally ascribes women's political exclusion to masculine coercion rather than 'natural' deficiency: 'by an opinion which I hope is but an erronious one in men, we are shut out of all power and Authority by reason we are never imployed either in civil nor marshall affaires; our counsels are despised and laught at, the best of our actions are trod[d]en down with scorn, by the over-weaning conceit men have of themselves.'[66]

Thomas Edwards thought he had dealt a devastating blow to the Levellers when he pointed out that, pushing Lilburne's argument about the franchise to its logical conclusion, 'all women at once were exempt from being under Government' (*Gangraena* III. 154). This argument had already been articulated by female enclosure-rioters forced to defend themselves in Star Chamber (chapter 2, n. 6 above): since 'women were lawlesse, and not subject to the lawes of the realme', they can be *lawless* in another sense, licensed to protest with impunity. Edwards now brings this unthinkable possibility into the public debate over Levelling. The political centre, the sense of masculine normality and legitimacy in troubled times, was thus held in place by two equal and opposite visions of extremity, the 'parliament of women' and the ungoverned female horde. In the light guise of a 'sociable letter' from a royalist to a Parliamentarian wife, Cavendish moves towards precisely this state of principled 'lawlessness'. Starting with conventional disparagement of her sex ('As to the matter of Governments, we Women understand them not'), she rapidly escalates into indignant complaint ('we are excluded from intermedling therewith, and almost from being subject thereto') and thence into the radical corollary that had so disturbed the judges of Star Chamber and the apoplectic author of *Gangraena*:

we hold no Offices, nor bear we any Authority therein; we are accounted neither Useful in Peace, nor Serviceable in War; and if we be not Citizens in the Commonwealth, I know no reason we should be Subjects to the Commonwealth: And the truth is, we are no Subjects.

Catherine Gallagher plausibly links this passage to the extreme solitude or monadism expressed in Cavendish's famous desire to be 'Margaret the First', arguing that 'exclusion from political subjecthood allows female subjectivity to become absolute'. But this emphasis on solipsism underestimates the bonding, networking role of female correspondence – announced in the title *Sociable Letters* – and the contradictory positions taken here and throughout the collection. In this letter to a Parliamentary friend, for example, the grumbling of the powerless turns into a collective celebration of female emotional dominance, the 'magical chaining' that Hall finds at the basis of absolutism. 'Nature' guarantees that 'we oftener inslave men, than men inslave us'; men merely 'seem' to rule, 'but we really govern the world, in that we govern men'. Indeed, true manhood *means* being 'govern'd by a woman more or less', whether by wives, mistresses, mothers, daughters, aunts, landladies, or hostesses. Exceptions to this gynocratic definition of masculinity – the 'dull Stoick' or the 'cold, old, withered Batchelor' – are frankly mocked for their impotence. Cavendish harnesses the long tradition of satyric sexual mockery – the word 'cuckold' flows easily and often from her pen – but reverses its gender politics, promoting an aristocratic version of the 'woman on top'. As she puts it in the *Olio*, 'a Gallant Man will never strive for the Breeches with his Wife, but present her with the whole Suit' (keeping his sword, however); 'it is more honour for a Man to be led Captive by a Woman, than to contend by resistance'.[67]

How then does this invisible and manipulative erotic-familial 'government' relate to the political realm? How does Cavendish evaluate the mobilization of female agency – hers included – provoked by the revolution she detested? The *Sociable Letters* offer two diametrically opposed models. The letter declaring women 'free' from subjecthood, a celebration of friendship between women whose husbands fought on opposite sides, absolves 'us' collectively from any responsibility for that disaster; here, as in the Oration that calls for a 'Combination' among women, Cavendish voices directly what the *Parliament of Ladies* could only express through satirical ventriloquism – the appeal to 'unite against the common enemy, their Husbands' (6). Indeed, she detaches women not only from 'the Civil War in the Kingdom' but from the 'general War amongst the Men' (28). This unmistakable echo of *Leviathan* shows Cavendish gendering the Hobbesian vision of human nature in its raw state, turning Hobbes's 'inference from civil war' into a critique of specifically masculine belligerence. Reversing her earlier reworking of Hobbes – the sonorous complaint about women's 'natural' weakness and technical incompetence – she now celebrates their peace-loving non-involvement. (Women had indeed formed their own anti-war movement, as we saw in our discussion of the petitions in section 2.) Elsewhere in the volume, however, Cavendish recalls a different vision of female power and influence: 'no question but Women may, can, and oftentimes do make wars, especially Civil wars; witness our late Civil war, wherein women were great, although not good actors'. 'Women in State-affairs' fret and distemper the body politic, inducing fevers they can exacerbate but not heal. This insider's view of women's political agency – by a Lady-in-Waiting to Queen Henrietta Maria and wife of the defeated royalist commander – revives the monstrous, devouring figure of porno-political satire: Cavendish blames 'their restless Minds, and unsatiable Appetites' (*Letters*, 12–13).

Cavendish's model of female political influence makes it difficult to distinguish the admirable *femme forte* – who 'governs as it were by an insensible power', and to whom every true gentleman submits – from the deplorable 'actor in some State-design' whose insatiable appetites foment civil war. Both express features supposedly common to all 'Women', but which are brought together most conspicuously in the powerful 'Courtesan'. Without Neville's comic exaggeration, Cavendish explores the same analogy between prostitutes and the Cromwellian 'Ladies' who constitute an alternative parliament. Politics and whoredom equally require the combination of 'cheating Craft' and 'unsatiable Appetite'. 'We are full of Designs and Plots', she asserts in the Civil War letter just cited; 'for deceiving Craft, Women are well practised therein, and most of them may be accounted Politicians' (*Letters*, 12). 'Unruly Appetite' drives them (or 'us'?) to fantasies of dominion and to the kinds of sexual-political excess that provoked the Skimmington ride, 'Striking and Cuckolding their Husbands' (49). But if 'Adultery is caused by unruly Appetites', what causes those appetites in the first place is the artificial education given to the 'Quality', the entire system of upper-class accomplishment that has produced Cavendish herself: 'it makes their Body a Baud, and their Mind a Courtesan' (50).

The destructive courtesan and politician, as Cavendish elaborates them, sound increasingly like the self-fashioning artist-heroine. 'We are full of Designs and Plots.' Aspasia's 'Power lay in her Tongue', so that the great men of Athens 'learned to speak Eloquently by her, [and] brought their Wives to hear her'; the modern courtesan exerts a 'Magick Power' by coordinating all the 'Arts' of behaviour, speech, music, dance, dress, and 'Artificial Shews'. These mistresses of action and 'Rhetorick' contrast favourably with the 'sighing' preacher, the beautiful but mute 'Statue', and the tongue-tied petitioner (pp. 82, 111, 112 above). Indeed, 'it would be well if Wives had more of that Art to keep their Husband's Affections'. A dialogue from one of Cavendish's late Interregnum plays asserts that 'most Stage-Players are Curtizans', 'most Curtizans are good Actors', and both should be hissed off the stage; as Tomlinson points out, however, this is precisely the fate she imagines for her own dramatic works. In 'this Age, wherein Courtesans are so Prevalent and Fortunate', when the *Sociable Letters* repeatedly allude to their success in marriage and 'petitioning', Cavendish's moralistic diatribes are tinged with grudging admiration for 'Wanton and Free Women'. Amongst her Female Orations, the most militant feminist insists that women must gain all the 'Strength and Wit' that men acquire by 'Exercise' in every social arena – in colleges and taverns, but equally in

'Brothels'. And in the decade of the Restoration itself, to which we turn in the next chapter, Cavendish adopts a 'free' and theatrical self-presentation that combines the extremes of *femme forte* and courtesan, drawing crowds 'as if it were the Queen of Sweden', 'her brests all laid out to view in a play house with scarlett trimd nipples'.[68]

CHAPTER 4

The wandering whore's return: the carnivalization of sexuality in the early Restoration

This full appearance of our Companions sets me all on fire, to talk a little bawdery and drollery amongst them . . .

(*The Wandring Whore* I.3)

They encourage all the vile excesses that the most profligate strip-ping Whore can act, yet at the same time they applaud, they must need entertain a secret hatred and scorn . . . They are solicitous for this wild diversion, as they are for the sight of a *Bartholomew Shew*, . . . but once a year.

(*The Whores Rhetorick*)

We have seen in chapters 2 and 3 how thoroughly sexual mockery imbued the period of Civil War and Cromwellian rule; following the collapse of that régime, a different aspect of pornotropism comes to the fore. As political commentary responds to institutional crisis and women's assertiveness by adapting ceremonies of abjection designed for the common whore, so the discourse of sexuality and the narrative of prostitution – the inheritance of courtesan-dialogues like Aretino's *Ragionamenti* and *La Puttana errante* – become shaped by political language. This chapter will take its cue from those 'pornographic' texts that appeared at the end of the Cromwellian period and during the first months of the return to monarchism, in particular the courtesan-biography *The Practical Part of Love*, the *Wandring Whore* dialogues, and other *Strange and True* pamphlets that describe the 'Offices' of notorious bawds like Mrs Cresswell and Priss Fotheringham. Together they define the conjunction of sexuality and politics at the moment of 'Restoration'. They stage spectacles of perversion-as-diversion that clearly act out the fantasies, and reveal the tensions, of the sexual counter-culture at a period of institutional flux that ideologues presented as the victory of carnivalesque hedonism over 'Puritan' repression. In the triumphalist outpouring of royalist literature that followed the roasting of the Rump, the radical City of London becomes a 'fading' and poverty-stricken harlot, the Goddess Victory is found to have been 'prostituted' and 'ravished' by Cromwell, and politicians are perceived as 'wonderfully enamoured of a *Commonwealth* because it is like a Common Whore, which every one may have to do with; but cannot abide *Monarchy*, because it is honest and confined to one'.[1] Conversely, institutional satire and a kind of perverse Utopianism flood into *pornographia* itself. In chapter 3 we saw political enterprise turned into whores' tricks; here we shall see the reverse.

What exactly was 'restored' in 1660? A Good Old Cause moralist like Lucy Hutchinson notices an immediate outburst of lewd discourse, but interprets it as an inversionary disguise for former Cromwellians: 'everyone hoped in this change to change their condition, and disowned all things they had before adored; and every ballad singer sung up and down the streets ribald rhymes made in reproach of the late commonwealth'. Milton of course denounced the return of the Sons of Belial, the 'barbarous dissonance / Of *Bacchus* and his revellers' (*PL* VII.32–3). Other serious poets greeted the monarch's return with a rapture not 'ribald' but equally sexualized: in Rachel Jevon's 1660 'Song of Exultation', for example, Britain is 'ravished with love' and the three kingdoms become three willing bedmates for the king, who comes 'to Reign a Lord / O'r hearts subdu'd by Love, not by the Sword' – just as John Hall had warned in his gendered satire against absolutism. But even royalists deplored the carnivalesque excess that followed the Restoration, after the first flush of panegyric had subsided. Samuel Butler, chief author of the anti-Puritan mockery that Hutchinson despised, nevertheless comes to endorse her inversionary model: Restoration libertines act as if they 'had no other Way but Sin and Vice / To be restor'd again to *Paradise*', replicating in opposite but equal forms the narrowness of the elect and the dionysiac frenzy and arrogance of the Antinomians, the 'forc'd Hypocrisy of Wickedness'.[2] Margaret Cavendish deplored (and emulated in her theatrical self-display) an age in which courtesans achieve the social prominence of duchesses and aristocrats become 'Pimps and Bawds' – an inversion of social order which shows 'that the Practise of their Lives is not answerable to the Degree of their Dignities'. The noble and the picaresque change places or compete for the reputation of immoral 'Wit'; a knightly acquaintance models his own autobiography on that of the Spanish rogue Guzman de Alfarache, provoking Cavendish to remark that his life 'hath been as evil as *Guzman*'s, but whether his Wit be as good as *Guzman*'s, I know not'. Gilbert Burnet saw the same conjunction of extreme wit and appetite in Rochester: his two ruling passions – 'a violent love of Pleasure, and a disposition to extravagant

Mirth' – were alike kindled and heightened by 'the humour of that time'.[3]

The final section of this chapter will therefore explore the affinities between the lower-stratum pornography of *The Wandring Whore* and the 'extravagant Mirth' of the aristocratic Sons of Belial. The removal of Lenten severity in some ways induced a perpetual and exaggerated 'Carnelevation'. The kind of inversionary violence that Jonson described in the induction to *Bartholomew Fair*, or that the Church courts prosecuted in disorderly villagers, returns in what Milton calls the 'riot' of the young gentry. The social and sexual mingling that used to be confined to Bartholomew Fair – 'Hither resort people of all sorts, High and Low, Rich and Poore, . . . and of all conditions, good and bad, vertuous and vitious, Knaves and fooles, Cuckolds and Cuckoldmakers, Bauds and Whores, Pimpes and Panders' – now blossoms into the newly fashionable turmoil of St James's Park as Wycherley or Rochester describe it:

> Unto this All-sin-sheltring *Grove*
> *Whores* of the *Bulk* and the *Alcove*,
> Great *Ladies*, *Chamber-Maids*, and *Drudges*,
> The *Rag-picker* and *Heiresse* trudges:
> *Carr-men*, *Divines*, great *Lords*, and *Taylors*,
> *Prentices*, *Poets*, *Pimps* and *Gaolers*;
> *Foot-Men*, fine *Fops*, do here arrive,
> And here promiscuously they swive.[4]

The wilder performative gestures of Dorset, Sedley, Etherege, and Rochester – famous as a privileged 'merry gang' or 'mob of gentlemen' – can in part be explained by the repressive hypothesis. Their defiant exhibitionism resembles a case of delirium reported in the *Philosophical Transactions*: after accidentally eating a pie made from opium poppies, the male and female servants in a Cornish inn 'stript themselves quite naked, and so danced one against the other a long time'; when their mistress returns home 'the Maid turn'd her Brich against her, and purging stoutly, said, There, Mistress, is Gold for you'.[5] But the Restoration culture of priapism cannot wholly be explained as a release from inhibition, a return to 'Merry England', a levelling submergence in popular culture, or a ritual expulsion of Puritanism by 'forc'd Hypocrisy of Wickedness'. Though aristocratic 'Frolicks' borrow the festive-violent 'bawdery and drollery' of the illicit or plebeian subculture, their purpose is to flaunt impunity and privilege. Their deliberate cultivation of perverse extremes, as Mrs Cresswell herself explains in the English adaptation of Pallavicino's *Retorica delle puttane*, expresses 'a secret hatred and scorn'.

1. 'NATURE'S GOOD OLD CAUSE': *PORNOGRAPHIA* AND THE TRANSITION TO ROYALISM

Already in the 1650s, political satire and the discourse of prostitution had become interchangeable at those moments when shameful persons (male 'whoremongers' or lower-class women) were thought to be entering the political process, or when the new régime tries to extend its power over illicit behaviour. The post-regicide *Newes from the New Exchange, or the Commonwealth of Ladies*, a product of the uncertain year 1650, ends with a printed catalogue of the women whom 'you may buy' in the Exchange, and his list of female transgressors mingles obvious satiric inversion (Lady Cromwell raising her glass '*To the best -------- in Christendome*') with plausible observations of the looser gentry; the exuberant gestures of Lady Sandys, for example, reappear in several accounts of glamorous debauchery from 1660 (3, 20–1). The Parliamentary legislation on marriage in 1650 – the first wholesale attempt to secularize the laws governing sexuality in England – generates the first of the wave of whore-pamphlets that would crest in *The Wandring Whore* of 1660–1, adapting the Italianate dialogue to the geography of the London underworld: the strangely hybrid *Dialogue between Mistris Macquerella, a Suburb Bawd, Ms Scolopendra, a noted Curtezan, and Mr Pimpinello an Usher* has them 'Pitifully Bemoaning the Tenour of the Act (Now in Force) against Adultery and Fornication'.[6] Their exaggerated concern seems designed to reinforce this formidable Act rather than to undermine it; contemporaries complained rather that its strict evidence-requirements in effect encouraged women's sexual freedom, or at least that it 'was made only or chiefly for guarding of women's credits, that lewd persons might not dare to boast of their own filthiness'. Clarendon believed that abolishing the Church courts left 'adultery and incest as unpunishable as any other acts of good fellowship', unwittingly exposing the convivial side of those transgressions. Thomas Ivie, the East India Company executive who published his acrimonious marital breakdown in *Alimony Arraign'd*, clearly blamed his wife's sexual adventurism on the ease of obtaining alimony under the new state jurisdiction – a motif that proliferated in whore-biography and comedy.[7]

The decade of godly rule in fact displayed many features of 'Restoration' lewdness and disorder. Edmund Gayton's comments on the 'Carnelevation' common to Ranters and Hectors (chapter 2, n. 2 above) remind us that riotous street gangs using that name were a familiar point of reference in 1653. When John Evelyn reports on wild debauchery and 'popular Libertinism' (section 4 below), he describes the late 1650s and not the years after the Sons of Belial had resumed control. As well as the bawdy petitions discussed in chapter 3, all kinds of low-libertine satire revived towards the end of the Protectorate, including risqué playing cards showing 'Joane hold my Staff Lady Protectresse' and 'The Lady Lambert and Oliver under a strong Conflict', obscene drolls, and the torrent of verse on the 'Rump' in 1659, celebrating constitutional change with excruciatingly obvious puns on sexual, edible, and Parliamentarian backsides. The *Mistris Parliament* dialogue was reprinted with the simple alteration of the title to *Mrs Rump*. In the power-vacuum that followed the death of Cromwell, John Tatham's topical farce *The Rump* juxtaposes the Committee of Safety with a gathering of women around Lady Lambert, clamouring to settle new honours and repeal the laws against fornication; these and other power-bids by Lady Lambert, a self-proclaimed 'Free Woman', lead only to ritual abasement, as she and all the Puritan leaders are forced to sell their wares in the street. Thus Tatham revives the lewd 'parliament of ladies' in order to associate activist women with what Paula Backscheider calls 'unofficial kinds of government, inappropriate kinds of influence, and illusionary forms of power'.[8] In these uncertain months, what other kinds were available?

The mock-official pamphlets of early 1660 continue this 'porno-political' process, mirroring the crucial debates of that time – the composition of Parliament, the exclusion of the regicides – by identifying the 'qualifications' of the MPs in sexual terms, or by solemnly appointing Henry Marten '*Custos Rotten Whorum* for the Suburbs of London'. Throughout the revolutionary decades, as we have seen, Marten's advocacy of women's petitions and Leveller reforms had made him the focus of pornotropic satire and the lightning-rod for sexual-political anxieties. He becomes the chief chartered libertine, the whoremaster-general flourishing his 'standard' over a female army, proclaiming a new freedom for 'all women who have poysoned their husbands, murdred their children, baudy house keepers, Whoores, secret and publick, and all others who desire to live as they list' – an astonishing catalogue of transgressors that reveals how closely prostitution was associated with agency-in-excess. This baiting of Marten continued into 1660 and beyond. John Phillips's comic almanac *Montelion* retails gossip about his involvement with a '*Beggar Wench*' (an allusion repeated in *The Wandring Whore*) and his supposed love-letters to this lower-class mistress were published in 1662. The revival of Aretino – an English adaptation called *The Crafty Whore* appeared in 1658 and the new Elzevier edition of the *Ragionamenti* in 1660, with the apocryphal dialogue now called *La puttana errante* – created new opportunities for slurring discredited leaders and marking certain spaces as erotic institutions, parodic social bodies founded upon a set of rules or constitutive document. When the satirist undermines Marten by wondering whether he 'loves the Kings Bench Rules better than *Aretines* Postures', he imagines the legal profession and libertine sexuality as two parallel worlds, each structured or 'chartered' by its own regulations.[9] In the 'Suburbs of London' – disreputable zones where 'Mother-Strumpets' keep their 'Courts' (as Dryden would put it in *MacFlecknoe*) – these two worlds converge, creating an entire republic of 'rotten whores' presided over by Marten as *custos rotulorum*.

The concept of the *counter-institution* goes a long way to explain the form taken by those 'lascivious, idle, and unprofitable books' that assail female agency and weave political discourse into pornography. The preposterous imaginings of low-libertine literature serve to model the world of illicit sexuality as an alternative establishment, either to integrate the marginal and forbidden into official culture, or to rehearse changes in the larger world at a time of social and political upheaval. The process did not begin in 1660, of course. Even before the 1640 *Parlament of Women*, the 'lascivious' work denounced in the Root and Branch petition (chapter 3, n. 25 above), Nicholas Goodman's *Hollands Leaguer* had described a quasi-institutional brothel arranged like a moated castle, halfway between the architecture of state power and the mock-castles of carnival; the resident prostitutes (significantly identified as 'the wicked Women of *Eutopia*') apparently designed their house as an imaginary state.[10] Many of the lewd petitions from the Civil War period, as we have seen, imagine whores, bawds, and midwives as an estate or organized corporation, with its own representative voice ready to defend its interests, complain about 'Want of Trading', and answer accusations. The 'wandering' pamphlets that greeted the Commonwealth's demise – often concerned with the governing rules and decorative programmes that turn the bawdy-house into a miniature nation – advertise this corporate voice on their title-pages. *A Strange and True Conference between Two Notorious Bawds, Damarose Page and Pris. Fotheringham* (1660) promises 'the Newest Orders and Customs of the Half-Crown Chuck Office, and the Officers thereto Belonging, with the

Practice of the Prick-Office'; 'Megg. Spenser' claims both authorship and authority, as 'Over-seer of the Whores and Hectors on the Bank-Side'. Likewise *Strange and True Newes* (another pamphlet about Priss Fothering-ham) displays a list of officers headed by Mrs Cresswell, and *The Ladies Champion, Confounding the Author of the Wandring Whore* announces that it is 'Approved of by Megg. Spenser, Damrose Page, Priss. Fotheringham, Su. Leming, Betty Laurence, Mother Cunny', as if these already-famous London brothel-keepers formed a semi-official Jury of Matrons, lending their names to vouch for the scandalous truths within – just as real mid-wives and doctors 'approved' and authorized publications that describe monstrous births.[11]

A specifically 'Restoration' sexual literature, then, results from the convergence of two discursive genealogies – the Continental 'Aretine' tradition of prostitutional expertise, and the indigenous tradition of festive-aggressive bawdy, evolving from individual whore-baiting into politicized mock-institutional satire. It erupts in the liminal period, after the Restoration itself had abolished the vestiges of 'Puritan' power in a rush of festivity, but before the new state had been fully defined and confirmed. In November and December 1660, for example, when *The Wandring Whore* appeared in multiple instalments, Pepys's diary registers numerous novelties and disturbances that ripple the celebratory surface: the first new Theatre Royal and the first visit to a coffee-house, the need to make up entirely new 'forms' for certain official promotions, debates and demurrals over the sentencing of the regicides (some still buried in Westminster Abbey), major financial problems involving royal revenue from the Excise and the seamen's pay, intrusive personal demands for Poll Tax, murmurs against corruption, shocked discussion of the Duke of York's marriage to the heavily pregnant commoner Anne Hyde, and the discovery of an armed insurrection by Major-General Overton. The most striking precursor of the *Wandring Whore* dialogues, *The Practical Part of Love, Extracted out of the Extravagant and Lascivious Life of a Fair but Subtle Female*, appeared in August 1660, a month of awaiting warrants from the king, 'fear of a turn', calling in accounts, speculation in offices, factions in Parliament, debates over indemnity and the status of Interregnum legislation.[12] The traditional *carpe diem* on the title-page ('You that would Love, pray now begin it, / And do not lose this present minute') seems to take on a new urgency, as the courtesan-biography takes stock of political changes through the satyric veil, and obliquely explores the possibility that the sexual régime might now correspond to the national culture, that the newly restored Court might call home the *puttana errante* and reinstate the *cortegiana honesta*.

Throughout *The Practical Part of Love*, transformations in the whore-narrative encapsulate the destabilization of hierarchy brought about by the return of an aristocratic culture once identified with the Whore of Babylon. In one episode, the Collier of Croydon (a chapbook character famous for dirty labour and rustic manners) travels to London to gaze besottedly at the Court beauties, becoming so aroused that ('by the strength of imagination') he passes their pride and lasciviousness to the daughter he fathers that night; the visual impact of the Court inspires the lower-class spectator to beget a hybrid, literally embodying the juncture of the old folkloric–proletarian whorishness and the new 'Quality' lewdness. The main narrative – in which Aretino's mother–daughter dialogue has been replaced by a third-person history covering two generations – spells out the prostitute's rising social aspiration. Lucia's initiation resembled a rough village carnival, as she 'stifly held out her Maiden-Castle' (chapter 2, section 1 above), but her daughter Helena receives a full training from the London equivalent of Aretino's Nanna, the bawd-midwife who passes under the double name of 'Ventricia' and 'Mother Cunny' – one of the authoritative matrons who would soon 'approve' *The Ladies Champion*. This preceptor figure borrows from Aretino's *Ragionamenti* the programme of cultivated demureness and artistic accomplishment that transforms Pippa from a raw *puttana* into an accomplished 'mistress'; on the threshold of the Restoration, the strapping plebeian whore character must be converted into a cultured Italian courtesan, more like Veronica Franco than Doll Common. After a career driven more by pleasure than avarice, Helena contrives an Aretinan marriage to a wealthy dotard. Exploiting the loopholes of the 1650 Adultery Act and the alimony it supposedly guaranteed to errant wives like Mrs Ivie, she finishes the book as 'a most triumphant rich now regnant Whore'.[13] This final oxymoron intensifies the conceptual dissonance of the *cortegiana honesta*, combining or 'restoring' the scattered extremes of the female hierarchy: the quean becomes queen; royalty merges with common prostitution.

The 'chartering' or institution-building impulse in *The Practical Part of Love* serves to envision both the internal literary history of libertine discourse, now flooding onto the London market, and the external political and social situation. The educational theme prompts the anonymous author to create an entire University of Love, its curriculum and library described in detail. Having passed through the gallery of 'amorous and lascivious Pictures', we find in the rare book room the inevitable

'*Aretines* postures in folio done to the life' (39) and beside it a mysterious volume with only two leaves, 'bound in murry leather, and red on the leaves', but 'very much beaten'. This is of course the 'two-leaved book' already flaunted in Carew's royal masque (chapter 1, section 4 above), the ultimate reduction of sexuality to textuality since it signifies the vulva itself; the version in *The Practical Part* (available 'in Folio, in Quarto, and so to the least Volume') combines the sex-as-book trope with the abject associations of penitence and hygiene, since the two labial 'leaves' are flanked by 'two white sheets of paper, one before, and the other behind' (40). Other titles in the library suggest the proliferation of sexual discourse rather than its grim minimalism. Here again Aretino provided a model; the original *Ragionamenti* had helped to form a libertine canon by citing parallel texts – the *Puttana errante* poem, the *Tariffa delle puttane di Venegia* – and by introducing scenes that advertise the 'Postures' or suggest new ones. Similarly the improbable-sounding book-lists in the University of Love serve as a catalogue of the underground book trade newly burgeoning in London, mingling current and projected titles: *Francions bawdy History* emphasizes the lewdness of Charles Sorel's *Histoire comique de Francion*; John Phillips's *Jovial drollery* reminds us of Milton's nephew and protégé; *Luteners Lane decipher'd* maps out the secret geography of the London pornosphere; *The Life of Mother Cunny* exploits the new fascination with naming notorious bawds; a *Catalogue* of London prostitutes imitates the Venetian *Tariffa* and anticipates *The Wandring Whore*; *Venus her Cabinet unlockt* introduces English readers to the term 'pornodidascalian'. The publisher, Henry Marsh, includes several of his own scandalous projects, like *Venus undrest* (the title under which he would reissue the *Practical Part of Love* in 1662) and *The crafty whore*, the loose translation of Aretino that he had brought out two years earlier; *The Errant Rogue*, a title that confers the qualities of the *puttana errante* on the picaresque hero, anticipates Marsh's 1665 publication of Richard Head's *The English Rogue Described in the Life of Meriton Latroon*.[14] In addition to lifting the entire pornodidascalian theme from Aretino, then, the English text establishes him as a point of origin for sexual discourse and a model for its proliferation in the marketplace.

The political-sexual metaphors of this representative mid-1660 *pornographia* suggest more than a mere trivializing hunt for *doubles entendres*. As Helena's story develops, *The Practical Part of Love* identifies the pornosphere sometimes with the new licence anticipated after the return of Charles, sometimes with the old Puritan order. Looking back to the revolutionary era and its mock-parliamentary satire, she discovers that 'a Baudy-house, or a community of two or three Bauds, and their well affected people the wenches, is as like our late Commonwealth as may be'; in both systems goods should be shared equally, but in fact plebeian whores toil with their 'Rumps' (an obvious topical pun) and the profits end up in the hands of a few unscrupulous grandees (43). When Helena commits herself to 'Nature's Good Old Cause' (73), the phrase links unlimited copulation with anti-royalism and the political activism of women, as if that were the only 'Cause' natural to them. On the other hand, her partners are not the hypocritical Puritans but the 'lewd Quality', the newly confident Cavaliers and courtiers who 'never yet made conscience to dispense and indulge with their codpiece' (44); their libertine sexuality lets them ignore the current debate over liberty of conscience and declarations of indulgence, but the sexual metaphor plunges the reader back into these issues. They seduce her, as we shall see, by induction into the 'Restoration' culture of rakish toasts and lewd frolics (section 4 below). And the brothel itself, in addition to resembling 'our late Commonwealth', encapsulates the political problems brought back with the king. Helena's dread of exploitation by the bawd who gains 'absolute sovereignty over her affections' (42), reducing her to 'slavery' and 'bondage', resonates with nostalgia for England's lost liberties and fear of Stuart absolutism.

2 . *THE WANDRING WHORE* (1 6 6 0 – 1 6 6 3)

The pamphlets of the *Wandring Whore* series, ostensibly by 'Peter Aretine' but written for the most part by Milton's enemy John Garfield, continue the discursive and political hybridization typical of early Restoration writing. They combine the native tradition of coney-catching and rogue literature with 'Aretino's Postures' and *La puttana errante*, forming a kind of literary grotesque or chimera. They advertise and define the internal landscape of the London pornosphere, but at the same time they mirror contemporary institutions in flux, before the settlement of a civic, ecclesiastical, and economic order. Garfield published his prostitutional miscellany in four teasing instalments between 28 November and 19 December 1660 – perhaps anticipating the first Christmas of the new era – and it spawned various offshoots and continuations even after Garfield himself was thrown into Newgate.[15] It borrows from, and contributes to, an interconnected group of scandalous texts that includes *The Practical Part of Love*, *Select City Quaeries*, *The Ladies Champion* mentioned above ('confounding the author of *The Wandring Whore*'), *Strange Newes from*

Bartholomew-Fair, or the Wandring-Whore Discovered, and *Strange and True Newes from Jack-a-Newberries Six Windmills, or the Crafty, Impudent, Common-Whore (Turnd Bawd) Anatomised* – whose exposé of Priss Fotheringham's notorious London brothel comes from the pen of 'Peter Aretine, Cardinall Of Rome'. True to the textual-promotional instincts of Aretino himself, and the library-sequence in *The Practical Part of Love*, the pimp character in *The Wandring Whore* advertises a parallel publication, promising the gull Francion that he will 'shortly' learn how to find more and better prostitutes in the *Strange and True Conference between Two Notorious Bawds*, authenticated (as we saw) by a leading denizen of the underworld (II.10).

These pamphlets borrow much of their form and content directly from Aretino (or perhaps from Marsh's 1658 adaptation *The Crafty Whore*). Many are written in the dialogue-form of the *Ragionamenti*, and all give the dominant role to female speakers, allegedly capturing the authentic voice of the prostitute; claims of female 'approval' or authorship alternate with the standard use of 'Aretine' on the title-page. Nanna's elaborate training-programme has been compressed into a farcically mechanical routine:

> give them Instructions to paint, Powder, and perfume their clothes and carkasses, have fine clean Holland-smocks, kiss with their mouths open, put their tongues, as all wantons do, in his mouth and suck it, their left hand in his Cod-piece, the right hand in his Pocket, commend his Trap stick, pluck their coats above their thighes, their smock above their Knees, bidding him thrust his hand to the best C--- in christendom, tickling the Knobs thereof till they burst out with laughing.[16]

The English pamphleteer finds equivalents for Aretino's demotic obscenity in the comic banter of Interregnum satires on the ladies' commonwealth; Lady Cromwell in *Newes from the New Exchange*, 'controller of the *Club* among the Ladies, is excellent at the beginning of healths, *viz. To the best ------- in Christendome*' (20). In *The Fifth and Last Part of the Wandring Whore . . . By Peter Aretine* (1661), Gusman the 'Pimping Hector' translates directly from Aretino when he explains to Julietta (the *puttana errante* or 'exquisite whore') that once she is married she can visit her 'Gentleman usher' in the night, pretending that she is getting up 'to piss' – an exact echo of Nanna's advice to Pippa in the fourth *Ragionamento*. The bawd Magdalena then praises Gusman as a tutor: 'I dare swear there's scarce a rule in all *Aretines Postures*, but thou hast it *ad unguem*, readier than thy *Pater Noster*.' (In *The Sixth Part of the Wandring-Whore Revived* (1663), the author/publisher Garfield himself is credited with having produced a translation of '*Peter Aretines Postures*' – an obvious assault on his

claims to be reforming, rather than promoting, the underworld of illicit
sexuality.) Throughout these dialogues Julietta infuses Nanna's boisterous
language – especially her travestic images of combat and jousting – with
the fairground spirit of English mockery, for example when she describes
how 'common Jades . . . will sit with their leggs spread over the sides of
a chair with their petticoates and smocks in their mouths, whilst their
Comrades run a tilt at their *touch holes* in that posture, paying twelve pence
a time for holing'.[17] The lewd inflection of carnival – the bawdy 'Holing Game' that outraged the Puritan authorities – is now permanently
installed in the brothels of London, inscribed into their metaphors for
the body.

In addition to these fragmentary borrowings from Aretino's *Ragionamenti*, the *Wandring Whore* pamphlets lift their name and characters from
the prose *Puttana errante* – just reissued as an authentic text 'di Pietro
Aretino', with a descriptive catalogue of thirty-six postures – and derive
their dramatic situation from the verse *Tariffa delle puttane di Venegia*: a foreign visitor intent on whoring begs information from a seasoned expert,
who then recites a list of names with commentary and anecdote. Fully half
of the *Sixth Part* is translated directly from the prose dialogue, incongru-
ously retaining the Roman setting but sometimes augmenting the Italian
original with touches of descriptive particularity or London colour; in
the Aretinesque description of the successful courtesan, for example, 'un
conno rilevato con certi peli biondi' becomes 'a clicking red-lipt Cunny,
beset with golden haires'. But unlike the narrowly pornographic *Puttana*,
these pamphlets are more concerned with discursive provocation – verbal
exuberance, satirical exposé, and comic story-telling – than with the *ars
erotica* itself. Again, the *Tariffa* provides a model, since its catalogue is
frequently interrupted and relieved by the 'novelle piacevoli da ridere'
promised on the title-page, and since the foreigner seems aroused ('tutto
di foco', all on fire) more by the promised description than by the physical gratification.[18] The first *Wandring Whore* begins in the same state of
incendiary anticipation: 'This full appearance of our Companions sets
me all on fire, to talk a little bawdery and drollery amongst them' (3).

Though the older bawd tries to impose order by listing the topics
for discussion ('Fifthly, The several postures of Dancing, Backwards,
Forwards, and every way . . . Ninthly, for bringing in all the profitable
Venetian Customs and Curtezans actions'), the dialogues of *The Wandring Whore* for the most part follow the free-associative pattern of drunken
conversation rather than the meticulous arithmetic of the posture-list or
the philosophic elaboration of contemporary French erotica. The *Fifth*

and Last Part is even organized as a Rabelaisian game in which each speaker must 'tell a Tale or let a fart' (8). Actual scenes of enticement and copulation play only a small part compared to transcriptions of local gossip, exchanges of comically reductive phrasing ('twelve pence a time for holing'), and rogue-narratives that stress extortion, malign ingenuity, and violence rather than erotic bliss. The text does aim to reproduce the whores' and bawds' arousal in the reader ('all on fire'), but they burn for hair-raising 'Newes' and bawdy 'Tales'. Some of these stories themselves hinge on the production of female language across the boundaries of decorum, and so epitomize the dialogue as a whole; one concerns a judge receiving testimony from a Jury of Matrons, who pretends not to understand the spokeswoman's euphemisms and so forces her to declare out loud that the plaintiff 'hath a *C*--- large enough for the biggest mans *P*---- in the Parish' (v.7). Laughter ripples through the court and the bawdy-house, presumably to be echoed in the space of reading.

If the *Wandring Whore* dialogues advertise their 'Aretine' heritage, the *Strange News* pamphlets – retailing the inventions of the celebrated madam Priss Fotheringham – emphasize the institutionalization of sexuality, and push it to new limits. The brothel becomes a 'Society' even before the foundation of the Royal Society, an 'Office' even before Pepys did his best to integrate the smooth running of the Navy Office with the supply of materials for his own libido. Fotheringham's posture-house-cum-tavern, the Six Windmills, becomes a parodic government, complete with a Council, Clerk and Treasurer, 'Orders', committees, ministries, and ancient precedents, even before the new constitutional norms of Great Britain had been properly defined. '*Priss Fotheringhams* Chuck-office', like the 'Prick Office' set up in another public house, mimics or rehearses the organization of a real Crown Office, with its elaborate regulations and extensive powers of punishment (castrating disloyal 'Hectors', sewing up the arses and 'water-gaps' of whores who betray their quasi-Masonic 'Manners and Customes'). This conceit serves double duty, since the 'Office' signifies both the venue and the sexual 'trick' it patents, where the vagina is inverted and exposed to a shower of coins. The institution and the body reduplicate the same tortured conceit – reenacting, in the hysterical theatre of the 'Chuck-office', the national panic over the profits of office, the direction and control of trade, the getting and spending of estates. By the same token commerce is sexualized: the influx of coinage ('French Dollars, Spanish Pistols, English Half-crowns . . . plentifully pour'd in') corresponds to the emerging heroic-erotic image of the Thames as the recipient of the world's trade, the staple of royalist panegyrics like *Cooper's Hill* and *Annus Mirabilis*. As Cowley remarked in his address to that river, under Stuart rule 'all the riches of the globe beside / Flow'd into thee, with every tide'.[19]

These parodic institutions aspire to regulate cultural consumption as well as physical and monetary behaviour. Like a miniature court, the whore's 'Offices' promote and control artistic production, appointing a poet laureate, setting up a panel of literary critics, and commissioning paintings. The oral poetry of the street, and the clandestine print culture of the Interregnum, erupt into the light of patronage: '*George Simpleton* the Hector and Extempory poet shall belong to this Office to make baudy drollery for the Sportive Wits among us.' Here the lewd publications of Milton's nephew John Phillips (*Lusty Drollery, Sportive Wit*) merge with a character listed in *The Wandring Whore Continued* as 'Pimp Singleton the extemporary poet', with perhaps an allusion to Charles II's snubbing of 'Singleton's Musique' in favour of a French orchestra. The most de-tailed of these mock-regulations, appropriately enough, concern books of 'Venery or Midwifery'. Taking its cue from the library-sequence in *The Practical Part of Love*, the Six Windmills 'Half Crown Chuck-Office' promotes an inverse canon of formative literature that includes the adap-tation of Aretino pillaged in *The Wandring Whore* and Humphrey Mill's didactic *Nights Search*, once praised as 'no bawdy-house, but a Bridewell' (chapter 1, section 3 above), though now considered more instructive than preventative:

Ordered that two Books entitled *The night Search* and *the Crafty Whore* be brought into this Office, and examined, to know what may be useful therein to train up the younger sort, and be taken notice of so as to make the older sort more exquisite, all others to be voted destructive to our Principles.

The brothel-world thus mirrors the state's concern with the social influence of reading, and enforces its own orthodoxy through the control of texts – just as the restored government of Charles II would soon order every householder, school-teacher, and apprentice to read the ultra-conservative Jacobean tract *God and the King*. ('Our only beloved Patron and singular Tutor *Peter Aretine*' is granted the monopoly of publishing.) The visual treasures of this imaginary anti-culture, authenticated by the Venetian *puttana errante* herself, include not only '*Peter Aretines* postures curiously painted, and several beauti-ful pictures stark-naked (not such Landskips as P----- in C---- at *Priss Fotheringhams*)', but also a uniform series of portraits of 'the principal

beauties of this our said Chuck-Office', such as Lely would later paint
for the court of Charles II and Kneller for William III.[20]

Given the time of their appearance, then, early Restoration pornogra-
phies might be expressing erotic-Utopian as much as satiric urges, reconstituting the illicit subculture as a 'Eutopia' or Blazing World. The
restoration of a libertine monarch – already seen in public endeavouring
to make the future Earl of Castlemaine 'a cuckold' (as Pepys reports on
13 July 1660) – would reconfigure the relation between the extremes of
society, redefining the prick-office as a *mundus alter et idem*, different from
the legal world and yet the same, 'in London separate from London'
and therefore all the more representative of the whole. The device of the
'wandering whore', the unfixed 'female' mouthpiece, allows the pornographer to imagine a new anti-Puritan order more tolerant of sexual
alternatives, a court that might come to resemble the courts of whoredom. As the 'English Rogue' would soon discover, even 'palaces' may
be 'courts of bawdry'.[21] Once this linkage has been made, however, it is
easier to reverse than to undo: in the great brothel riots of 1668 (chapter 5
below), when the apprentices direct their stones against the little bawdy-
house and murmur that they should be pulling down the 'great bawdy-
house at White hall', they act out an image rehearsed in the brothels of
literature.

Beyond these specific allusions to courts and offices, the collective
subject of the *Wandring Whore* genre is London itself, its liberties, markets,
neighbourhood disparities, and systems of regulation. To this extent
it revives, and pushes to new extremes, the Elizabethan attempt to
'resituate writing in relation to the streets of London' (as Lawrence
Manley puts it). In Greene's coney-catching pamphlets, for example,
Manley finds 'the force of discursive heterogeneity that opens a closed
environment to new possibilities of exchange and combination'; that
'heteroglot' effect (posited in the reader as well as the text) certainly
describes these 1660 whore-dialogues, which create an obscene,
demotic form of the 'urban eloquence' that London was developing.
As Greene and Dekker abandon their official, disapproving voices
for a more comic delight in the fiction of roguery 'the in-law world
is implicitly challenged' and its 'instabilities' revealed. As we shall see,
early Restoration underworld literature blurs this over-sharp distinction
between official and subversive discourse. But its institutional parody,
festive-violent humour, and constant appeals to 'vagabond lust' illuminate Manley's thesis that 'fictional "diversion" is a serious de-railing

of more privileged forms of discourse, a low-life "roughing-up" of monological structure that yields a more heterogenous urbanism'.[22]

La Bruyère's neoclassical complaint about Rabelais ('c'est une chimère, . . . un monstrueux assemblage') applies equally well to these pamphlets; they are promiscuous in their textual strategy as well as their content, stylistically as well as sexually libertine.[23] The *Wandring Whore* dialogues mingle discursive levels and jumble together the comical, the serious, and the pornographic much as they were juxtaposed in the streets of London or in a typical entry of Pepys's diary. On the lowest level, the representation of sexuality is dashed with 'drollery', coffee-house banter, disreputable medical advertisements, 'city queries', and 'low-style satire'. The relation between text and speaker likewise veers suddenly from the invitational to the repulsive: at the very beginning of the third part, Julietta promises Francion 'I will show thee a pure pair of naked breasts, smooth Buttocks, Lovely and ivory thighes whiter than untrod Snow, with the best red-lip't C--- in *Christendom*', tempting the reader as well as the customer into the untrodden snow of the first page, but Magdalena provides an alternative paradigm, more in keeping with the ugly and violent episodes, in her tale of the gentlewoman who shows her cancerous breast to an over-eager suitor. This anarchic mixing of themes and modes operates vertically as well as horizontally. The various low styles alternate with moralistic warnings against prostitution (the middle style) and high-cultural touches such as effusions in heroic couplets or quotations from Claudian and Martial in the original Latin.[24] What Manley says about the social structure in Elizabethan crime-literature applies to the discursive hierarchy here; it is not so much inverted as 'turned on its side to yield a proliferation of quasi-theatrical roles' (348).

The *dramatis personae* of these dialogues exhibit the same demented heterogeneity. Libertine discourse breaks up into a kind of circus or music-hall, with an all-European cast as varied as the vocabulary of Pepys's sexual confessions: Julietta and Magdalena (the original whores from the Italian *Puttana errante*), Francion from Sorel's '*Bawdy History*', and Guzman de Alfarache from the Spanish picaresque (trained in 'the School of *Venus*' and expert in '*Aretines Postures*'), join with English folk-characters like Ruth the Buttock and Bonny Besse of Whore and Bacon Lane. To complete the circle, the later sixth dialogue includes 'Eubulus', the *nom de plume* of the author/publisher Garfield himself (III.15). These interlocutors in turn allude to a swarm of named characters from the coney-catching London underworld, who then find themselves listed at the end of each pamphlet. This apparently genuine catalogue is headed by the celebrated prostitute-managers Damarose Page and Priss Fotheringham, who preside over their own Offices and star in their own pamphlets, and many of the other names resonate with anecdotal or literary significance: Mother Cunny launched the 'practical part' of Helena's career and 'approved' the subsequent flow of pamphlets; Mrs Cresswell, here credited as one inventor of the genteel portrait-gallery–brothel, is constantly cited by Restoration wits and achieves her own dialogue in *The Whores Rhetorick*; 'fair *Rosamond*' and 'Queen of Morocco' anticipate the tragic heroines of theatre. Other nicknames suggest the grimmer realities of the street ('Gridiron', 'Sugar C--- a constant wanderer and night-walker', 'Satchel C--- *Greens* wife who has both holes broken into one'). Even the originary title 'the Wandering Whore' shows up as a professional name, transferred from person to text and from text to person in its 'wanderings' around Europe. Mercurius Philalethes gossips about '*Betty Lucas (La Puttana Errante)*', reenacting the moment when the Venetian *Tariffa* identifies the real-life name of Lorenzo Venier's 'whore errant'. Just as the title *Puttana errante* shifted from Venier's poem to the prose dialogue that disseminated the list of 'Aretino's Postures', so the old nickname adheres to new characters in print; Mercurius Democraticus's *Wandring-Whores Complaint for Want of Trading*, for example, brings into the dialogue not only 'Gusmond' and Ruth the Buttock but *Isbel the Wandring-Whore*.[25]

This 'monstrous assemblage' of characters and discursive modes corresponds to the profusion of cultures and sites within the text. The Italian heritage brings in frequent references to 'Aretino's Postures' and recycled descriptions of Venetian and Roman prostitution (in the mouths of those characters who have wandered in from the prose *Puttana errante*). The *Sixth Part* even promises on its title-page 'a History of the Noble Conversation and various Couplings of the *Wanton Curtezans* of *ROME* and *VENICE*', most of which is teasingly deferred to a seventh part that never materialized (8). The range of erotic experience has nevertheless been trimmed to fit English cultural expectations; the anal perversions – ubiquitous in the original dialogue and distinctively 'Italian' in the popular mind – are reduced to hints and whispers. (Other English adaptations of Italian *puttana*-literature explicitly reject Aretino as suitable only for 'a hot Region a little on this side *Sodom*', but here the anti-sodomitical stance cannot be explained in terms of 'Mediterranean' acceptance versus 'Northern' disapproval, since it is taken by the Spanish Gusman during a heavily Latinate lecture on the sexual habits of the ancient world.) In their overall manner, the *Wandring Whore* pamphlets do resemble the German picaresque and the Dutch genrescene, the tableau of low companionship and creaturely detail that hovers between didactic condemnation and amused participation; references to the body's 'hot Low-country', and to the antics of 'the Dutch whore' and 'the Dutch wench', reinforce this similarity. 'Monsieur Francion' embodies Frenchness by being lecherous, extravagant, and gullible – in the same way chastity belts are 'Italian' and artificial stimulants 'Scotch' – but he can already rattle off the localities of London and embroider his speech with neighbourhood gossip.[26] Sexuality is dispersed but at the same time localized in this discourse of 'heterogenous urbanism', associated with particular 'Regions' and with particularly notorious quarters within the city.

Low-libertine pamphlet titles often sharpen curiosity by linking some fascinating vice to a specific urban zone – *The London Jilt*, *'t Amsterdamsch Hoerdom*, *Holborn-Drollery*, *The London-Bawd*. The title-pages of these early Restoration scandal-sheets promise 'strange news' from even more specific places: Bartholomew Fair, Newgate jail (where Page and Fotheringham conduct their 'Conference'), the 'Prick Office at the Last and Lyon in East Smithfield', Whore and Bacon Lane, the Six Windmills public house in Upper Moorfields, site of the Chuck-office and formerly named after the low-literary hero Jack of Newbury (featured in chapbooks, bawdy ballads, and Thomas Deloney's novel). Some of these pamphlets exploit neighbourhood rivalries, the urban equivalent of the village battles in *Gargantua*: Jonson's Ursula and Punk Alice hurl topographical insults ('Thou Sow of *Smithfield* . . . Thou tripe of *Turnebull*'), and likewise the *Strange and True Conference*, which details scandals in northeast London, was supposedly authored by the governess of the older southern prostitution-zone 'on the Bank-Side'. Titles like *The Womens Brawl, or Billingsgate against Turn-Mill-Street* continue this slanging-match and confirm the proverbial association of certain areas with certain freedoms and vices, shorthand designations that helped Londoners 'to define their own protean and mobile environment'. Legal documents show that areas such as Turnmill or Turnbull Street were so shameful that suggesting a neighbour move there provoked actions for defamation; in the same spirit, Maffio Venier could vilify Veronica Franco merely by alleging that she lives 'between Castello, Ghetto, and Dogana', and Dryden could put Shadwell in his place between Pissing Alley and the Barbican, 'Where their vast Courts the Mother-Strumpets keep'. These pamphlets evoke an individual city underworld, as Aretino and his followers had done for Rome and Venice. Gusman recites the localities of his trade

like a farmer counting his fields, lamenting that private fornication has
drawn consumers away from 'our Cattel in *Dog and Bitch Yard, Drury-lane,
Luterners-lane, Parkhurst-lane, Bloomsbury, Hatten-wall, &c*'.[27] Continuing the
topographical realism of the prose *Puttana errante* and the Venetian *Catalogue of Courtesans*, the printed lists in *The Wandring Whore* often give street
addresses, to intensify the localizing effect.

   This sexualization of urban geography brings with it a corresponding urbanization of sex – a reconstruction of the city, teeming with foul
energies, in the grotesque or scandalous details of the body. In these
whore-dialogues the 'Chuck-office' refers interchangeably to the institution and the orifice, a pock-marked face resembles 'an *Islington*-Cake
with the plumms pickt out', the space between anus and vagina becomes
'Narrow-bridg, where so many passengers croud and thrust to enter one
after another'. Vigorous urination, described in some detail after Julietta's
bout with Francion, seems to unite the two cities that engendered the
Wandring Whore dialogue: Julietta, Magdalena, and Gusman endorse it as
'an excellent way to raise lechery' as well as 'to prevent the French Pox'
and 'getting with Childe', citing this as an 'approved maxim amongst
Venetian Courtiers and Curtezana's'; but this 'Venetian' habit (charac-
teristic of grand and careless courtesans like La Zaffetta, according to
the *Tariffa*) becomes a local spectacle, as Julietta tells how she makes the
chamberpot 'whurra and roar like the Tyde at *London-Bridge*'. In Phillips's
Sportive Wit anthology, disgusting details of the genitals are compared to
Fish Street, Thames Street, and 'a Tanners pit', or else advertised as
'*Cunny-hall*', a tenement for rent. This Thames-side imagery flourishes
even after the literal referent had been purged by the Great Fire: *The
Whores Rhetorick* advises courtesans to use a 'drying Pessary' after each
customer, since 'the Stairs will be wet and the Passage slippery'; the sexual tableaux displayed by the famous 'Posture Moll', like the urination
scene staged by Julietta, combine topography and pornography by acting out 'how the Water-men shoot *London-Bridge*' and 'how the Lawyers
go to *Westminster*'.[28] Eros may be called 'builder of cities' in Auden's elegy for Freud, but these examples suggest the reverse: the city builds its
own forms of sexuality, its own erogenous zones, its own correlations of
posture and place.

The provocation of discourse and the localization of sexual display
combine when the English whore-pamphlet imitates, or emulates, the
sounds of city marketing and seasonal fairs. Several *Wandring Whore* dialogues begin with bawdy versions of the Cries of London; the alliterative

jingle 'the best C--- in Christendom', often repeated in these pamphlets, seems to have become a formulaic cry itself, like 'Cherry Ripe' or 'Alive, Alive-O'. Gusman acts the mountebank, the town crier, and the market vendor as he lists the cures performed by individual whores (II.3), 'proclaims' the monstrous spectacle of a woman who 'grindes Ginger in her a---hole' (II.12), or advertises 'Fine *Oranges*... for provoking lust and lechery' (IV.3). (The *Fifth and Last Part* begins with a different cry, '*Silence in the Court*' (3), perhaps echoing the popular-festive 'Jury of Whoremongers' routine and certainly alluding to the author's imprisonment in Newgate.) In the *Sixth Part* Gusman complains (as Punk Alice already complains in Jonson's *Bartholomew Fair*) that private lechery has so flourished since the Restoration that the more visible street-whores can find no customers, despite their 'sweetest Oratory and loudest calling' (4). This low-style 'Oratory' – modelled on the cries of the Billingsgate market trader and the fairground barker, the voices of London's criminal margins and zones of tolerated misrule – runs throughout these pamphlets, even in descriptions of the sexual body. When Magdalena invites the reader to enjoy the courtesan's 'clicking red-lipt Cunny', the organ itself duplicates her enticing speech, like a *bijou indiscret* – 'clicking' being a cant word for 'snatching' or 'calling in customers at a shop door' (*OED* 'click' *v.*[2], 'clicker'[2] 1).

As we might expect, the fusion of sexual display and market vocalization reaches a blatant climax in the 1661 *Strange Newes from Bartholomew-Fair*, supposedly authored by 'Peter Aretine' but dominated by the voice of yet another 'wandering whore'. Though Londoners told themselves that 'the Faire lasts all the yeare', woven into the urban fabric rather than confined to a specific season, Bartholomew Fair still constituted the major festive event of the calendar and the closest London came to a metropolitan carnival. (As we have seen, Charles II encouraged it to expand after the Restoration as part of his policy of reconstituting Merry England.) The fair's association with prostitution and 'Carnelevation' had long been an open secret, as if (under the patron saint of butchers) all the meanings of *flesh* could be collapsed together – confirming, by literalizing, the Puritan denunciation of a place whose 'very *Booths* are *Brothells* of iniquity' (p. 78 above). In Jonson's comedy Alice complains that upper-class courtesans 'lick the fat from us', and Ursula's booth offers 'your Punque and your Pigge in state,... both piping hot'; this conjunction, already compressed into the facetious placename 'Whore and Bacon Lane', is spelled out by a character with the mock-official title 'The Ranger of Turnbull'.[29] By thus levelling these two greasy commodities, Jonson achieves what the Induction complains that he failed to do (chapter 2, n. 21 above); he inverts and 'pumps' the whore for entertainment. And like the fair itself, he creates a further marketing opportunity in the place where other unwholesome desires converge. Texts as well as flesh were produced there. 'Bartholomew fairings' included not only the 'rare' and gamy play – which Jonson at once disciplines and emulates – but the lewd pamphlet, available as a souvenir. In the pre-Restoration decades these publications still served as a vehicle for 'licensed' commentary and porno-political satire: in one, *A Bartholomew Fairing, New, New, New* (1649), godly ladies exult over the sexual rewards that Henry Marten will provide in exchange for donating their family silver; in another, with surprising frankness for a text published in 1641, the sexual meat-market is identified as 'a fucking Exchange'.[30]

In *Strange Newes from Bartholomew-Fair* (subtitled *The Wandring-Whore Discovered*) the main character gives her fellow-dialogists – and by extension the hungry reader – a vivid example of the self-commodifying 'cry' that combines lower-stratum market vending with prostitutional invitation. She boasts about how she calls out '"Lads, here's a can of the best liquor in the fair", claping my hand on my market-place', while her meaty colleague Peg of Pie-Corner adds 'I for my part cry, "here boys, here's the best Pigs head in the Fair, a rare quarter of Lamb, pure Mutton, and the best buttock bief in England"' (3). In a related image from the *Wandring Whore* series, a prostitute called Ursula – the same name as Jonson's pig-woman – earns five shillings for exposing her 'Twit-twat' and 'stroaking the marrow out of a mans Gristle'. Fairground patter here combines with the aggressive Rabelaisian bawdy associated with butchers and sausage-makers, already exploited in the Interregnum *Sportive Wit*.[31] In recounting her own sexual adventures, the 'Wandring-Whore' in *Strange Newes* intertwines this metaphorics of gross consumption with allusions to the European picaresque, the low literary genre mingling with the imagery of pig-roasting, the fiery, sooty work of the 'blackguard': 'I spread my Colours, and receive the Spanish Rogue into my *French* quarters, where he turn'd the Pig so long till one of his best members was lost in the dripping-pan' (3). In this latest incarnation, the original *puttana errante* – displaying her military 'Colours' as she opens her legs – combines with the carnival figure of the cook rampant, the female trooper marching behind Masaniello with her roasting-spit, the female Leveller 'Kate of the Kitchen'. The genitals, the Mediterranean zone of the politic body, become synonymous with the 'hot Low-country' topography of market-place and roasting-tent – areas of licence, 'Carnelevation', and unbridled plebeian commerce. The grotesque association of sexuality with low and dirty technology (spit-roasting, chimney-sweeping, and other activities of the 'blackguard') proliferated throughout 'satyric' and clandestine literature.[32] In *Strange Newes from Bartholomew-Fair* the 'wandering whore' uses this trope to 'discover' a new country, a wonderland of carnival inversion. In this régime the active, priapic male metamorphoses first into a dog in a wheel – turning the spit that roasts the Pig – and then into the roast itself, its fat and marrow 'lost in the dripping-pan'.

3 . THE LIBERTINE ABJECT: VIGILANTISM AND VOYEURISM

In Bakhtin's reading of Rabelais, the 'carnivalesque' language of fairs and markets reveals a festive and untamed people for whom sex and excrement still evoke cheerful fertility, converting the horrors of death and disease into a 'gay monster' for their entertainment.[33] This sympathetic but misty-eyed interpretation underestimates the edge of real violence in carnival, sometimes directed against the authorities but often unleashed on their behalf. As we have seen in the case of local Skimmingtons or charivaris, the festive-aggressive goal of mocking the assertive wife or exposing the 'wandering whore' frequently spilled over into sadistic excess, or evolved into a riot against unpopular officialdom. Urban carnivals could be seen as dangerous uprisings – like Masaniello's rebellion or the London 'Evil May Day' of 1517, held in check only by Sir Thomas More's famous intervention – or they could include harsh enforcement of conventional hierarchies and sexual norms. The 1580 carnival at Romans (made familiar by Le Roy Ladurie) erupted into a massacre of the lower orders. Even the more stable and stylized seventeenth-century carnivals suggest a narrow boundary between festive tolerance and rage: when Jean-Jacques Bouchard visited the Roman carnival with a group of *libertin* friends in 1632, he was delighted to be pelted with hollow eggshells filled with perfume – but the moment his group stepped out in *female* dress they were assaulted with real eggs and stones, and fled to escape injury. To use Théodore Tarczylo's phrase, the 'connivances' of carnival were 'momentary and limited'.[34]

The violence of the behaviour depicted in these Italo-English pamphlets, the cruelty of their humour, and their persistent objectification of sexuality as a gross 'Commodity' for sale, support this critical and revisionist interpretation of the festive low style. As in Rabelais's original 'monstrous assemblage', the sexual/verbal liberties of early modern London were hemmed in by official power and shot through with aggression and suspicion. The 'Conference' between Page and Fotheringham takes place not in a sunlit Italian orchard but in Newgate, and Fotheringham had to change the name of her tavern-brothel 'for fear of the multitude'; the 'Jack of Newbury' (a popular hero of the militant apprentices who might attack and demolish her house) becomes the innocuous 'Six Windmills', but this will not protect her from the '*Shrove-Tuesday* Boys'. The interlocutors of *Strange Newes from Bartholomew-Fair* worry about police informers who might send them to the beating-block or the transportation-ship, and the dialogue ends when the house is raided by the Beadles (2, 6). The pamphlet itself may pretend to act as informer or policing agent, hypocritically condemning the sexual and verbal play it revels in – just as the 'rascal beadle' in *King Lear* lashes the whore he lusts after. *The Constables Hue and Cry after Whores and Bawds* (*c.*1700) calls for their punishment and yet amuses the reader with jokes on 'Commodity' and 'Flesh' (6–7). According to the title-page of *The Wandring Whore*, Garfield 'Publisht to destroy' the vermin of prostitution, though his pamphlets clearly belong to the disorderly substratum; since they threw him into jail for publishing them, the authorities evidently failed to believe Garfield's moral-crusading front. The equally scurrilous *Ladies Champion* blames *The Wandring Whore* for having caused the arrest or beating of numerous people, but still threatens Garfield with burning at the stake for publishing obscenity, just as Aretino himself was burned (the 'Champion' assures us) for inventing 'the six and thirty several ways and postures of occupying'.[35] The pamphlet goes on to undermine its own mock-moralist stance with a praise of whoring and a defence of polygamy.

The explicit naming of prostitutes, locations, and agents brings out with particular sharpness the contradiction between celebrative and punitive impulses, proscription and promotion, endemic to the satyric mode and already rife in earlier 'Catalogues' like the *Tariffa delle puttane di Venegia*. Exposé and procurement intermingle at every level in these texts, even in the meta-textual self-justifications that Garfield transcribes into the forematter and the last dialogue. The idea of mapping the pornosphere with printed lists of names and addresses probably came from the *Tariffa* via *The Common-Wealth of Ladies* and *The Practical Part of Love*, where the University Library includes a '*Catalogue of all the Whores of the Citty covering thirty sheets of paper*'; here the intention is obviously to celebrate the mutual self-promotion of the sexual underworld and the clandestine print culture. Gusman in *The Sixth Part of the Wandring Whore*, the author's surrogate as master of all discourses, makes exactly the same assumption, that setting 'our Lists' in print was intended to boost sales (indeed, 'that List sent us Trading from all parts of the Nation, of all sorts and from all Countries' (4)). But Eubulus – the disingenuous Garfield himself – sidesteps the issue, and repairs his vigilante credentials, by railing against the secret adulteries of certain London women fit only to be 'pinn'd up in a publick ducking stool for a common Scold' (5).

Earlier in the *Wandring Whore* series Garfield/Eubulus claimed to be using print as a kind of unofficial pillory, a speculative free-market version of the presentment of immoral neighbours; 'publication' here retains some of its older meaning, the placarding or display of a criminal. (Eubulus should be quite aware of this ironically appropriate double meaning, having been jailed for 'publishing' in the typographical sense.) Like the Elizabethan 'coney-catcher' before him, Garfield boasts that his lists have forced the guilty to change their names, leave the parish, or offer him 'gratuities to be obliterated' – the basis for a thriving career in blackmail.[36] (In *Six Windmills* furtive customers are similarly warned on the title-page 'lest their names be rendred in Capitalls, of whom there is a large Catalogue', and a few are later identified by their trades and initials (6).) A third meaning of 'publication' upsets this easy equation of print and vigilantism, however; the word could also be used as a synonym for whoredom, as in Jeremy Taylor's call 'to redeem maydens from prostitution and publication of their bodies'. Within the dialogues themselves most of the speakers reinforce this lewder association by assuming, with the pimp Gusman, that naming and locating specific prostitutes *invites* the customer rather than deterring and exposing him: 'If you fancy variety of faces, Mounsieur *Francion*, visit the Cherry-garden, Hatton-wall, Blomesbury' (and so on for seven lines); 'Show him into a convenient Room, and send in Mrs. *Cupid*, the Dutch whore, fair *Rosamond*, Sugar C---...' Julietta assumes that whores positively seek out this publicity, and that masses of them are waiting for the chance to apply ('they are but a handful in comparison of those are yet to enter themselves amongst us'); Gusman replies, in a kind of wonderment at the proliferation of sex-in-print, 'I do not think that all my leaves and pages in folio are able to contain them.'[37] The Advertisement that Eubulus/Garfield attached to the third issue of the *Wandring Whore* (above a Wanted notice for a thief) suggests that this libertine, pimping interpretation was shared by many readers; like Milton confronting the Sons of Belial, he expresses indignation that 'some libidinous wretches' have read these pamphlets as if they intended 'propagating of whoreing, and tempting Customers to go amongst them, instead of destroying them' (III.15). This 'libidinous' reading derives, of course, from his own dialogic creation; pamphlets that begin by promising 'smooth Buttocks, Lovely and ivory thighes whiter than untrod Snow, with the best red-lip't C--- in *Christendom*' can hardly be divorced from the construction or 'propagating of whoreing'.

These double-dealing texts thus amalgamate a 'Gusmanic' realism (which provides a titillating, vicarious familiarity with the erogenous zones of London) and a 'Eubulan' vigilantism that equates description with denunciation and authorship with police work. Like most products of Mercury, this compound is slippery and unstable: 'the official sobriety of taxonomy' (in Manley's terms) cannot be clearly distinguished from the 'outlaw point of view', the language of power from what Bakhtin called 'the language of the merry rogue'[38]. This blurring or slippage may be seen throughout the low-libertine discourse we have been studying. The rural naming-lampoons associated with charivari sometimes evoke parodic merriment (as in the 'litany of the whores of the village, with *ora pro nobis* . . . pronounced after each name'), but sometimes take on a more menacing tone, urging local officers to 'look to it'. Claiming a moral duty to expose vice became a convenient excuse for neighbours accused of foulmouthed defamation. Conversely, when godly reformers like Ignatius Jourdain or Humphrey Mill list the 'places of open bawdry' throughout London, their maps of iniquity sound uncannily similar to the recommendations of Gusman; the Commons frequently hooted Jourdain's campaign-speeches, diverting reform into mirth, and Mill's *Nights Search* – soon to be elevated to text-book status by Priss Fotheringham – gives detailed instructions for night-walking in Bloomsbury, Islington, and Turnbull Street. The regulatory mechanism of the state and the informal discourse of the subculture mirror one another, just as official punishment and popular shaming ritual converged in 'cruel carnival'. In the 1632 fiscal census of Florence, for example, the bureaucratic document is sprinkled with strangely non-objective expressions of familiarity and malevolence, such as 'boorish whore' or 'made-over, liquefied whore and witch'.[39] Conversely, *pornographia* identified with the mapping-impulse of official codification. Promising Francion a fuller directory, Gusman explains the similarity between the self-advertisement of prostitutes and the state taxation-survey, the Poll Tax that Pepys found so intrusive: 'by the advice of one of their own society, I took a rough draught of them, from the Collectors List for Poll-mony about Dog and Bitch-yard, Turnbull-street, Cress-lane . . . ' (II.10).

In a sense Garfield is right to claim a policing function for his shifty, lubric, heterogenous, seriocomic, Veneto-Cockney whore-pamphlets. The 'roughing-up' of privileged discursive forms does not necessarily 'derail' them, since power already had its rough edges and its grim diversions. The institutional boundaries of public and private, police and citizen, remained broad and indistinct as long as regulation depended on neighbourhood cooperation. The gossipy questions that fill the whore-pamphlets (and parallel works like *Select City Quaeries*) can be interpreted as pure comic invention, as sexual inquiries in the tradition of *Aristotle's Problems*, or as the printed equivalent of vigilantism, the denunciation of neighbours for sexual crimes heard and seen through the thin walls of a crowded tenement. Eubulus's list of private vices – 'Who has been in Loves Fundamental, who makes *Pegoes Nightcap* of a Leather Purse, who has been squirted and flirted with *Venus* Pocket Pistol?' and so on – works on the level of comic patter and bawdy farce, but it also sounds like a blackmail-list, matching specific people to familiar but forbidden sexual practices in the prying spirit of a neighbour gathering information for the Church courts.[40] These cryptic comments seem to indicate contraception with condoms and syringes, and anal intercourse; even in the early eighteenth century, the verbal accusation of heterosexual sodomy could raise a violent mob. Throughout the series, the gossip of Magdalena and Gusman turns from famous bawds to the secret adulteries of married women (with names and addresses), tearing the urban fabric by stirring up trouble and strife in the family. They even provide a vividly descriptive list of wives who beat their husbands as well as cuckolding them – the classic occasion for a riotous Skimmington or charivari (v.9). Lower-stratum 'urban eloquence' provides the rough music.

Later versions of the English whore-dialogue discover an irredeemable hostility, not just in the 'publication' of prostitution, but in the entire 'carnivalization' of sexuality. In the 1683 *Whores Rhetorick*, the procuress-mentor Mrs Cresswell urges her protégée to fashion herself as a discreet and refined courtesan rather than a vulgar whore. She must resist the customer's desire to force her down to fairground level. In advising young prostitutes never to 'rashly addict themselves to a scandalous liberty in drinking, lewd swearing, and open ribaldry', Cresswell evokes the lower stratum of London sexual discourse, the punitive-comical bawdy of the fairground and the *Wandring Whore* pamphlets where she herself had been 'published' twenty years earlier. And she associates this ribaldry not with 'free' merriment but with the brutal policing of plebeian sexuality. Rather shrewdly, she explains that men 'encourage all the vile excesses that the most profligate stripping Whore can act, yet at the same time they applaud, they must need entertain a secret hatred and scorn . . . They are solicitous for this wild diversion, as they are for the sight of a *Bartholomew*

Shew, . . . but once a year, and then too the Farce grows nauseous before it is half ended.' Only by expert simulation of upper-class respectability can the prostitute escape this 'nauseous' celebration-with-contempt – a device to keep her in her place, equivalent to 'the Constables Staff, or the justices Warrant, a publick whipping, or a private one in *Bridewel*' (37, 177–8).

The menacing conjunction of farcical humour and pillorying display, shared by the whore-pamphlet and the fairground, comes to a climax in the *Wandring Whore*'s descriptions of the sexual perversions currently performed in London brothels. Here low-libertine discourse finds a textual equivalent for the 'monsters' or raree-shows of Bartholomew Fair, the 'wild diversions' that express hatred more than desire. Earlier libertine dialogues like Aretino's *Ragionamenti* had initiated this tendency toward the grotesque by staging spectacular tableaux of what Evelyn called 'unnatural figures and usages': distorted postures imposed on whores by their aristocratic clients, a complex chain of interlocking nuns and abbots that Nanna compares to the Laocoon, a disturbing description of gang-rape that reminds her of the Sack of Rome.[41] Both the *Ragionamenti* and the verse *Puttana errante* include self-consciously monstrous episodes which operate less as 'postures' than as quasi-allegorical representations in the tradition that led to Milton's Sin. But the English *Wandring Whore* pamphlets turn their most obscene descriptions into what the pimp Gusman calls 'mad tricks' – performative routines or tavern 'holing' games, offered to the dialogists (and thence to the reader) both as bizarre entertainments and as instructive exposées of sexual reality. The 'trick' or *beffa* had long provided comic and narrative relief in prostitutional discourse; the trickster-tales that interrupt the *Tariffa* (chapter 1, section 3 above) all concern the pecuniary or scatological devices that confound the rival courtesan or divert the foolish client from his sexual purpose. In contrast, the 'mad tricks' retailed by Magdalena and Gusman *are* the customers' goal, the product hawked by the 'wandering whore', and by extension the hook that draws the reader in. Arousing both prurience and freakish fascination, these market-criers extend their professional roles into the narrative, at the same time procuring and threatening. The reader is invited to become at once spectator, victim, customer, and constable.

The most frequently mentioned routines involve postures that invert the female body and convert it into a target or receptacle. 'The Dutch wench' would 'show tricks upon her head with naked buttocks and spread legs in a round ring', and women at the Six Windmills receive official orders to 'stand upon their heads . . . with all their cloathes and smock about their ears bare breeches to the cold wall (like Monsters) leggs spread at large with the door of their Chuck office open'. Even the owner and 'Governess', Priss Fotheringham, 'stood upon her head with naked breech and belly whilst four Cully-rumpers chuck't in sixteen Half-crowns into her Comodity', initiating and leading the process of 'de-monstration'. This most notorious of the 'figures' – the device that triggered the entire series of pamphlets – obviously alienates and commercializes female sexuality; clients fling their money rather than their seed. As Steven Marcus remarks of a similar perversion in the Victorian *My Secret Life*, the physical insertion of cash into the vagina is the 'logical conclusion' of a system in which sex and money have become the agents of masculine power, and in which sexual acts must maintain 'the maximum distance' between partners ostensibly engaged in an intimate union.[42] The exhibitionist games described in *The Wandring Whore* – what Gusman calls 'the maddest tricks that ever I saw acted' (1.7) – correspond quite closely to the parodic and ludic actions prosecuted in the Church courts, which turn the body into a kind of theatre; the defiantly bawdy shaming gesture ('showing her arse before the King') has been tamed by inversion and compulsion, and the customers' actions resemble more the chucking and smearing assaults of male rioters. In the *Wandring Whore* dialogues we encounter these rituals of humiliation and display in *consumable* form, as commodities. They are represented as a range of specialities available to the customer at the appropriate price, according to the amoral principle that 'no one of this Society refuse to do the deed of nature either backwards or any other of *Peter Aretines* postures so long as shee's pay'd for it'.[43] And this 'pimping' arrangement extends to the discursive relation between text and reader: perversions become narrative 'tricks' to draw the customer in, 'all on fire' to buy further instalments.

 The listing of these spectacular-sadistic 'postures' constitutes a thorough *psychopathia sexualis*. The customers who keep Magdalena busy, for example, include 'a *yong Merchant* in L---- street, who will not be contented with doing the business, but will have half a dozen Girles stand stark naked round about a Table whilst he lyes snarling underneath as if he would bite off their whibb-bobs, and eat them for his pains'. Again, similar canine play-acting can be found in court records of unruly behaviour (chapter 2, n. 6 above), but now the old collective 'expressive violence' – the pack-hysteria of a sexually rampant youth gang – has been fixed and concentrated into an individual speciality. Another customer 'will needs shite in one of our wenches mouth's (which is odd

lechery)', a gesture far removed from the fecund and genial scatology
that Bakhtin thinks he finds in Rabelais. Another 'will needs be whip't
to raise lechery', while 'a fourth would fayn be buggering some of our
wenches, if the Matron could get their consent, but had rather be dealing
with smooth-fac'd Prentices'. Julietta is shocked by such 'unseen and unheard of Monsters', but Gusman explains that poverty-stricken whores
will 'endure any annoyances, punishments or extremities to get mony
by it' (III.9–10). These comments might suggest some compassion in the
characters of the dialogue and hence some direction for the reader's
response, but such moments of empathy rapidly vanish in the general
atmosphere of farcical 'drollery'.

Other aggressive-erotic 'mad tricks' reveal the brothel as the locus of
masculine drinking and smoking rituals rather than direct sexual encounters. The flow of coins into Priss Fotheringham reminds the narrators of
another game, which involved pouring 'smarting and searching' white
wine into 'the Dutch wenches two holes till she roar'd again', and this
in turn recalls the routine of blowing pipe-smoke into both openings of
a 'Girl that was terribly pepper'd with herds of Crabblice' ('one of the
maddest tricks' that Gusman ever 'saw acted'). Another of these supposedly authentic tricks involves pouring sack into one orifice and sucking
it out of the other, turning female anatomy into 'a new fashioned Cup
for roaring boyes to drink in'. In a more fetishistic variant – recorded
in contemporary gossip and memoirs as well as in 'roaring' fiction like
this – customers 'drink straind Sack thorough our Madams Smocks till
they drop again'. (Already in the 1650 *Newes from the New Exchange* the
ladies demand the right to 'convert their smocks into *Colanders*, to strain
healths of *Sack* into *Beer-glasses*, and take them off astride upon mens
shoulders' (1–2).) These intimate minglings of mouths and genitals, wine
and bodily fluids, simultaneously affirm and deny sexuality. They 'divert' in every sense. The drinker performs a sort of cunnilingus at one
remove, an aphrodisiac ingestion of sexual matter that adds 'Zesto' to
his toast. Such practices were quite conceivable at the time: *The Practical Part of Love* recommends 'carousing' a young beauty's urine, and *The
Wandring Whore* gives recipes for aphrodisiac drinks incorporating dried
menstrual blood or nutmeg marinated in vaginal juice – a depotenti-
ated remnant of the sex-magic taken seriously in Renaissance Venice
and celebrated by Aretino's Nanna? In the 'mad tricks', however, intimacy is held at arm's length, literally and metaphorically; the male
maintains a 'diverting' spectatorial distance, a histrionic sense of role-
playing, and the female is reduced to a mere channel or instrument of

homosocial bonding. Such lewd drinking rituals confirm Evelyn's belief that his countrymen increasingly devoted themselves to 'speculative
Lusts', which feast the imagination and turn sex into a performative
display.[44]

The *mise-en-scène* of these performative routines clearly compromises
the ostensible philosophy of the pornosphere – recreational hedonism
and 'free' participation for both sexes. The spectatorial position, and
the somewhat strained emphasis on 'diversion' and entertainment in
the narration, suggest a desire to emulate the attitude taken in Bruno's
jocoserious description of the antique gods who read Aretino, a detached
pleasure in all kinds of actions and representations however extreme
and 'nauseous' (chapter 1, section 4 above); that detachment converts
the customer into a voyeur and the courtesan into a mere prop in the
theatre of abjection. Gusman and Magdalena express contempt for 'idle
whores who F--- for necessity, not pleasure' (IV.10), implying a higher
pleasure-motive that applies equally to the female participants in this
game. Julietta, the character closest to the Italian *Puttana errante* dialogue,
certainly enjoys her sexual 'recreation' with Francion, wishing (like the
woman in Aretino's tenth sonnet) that it could last for an entire year
(I.11–12). Yet it is impossible to imagine what satisfaction she could derive
from the monstrous scenes that make up the bulk of the *Wandring Whore*.
The customers shown in these vignettes seem engaged and driven by
desires quite different from the pursuit of pleasure. Under the guise of
festive trickery, they not only debase the female body but parody those
official agencies and rituals that shape the more serious parts of civic
life. In one particularly mortifying improvisation, a prostitute passes out
from too much drinking and her customers 'lay her belly naked upon a
Table, like as if she had been layed out for buryal, thrusting or sticking
a Candle in her Comodity, and drinking healths over the dead drunk
party'; when her hair bursts into flames, the fire 'was quickly abated by
drawing a codpiece engine, and giving her two or three Coolers' (I.6–7).
In this grotesque little drama the male revellers take on the institutional
roles of minister and fireman, appropriate in a city soon to be ravaged
by plague and conflagration.

Reading below the carnivalesque surface reveals an element of realism in this literature of 'mad tricks'. Even the most extreme practices
recounted by Magdalena can be matched in prosecution documents,
records of the breakdown of the festive-violent synthesis that allow us
to glimpse actual behaviour behind the recreational account. The client
who demands anal intercourse with women but 'had rather be dealing

with smooth-fac'd Prentices' has been prefigured by Jacques Rossiaud's sixteenth-century examples: the apprentice buggered by his masters while being instructed that 'this was a good way to have girls', or the man arrested for sodomizing a female apprentice. Though Rossiaud describes France, scattered evidence from England supports Magdalena's assumption that the perversions of London are shocking but not foreign: one frequently cited case of sexual assault in Somerset involved a twelve-year-old male apprentice.[45] Heterosexual aggression can likewise be documented in the courts. Husbands at all social levels punched and kicked pregnant women; one defendant always withdrew from his wife before orgasm and 'threatened if she were with child he would slit the gut out of her belly'. Historians might assign such violence to an older and more primitive construction of masculinity, and perhaps to a Mediterranean culture of gang-rape and sodomy never endemic in England. Even in the Elizabethan homily on marriage, as Susan Amussen shows, Christian manhood (based on moderation and gentleness) was starkly opposed to the 'common' belief that violence towards women best 'becomes a man'; the relative infrequency of sexual assault in the prosecution-records she studies, and the shame occasioned by the accusation, lead her to conclude that sexuality played only a small part in English masculinity.[46] Clandestine discourse complicates this argument from statistical prevalence, however, since by 'publishing' extreme cases it makes them available as defining instances. Culture acquires new paradigms when criminal records and 'pornography' concur, when plaintiffs describe 'tricks' that resemble those of the *Wandring Whore*. Even in the early eighteenth century, London prostitutes accused unruly clients of forced heterosexual sodomy, flagellation, assault by throwing urine, and torture with a knife; in one case a woman accused of theft claimed that the man had paid her 'to let him spit in her Mouth'. Nor was this confined to the 'wandering whore' subculture, which might have served as a repository for all those 'perversions' eliminated by the civilizing process. The accounts of marital breakdown gathered by Lawrence Stone confirm that sexually motivated violence – particularly against the pregnant body – boiled up throughout the Restoration and Augustan periods, in 'middling' and 'polite' society.[47]

Magdalena's catalogue of 'odd lechery', and Gusman's repertoire of 'mad tricks', thus define the repressed modes of 'acting' masculinity that flare up at moments during the Interregnum and return en masse at the Restoration – 'unseen Monsters' now all too visible. Publishing them in 'pornographic' form no doubt tends to maintain them at a safe distance, as an entertainingly marginal 'diversion'. But legal records break down this *cordon insanitaire*. Heterosexual sodomy for example – a constant theme of Italian sources like Aretino and *La puttana errante*, hinted by these pamphleteers in comments about 'Loves Fundamental' and 'doing the deed of nature backwards' – formed the basis for several highly visible law suits, locating it in the marriage-bed and not only the brothel, among the élite rather than the pimps and Hectors of Smithfield. The indictment of Thomas Ivie, in the most visible alimony case of the 1650s, accused him of having 'bugger'd his Wife'; later in the century, no less a figure than the Duke of Buckingham found himself prosecuted in court for sodomy – clear evidence of the credibility and danger of sexual defamation. Decades later the suspicion of intramarital sodomy could still trigger riotous protest. Whore-literature expropriates and embroiders scandals such as these: Helena in *The Practical Part of Love*, for example, achieved her independent wealth and status as 'regnant Whore' by extracting alimony precisely as Mrs Ivie did, alleging 'some obscene unnatural attempts of his towards her; a practice that had pretty well succeeded in that Court before'.[48] The case of Marie Hobry, the 'French Midwife' burnt at the stake for petty treason in 1688, embodies and sums up this whole repertoire of no-longer-festive violence. At times her English husband 'attempted the Forcing of [her] to the most Unnatural of Villanies, and acted such Violence upon her Body in despite of all the Opposition that she could make, as forc'd from her a great deal of Blood'. On other occasions, like the 'Mastiff' apprentice worrying his whore or the Lombard Street merchant snarling under the table in Magdalena's brothel, he 'Bit her like a Dog'.[49]

When the *Wandring Whore* pamphlets narrate encounters between the sexes outside the stylized routines of the brothel, they confirm the sense of dehumanizing injury and display. In the *Fifth and Last Part* we hear of 'a fellow who helping a Gentlewoman on Horse-back, slipp't his hand under her belly and tore a tufft of hair off her Commodity, wearing it in a *Bravido* in his hat'. (This yeoman ancestor of the Baron in *The Rape of the Lock* may have been inspired by Aretino's suggestion that the genitals should be sported on the hat, but in Aretino this trophy is an ornamental representation, not something torn off the body.)[50] Julietta tells this story immediately after the courtroom scene in which a respectable matron is forced to speak dirty words in public (section 2 above), implying an equivalence between two episodes where 'Bravido' consists in hoisting sexual matter into view, to derive pleasure from women's pain and embarrassment.

In another story-capping dialogue, Gusman produces an even more painful episode to provide a modern equivalent to the hair-raising perversions of the ancient world, like incest and sodomy. Now, however, the agent of violence becomes the prostitute herself, 'wandering' dangerously free from the constraints of comic routine, a Hobbesian figure awakened to the logic of aggression and the necessity of retaliation in a lawless subculture. The incident takes place, both literally and metaphorically, in 'a dark passage'. A drunken gentleman, meeting a 'wandering whore', starts 'feeling her with freedom'; after encouraging his erection, 'she drew out a sharpned knife . . . and holding of his P---- close by the root, she cut it cleer and sheer off, leaving him his member and knife together, where he continued dancing and roaring till some company brought forth lights.' Before he dies the gentleman 'confessed that he had given a wench the *running of the reins,* and he believed she had returned him that for his pains'. Her gesture recapitulates and reverses the ill-treatment of whores by their customers, not only the spreading of disease but the mutilation of the face which simultaneously defines and incapacitates the prostitute: she now does the same to the whoremonger. The state of warfare implied in the scenes of 'roaring' merriment becomes explicit in this 'dark passage', and Magdalena's sober response brings out the paradox of the monstrous, which is at the same time normative and freakish. She first exclaims 'that was a *whores trick* indeed', revealing the standard association of prostitution with evil agency. As in the sensational murder-pamphlets that enjoyed a quasi-pornographic vogue throughout the century, or the royalist propaganda that equated the *puttana* with 'women who have poisoned their husbands [and] murdered their children', 'whore' becomes synonymous with murderess and violent assault a paradigm of the entire enterprise. Castration is the ultimate 'trick'. Magdalena then reflects, however, that the whole business of the 'wandering whore', and the whole readership of the pamphlets that celebrate and punish her with display, would collapse 'if our Customers were so dismembred'.[51]

4. 'THEN WANDER FORTH THE SONS OF *BELIAL*'

Despite the restored hegemony of the monarchy and the royalist nobility, it became increasingly difficult to demarcate the boundaries of high and low status in representation, to separate 'popular' libertinism from aristocratic excess. During the first year of the Restoration, even the most abject whore-pamphlets focus on areas of ambiguity or slippage between low and high, poor whoredom and great. In *The Practical Part of Love*, as we have seen, the blackguardly Collier of Croydon can now gaze directly at the Court beauties in Whitehall and beget a new kind of prostitute who combines plebeian sluttishness and courtly hauteur; restoring a spectacular monarchy fastened 'magic chains' on the English, as John Hall had warned (chapter 3, section 3 above) – inducing visual fixation, cross-class identification, and sexual hybridity. Francion and Julietta in *The Wandring Whore*, figures of a new sexual and social mobility just arrived from the Continent, project into the future a heady but chaotic assault on genteel society, which they imagine as a dislocated world where high status is manifested, paradoxically, by disease, violence, and excess. Like Rochester preparing for a 'ramble', the gullible Francion declares his intention to scale these heights by plunging into the lowest depths; he will frequent the scurviest whores, and 'visit their Quarters one after another, though I'me clapp't three times over with the Pox, and so become a Gentleman'.[52] As Pascal observed at precisely this time, perhaps echoing Giordano Bruno, the libertine strives to rise above common humanity by cultivating the bestial.

The 'wandering whore' herself recognizes the folly of Francion's ambition, like her real-life counterpart in the Roman lawsuit who denounced one troublesome client as a mere 'papier-maché gentleman', an empty simulacrum who reveals his class hubris by demanding anal intercourse (chapter 1, n. 32 above). Nevertheless, Julietta can use his delusion to advance her own social climbing. At times she appears so plebeian that when she recommends 'honest whores' she means simply those who will not pick pockets (III.7), but the prospect of exploiting Francion gives her the higher cultural and economic pretensions of the *honesta cortegiana* or the royal mistress. Like the ambitious mistresses circling in on Charles II, Julietta plans a lucrative match that will allow her to become a great rather than a poor whore: 'Ile have him sign and seal these following *Articles* for an *Assurance* of his future *Affections*', listing her demands with the full legal terminology of '*Imprimis*' and '*Item*' (£300 per annum, a coach and four, male visitors, and 'free liberty to make choise of her own *Chamber-maids*'). She will undo her own commodity status by commodifying others, adding to her list of luxury accessories a '*Lusty Black*' footman; as a fall-back plan she will accuse her husband of sexual abuses and sue him for maintenance, like Mrs Ivie and her fictional disciple Helena.[53] In this proviso-scene Julietta is fashioning not merely another rogue-and-whore trick, but a whole institution of aristocratic 'liberty' – precisely the 'indulgence' that would stir popular fury in the coming decades.

Judicial reactions to those protests – as we shall see in chapter 5, on the bawdy-house riots and the treason trials they occasioned – suggest that the cycle of transgressive sexuality, violence, and counter-violence operated not simply within a clearly defined 'popular' sphere, but across hierarchical boundaries, threatening property and authority. The violent encounter in the 'dark passage' involves a whore and a gentleman (section 3 above), and their murderous exchange of disease and wounds anticipates the stories told in Court about Robert Carnegie, Earl of Southesk, deliberately infecting the Duke and Duchess of York with the most virulent pox in revenge for his cuckolding: the disease, like the story, 'communicates' between the brothel and the throne, generating 'great glory' for the contriver despite the abjection it visits upon him.[54] The entire episode – gleefully 'owned' by the husband who conspicuously did not own his wife – reads like one of the 'mad tricks' recounted by Gusman, and displays the same unstable mixture of vicious purpose and pointless entertainment. 'Rogue' and 'whore' literature might seem confined to the lower stratum of discourse and the underbelly of London, areas demarcated by their associations with food markets, prostitution, and corporeal punishment (Smithfield, Billingsgate, Newgate). But Francion's urge to 'become a Gentleman' by wallowing in abject debauchery, or Julietta's desire to promote herself from 'exquisite whore' to the life of wealth and luxury, break down these boundaries: *puttane errante* become *grandes dames*, who in turn perform like orange-sellers; whoremongers acquire the 'glory' of gentlemen by acting like 'Hectors' and hoodlums.

Equally concerned to dissociate themselves from the stolid 'middling sort', the 'disengaged' style of the idle classes could resemble the 'loose' or 'vagabond' behaviour of the shiftless underclass, and vice versa. The exchange of manners between 'Restoration' aristocracy and popular misrule had been brewing during the Protectorate – as we learn from parliamentary satires on the ladies' commonwealth and from Evelyn's *Character of England* – but the promiscuity of the newly restored king and duke threw public morality into deeper confusion; in particular, the category of Royal Mistress obstructed the attempt to corrall illicit sexuality into a nether zone. 'Manly' behaviour evolved correspondingly. The violence rehearsed in the *Wandring Whore*'s 'mad tricks' reappears not only in subsequent low-style narratives like *The English Rogue* or *The London Bully*, but in the 'rambles' and 'frolics' of the Court Wits around Charles II – setting a pattern to be echoed in the Mohocks and Tumblers, street gangs described (or perhaps invented) by Sir Richard Steele, and faithfully imitated in the 'blackguard' debaucheries of James Boswell.

When Milton characterized the libertine opposition in the 1640s, re-sponding to the ribald laughter that greeted his attempt to rethink sexual relations from first principles, he conjured up a ruffian subculture where all proprieties and distinctions collapse: when he imagines his divorce tracts celebrated by 'the brood of Belial', he means the very dregs of society 'to whom no liberty is pleasing but unbridl'd and vagabond lust without pale or partition' (*CPW* II.225). In the charivari of sexual and anti-sexual abuse – the physical violence of Skimmingtons and appren-tice riots, the textual violence of the *Wandring Whore* pamphlets – the 'pale or partition' of decorum seems to collapse and the manners of the 'vagabond' seem to prevail. Whether or not one accepts their reforma-tory purpose, their 'music' remains 'rough'. By the time he writes *Paradise Lost*, however, Milton has detected a significant change; now he locates the Sons of Belial among the upper classes of 'luxurious Cities', and especially in 'Courts and Palaces'. When Milton first presents Edenic intercourse, defining it by contrast with the most corrupt and 'Casual' form of modern sexuality, he deliberately equates 'the bought smile / Of Harlots' with the 'wanton Mask', the 'Midnight Ball', and with every-thing that can be expressed in the phrase 'Court Amours'. When he describes Belial in the epic catalogue of fallen angels he slips from the narrative past into the present tense, and transfers the social setting from the lower depths ('vagabond lust') to the highest echelons:

> In Courts and Palaces he also Reigns
> . . . And when Night
> Darkens the Streets, then wander forth the Sons
> Of *Belial*, flown with insolence and wine.

Milton's acoustic portrait of a city terrorized by drunken aristocrats fits Restoration London far better than the Old Testament examples that he cites as 'witness'; Sodom and Gibeah were not noted for their 'Courts and Palaces'. This shift in the placing of 'Belial' – a direct riposte to the official Restoration prayer-book, which forced that name on the late regicides – identifies social disorder with the oxymoronic conjunction of criminal 'riot' and courtly arrogance. In *Paradise Regained*, when Belial proposes tempting Christ with modern courtesans 'Expert in amorous Arts', Satan himself confirms Milton's class-analysis by accusing Belial of lurking 'in Courts and Regal Chambers'. [55]

Extending Milton's insight, we might locate the source of libertine unruli-ness in two volatile and amphibious groups of young males on the thresh-old of enlarged privilege, where the boisterous sexual violence associated with bachelor gangs combines with the reckless ambition that turned Francion's head. The 'merry gang' of Wits around Charles II – newly exalted by personal association with the king, but too young or footloose to assume the high offices their class-position entailed – formed what Pope would later call a 'Mob of Gentlemen', like Milton's Sons of Belial at once riotous and aristocratic. And the '*Brave London-'Prentices*', many from upper 'middling' families or the younger sons of gentry, yearned to assert their political power and reclaim traditions of seasonal misrule that had been suppressed during the Puritan ascendency.[56]

Even in England, apprentice boys (and girls in the luxury trades) exemplified the amphibious sexuality of the early modern adolescent, beginning their term as an *object* of desire (Magdalena's client 'had rather be dealing with smooth-fac'd Prentices') but rapidly becoming a *source* of pubescent libido, severely restricted by the regulations that forbade marriage and kept them in dependency. Laura Gowing concludes that sex between the London apprentice and his mistress is 'the most well-rehearsed scenario of adultery'. The air of licence they generated can be felt even in the severest authors; the chaste Jane Barker, for instance, allows herself sly jokes about the sexuality of City wives and apprentices.[57] Though their attacks on brothels seemed to express hostility to the values of the new Court, apprentices also acted as a royalist mob and clearly aspired to resemble the newly enfranchised bachelry of the upper class, moving into the fashionable milieu of the Wit. Contemporary satire shows them frequenting 'the Play-houses, *Spring-Garden*, and the Park' with their hired mistresses, and crowding into the Pit with the other fops and critics.[58] Their rituals of release converged on those of higher-class youths in their combination of lechery and aggression: the habit of storming the very brothels they frequented, in a kind of fraternity riot that could easily boil over into real disorder, linked the apprentices and their social betters.

In Restoration adaptations of lower-stratum literature, the traditional *picaro* takes on the doubly amphibious character of the modish apprentice or gentleman-rake. Just as the word 'rogue' improves in meaning, denoting sexual liveliness or sparkish wit, so the representative of 'vagabond lust' starts to emulate fashionable vices that might be interpreted as genteel transgressions rather than plebeian mutinies. Richard Head's *English Rogue Described* carries the significant subtitle *The Witty Extravagant*, a term that suggests the conspicuous consumption of the prodigal gentry as well as the deviant wanderings of the *vaga*bond and the *puttana errante*. (Meanwhile the 'extravagant rake' of Restoration comedy claims an affinity

with the lower-stratum carnival.) Head's rogue modulates from wholly
vulgar tricks – throwing a turd at his school-teacher, glueing a girl's vagina
together – to glamorous exploits in a 'new-fashion Bawdy-house', where
business is run on hedonistic rather than mercenary principles, and mistresses are selected by connoisseurship from a gallery of paintings; if he
takes his cue from the cruising-guides in *The Wandring Whore*, he clearly
steers away from Dog and Bitch Yard towards Mrs Cresswell's house
in Upper Moorfields, where she has recruited 'Citizen's wives, whose
Pictures you keep in readiness for your best Customers to chuse on, and
trade with'. His sexual adventures on the road may be no less destructive
and disgusting than his earliest pranks, but he now performs them with
a gentlemanly hauteur designed to drive home his superiority. Even the
name of the rogue, Meriton Latroon, suggests in miniature his combination of low and high debauchery, the first name evoking social advancement and the second thievery and excrement (*ladrone*, latrine). Evoking
the new fusion of picaresque with aristocratic libertinage – and perhaps recalling the exaltation-through-abjection expressed by Francion
in *The Wandring Whore* – one dedicatory poem to Head's *English Rogue*
places it in the tradition of Rabelais, 'Guzman', and 'Francion'.[59]

This suffusion of low-life sexuality with genteel aspirations continues
throughout the literature of the apprentice-rake. In Ward's *The Rambling
Rakes, or London Libertines* (1700) the narrator scours the city's zones of
misrule 'in quest of Common Game, that the Wickedness of the Night
might Crown the Debaucheries of the Day, and that I might continue a
Fashionable Libertine in a hot pursuit of Vice without any Cessation' –
though this desire is mortified, quite literally, when the bawd tricks him
into spending the night with a corpse (12–14). Another young anti-
hero, the 'London Bully', explicitly links his bursts of sexual violence
with the social elevation his apprenticeship will bring ('we shall never
be in a way to become good Master-Chirugeons unless we be extraordinary Debauchees'), and so adopts a demeanour not proletarian but
gentlemanly and 'Sparkish'. His most disturbing frolic, when he and his
companions force a lady to copulate with her steward on Hampstead
Heath, combines elements of the charivari and the gang-rape traditionally performed by the *confréries de jeunesse*, but these young men assume
the attitude of a Horner or Lovelace ('When I was drunk, I imagined
all Women were Whores') and threaten their victims with aristocratic
'Swords', not plebeian stones and faeces. Indeed, the 'Bully' explicitly
ascribes the warping of his earlier character to his parents' social pretensions, aping the gentry by sending him first to a wet-nurse ('I always loved

that Woman more than my Mother') and then to Westminster, where his 'love' is transferred to his fellow schoolboys. Even when his parents die, his 'Libertine Humor', as he significantly calls it, 'did not allow me to shed tears'.[60]

In parallel with this gentrification of the lower stratum, the 'high' libertinism of the Restoration aristocracy deliberately simulates the sexuality and violence of the streets. To 'keep himself superior', as Bruno said of the pagan gods (chapter 1, section 4 above), the rake 'made himself into a beast'. Lords behaved like 'London Bullies', whipping off their clothes, uttering obscenities, assaulting the watch, 'tumbling' to the ground and even raping unprotected women, slashing faces, and smashing the windows of brothels – a symbolic attack on the face or front of the house. 'To such a degree of madness the nobility of this age is come', Pepys observed as early as 1663 (15 May). Whereas the 'roaring blades' of Caroline comedy would 'break windows, fright the streets / At midnight worse than Constables', their post-Cromwellian descendents felt themselves exempt from police control, attacking the constables as well. Evelyn's *Character of England*, published after the death of the Protector but before the actual Restoration, shows the chaotic mélange of English society and the destruction of all decorum in 'popular Libertinism'; in this atmosphere of 'Carnelevation', the younger sons of gentlemen profess atheism, drink madly, 'stile themselves *Hectors*' (as if that were an aristocratic title), 'pierce their veins to quaff their own *blood*', and turn into street desperados. Significantly, Evelyn finds a female counterpart to this performance of status-confusion: the high-born ladies retailed in the *Character of England* – like the Cromwellian élite satirized in *Newes from the New Exchange, or the Commonwealth of Ladies*, or the loose-tongued swaggering women criticized by Margaret Cavendish – play whorish games like drinking rude healths in wine strained through their underwear, in taverns 'where a *Curtesan* in other *Cities* would scarcely vouchsafe to be entertain'd'.[61]

   In the unsettled months that ended the Interregnum, then, the younger gentry were already borrowing their drinking rituals and their 'roaring' demeanour from the milieu that generated *The Wandring Whore*. Face-slashing and blood-drinking anticipate the 'extravagant' and politically inspired merriment that led two London debauchees to devour the liver of an executed regicide (chapter 5, section 2 below). Less violent games such as straining wine through the smock and drinking off lewd toasts – explicitly mentioned by Gusman in *The Wandring Whore* (1.7) – transgressed verbal propriety and apparently allowed women of the 'alamode' classes to play with the 'pale or partition' that distinguished them from the illicit subculture. Evelyn may refer specifically to Lady Lucy Sandys, third daughter of Lord Salisbury and a friend of Nell Gwyn, whose low-libertine escapades earned her a mention in the 1650 *Commonwealth of Ladies* and prompted Henry More to ask 'Whether that comedie *The Costlie Whore* was not intended for the life of Lady Sands, and was written by Henry Marten?' *The Practical Part of Love* identifies her with precisely this aggressive-erotic trick: a group of upper-class revellers, apparently taking their cue from a fashion set by Lady Sandys, mob Helena by pulling up her skirts,

while she tugs and struggles to let down her coats and cries, *fie Gentlemen*. This flusters and animates the Gallants, and therefore we must now see her linnen, and kiss the hem of her smock, and *a la mode Sandys*, strain the Sack through the fore part of it, and drink a health to the best in *Christendome*.

Though the episode largely concerns male solidarity in sexual aggression (slipping into a conspiratorial 'we' to involve the reader in this flustered and animated circle), the dominant, formative figures remain Lady Sandys and the courtesan-heroine herself. Even before the public elevation of Lady Sandys's friend to the royal bed, then, Grub Street was circulating characters of high-born and influential ladies who borrow their gestures from Gusman in *The Wandring Whore* and their language from the 'clicking' vendors of Moorfields and Bartholomew Fair ('I will show thee . . . the best red-lip't C--- in *Christendom*').[62]

The 'mad tricks' enacted in pamphlets like *The Wandring Whore* cannot be dismissed as fictional, marginal, or exclusively 'low', therefore. They express a nonchalant bravado evidently compatible with high social status, and they extend the normal pattern of male conviviality in which men would establish their solidarity by drinking to the absent female or to the 'best cunt in Christendom'. (The commonwealth-women in 1650 had already taken over this phrase, and the gestures of lewd female companionship cited by Thomas Ivie to discredit his estranged wife include drinking to 'the Best in the house' – that is, to his own penis.) Evelyn clearly disapproves of the inversionary behaviour reported in the *Character of England*, just as his diaries and letters denounce (and thereby record) the 'Libertine Libells' circulating in the apprentice world and the 'speculative Lusts' tempting his son; other gentleman-memoirists, however, recall these diversions with pride and amusement. Wycherley, for example, told his friend Major Pack that '*Persons of Better Condition*' would gather at a particular house of pleasure with their mistresses, '*take hold of the Bottom of their* SMOCKS, and, *pouring the* WINE *through that Filtre,* feast their *Imaginations* with the Thought of *What* gave the *Zesto,* and so *Drink a Health* to the TOAST'.[63] Wycherley recalls precisely the trick described in *The Wandring Whore,* and even relishes the aphrodisiac infusion of spice and sexual juices that Magdalena recommends mingling into the wine. His word-choice is revealing: these ritualized gestures do indeed constitute a '*Filtre*' – both a philtre to stimulate desire, and a permeable partition or filter to keep it at a controllable distance. Perhaps unwittingly, Wycherley conveys the simultaneous alienation and intensification that characterizes libertine sexuality.

When the Sons of Belial expropriate the carnivalesque mockeries and pornotropic satires of popular culture for the upper-class 'frolic' and the Court lampoon, they recapitulate the upward mobility of abjection. Already in Henry Neville the social focus of misogynist satire had shifted from fishwives and orange-sellers to the 'parliament of ladies', from Billingsgate to Spring Garden. In their lewd verses and in their festive-violent gestures the new unruly bachelry 'lift' the rituals of street and village, rituals that in their original form were now classified as amusingly rustic or intolerably seditious. The treatment of Sir John Denham typifies this *Aufhebung.* The once-glorious poet of *Coopers Hill,* father of Caroline poetics in an earlier generation, now finds himself a ridiculous Court-cuckold, mocked for his marriage to an eighteen-year-old who had quite openly become mistress to the Duke of York (apparently at Lady Castlemaine's instigation). Marvell parades Denham as the leader of the wittolds in *Last Instructions* (line 174), turning back on the Court its own taste for slumming entertainments like the Skimmington. Less subtle lampoons launch a typical bachelor satire against the mismatched couple, which weaves into the narrative of Court scandal the 'rough music' of charivari ('O Denham, thou had'st better bin brain'd with a Bricke / Than marry a young C. without a stiffe pricke') and the pornographic trope of the sexually rampant female parliament, adapted for the political conflict now supposedly laid to rest:

> The Ladys of London have lately agreed,
> And in their new parliament stoutly decreed,
> A tryall of skill of the sound, and the Lame,
> And hee that Fuckes best, shall carry the Dame.[64]

In a counterpart to this lampooning, an urban equivalent of the village shaming ritual, the 'local populace' also offer to break his windows.

Upper-class window-smashing – part youth riot and part vigilante protest – predates the era of *politesse*, but only now does it acquire associations of genteel amusement. When the Earl of Surrey describes breaking the windows of wicked London with a stone-bow in 1543 (an offence for which he was imprisoned in the Fleet), he adopts a grimly jeremiad tone that editors try in vain to explain as parodic.[65] Early Restoration 'riot', in contrast, comes wrapped in an aura of indulgence. This gentrified version is perhaps first embodied in the character of Sir Frederick Frolick, the cousin of Lord Beaufort in Etherege's immensely successful comedy *The Comical Revenge, or Love in a Tub* (1664). As the victim of one of his house-raids complains to the eponymous Frolick, 'You and your rude ranting Companions hoop'd and hollow'd like Mad-men, and roar'd out in the streets, *A whore, a whore, a whore*' (I.i.4–5). Multiple associations combine in this characterization: the Antinomian Ranters who declared themselves above the law and joined the Hectors in 'Carnelevation'; the roaring boy of Jacobean comedy; the hunting-cries of rural shaming rituals ('à whore! à whore!'). A decade before Rochester's disabled debauchee celebrates 'Windows demolish'd, Watches overcome' (45), Etherege's comedy identifies these infractions as amusing 'frolicks', expressing ebullient sexual energy rather than pathological hatred.

Riotous *pornographia*, marking the whore's house, enforces economic as well as sexual ruin. Gestures like shouting 'à whore' and window-breaking – defacing the façade both literally and metaphorically – redefine the occupant as a prostitute to punish her for resisting, which not only impoverishes the independent woman (making profitable work for the glass-merchant) but destroys her 'credit' in every sense. The nocturnal assaults of Sir Frederick have the effect of stigmatizing his mistress and her servants in the community, destroying her economic viability: as her chambermaid complains, 'We had so much the good will of the Neighbours before [this attack], we had credit for what we wo'd; . . . but this morning the Chandler refus'd to score a quart of Scurvy-grass' (I.i.5). Court records show that sexual defamation did have serious economic consequences, particularly for women in employment or business: men were acquitted for smashing the windows and furnishings of women's houses when neighbours could be found to assert the victims' reputation for prostitution. Even hearsay evidence of a woman's 'light conversacion' could disqualify her as a plaintiff and allow the authorities to dismiss her narrative of rape and robbery as mere fiction.[66] In the case of the bachelor's 'frolic' the attack itself, often motivated by the woman's *refusal* to yield, was meant to create such a reputation, to mark the house as a military officer would mark houses for free-quarter. Those who 'won't be civil', those who have ideas above their station (such as resisting rape by drunken aristocrats) are thereby isolated from their civil neighbours and written into an exclusively sexual script, a 'light conversation' in another sense. Etherege's chambermaid-character states the case quite forcibly – 'Unhand me; are you a man fit to be trusted with a womans reputation?' – yet the audience is invited to align, not with her complaint, but with Sir Frederick's immediate response; he claims 'intimate acquaintance' and makes a sexual advance (4). Such moments conceal, by a process we might call 'comedification', the truth they put into words: that discourse and gesture actually did control reputation, and that reputation translated directly into financial life or death, credit or ruin. This imposition of a gentlemanly perspective simultaneously turns 'good credit and reputation' into a jest and makes it the gift of the upper-class male; in fact, both men and women participated in the legal struggles that destroyed or restored this vital attribute, and the majority of all defamation cases were brought by women against other women.[67]

Etherege treats this ruinous house-shaming ritual with the maximum indulgence, clearly inviting solidarity with Sir Frederick Frolick. The woman's complaint continues in a mock-heroic vein that simultaneously exposes and excuses the violence: 'pray tell . . . how you gave defiance, and then wag'd a bloody war with the Constable; and having vanquish'd that dreadful enemy, how you committed a general massacre on the glass-windows.' (Glass windows being relatively new and expensive, this 'massacre' constitutes an economic retaliation against ambitious Julietta-like prostitutes who should have remained in the 'wandering' state, rather than fixing themselves in respectable-looking houses.) The same playfully martial language applies to the window-smashing raids of Sir Frederick and to the act of penetration itself, continually militarized in pornographic discourse; the Debauchee boasts of 'Bauds Quarters beaten up', and *L'Escole des filles* advises 'Be not afraid of having thy Quarters beaten up, though the Prick be never so big, indeed it may scare a tender young Virgin'.[68] In the whore-pamphlet, as we have seen, the 'war' between the gentleman and the prostitute could become horrifyingly explicit, but in the comedy we are supposed to find it hilarious; the recipient of the assault teases him only mildly, and invites him back for a second visit (I.ii.6–7). As the play develops, we are invited to look ever kindlier on Sir Frederick as he becomes the *magister ludorum* and the dispenser of justice, tricking all the wronged parties into marriage.

What Milton called the 'injury and outrage' of the privileged classes should not be regarded merely as a comic trope, however; the 'violent love of Pleasure' that Burnet noted in Rochester easily turned into a pleasurable love of violence. Captain Henry Goring, for example, died in an actress's dressing-room with his throat cut. The seventh Earl of Pembroke kicked a man to death in a tavern, only to be pardoned by the king. The frolics of Lord Buckhurst (later Earl of Dorset), the dedicatee of Etherege's *Comical Revenge*, included killing a tanner in Stoke Newington.[69] Not all his amusements involved manslaughter (for which he was acquitted), but they frequently assaulted public morality and provoked a breach of the peace. When the Duke of Buckingham killed the Earl of Shrewsbury in a duel, the king intervened to guarantee his pardon; Buckingham then brought the widowed Countess of Shrewsbury to live with him, kindly offering his own wife a carriage to take her to her father's. In striking contrast to this contempt for the law – reprimanded by both houses of parliament, but only after six years had elapsed – when Buckingham found *himself* the injured party in sexual matters he mustered the full forces of legal and social privilege, ordering a near-fatal assault on Henry Killigrew for spreading rumours about Lady Shrewsbury, and prosecuting his detractors for *scandalum magnatum*, a wholly class-defined offence that consisted of speaking ill of a peer; his victims, including those who had prosecuted him for sodomy, were pilloried, fined, and imprisoned for several years.[70]

Dorset's bonding with other Wits – constituting the 'merry gang' that commoners perceived as the inmost circle of Charles II's friends – produced one memorable scene, on the balcony of the Cock Tavern in Bow Street. A group including Dorset and Sir Charles Sedley stripped naked, performed a mock-sermon (as village roisterers did earlier in the century), simulated a mountebank selling aphrodisiacs, washed their penises in wine and drank the king's health in it, defecated in public view and flung bottles of urine onto the 'thousand people standing underneath to see and hear them'. According to Pepys, who accentuates the visual theatricality of Dorset's and Sedley's transgression, they were seen 'acting all the postures of lust and buggery that could be imagined'.[71] (Sedley's love of 'acting' did not extend to others, however; when the actor Edward Kynaston began imitating him off-stage, the 'real' Sedley ordered him to be 'exceedingly beaten' by assassins who pretended not to penetrate the disguise.) This aristocratic behaviour suggestively parallels that of the servants described in the *Transactions* of the Royal Society (p. 1 20 above), released from their customary deference by hallucinogenic drugs: frenzied nudity, simulated copulation, and public defecation as defiance.

Whatever affinities this balcony performance might have claimed with popular forms of festive violence, the London crowd perceived it as an affront, smashing the tavern's windows and threatening to wreak justice on 'the preachers' who had literally smeared them and talked down to them. Showers of excrement, normally hurled *against* the exposed malefactor or the mismatched couple, had flowed *from* the balcony into the audience, imitating but reversing the cruel carnival of charivari – and perhaps forcing the commoners below into the coprophagic 'posture' practised in Magdalena's brothel. On the occasion of this Bow Street display the nobleman Dorset enjoyed complete impunity. Though Sedley (a mere baronet) *was* prosecuted and fined, he managed to turn the courtroom into another theatre of obscene and confrontational amusement; when the Lord Chief Justice asked whether he has read Peacham's *Compleat Gentleman*, Sir Charles condescendingly claimed to have read more books than his lordship, and brushed aside the sentence with the witty retort 'he thought he was the first man that paid for shiting'. When Dorset and Sedley were later arrested for running naked through central London, the *constable* was thrown into jail and heavily fined. Pepys felt certain that this 'horrid' and shameful inversion of justice stemmed directly from the king's favouritism, and he links it to another episode of broken decorum and upper-class expropriation of the lower stratum, when Dorset, Sedley, and their sovereign ordered the fiddlers of Thetford 'to sing them all the bawdy songs they could think of'. Such was 'the ill posture of things at this time'.[72]

It should not surprise us, then, that the 'tricks' of *The Wandring Whore* should migrate into higher-status discourses, where they serve simultaneously as 'diverting' side-shows and emblems of aristocratic extremity. Magdalena's dog-perversion for example – in which 'Girles stand stark naked round about a Table' while the Lombard Street merchant 'lyes snarling underneath as if he would bite off their whibb-bobs' – apparently recurs as a mode of domestic violence among the middling sort; it is listed among the cruelties that prompted Marie Hobry to murder her husband and suffer the aggravated penalty of petty treason for inverting 'natural' hierarchy. But it also recurs in texts with higher moral and literary pretensions than *The Wandring Whore* and the crime-pamphlet. In *The Fifteen Real Comforts of Matrimony . . . by a Person of Quality of the Female Sex* (1683), purportedly a feminist counterblast to male debauchery, indignation dissolves into mirth, as the elderly lecher not only snaps at the naked women dining at the table above, but crunches the bones they throw him (47). In *Erotopolis, or a New Description of Bettyland*, the dog-perversion likewise creates a travesty of domesticity, with anti-Puritan overtones suitable for a time that feared the return of 1640; the brothel must be a 'family of love', since 'there are few Families without a Cur'. When the time-travellers (transposed from Petronius's Rome to modern London) witness this canine behaviour, their response suggests not moral outrage but the neo-pagan amusement and detachment recommended by Bruno when reading Aretino: 'the Gods that only smil'd to see *Mars* and *Venus* so entangled as they did, would have laugh'd themselves out of their Immortality, to have seen this Extravagant Divertisement' (105–6).

In the cyclic return of oppositional politics (as we shall see in the Epilogue) pornographic tropes once again serve as signs for 'the ill posture of things' – particularly in Tory satires against the Earl of Shaftesbury. To figure him as a hubristic aristocrat who descends into populism, his enemies match him to those sexual inversions of the Chain of Being that express hauteur by 'acting the beast' (as Bruno or Pascal would put it). The antics of Antonio in Otway's *Venice Preserved* – who growls and barks under the table in a brothel, begs to be kicked, and then gives his mistress a vicious bite (III.i) – provide a satiric counterpoint to the evil rebellion of his co-conspirators. Yet even these scenes of abjection prompt a comic rather than a tragic or psychopathological response. Otway's prologue winks at the audience's familiarity with the brothel-world, inviting them to 'match' these antics of Antonio with their own knowledge of what goes on 'at Mother *Creswolds*' – a standard point of reference ever since she featured in *The Wandring Whore* and *The English Rogue*, and soon to be depicted among the Cries of London (fig. 2b above). From the opening moment, Otway thus establishes an ethos of knowing indulgence and erotic consumerism, an atmosphere that suggests laughter rather than horror as the verdict on Antonio. Restoration culture remained critically unable to distinguish between the 'dark passage' and the *divertissement*, 'unseen Monsters' and extravagant entertainments, popular libertinism and treason. Would 'riot' be interpreted in the comic spirit of Sir Frederick Frolic or the grim 'dissonance' of Milton? The disturbances of 1668, to which we now turn, put this hermeneutic ambivalence to the test.

CHAPTER 5

Monstrous assemblies: bawdy-house riots, 'libertine libels', and the royal mistress

> *Belial* came last, than whom a Spirit more lewd
> Fell not from Heaven, or more gross to love
> Vice for itself...
> In Courts and Palaces he also Reigns
> And in luxurious Cities, where the noise
> Of riot ascends above their loftiest Tow'rs,
> And injury and outrage: And when Night
> Darkens the Streets, then wander forth the Sons
> Of *Belial*, flown with insolence and wine.
>
> (*Paradise Lost* I.490–502)

> Some blood hath been spilt, but a great many houses pulled down; and among others, the Duke of York was mighty merry at that of Damaris Page's, the great bawd of the seamen... These idle fellows have had the confidence to say that they did ill in contenting themselves in pulling down the little bawdy-houses and did not go and pull down the great bawdy-house at White hall.
>
> (Pepys, 25 March 1668)

It would clearly be naive to regard *pornographia* as a record of what really happened in the world of illicit sexuality, or as the direct cause of the numerous explosions of sex-linked violence – individual and collective – that disturbed the uneasy peace of the 1660s. On the other hand, we should not allow a false literary sophistication to interpret whore- and rogue-pamphlets as 'purely' textual, nor lose sight of the 'cultural operation' that brings text and action closer together. Throughout the edgy first decade of the Restoration, and again at the crisis-ridden close of Charles II's reign, low-libertine publication and carnivalesque insurrection converge at the point where bawdy 'merriment' turns violent, feeding each other in a mutually provocative cycle of performance and representation. This chapter will concentrate on the most dramatic manifestation of this expressive and performative synthesis, the apprentice riot of

Easter 1668, a massive and destructive charivari against the houses of established whores which threatened to engulf 'the great bawdy-house at White hall'. The twin revival of folkloric unrest and prostitute discourse – as 'whores' petitions' accompanied the riots – provoked the most fearful response from the authorities, who classified it as full-blown treason.

When Milton describes the newly assertive Sons of Belial, he gives their 'riot' a specific urban location. Sitting in darkness, he can compute by the 'noise' the place and direction of misrule. It emanates *from* courts and palaces, and the unruly bachelry 'wander forth' from that privileged location, at once sinisterly purposeful and insolently casual. Aristocratic errancy, like the equally lust-driven wanderings of the *puttana errante*, perverts the chivalric ideal that leaders should maintain. Milton's description inevitably recalls his self-portrait in *Paradise Lost* compassed around with 'evil tongues' and 'dangers', barely protected from the 'barbarous dissonance' of drunken revellers; this phrase, originally said of Comus in a wildwood setting, now expresses the festive aggression of the 'luxurious city' – and the poet himself is its target.[1] The demonstrations of 1668 reverse this directionality. A politically radical crowd takes back the 'riot' that had been lifted from the popular stratum by the likes of Dorset, Sedley, and 'Sir Frederick Frolick'. Disorderly apprentices parody the Court's parody of themselves. Like the Fire in Dryden's *Annus Mirabilis*, tumult moves from the mean streets *towards* its origin in Whitehall, the royal palace turned brothel.

This 'Court' focus centres the blame squarely on the monarch whom an eighteenth-century liberal defined as 'that riot-prince Charles the Second' – as if he were a living oxymoron of disorderly order, a carnival lord of misrule. Though James I had been denounced (by Puritans like Lucy Hutchinson) for encouraging 'bawds' and 'catamites', corrupting the entire country by 'conformity with the court example', not since Henry VIII had a monarch openly acknowledged his mistresses and pardoned the 'injury and outrage' of his courtiers.[2] (Henry had also instituted the 'Gentlemen of the Bedchamber', breeding suspicion of his dissolute and overprivileged 'minions'.) The 'loose' and all-too-visible behaviour of Charles II's entourage – recorded and furtively emulated by Pepys – opened up a conceptual channel between zones of licence widely separated by social status. The subculture of whoredom and the superculture of the Court exchange features; Whitehall can be perceived as a 'great bawdy-house', and the brothel as a little Court with prerogatives and 'Offices'. As Stallybrass and White observe, 'the Restoration court projected a collective image of living in ironic and even defiant incompatibility with its inherited forms of public representation . . . The Court was *both* classical and grotesque, both regal and foolish, high and low.' 'The Practise of their Lives', as Margaret Cavendish would say, was 'not answerable to the Degree of their Dignities.'[3] To Pepys, and indeed to every eager consumer of gossip and lampoon, the Court presented a monstrous spectacle of 'wanton talk' and obscene writing, drunken brawling, riot, injury, outrage, window-smashing, and wife-snatching – a general state of warfare, both verbal and physical, in which sexuality and disease are the weapons. The age that coined the 'noble Savage' also produced the savage noble.

But the principal source of grievance and fascination, summed up in the 'petition' satires spun off by the bawdy-house riots, was the shocking rise to wealth and influence of 'the most Splendid, Illustrious, Serene and Eminent Lady of Pleasure, the Countess of Castlemayne'. The figure of the king's principal mistress, Countess of Castlemaine and later Duchess of Cleveland, will recur throughout this chapter, in Pepys's diary and in the riots and satires that punctuate the decade it chronicles. In the rioters' mock-petitions as in Marvell's *Last Instructions*, Castlemaine focusses (and sexualizes) popular resentment against Catholicism, foreign armies, Stuart tyranny, and the inappropriate liberties taken by the Court while dissenting religion was crushed by the repressive Clarendon Codes. Porno-political satire against the royal mistress continues into the 1670s, and forms an essential thread in the Restoration culture of priapism. Leading on from the physical and textual insurrection studied here, chapter 6 will begin by exploring the representation of Castlemaine in William Wycherley, a discarded lover of hers and thus particularly subject to the erotics of outrage; we will see that his sly evocation of élite transgression and 'the great bawdy-house at White hall' revives the mock-petition and the memory of the 1668 riots.

1. THE COURT, THE NATION, AND THE HUNT FOR 'SATISFACTION'

Royal mistresses – with their shameless sexuality and their exuberant 'frolics' (such as the lesbian mock-marriage staged by Castlemaine and Frances Stuart for the king's voyeuristic pleasure) – provided a female equivalent to the Sons of Belial, like the Daughters of Men in *Paradise Lost* 'Bred only and completed to the taste / Of lustful appetence' (XI.618–19). In a *Secret History* sometimes attributed to Milton's nephew John Phillips, Charles seduces the future countess (already married to Roger Palmer) on 'the very first Night' of his return to Whitehall, committing incest as well as adultery since she was allegedly the daughter of Queen Henrietta Maria by her lover Henry Jermyn.[4] (Another persistent rumour made the king himself a bastard of this union.) Nor did Charles renounce these indulgences after leaving behind the bachelor stage. Lady Sandwich was 'much troubled' to discover that after marrying Catherine of Braganza 'the King comes often to [my lady Castlemayne] as ever he did', though when Pepys hears the news he exclaims in a burst of adulterer's solidarity 'God forgive me, I am well pleased' (6 July 1662). The king's own correspondence shows him pursuing his intention to install Castlemaine as Lady of the Bedchamber to the new queen – flaunting his illicit sexuality in the face of the world and publicly humiliating his bride only a month after their wedding – with all the zeal and determination of Oliver Cromwell at the battle of Naseby: 'I wish I may be unhappy in this world and in the world to come, if I faile in the least degree what I have resolved . . . which againe I sweare before Almighty God.' Such endorsement generated the spirit of the 'age' that Margaret Cavendish criticized, when 'Courtesans' not only join the élite but provide a model for successful relations between the sexes that extends even to marriage: men now 'love the Company and Conversation of Wanton and Free Women, insomuch that a Courtesan shall have a greater and stronger Power, . . . nay, many Men love a Whore so much more than an Honest and Chast Woman, as many make better Husbands, and are more Fond and Kinder to their Wives if they be Libertines, than if they were Honest and True to their Marriage-Bed'.[5] Yet Cavendish herself, in her *Sociable Letters* and in her Utopian *Blazing World*, imported the notion that true manhood consists in surrender to the rule of women; could not Charles be simply acting out this Gallic conception of gallantry?

Pepys's 'pleasure' in the great courtesan soon modulated into a tense mixture of indignation and arousal. The spectacular prominence of the royal mistress clearly troubled him, confounding the public–private dichotomy and the status-hierarchy that separated courtesans from countesses. He acquires her portrait and gazes wonderstruck at her beauty 'though I know well enough she is a whore'. But as he records popular 'content or satisfaction' waning after the euphoria of the Restoration, so his enthralled pursuit of Castlemaine becomes increasingly shadowed by a sense of national disaster. As we saw in chapter 1, he is fascinated to learn that she 'hath all the tricks of Aretin that are to be practised to give pleasure', but the observation occurs in an ominous conversation 'upon the unhappy posture of things at this time', where he worries 'that the King doth mind nothing but pleasure and hates the very sight or thoughts of business; that my Lady Castlemayne rules him'. Rapturously describing a dream in which 'I had my Lady Castlemayne in my armes and was admitted to use all the dalliance I desired with her', Pepys still recognizes how intimately this vision is linked to the fear of death in the Great Plague. Though he relished his participation in the riotous superculture – not only in his fantasies of cuckolding the king, but in lewd gossip with the Court Wits – the inner Puritan laced his excitement with an almost physical sense of dread: 'mad bawdy talk' with one of the Duke of York's Grooms of the Bedchamber 'did make my heart ake', and the night before the Great Fire (apparently without intending a pun) he records being 'horribly frighted' to see the same courtier 'with a great many more young sparks'.[6]

During the equally traumatic war of 1667, when the Dutch navy broke the defensive chain and burned the British fleet in the Medway, Pepys weaves even closer this association of political catastrophe, aristocratic riot, and sexual transgression. In an almost continuous spasm of free association, he juxtaposes the idiotic violence and debauchery of the upper classes ('a kind of emblem of the general complexion of this whole Kingdom at present'), the universal fear of absolute monarchy, and the pornocratic subjection of the king – 'only governed by his lust and women and rogues about him'. The humiliation of naval defeat floods into Pepys's perception of the royal liaison, turning his scopophilic 'desire to see' Castlemaine into an all-encompassing embarrassment; glimpsing the illicit couple together, he shrinks from encountering 'the King (whom I have not had any desire to see since the Dutch came upon the coast first at Sheerness, for shame that I should see him, or he me methinks, after such a dishonour)'. Other commentators make the same connection. Marvell's *Last Instructions to a Painter* combines the gross sexual adventures of Castlemaine with a mock-heroic description of the Dutch admiral's triumph, creating a 'spectacle' of disgrace explicitly modelled on the Skimmington ride (chapter 2, section 3 above). Another 'painter' satire extends *pornographia* for the first time to Charles II himself, figured as a Nero 'swiving' Lady Castlemaine rather than fiddling as the Royal Navy burned: kindly offering to 'extinguish those flames with his seed', his efforts fail because 'His pr---- then prov'd as useless as his chain.' The linkage between royal adultery and the collapse of the coastal defences even filtered upwards into official discourse, when the king's own chaplain made the same point in a thunderous and outspoken sermon. But despite this rebuke Charles continued to consort with Lady Castlemaine, whose influence and prestige had even spread to the Church. Pepys anticipates the post-riot satires of 1668 by imagining the most senior ecclesiastics sharing in the royal debauchery and enjoying the same favours: not only has the Archbishop of Canterbury become 'as very a wencher as can be', squabbling with Sir Charles Sedley over one of his 'girls', but (more 'astounding' still) 'my Lady Castlemayne hath made a Bishop lately'.[7]

The riots and 'petitions' thus assailed precisely what disturbed Pepys and his sources – Castlemaine's absolutist politics, unorthodox religion, and supposed influence over patronage and policy. (Marvell, who initiated sexual satire against her in *Last Instructions*, concluded that 'all Promotions, spiritual and temporal, pass under her Cognizance'.) Satyric or pornographic, representations of the royal mistress focus national fears and translate them into modes of 'public' sexuality, as we have seen in Pepys's Aretinesque dream and prurient-indignant gossip. One anecdote (supposedly taken from an eye-witness) typifies this conflation of political anxiety and the sexual violence projected onto the 'wandering whore'. Lady Castlemaine goes to view the mummified body of a mediaeval bishop unearthed during the Great Fire (perhaps an emblem of the regeneration of continuity of England despite catastrophe). After reverently crossing herself (a typical anti-Catholic detail) she asks to be alone with the bishop, but then treats him 'like a Turkish Eunuch'. Using her teeth 'for want of a circumcising Pen-knife', she promptly 'dismemberd as much of the Privity as the Lady could get into her mouth to bite'. Narrator and informant then trade witticisms rich in unspoken political analogies: the teeth of time could not achieve in three centuries what Castlemaine performed in an instant; 'some Ladys of late have got Bishopricks for others', but now she has one of her own.[8]

More is at stake here than merely wielding 'the phallus' in the generalized or symbolic sense used by psychoanalysts. That small pun on 'Bishoprick' contains a large concern, not over signification-in-general but over patronage and dependency, control of the institutions that control subjectivity and social status. Like the virago in Butler's Skimmington (chapter 2 above), Castlemaine inverts patriarchal norms and expropriates the '*Bulls pizzel*' as an instrument of chastisement. But she is a grand courtesan, not an errant wife; her sphere of operation is not the cottage but the Court. As Cavendish points out, 'when Beauty is attended with Insinuating Arts . . . it becomes Victorious, and makes its Triumphs in many Hearts, like as in many Nations'; seduction and emasculation become national rather than personal moments, emblems of political servitude or disintegration. Now that 'Libertines' can be female, Cavendish further complains, they can enjoy the privileges of both the wife and the courtesan. Castlemaine is both a 'public' woman and a great lady who could influence foreign policy, secure a promotion, or launch a new career, in the theatre as well as in the Church. Several playwrights including Wycherley – as we shall see in chapter 6 – accept her cultural patronage but translate it into sexual dependency. Marvell's phrase 'new Whore of State' epitomizes the politically intrusive figure constructed by hostile satirists, contrasted with actresses like Nell Gwyn who might 'handle' the king's 'p----, / But never lays hands on his sceptre'. Castlemaine raised the same conceptual confusion as the *cortegiana honesta*, but on a larger scale. 'State' here means more than social *status* or *stateliness* in dress and manners; in effect, the titled mistress declares *l'état, c'est moi*. When Whitehall became a great bawdy-house, 'When *Love* was all an easie Monarch's Care', then (as Pope would later put it in a cluster of contemptuous monosyllables) '*Jilts* rul'd the State'.9

Though they cannot be collapsed together, gestural and discursive 'riots' share a fundamental (and often convenient) ambiguity concerning purpose. As we have seen throughout the Caroline and Cromwellian years, disorderly assemblies and 'monstrous assemblages' resemble one another not only in the targets of their 'satyrical' representation, but in their evasiveness and slipperiness. Do 'carnival' representations have a *point*, or do they merely entertain? Are they transitive or intransitive? Do they express an anarchic hunt for spectatorial pleasure and vicarious arousal – a loose and lubricious 'Carnelevation' appropriate to the seemingly chaotic 'assemblage' of their form – or do they conceal a purposeful activity with a distinct ideological agenda? This contradictory doubleness serves to justify both 'pornographic' texts, which obviously provide titillation and comic participation while claiming a didactic purpose, and 'disorderly' gestures: the spontaneous viciousness of the drunken customer and the victim of disease, or the more institutionalized sadism of the 'mad tricks' performed in the brothel, or the ritualized violence of the charivari and the bawdy-house riot. The serious and the 'extravagant', the purposive and the nugatory, meet at a permeable border, where perpetrators can take evasive action if challenged. As in earlier prosecutions of the charivari (chapter 2 above), sexual aggression can be passed off as moral reproof, but conversely dangerous riots and critical lampoons can be excused as customary merriment. Carnivalesque enterprises like *The Wandring Whore* mingle lewd entertainment and menacing vigilantism. Purveyors of outrageous whore-biographies like *The London Jilt* claim a severe moral purpose, while still assuring the reader that 'this Narrative . . . will afford thee a peculiar delight and satisfaction'.[10] Sexuality encourages a 'loose' relation between representation and responsibility, expressive means and didactic ends.

If the Restoration culture of priapism had any obvious purpose, it was to legitimize the new régime by contrast with the repressive Cromwellian period. Looser times, ushered in by a carnivalesque min-gling of high and low, would create allegiance through solidarity in pleasure, making a kind of bachelor fraternity out of the citizenry, and inspiring an eroticized loyalism among independent but male-identified women like Aphra Behn. (The most sophisticated expression of liber-tine recruitment must be the opening of Dryden's *Absalom and Achitophel*, where the reader is teased into sharing an indulgent and generous view of Charles II's bastard-making.) The stratagem could easily back-fire, however. The godly remnant, of course, seethed with disgust and indignation against such irresponsibility in the Head of the Church, and courtiers seeking to restore aristocratic privilege and high-cultural hegemony found low-libertine sexuality a mixed blessing at best. Their expropriation of riot could in turn be reappropriated and turned back on them, as we shall see in Court reactions to the 1668 disturbances. In this renegotiation of the porno-political, 'Puritan' demands for liberty of conscience take on the low-libertine style of festive mockery.

The insecurity of 1660s London – articulated most abundantly in Pepys's diary but confirmed in other memoirs and legal documents – stems from the inadequate fit between 'unbridled' pleasure and the political stability it supposedly betokened. Though frenetic hedonism became a badge of anti-Puritan loyalty, Pepys could still report, in the afterglow of the Restoration, 'no content or satisfaccion anywhere in any one sort of people'. The obscene frolics of Dorset and Sedley provoked violent anger in the crowd, as we saw in chapter 4. The large-scale tensions that erupted in the 1668 riots can be detected already in the microscenography of the diary: when Pepys fondles a woman in a tavern, an angry passer-by stages a one-man bawdy-house raid, smashing the window with a stone. Another encounter reads like a genteel version of the 'dark passage' in *The Wandring Whore*; when he starts to grope a complete stranger in church, she takes out a set of pins 'to prick me if I should touch her again'. As in his ambivalent reactions to the sexual glamour of Charles and Lady Castlemaine – the object of his erotic gaze but also the source of his fears for the nation – Pepys transcribes and emulates the royal search for 'satisfaction' but darkens it with an ominous awareness of social unrest, not entirely managing to suppress his own recurrent sympathy with the Good Old Cause. The two loci of his anxious fascination – the Court and the street, the aristocratic whore and the popular carnival – even combine in a single episode, when Lady Castlemaine visits Bartholomew Fair. As she watches the puppet-play – which tells the story of the long-suffering and obedient wife *'patient Grizill'* – the spectacle-hungry crowd patiently watches for her reappearance. For Pepys, however, this benign glamour-smitten 'street full of people' conjures up the counter-image of an angry 'police crowd': 'I confess I did wonder at her courage to come abroad, thinking the people would abuse her; but they, silly people, do not know her work she makes, and therefore suffered her with great respect to take coach; and she away without any trouble at all, which I wondered at I confess.'[11] His awkward, repetitive, 'confessional' narrative supplies the missing popular outrage from within. The whole account of this visit to the Fair sounds guilty and conflicted, as if responding to a silent interrogator, as if Pepys has shed his precarious gentility and wallowed in the lower stratum, sharing its foul pleasures and surges of vigilante aggression. Half-acknowledged impulses lead his imagination in two directions; like the apprentice, he simultaneously wants to enjoy the 'punk' and to cast the first stone.

Pepys's erotic relationship to 'the people' has clearly been constructed by his reading as well as by the customary 'liberties' of London. Like the pseudo-Aretine 'wandering whore', he narrates his sexual activity as a series of tricks performed in unexpected places, boats, churches, taverns, coaches, and odd corners of the office. In the story he tells himself desire is manifested as a kind of picaresque mobility, shuttling him back and forth across London to lie with his carpenter's wife, glimpse an actress's breasts, feel a neighbour's thigh, or lure a servant-maid to his garden gate. In *La puttana errante* and in English imitations like *The Wandring Whore*, Pepys could find the teeming, random, bawdy life of the heterogenous city that lapped against his own back door, and in turn he modified his own 'pleasures' to match their perversions: Gusman defines the adept whore as one willing 'to do the deed of nature either backwards or any other of *Peter Aretines* postures'; Pepys dreams of performing those postures with Lady Castlemaine, and tabulates his own performance in the didactic spirit of the Italian dialogue – copulating with Mrs Martin, for example, 'both devante and backward, which is also muy bon plazer' (3 June 1666, Whit Sunday). The timid civil servant felt strongly drawn to the common brothels featured in *The Wandring Whore*, despite his fear of violence, extortion, and disease; he finds himself tempted to enter one particular house in Fleet Alley, not for sexual enjoyment, but to 'see' with his own eyes 'what formerly I have been acquainted with' – the inflation of the reckoning and the instant change in demeanour when he pretends to be penniless. His expectations, and his treatment, correspond precisely to the pamphlets he might have been reading, which pay far more attention to the postures and cheating tricks of London bawdy-houses than to 'holing' itself, and recommend that the customer who runs out of money should be kicked out with 'no more respect than a Sr. Reverence'; their philosophy is summed up in the market-vendors' phrase that recurs throughout the whore-literature, 'No money, no Coney'.[12] We can assume that his 'acquaintance' came from the low-life print culture, and that he felt the compulsion, typical of the age, to act out or witness as a scene what he had hitherto read in the privacy of the forbidden text.

Pepys responds similarly to the discursive and erotic provocations of Bartholomew Fair, translating pornographic tropes into performative routines. Like his idol Lady Castlemaine – reputed lover of the rope-dancer Jacob Hall – he was attracted to this 'low' theatrical space as a libidinous zone, or more precisely an occasion for lowering his threshold of sexual fastidiousness. In 1668, the same year that he records ejaculating while reading *L'Escole des filles*, he describes kissing 'a mighty belle fille' at the Fair. Suitably excited, he then went in search of the famous 'Horse of knowledge', the same side-show that Wordsworth recorded at Bartholomew Fair over a century later. Whatever it meant for the Romantics, in Restoration festive culture the 'knowledge' produced at the carnival was exclusively carnal; when the horse had to identify which man in the audience 'most loved a pretty wench in a corner', it picked out Pepys, and received a shilling reward. Following the subterranean logic of the fairground pamphlets, the feverish association of cash, sex, and publication, Pepys then gave another shilling to a common prostitute for mas-turbating him in a coach – was this 'Ursula', stroking out his 'marrow' as promised in *The Wandring Whore*? – and then made straight for a bookshop in Duck Lane, where he tried to seduce the bookseller's wife. Perhaps he was again acting out a fantasy schooled by his bawdy reading; 'Moll of Duck Street' is one of the dialogists in *Strange Newes from Bartholomew-Fair*.[13]

Pepys clearly enters these hot zones with the same appetite for 'bawdery and drollery' that propels the *Wandring Whore* dialogues, an expectation of amusement mingled (as in the pamphlets themselves) with distance and distaste. The term 'drollery' denoted not only a literary genre (risqué anthologies like *Covent Garden Drollery*, or the lewd playlets called 'drolls' performed at Bartholomew Fair), but also a social practice – what Marchamont Nedham called a 'knack of living in the world' by remaining 'Betwixt Earnest and Jest' – that apparently had migrated from the disreputable 'suburbs' into the mainstream. Pepys loved to have men working in his house, for example, because he felt it was 'my luck to meet with a sort of Drolling workmen upon all occasions', and he reached for the term also when first encountering the irreverent, roving wit of the king's inner circle. (On the boat bringing Charles back to England, Thomas Killigrew's comic anecdotes about royal sexuality earned him the epithet 'merry droll'.) 'Drolling' allowed non-threatening communication between higher and lower classes while at the same time confirming the hierarchy of styles that equated 'mechanicals' with the comic and the creaturely. Roger Chartier shows that the popularity of rogue-literature in Paris stems directly from the close proximity of the underclass, seen simultaneously as an 'intolerable threat' and as 'pools of picturesque characters whose immorality was reprehensible but attractive and whose ruses were found captivating'. The same applies *a fortiori* to the vaster and more heterogenous London, a city of diverse cheek-by-jowl neighbourhoods and constant exposure to the 'popular Libertinism' of the milling crowd (as Evelyn remarks in the persona of a Frenchman). Disorder-as-entertainment provided a temporary and relatively safe identification with the bawdy rogue, and sexual literature often appealed to this desire for vicarious criminality: *Rare Verities*, for example, explicitly offers the 'recreation' and 'drollery' of pseudo-scientific prurience, and weaves together associations of thievery and procurement when it promises the reader 'the pick-lock of *Venus* her Cabinet, to let you with more ease enter and rifle and despoile her inestimable treasure'.[14] This imagery of sexual breaking and entering – replicated in the subtitle *Venus Cabinet Unlocked* – flourishes again on the title-pages of *The Wandring-Whores Complaint* and *Strange Newes from Bartholomew Fair*, which lure readers with the spectacle of *The Wandring-Whore Discovered, Her Cabinet Unlockt, Her Secrets Laid Open, Unvailed, and Spread Abroad.*

2. TAKING LIBERTIES: THE RIOTS OF 1668

The bawdy-house riots inspired, in Pepys and many others, the same spectatorial desire that the whore-pamphlets had instigated, the prurient-censorious compulsion to witness the 'spreading' or 'displaying' of secret parts. When Pepys hears that a crowd of apprentices have been celebrating Easter in the pornosphere, 'taking the liberty of these holidays to pull down bawdy-houses' (24 March 1668), he makes his way across London to see the spectacle. As with his other visits to red-light districts and disorderly carnivals, he wants to enjoy the 'liberty', to create his own 'holiday', as if he were crossing to Smithfield to see the 'droll'. These expectations of entertainment had clearly been formed by lower-stratum literature as well as by memories of traditional Shrove Tuesday customs and by the new association of riot with fashionable 'frolic' and amusement. Tracing the 'restoration' of brothel-storming rituals allows us to see the dialectic interchange between discourse and behaviour as a 'cultural operation' in progress. Bawdy-houses and loose texts, disorderly gatherings on the street and 'monstrous assemblages' in print, generate one another. Charivari – which always combined action and representation and always generated performative texts – was evolving into a literary category; it comes to mean an enlivening farrago or risqué miscellany as well as a shameless shaming ritual. (This reader still remembers when the title-character of *Punch* magazine, subtitled *The London Charivari*, sported an immense phallus.) Pepys is drawn to the apprentices' rampage by the quality that Margaret Doody discovers in Butler's Skimmington ride, 'the energy and fascination of the misrule'.[15] We still use 'riot' to mean outrageous comedy.

From the 'wandering-whore' craze of 1660 to the *évènements de '68*, the mutual provocation of text and action unfolds as follows. The dissolute houses of Priss Fotheringham and Damarose Page subsist in the shady subculture of the Interregnum. Their increasing prosperity in the 'loose' threshold-period of the Restoration stimulates gossip and reportage about their extravagant 'tricks', leading to their arrest and imprisonment in Newgate. This enforced publicity generates the *Strange and True* newsbooks and *The Wandring Whore*, texts that introduce their specialities to a broader reading public and graft the European picaresque onto the English literature of roguery. Within a few years, this pornopicaresque fusion produces Richard Head's *English Rogue* (1665), where the *picaro* or 'Hector' has become a socially ambitious London apprentice, a sexual tourist who visits, names, and exposes the brothels of Mrs Page and Mrs Cresswell – one already famous from the *Strange and True Conference*, the other listed by Garfield and shortly to feature in *Venice Preserved*, *The Whores Rhetorick*, and *The Cryes of London*. These visits in turn revive memories and descriptions of the customary Shrove Tuesday riots – fallen into abeyance since 1641, but ominously evoked in the 1660 *Strange and True Newes from Jack-a-Newberries Six Windmills*. On this date, as

Head recounts it, the apprentices (generally described as the prostitute's most eager customers) suddenly turn into moralistic vigilantes, pulling down the walls of bawdy-houses and rolling their inhabitants and belongings in the dirt. As one old bawd tells the rogue-hero, 'the Apprentices pulled down my house', showered her with 'rotten Eggs ... with which I thought they would have pelted out my brains', 'dragged me sufficiently, and worried me (as a Mastiff would a Cat)', finally pitching her into a public latrine.[16] This memorial reconstruction combines the real violence recorded in riots and Skimmingtons – smashing windows and walls, hurling eggs, trampling the scapegoat-victim in the mud or the sewer – with the dog-like harassment that had already become one of the 'tricks' in the brothel repertoire. This violent amplification of the house-shaming ritual collapses the distinction of outside and inside in the most literal way, making concrete the titillating and censorious breaking open of a secret world promised in the subtitles of pamphlets like *Strange Newes from Bartholomew Fair*.

Three years later, Richard Head's textual reenactment of a rough popular entertainment is translated back into reality by a huge crowd in which eye-witnesses thought they saw apprentices, artisans, and sailors. Flourishing aprons and sheets as their 'Colours', they demolish brothels, open prisons, and storm all the zones of tolerated misrule. The composition and purpose of this mob prompted diverse explanations that would soon become (literally) a matter of life and death for those arrested. Were they indeed young apprentices 'taking the liberty of these holidays', or were they undercover revolutionaries and discontented sailors? Did that 'liberty' constitute a customary amusement, a moral crusade, or a dangerous breach of the peace? Since the sureties who stood bail for the rioters include one 'gentleman', could this tumult claim some affinity with the 'frolics' that were treated with indulgence when associated with the élite? Arguments at the subsequent trial centred on the innocence of 'custom' and spectatorial curiosity. Though the violence closely resembled what Head depicts – a house 'broken down so that you might have ridden a Horse thro' it', a woman 'dragg'd' into the street while protesting that she did not keep a bawdy-house – sympathizers (including one Justice of the Peace) justified it as a legitimate protest against a 'grievance' that should have been suppressed by the magistrates. On the other hand, members of the crowd did cry 'Reformation and Reducement' and their campaign did take an increasingly militant turn, attacking the injustice of suppressing 'liberty of conscience' while condoning aristocratic libertinage. Apprentices themselves presented a hermeneutic dilemma:

it was unclear whether their public actions represented a renewal of 'Merry England', a heroic assertion of traditional values, or a dangerous invasion of the political sphere; though publications like *The Out-Cry of the London Prentices for Justice* (1660) enforce the new royalism (and launch a vicious personal attack on Milton), their 1660 rising in support of the soldiers' mutiny led to mass arrests, and their 1664 riot against the pillorying of two of their number mobilized the trained-bands throughout London.[17] Speculations triggered by the 1668 riot revived questions that had already been raised before the Civil War, when Taylor the Water-Poet – adopting the bawd's point of view – denounced the 'uncivill civill hostilitie' of 'the unruly Rabble', who 'did falsely take upon them the name of *London* Prentices'. In 1640, when the apprentices start to combine rioting with legitimate political protest, Lord Conway guessed that it might prove only 'a Shrove Tuesday business' (chapter 2, nn. 28, 38 above).

At the trial itself, Lord Chief Justice Keeling – the same Keeling who persecuted John Bunyan, ridiculed the subject's rights as 'Magna Farta', and only a few months later imprisoned the constable who tried to tame the rioting Dorset and Sedley – denied that many real apprentices had taken part. Quashing any association with youth and holiday merriment, he did his best to distinguish this uprising from the licensed adolescent violence unleashed by apprentices against bawdy-houses. Keeling constantly refers to the danger of a 1640-style rebellion starting up again under the cover of a slight and moral-seeming cause, and presumably this paranoia led him to abandon the usual evidentiary requirements and to argue that anyone caught up in such a tumult was guilty of treason even if he was ignorant of any such intention; even a man who whooped and threw up his hat was found guilty, though he was later discharged on the grounds that such merriment denotes 'Curiosity to see' rather than zeal to overthrow. Keeling sought to define the dangerous rioter *against* the jovial festive crowd, arguing for acquittal in one case by pointing out that 'many People are walking abroad in the Holidays'; his indictment painted the defendants as revolutionary agitators using the acceptable ritual of brothel-smashing 'to colour their Design'.[18] Eyewitnesses, however, report that the crowd progressed seamlessly from one 'Design' to the other: 'they did ill in contenting themselves in pulling down the little bawdy-houses', some of these 'idle fellows' were heard to declare; they should rather 'go and pull down the great bawdy-house at White hall'. If 'displaced abjection' had focussed traditional apprentices' rage against the brothels that entertain and exploit them, the new institution of royal whoredom allows for a reversed transference – from small to large, from the neighbourhood brothel to the state and the 'Jilt' who rules it.[19]

As if to complete a cycle started by *The Wandring Whore*, the rioters begin by smashing the house of Damarose Page in Poplar. In the 1660 pamphlet Magdalena had dropped ominous hints about Mrs Page's having saved enough to build 'Houses in *Radcliff-high*-way', and the indictment of one 1668 rioter uses the identical phrase to describe the 'Rebellion in *Poplar*' and its bawdy-house targets. (Significantly, no witnesses appeared against this defendant and Page was never mentioned in the treason trial, presumably because it would dissolve the draconian atmosphere into merriment.) Other detachments of rioters take over the brothel district of Moorfields, where Mrs Fotheringham had set up her 'Chuck-office' and sent out orders for books to make her whores 'more exquisite'. Targeting those 'houses' that had already been imagined aspiring to institutional status, the rioters rehearse their subsequent attacks on actual institutions – the prisons where colleagues had been held, the Royal Horse Guards supposedly led by the hated Duke of York, and ultimately the 'great bawdy-house' at Whitehall, where a break-in occurred on the last day of the disturbances. This logic of institutional association is spelled out when these turmoils generate fresh disorderly texts, emulations of the vicious wit and performative drollery associated with apprentices. The bawdy mock-petition had earlier sought to degrade the 'middling sort' who demanded the right to influence policy, but now the genre aims at the royal mistress herself. In the petition to the chief whore Lady Castlemaine that appeared immediately after the riots, the characters of Damarose Page and Mrs Cresswell (who else?) complain about their rough treatment, beg their noble patroness to call in 'French, Irish and English Hectors' to protect them, and reveal their *puttana errante* ancestry by promising to contribute to Castlemaine's personal wealth 'as our Sisters at Rome and Venice to His Holiness the Pope'. In her mock-replies the king's mistress accuses the apprentices of 'the highest Treason', striking at 'the roote of the Government as now-established' – that is, the new pornocracy. How dare they question the principle that only 'the most exquisite Whoores' should rule the Church and the state?[20]

As he hurried over to Moorfields, Pepys evidently hoped to share the experience reconstructed (for the crowd and for the reader) in Richard Head's *English Rogue*, to derive 'a peculiar delight and satisfaction' from a monstrous display of monsters. In the old Shrove Tuesday ritual, as recalled in Head's fiction by one of its whore-victims, 'the street was filled with people looking and laughing at my sad disaster, but none daring to come near me'.[21] Spectatorial desire, like the sublime, requires a controllable mixture of pleasure and danger, a vicarious participation in some 'sad disaster' framed and distanced as visual spectacle. To derive 'delight and satisfaction' from seeing houses pulled down by a wrecking crew and prostitutes mauled like the quarry in a blood sport, the audience must endorse the unleashing of violence against an alluring but tainted 'other', perhaps a scapegoat for the recent Fire and Plague; the apprentices would stage a miniature Sack of Rome, with the 'lascivious' city conveniently localized in a few streets and personified in a few notorious bawds. This malicious carnival deflects the fascination of the courtesan into 'looking and seeing', and the vigilantesque element sets up a warning barrier against fellow-feeling ('none daring to come near me'), a line of demarcation that guarantees the entertainment. This dichotomy of spectator and actor provided a life-saving defence for two of the rioters arrested at the scene, who described being drawn there by the irresistible invitation 'Brother, will you not go and see what they do in the Fields?'; though they were found guilty, they were discharged at the last minute because visual 'Curiosity' might have explained their presence. For more respectable witnesses, however, the proportions of terror and amusement went into reverse as this 1668 Easter rising gathered momentum. Driven by an intense desire to see, Pepys made several attempts to visit the riot-torn areas for entertainment, but was deflected either by the Horse Guards or by his own 'fear of meeting the prentices'. His pent-up spectatorial prurience was likewise diverted into a form of safe sex that he seems to have associated with contaminating carnivals: as he did later when returning from Bartholomew Fair, he persuades a Mrs Daniels to masturbate him in a coach, rewarding her with eight pairs of gloves.[22]

The same combination of merriment and panic – a suitable response, perhaps, to an ambiguous blend of bawdy carnival and revolutionary menace – ran through the minds of the authorities. James, Duke of York, waxed 'mighty merry' at the news that Damarose Page's entire house had been demolished (as Pepys reports on 25 March 1668), and joked about the profits he lost as 'landlord' of several of the brothels destroyed (since he had received the revenue from their wine licences). This sailor's jest shared with the Clerk of the Navy – our only evidence that Page was considered 'the great bawd of the seamen' – tries to establish a kind of Falstaffian community between James and the salty world of *The Wandring Whore*, between the 'Court' and the 'Mother-Strumpet'. (The same taste for participation in licentious folk-culture led courtiers to visit the Skimmington ride that Marvell so effectively turned against them in *Last Instructions*.) The king himself dismissed the bawdy-house riots with a joke about the apprentices as customers, 'going to' the same prostitutes they now pretend to abhor – a feeble attempt to redefine the situation as 'bawdery and drollery'. Even as heavily armed Guards rather than the usual trained-bands were brought in to quell the riot, the voices of those in power tried to merge with 'the language of the merry rogue' rather than maintaining the hierarchic difference that Bakhtinian theories assume (chapter 4, n. 34 above). But fears of insurrection soon made the Court 'ill at ease' despite their casual dismissal of the consequences. The rumour ran that former Cromwellian troopers orchestrated the crowd, who certainly chanted the slogans of radical 'Reformation' and religious 'liberty': 'Now or never' (already used as the title of a 'parliament of women' pamphlet); 'Down with the Redcoats'; 'we have been Servants, but we will be Masters now'. Crowds of onlookers prevented the soldiers from intervening – declaring that 'it was only for pulling down of bawdy-houses' and thus should not be disciplined – and in a few cases drove them back with stones. Prisons were broken open as they would be in later riots: as late as 1756, a crowd issued forth from Bartholomew Fair to storm the gates of Bridewell, the Bastille of the sexual underworld.[23]

The frolicking playfulness of the Court soon turned to vindictive fury, fuelled by precisely those individuals targeted by the angry crowd: the Duke of York and Lady Castlemaine, branded in the mock-petition as 'the most Splendid, Illustrious, Serene and Eminent Lady of Pleasure', natural leader of the guild of whores. The Crown took the astonishing decision to charge the rioters with high treason, on the grounds that storming the brothels levied war against the king and destroyed 'Inclosures'. Sir Matthew Hale was the only law lord who dissented, arguing that such eruptions were sanctioned by 'custom'; the others agreed that the assault targeted 'bawdy-houses in general' and thus private property in general. None expressed concern for the rights and feelings of the prostitutes themselves, and indeed the one apprentice among the defendants at this treason trial got off easily by painting himself as an angry vigilante: 'My Lord, there was a Whore that clapped hands on me, and I wrung my self from her, and told her that her House should be pull'd down.'[24] Specific aggression was thus pardoned, when it fitted the festive-moralistic paradigm associated with the apprentices, but more 'general' hostility raised the spectre of revolution. After

Lilliputian displays of leniency, four of the eight indicted rioters actually suffered the penalty for treason, which still included public castration. This draconian response thus unwittingly confirms the satirical trope that fuels both the original riots and the whore-petitioning: protesting against illegal prostitution does indeed constitute 'the highest Treason', since the state and all its institutions have become one great bawdy-house.

3. 'THE FEMININE PART OF REBELLION'

The bawdy-house riots and mock-petitions can thus be understood as the fullest manifestation of punitive-festive-prurient arousal, erupting in the ambiguous zone between righteous indignation and dirty fun, diversion and subversion. Informants at the time noted the sentiment on the street and in the taverns as a quasi-erotic bond, an exchange of pleasure, entertainment, and story-telling, between the two distinct groups whose interest converged in these riots and satires: the apprentices 'pander' to the radical conspirators; the sectarians are so pleased with 'those storyes of the prentices that they cannot contain themselves'.[25] This merriment was nonetheless unmistakably political. The seriocomic 'riot' throws into confusion the legalistic, top–down attempt to separate pardonable pleasure from treasonable critique, 'holiday' simulacra from purposeful actions.

Even the most extravagant combinations of sexuality and violence could claim a reformatory purpose, as we saw in the case of gang-rape (chapter 2, n. 24 above). And even hostile witnesses recognized some cohesive form within the riot, an order in its disorder. Skimmington rides, as Martin Ingram points out, are 'highly stylized representations of anarchy'. Shakespeare brings out this paradox in his rendering of Sir Thomas More, who quells the May Day rioters by pointing out that even they, 'whose discipline is ryot', require obedience to organize their tumult. In James Harrington's *Oceana* the facetious, reactionary Lord Epimonus tries to discredit alternative systems of government by associating the Oceanic constitution with rough village festivities of misrule; a rotating legislature would create a Commonwealth of football- and cudgel-players led by King Piper, a rabble even worse than 'the *Prentices* in their ancient administration of Justice at *Shrove-tide*'.[26] In invoking this image of plebeian chaos, however, Epimonus inadvertently elevates it to a legitimate cause, an 'administration of justice'. A similar retroactive structuring takes place in 1668 when the Lord Chief Justice, to render his catch more formidable, reconstructs the bawdy-house riot in quasi-aesthetic terms – 'Colour' and 'Design'.

Given that even the most anarchic effusions of merriment can display purpose, 'design', and 'discipline', the question then becomes *which* purpose? What is being disciplined? In the early Restoration, the most obvious political goal of riotous sexual humour is triumph over the defeated Puritans – the source of endless jests about the Rump and the bestiality of Quakers, endless genital puns using godly and radical dialect, constant reminders of women's contributions to the Great Rebellion. A typical lampoon combines this anti-Puritan mockery with the conservative, regulatory impulse of the Skimmington ritual, always directed against supposedly compliant husbands: the fallen hero died fighting for

> the good old cause
> Of suffering Husbands under Ruling Wives . . .
> Nor was't by force of Armes, by pike, and Drumm
> He did resist, but with his naked Bumm.[27]

As with Hudibras's over-eloquent defence of women (chapter 2 above), this vein of humour reveals the shakiness of the new régime as much as its confidence. After the armed insurrection of the Fifth Monarchists under Thomas Venner in 1661, for example, the Fifth Monarchy movement became associated with insubordinate female libido, perhaps because two of its leading writers were women (Anna Trapnel and Mary Cary), perhaps because women provided logistic support and cheered on the actual fighting. According to a 1661 pamphlet, to abet Venner's rising 'a woman in *Cheapside* sp[oke] most horrible and malicious speeches against his Majesty and people, for which high piece of impudence she was cruelly maul'd with stones in the street by the boyes'. Other ephemera reenact this apprentice 'mauling' using the common stock of porno-political satire. An engraved portrait of Venner, 'Orator, Seducer, and Captain of the Libertines', superimposes (at a suitably crazy angle) the scene of a 'Conventicula Curiosa Anabaptistarum et Quackerorum', where a woman in the congregation strips naked in response to a female preacher (fig. 9). In an obscene narrative poem from the Rochester circle, a rampant sectarian woman, who travels to the 'Warm Water' of Bath to initiate an Aretinesque orgy with twenty-four men, 'came to set up C--ts Fifth Monarchy'. The 'thirty-one' or enumerated gang-rape, which Aretino himself had used as an oblique representation of the Sack of Rome, has now come full circle; orgiastic mass copulation signifies not humiliation and defeat, but female

Figure 9. Artist unknown, *Thomas Venner* (1661), engraving

insurgency. Indeed, when the eponymous 'Cunt' emerges victorious her political associations extend even wider: the citizens cheer her on 'As if *Bath*, gratefull for her Trade, had sent/Too powerfull C--t to vote in *Parliament.*'[28]

The search for what Pepys called 'satisfaction' in the monarchal régime extended deep into the body politic, and at certain ritually heightened moments this 'body' became literal. The anti-Lenten associations of the triumph over Puritanism bred a coarse 'Bartholomew Fair' humour, which Charles himself exploited by gearing his anti-dissenter campaign to the butcher's festival of St Bartholomew and continuing to use Smithfield as a site for executions (chapter 2, section 2 above). The festive and 'extravagant' component of Restoration triumphalism is vividly captured in an incident reported at the execution of the regicide Sir John Barkstead, who had provoked particular resentment as the draconian ruler of London under Cromwell. His moralistic purges, including the arrest of 'several hundred prostitutes', probably prompted the various 'bawds' petitions' and 'women's parliaments' of the later 1650s, and one radical attack, *Invisible John Made Visible, or A Grand Pimp of Tyranny Portrayed* (1659), had compared him to the catamite of a Roman emperor. This gendered theme reenters the pamphlet-literature after his arrest in 1662: the '*Enamorato*' and impregnator of Fortune is now ridden by her; the grandee who once received the petitions of 'Ladies' cannot even win the support of a '*Billinsgate* woman' at the scaffold. As he was dragged through London, then, Barkstead drew the attention of an audience already primed to find significance in his physical disposition. Pepys noticed that he remained 'cheerful' and unrepentant ('which is very strange'), and other witnesses saw him eating and drinking spirits from a silver flask.[29] His enemies in the crowd evidently felt the need to whip up a countervailing cheerfulness and strangeness. Two in particular, 'rejoycing that now they should see him die, . . . got very near the fire wherein the Bowels were to be burnt, and having a convenient opportunity, did cut off a piece of Col. *Barkstead*'s Liver, and put it up in a Cloth'. During an afternoon spent 'making merry' in the alehouse, this relic

was produced, to heighten their mirth the more. At length, these two fellows drinking themselves almost drunk, began to be very extravagant, and resolved they would eat up this piece of Col. *Barkstead*'s Liver; and accordingly prepared it for the Coals, then laid it on and broyled it, and then did eat up a good part, if not all of it.

'Extravagant' transgressive humour, extending the official punishment of the traitor and incorporating the dismembered enemy into the feast, intensifies the political focus rather than diffusing it. The narrative framing of this anecdote, however, reveals a diametrically opposite politics and a different kind of 'satisfaction'. It appears in a clandestine anti-royalist publication, and ends with God's instantaneous judgement: both revellers 'immediately fell desperately sick, and within a few hours one of them died'. To disarm incredulity, the compiler adds that 'this Relation is sufficiently attested by the Neighbourhood, who will give satisfaction to any that will enquire after it'.[30]

The bawdy-house riots and petitions warn us, however, not to polarize Restoration political culture into royalist 'mirth' and sober 'Puritan' truth. Despite official efforts to equate dissidence with the Lenten caricature, elements of carnival drollery continue to appear in oppositional demonstrations: in one anti-Catholic 'Mock Procession', for example, the anti-Parliamentary 'Abhorrer of Petitions' was placed backwards on a horse or donkey, like the cuckold in a Skimmington ride. The rioting apprentices and radicals of 1668 launch a grand charivari against the king, 'defacing' the institutions of whoredom and attacking by analogy the dominant pleasures and policies of Lady Castlemaine. Creating an infinite regress, the dissenting subculture now reappropriates the pseudo-plebeian elements of aristocratic hooliganism in order to protest *against* the sanctioned 'riot' of the Sons of Belial. This attack becomes explicit in the mock-petition and the 'Answers' that define her as the sovereign whore. The channels of 'traditional' merriment easily lubricated sedition; ever since the 'Evil May Day' pacified by More, the authorities grew nervous around festive holidays and strengthened their armed guard, however much they promoted 'Sports' as an expression of loyalist merriment. The bawdy-house rioters explicitly recall that alternative possibility, expunging more recent memories of royalist May celebrations, when they threaten 'that if the King did not give them Liberty of Conscience, . . . *May-day* must be a bloody Day'.[31]

To maintain the uneasy authority of Charles II, Restoration censors scrutinize the casual spoken word as well as the clandestine pamphlet and the unruly gathering, trying to associate 'lubric' sexual chatter with resurgent revolutionary sentiment. (These reports may merely reflect what the spy wanted his employer to hear, but the evidence still had to be sufficiently plausible to satisfy a jury.) Throughout Charles's reign, government spies pick up vividly obscene phrases from the oral culture of dissent, railing at the king as a whoremonger and a bastard, continuing the Civil War hostility to Henrietta Maria by recycling the rumour that he had been conceived in adultery with Henry Jermyn, Earl of St Albans. In the insecure days of August 1660, Pepys records that Phineas Pett was suspended from his job to answer charges that he formerly did 'say that the King was a bastard and his mother a whore'; the same family produced the '*Phanatick*' Peter scapegoated for the Navy's failures in 1667, and vindicated by Marvell's unforgettable series of rhymes on his name. One dissident adds a Miltonic twist by asserting that the king copulates with his own mother, another cryptically remarks that he 'did bugger this Parliament much like the buggering of an old woman'. As Paul Hammond points out, 'this idiom is a popular appropriation and reversal of the two key elements in the royalist rhetoric of legitimation, the hereditary principle and the sacredness of the king's person'. But it also taps into a more ancient discourse. With his visible dalliance and lack of what Pepys called 'command' over his sex, the restored monarch literalized the old religious vocabulary of whoredom and fornication as synonyms for tyranny and idolatry. The seditious criticisms recorded by the secret police make an unanswerable case: how can good government flourish 'when the King keepeth other mens wyfes and makes them his Concubynes'? Rather than spying on honest citizens, the informant himself 'should inform against the King for lying with so many women'. Less forthright critics take refuge in the protective slipperiness of bawdy tavern discourse, blurring opposition and celebration: one government agent records a Londoner seditiously complaining about the king keeping whores, then 'drinking a Health to the King and all Whores' – perhaps confirming the charge, perhaps dissolving it in merriment.[32]

Sly foul-mouthed murmuring of this kind reverberates in Restoration literary satire, when the élite author simulates the 'popular' combination of political critique and audacious obscenity. Notable examples would be the burlesque of royal absolutism in *Sodom* ('I have fuckt and buggerd all the land'), or Marvell's allegory of the Excise – whose inventor 'Bugger'd in Incest with the mungrel Beast'. This pungent line expresses generations of hatred; in the 1640s the Excise had been opposed by Skimmington-like riots, and in the 1660s popular-libertine verses would brand prostitution as 'The Excise of Flesh and Skin'. Marvell's *Last Instructions* in fact draw together a whole network of sexual–political tropes from the clandestine subculture of libels and whispers. Royalist allegories of Sedition – like the 1648 *Mistris Parliament Brought to Bed of a*

Monstrous Childe of Reformation (chapter 3, section 1 above) – return in the painful birthing scene of the Excise, which 'Frighted the Midwife, and the Mother tore'. (This lacerating childbirth, followed by the incestuous coupling of father and daughter, resembles so closely the Sin-episode in *Paradise Lost* that we can posit mutual influence, perhaps even a political subtext in the epic.) Marvell's portrait of Jermyn – 'The new *Courts* pattern, Stallion of the old' – builds on the worst of the seditious slanders, that he slept with the supposedly virtuous Queen Henrietta Maria and fathered the bastard king. As the Court stud (first a 'Stallion' and then a mere 'Mule') he had been chosen by Fortune 'for her pleasure salt', an indirect allusion to the old queen and an inversion of Machiavelli's idea that the successful statesman should master Fortune by ravishing her. Appropriately, Marvell's character-sketch focusses on the ponderous phallus (the 'Instrument of Peace', the '*Plenipotence*') that epitomizes Jermyn's sensual person and courtly politics. He thus fulfils the promise to match lower-stratum visual effects in words, drawing 'prodigious tools' in a smutty medium. The following portraits in this gallery of iniquity likewise fuse sexual and political transgression: the fornications of Anne Hyde and Lady Castlemaine express and prefigure the corruption that gives us 'a new Whore of State' in the Excise. Each of these ecphrastic characters finds a visual equivalent to the subject's violation of patriarchal sexual norms: the arriviste daughter of the hated chancellor exemplifies the Bakhtinian grotesque body, with a vast rump that causes her to be mistaken for her own coach and a 'Wide Mouth that Sparagus may well proclaim'; Castlemaine, by sinking to an affair with her footman but transforming him into a kind of dildo-statue, travesties the libertine connoisseurship of a corrupt Court.[33] Marvell thus prepares for the ritual of sexual mockery even before he deals explicitly with the Skimmington ride, turning its claim to moral and didactic force against the government – and thereby countering its Hudibrastic associations.

Both Marvell and the bawdy-house rising exploit the conjunction of charivari and 'lubric' satire, switching between the literal and the metaphoric, using transgressive sexuality as an instance and an allegory of corruption. The mock-petitions that cluster around the 1668 riot share this 'porno-political' theme with more sophisticated insider satires from Westminster and Whitehall, particularly when they single out Lady Castlemaine's Catholicism, anti-populism, and collusion with the corrupt clergy. Thus Court lampoons about the Bishop of London's amours with Lord Mohun use anti-sacramental vocabulary to associate the prelacy with the Italianate vices of the Papacy. When that same bishop shares a mistress with the king, the satirist blithely justifies it by collapsing the political and the sexual together: since they 'club' their votes already, why not their seed? Libels against the royal mistresses move effortlessly from sexual to constitutional politics, and back again. In one 'Ballad', for example, Lady Castlemaine becomes 'That prerogative Queane', a dense phrase which combines the old pun on quean/queen with a new sense of the complicated relation between political and sexual 'prerogative' – a theme already broached in the libertine 'rebellion' of John Phillips's *Sportive Wit* (chapter 3, section 1 above). Here libertinism equates directly with tyranny and excessive privilege, a charge that would soon be brought against the king himself ('Out Flyes his Pintle for the Royall Cause / Prick foams and swears he will be absolute'). In the same ballad, however, Castlemaine's promiscuity collapses the social and natural hierarchy: a flurry of hostile images turns her into a 'Bitch' who needs spaying, a 'stoate' who never stops 'swiving', and a common gamester who plays 'Levell-Coyle with a prince, and a player'.[34] ('Level-Coil', the name of a popular card-game, suggests the Levelling effect of unbridled sexuality despite its previous association with hubristic 'prerogative'.) Satyric obscenity encourages a metaphorics as slippery and polymorphous as the sexuality it parades, and the political referent likewise swivels uncontrollably: Charles II's polymorphous libido allows him to embody absolutism and anarchy at once, too much and too little government; lewd mockery simultaneously triumphs over the old order ('Puritans', Levellers, and regicides) and articulates complaints about the new pornocracy.

The concern with female agency provides one stable referent in this polysemic tangle. Significantly, the petitions and the 'Answers' ventriloquize the voice of the whore at its two social extremes – the rampant mistress who rules the country like an illegitimate 'sovereign', and the corporation of Poor Whores whose houses have been split open and defaced. Radical and conservative might be seeking common ground in the mocking expropriation of women's political expression. On the other hand, female participation had been a distinctive marker of the Good Old Cause, and male activists often assumed female disguise for anti-authoritarian rather than misogynist purposes – for example, in protests against enclosures. As we have seen with the Fifth Monarchists, female militants continued to work for seditious causes and to voice 'horrible and malicious speeches against his Majesty'. Less than a year before the riot against 'the great bawd of the seamen', sailors' wives 'cried publicly' about their grievances (provoking Pepys to fear that they would fire his office) and Clarendon's house was 'forced by the women, his windows broken' and a gibbet set up with a shaming couplet that blamed him for the queen's barrenness. The loose-tongued, horn-throwing, distinctly un-Puritan spirit of radical women on the festive fringes of the revolution (chapter 2 above) still boils up occasionally in the conversations recorded by secret agents, sexual flytings by salty-tongued women who sound like something invented for the Bartholomew Fair or Billingsgate pamphlets: Margaret Dixon of Newcastle declares that only 'drunk whores and whoremongers' could love the king; Mary Greene of Middlesex 'did not care a t--- for never a Kinge in England, for she never did lie with any.' These assiduously reported outbursts must have contributed to the gendering of dissent in the minds of the royalist authorities, already threatened by those women like Elizabeth Calvert who continued to play a leading part in printing and distributing oppositional literature, or who continued to claim the right to speak in religious meetings, using arguments codified in Margaret Fell's *Womens Speaking Justified*. In a famous essay, Bacon described 'licentious Discourses against the State' as a kind of wandering whore ('running up and down, . . . and hastily embraced'), declaring 'that *Seditious Tumults*, and *Seditious Fames*, differ no more, but as Brother and Sister, Masculine and Feminine'. Such gendered terms came easily to mind in the Restoration: as the prosecution put it at one printer's trial, 'Raising of Tumults is the more Masculine, and Printing and Dispersing Seditious books, is the Feminine part of every Rebellion.'[35]

The most deliberate expression of political will through the voice – the petition – aims to fuse together action and discourse, the 'masculine' and 'feminine' parts of rebellion. Simulating the petition in a scandalously female voice ostensibly neutralizes dissent, but under that 'Colour' it may promote the rebellion it impersonates; the prosecutors and censors of the state assumed that this had happened in 1668. The 'petition' genre had continued to flourish after the collapse of the Commonwealth, its polymorphous bawdry allowing simultaneous attacks on the sectarian-Parliamentarian rump and the hubristic aristocracy. Thus *The Phanatick Intelligencer* invents a mock-petition to the Parliamentary Convention, then debating the entire constitutional future of the nation; in the godly dialect of inner light and 'tender Consciences', the scandalous Mrs Ives – who had just left her husband to become the highly visible mistress of the Earl of Pembroke – requests that the new house of Parliament be officially renamed 'a *Bawdy-house*', since the sisters 'had found much delight and comfort in such Houses'. (The 'Conventicle' rejects this new 'publick' title but instead sets up a weekly series of private orgies for the faithful, to compensate for their 'blasted' political hopes.) This two-faced little satire thus anticipates the murmurs of the crowd against the 'great bawdy-house at Whitehall', and forges an association between brothel-shaming ritual and the comic petition that would resurface prominently in 1668.[36]

These pseudo-female petitions generated by the bawdy-house insurrection proved to be the most conspicuous and the most infuriating to the authorities. In that year alone there appeared in prose *The Poor-Whores Petition to the most Splendid, Illustrious, Serene and Eminent Lady of Pleasure . . . the Countess of Castlemayne*, purportedly written by Damarose Page and Mrs Cresswell; *The Gracious Answer of the Most Illustrious Lady of Pleasure, the Countess of Castlem----- to the Poor-Whores Petition*; and *The Most gracious answer of Dame Barbara Countesse of C. to the peticion of undone, poore, and distressed company of Whores*, a significant variant preserved in an MP's manuscript anthology.[37] In a less satirical vein, the uprising also produced three broadsides in solemn doggerel verse: *The Whores Petition to the London Prentices*; *The Prentices Answer to the Whores Petition*; and *The Citizens Reply to the Whores Petition, and Prentices Answer*. As we have seen in section 2, the event itself inspired in Pepys and in the nation's leaders an ambivalent blend of carnivalesque merriment and tyrannical fury, culminating in the wholly disproportionate charge of high treason. The Castlemaine petition and her answers likewise mingle 'extravagant' mirth with savage indignation, as if to evade precise identification. We might be tempted to read them as an insider's exercise in bawdy wit, circulated in the coffee-houses by some side-kick of Sedley or spy from Castlemaine's entourage. But these broadsides were indeed printed, distributed, and enjoyed by the radical underground; by changing their style from fiery sermonizing to sexual mockery and ventriloquistic parody, anti-monarchist dissidents exploit the amphibiousness of festive-aggressive satire, smuggling in an explosive idea (the equation of the Court with the Great Whore) under the guise of a trivial divertissement, flattering by assuming the taste of that Court. The censor L'Estrange duly arrested the printer, but despaired of securing a conviction – precisely because of this 'lubric' slipperiness: 'I can fasten nothing on *The Poor Whore's Petition* that a jury will take notice of.'[38]

Contemporary attempts to 'fasten' signification onto these riotous simulations of the woman's petition only confirm the difficulty of fixing their specific point or programme. Evelyn described them as 'Libertine Libells', collapsing any distinction between the transgressive satire and the scandalous behaviour it attacks. Pepys notes that the real-life Castle-maine was 'horribly vexed' by the Page–Cresswell petition – a far different response from her amused participation in the popular drolleries of Bartholomew Fair – and he wonders in shocked tones 'how it durst be printed and spread abroad'. Even though similar or worse libels flow constantly from Pepys's gossiping tongue into the pages of the diary, he still finds such dissolute publication alarming, proof that 'the times are loose, and come to a great disregard of the King or Court'. 'Loose' adherents of the Court like Wycherley, no sympathizer of radical Republicanism, nevertheless align themselves with the sexually loaded misogynist humour of these petitions, alluding to them in their own bantering reminders of Castlemaine's whore status (chapter 6, section 1 below). Despite this appeal to insiders, which might suggest an affinity with libertine decadence and a determination to neutralize social disorder by sexual mockery, the historian of the bawdy-house riots interprets the petitions as direct evidence of the grievances that spurred the insurrection, almost a 'manifesto'.[39]

Radical dissent is certainly *one* interpretive strand that could be pulled from this monstrous assembly, but they raised many other issues endemic to the internal history of *pornographia*. The vigilantesque, pro-apprentice, anti-Catholic, anti-absolutist note already rumbles below the mock-grievances in the first petition, though only fitfully. The whores disparage the 'mechanick, rude and ill-bred Boys', promise to subsidize Lady Castlemaine as Roman prostitution funds the papacy, and call for draconian action against 'the Ringleaders and Abetters of these evil-disposed persons, that a stop may be put to them before they come to your Honours Pallace, and bring contempt upon your worshiping of *Venus*, the great Goddess whom we all adore'. This comes very close to the rioters' own threat to march on the 'great bawdy-house at White hall'. When Page and Cresswell ask Castlemaine to send foreign troops (or '*Hectors*') to protect them against rioters, they appeal to her self-interest as well as professional solidarity: 'should your Eminency but once fall into these Rough hands, you may expect no more Favour than they have shewn unto us poor Inferiour Whores'.[40]

These hints of anti-Whitehall resentment prompted L'Estrange to take *The Poor-Whores Petition* seriously as a seditious document, and they are greatly amplified in the subsequent 'Answers'. At the same time, however, the three poems that continue the 'petition' motif show that the riots could be interpreted in an entirely different spirit, with no trace of political message except for the conservative reassurance that the people should never take justice into their own hands, that the authorities can be trusted to suppress the crying evil of prostitution – exactly the point questioned by the defence at the treason trial. These clumsy City poems also take the riots seriously, but they emphasize other issues: the economic hardship of the prostitute, the moral chaos that ensues when '*Vice* shall undertake to punish *Sin*' and '*Order*' is enforced by '*Confusion*', the shame brought on the glorious City of London, the threat of 'Misrule' turning into 'sedition' or 'Rebellion', and the identity of the rioters. As in Taylor the Water-Poet, the perpetrators are declared to be rabble disguised as apprentices, while the *Prentices Answer* haughtily claims that they themselves scorn such base actions, however much they despise the 'pocky Jades', always keeping in mind that 'we shall Masters become in time / *And that Rebellion is* a scurvy crime.' The supposed eye-witnesses limit the action to Moorfields and Whetstones Park (a prostitution-street mentioned in lampoons but not in the trial proceedings), and describe it almost exactly as Taylor does, emphasizing the feather-beds ruined, the bedding '*open* shown for *hiding* Leacherous Dalliance', the windows broken to make work for the glaziers. Rather than appealing for royal protection, the whores in this verse-petition fall back on traditional moral reproof, threaten their foes with the common hangman, evoke Evil May Day with unmixed disapproval, and compare the rioters to the followers of Masaniello in Naples, a well-tried method of discrediting attempts to renew the militancy of the English Civil War. (The 'Prentices' endorse this analogy completely.) Equating these 'bawdy' London riots with the 1647 popular revolt in Naples appears to confirm the Crown's case for prosecuting them as high treason, but any solidity in this argument melts into air when placed in the mouth of 'Whores', 'Citizens', and 'Prentices' with the reputation of sexually rampant adolescents; even the earnest *Whores Petition* hints that, had the apprentices come to discuss their grievances beforehand, 'We would have eased you of all your trouble.'[41] Such ventriloquism returns the Naples–London parallel to its origins in the world upside down of urban carnival.

Hovering between conservative and radical, then, this mock-petitioning draws upon the ambiguity inherent in the disorderly festive culture, and uses the prostitute persona simultaneously to voice and to trivialize the weightiest concerns. The prose 'Answers' to Page and Cresswell take this one stage further by speaking through the ventriloquized figure of Lady Castlemaine herself, mingling the political protest against absolutism and corruption with the misogynistic hatred of 'female' secrecy, passion, and influence. Castlemaine becomes a figure of extravagance and carnivalesque theatricality, an embodiment of the kind of government-by-glamour that John Hall had satirized under the trope of female domination (chapter 3, section 3 above): 'on Shrove Tuesday last, splendidly did we appear upon the Theatre at W[hite] H[all], being to amazement wonderfully deck'd with jewels and diamonds, which the (abhorr'd and to be undone) Subjects of this Kingdom have payed for'. This targets not only her avarice and her 'exhibitionism at the theatre' but her taste for calendrical festivities like Bartholomew Fair, adding an undertone of incitement to violence since 'Shrove Tuesday', rather than Easter, was the customary date for ritual assaults on prostitutes.[42]

Simulating the voice of the Great Whore opens a flood of grievances, articulated with various success. Many of them are indeed topical: Anglican churchmen pawning their vestments in the brothel; the Archbishop of Canterbury (a 'wencher' according to Pepys) giving 'Episcopal Allowance' to her liaison; a foreign standing army ready to invade, abetted by French secret agents already in residence; 'Hectors' pardoned even when they turn highwaymen; repression of 'Fanaticks' and 'Conventicles'; '*L.C.J.K.*' (Lord Chief Justice Keeling) praised for launching the treason trial and assembling a jury of implacable 'Gentlemen'. Castlemaine even appoints her own close committee to oversee the 'happy Restauration' of whoredom – an incongruous gaggle of Court insiders including the archbishop, the Earl of Lauderdale, and Tom Killigrew. She exults in the prorogation of Parliament, but at the same time offers sexual favours to those MPs who vote lavish funds for the king (which she salts away in jewellery and overseas funds). Seditious satire and ponderous anti-Catholic cliché mingle with classic *pornographia*. The original *Petition* rather heavy-handedly juxtaposed the diseased, ulcerous condition of the London whores with the aristocratic status of their clients: the riots have set back their cures and made them 'uncapable of giving that Entertainment, as the Honour and Dignity of such persons as frequented our Houses doth call for'. The idea of contagion here fuses together the abject and sublime ends of the spectrum, the pocky whore and the status-confusing *cortegiana* who absorbs *honestà* from her noble protectors. Many of Castlemaine's counter-proposals, which sound like the mock-official decrees in the *Wandring Whore* and *Strange News* pamphlets, try to obliterate the stigma of poverty and disease: 'full Toleration of all Bawdy-houses, Play-houses, Whore-houses, &c.' (while all prayer meetings are shut down); whores to be made into a 'Corporation' with 'all their former Liberties, Priviledges and Immunities', so that the world will respect their high breeding, 'Ingenuity and Gentility'. But the recurrent theme is still the Great Fire, completing a chain of association that began with venereal Plague. Concern with the hot zones of London, the bawdy-houses at each end of town, dissolves into paranoid speculation about the burnt-out centre, dark suspicions about those who started the Fire, who let it burn, and who now block all attempts to rebuild the City.

Castlemaine's 'Answers' dissolve the boundaries of Queen and Quean, expressing arbitrary authority as a limitless power to dispose and rearrange the sexual body. By addressing her petitioners with their 'Titles of Honour' and repeating the addresses appended to the original petition – 'Right Trusty and Well-beloved Madam *Cresswell* and *Damaris Page*, with the rest of the suffering Sister-hood in *Dog and Bitch Yard, Lukeners Lane, Saffron-Hill, Moor-fields, Ratcliff-Highway*, &c.' – she reiterates *The Wandring Whore*'s mapping of London, defining that underworld as a little kingdom with its own estates and domains. She speaks throughout in the royal 'we', and by signing her response 'In the 8th yeare of our Royall Whoredome' she assumes the monarch's prerogative of dating an epoch from the start of a reign, with a strong hint that the Restoration itself had been an act of whoredom, eight years before. (She also refers to it as 'the Day that *Mars* was so instrumental to restore our Goddess *Venus* to her Temple'.) The threats and counter-remonstrances put into the mouth of the 'Premier' mistress vividly illustrate contemporary fears of domination by an unaccountable power gendered female. And this unruly agency is associated with castration, transposing the 'dark passage' scene of *The Wandring Whore* onto the large screen of national politics.

As in other gossiping projections of Castlemaine's secret desires, generic images of the disorderly and uncontrollable woman sharpen to focus on specific complaints against her Catholicism, her defiance of moral rebuke, and her corruption of the Anglican hierarchy. In the supposedly true story of Castlemaine and the bishop whose corpse came to light after the Fire (p. 169 above), she actually bites off the mummified organ and by analogy feeds on the 'Bishopricks' of the kingdom. The Castlemaine figure in the 1668 'Answers' likewise exults in her destructive power over religious leaders and moralistic rioters, boasting of her recent conversion and her ability to prosecute and destroy even an archbishop, if he dare suggest that 'exquisite' whores might not be the best advisors to the Church and the state. When she turns to the vigilante apprentices, this punitive threat focusses on their sexuality. We have seen how she equates the attacks on brothels with 'the highest Treason', an exaggeration that proved hideously prophetic when four of the rioters actually suffered the penalty for that offence. Grim triumphalist humour played freely with the body parts of executed revolutionaries, excised and thrown into the fire during the ultimate shaming ritual imposed by the state. Devouring the regicide's liver is only the most 'extravagant' and literal instance of this comic trope; Milton's nephew, for example, joked about the 'gelding' suffered by Hugh Peters on the scaffold. It seems particularly appropriate that the Castlemaine character – in a *Gracious Answer* dated April Fool's Day, four days before the actual trial began – orders the apprentices to 'bee deprived of their Testicles, as unworthy to weare them, and then to bee cast into the Fire, as a burnt offering to appease the anger of our great Goddesse'.[43]

These riotous images of absolute female dominion resonate, strangely enough, with the fictions of female authority published two years earlier by Margaret Cavendish. *The Description of a New World, Called the Blazing World* (1666), which expands the Utopian speculations of the Interregnum (chapter 3, section 4 above), draws much of its narrative impulse from sexual transgression and theatrical glamour. The heroine is first abducted by a foreign admirer, who loses his life when his ship is sucked across to a neighbouring planet by polar winds, and she then becomes the absolutist empress of this new Blazing World because the reigning monarch is absolutely taken by her beauty. In the *Sociable Letters*, Cavendish identifies the hyperbolic exaltation of a woman to 'Empress' as a delusion peculiar to the male, an example of 'how the Passion of Love had bribed his Tongue' (25); in this fictive kingdom, by contrast, such gallantry becomes the global norm. Not only does the empress rule at home unchallenged, but during a visit to England she even sets up an unconventional, Bloomsburyesque *ménage à trois* with her lover – 'honest Margaret Newcastle' herself – and her husband the duke. Though she assures us that these affairs were 'platonic' and disembodied, Cavendish's letters suggest her familiarity with more physical manifestations of triadic desire: 'it is a temptation to an Husband, to see two She-friends Imbrace, and Kiss, and Sport, and Play, which makes the Husband to desire to do the like, not with his Wife, but his Wives Friend'.[44]

As monarch of the Blazing World and ally of her original country, she excels in two activities for which Lady Castlemaine would soon be denounced in the 1668 petitions: innovation in religion, and deployment of an international military force. In both areas she reclaims the 'Artificial Shews' and the 'Art of Allurement' for which Cavendish half-admired the courtesan, the spectacularity for which the royal mistress was castigated: using deliberately theatrical displays of jewellery and lighting to captivate her audience, she establishes herself as the head of a new religious cult for women, and later in the novel – returning to her native land with the military technology to make it a world power – she uses the same effects to strike amazement into her countrymen, who worship her as a 'goddess'. As a *political* leader the empress makes very few changes in the paradisal world she comes to rule, since it already enjoys the Utopian uniformity of culture, language, and government that Europe so conspicuously lacked during the decades of religious war: she alters the state religion to involve women, and she fosters Royal-Society-like institutes for scientific research (which the duchess finally advises her to suppress, because they foment civil dissention). One extraordinary institution remains intact and unchallenged, however: in this peaceable kingdom, dominated by an absolute empress, all priests and governors must be castrated, 'made eunuchs'.[45] The conventional explanation that wives distract men from politics, though consonant with Cavendish's earlier account of the origins of civil war, can only appear ironic in the empress's testosterone-free régime. What the mock-petitions had projected onto Lady Castlemaine in an atmosphere of riotous transgression, Cavendish calmly incorporates into the ground-rules of the ideal state, the absolutist gynocracy.

CHAPTER 6

'Making yourself a beast': upper-class riot and inversionary wit in the age of Rochester

As Mr *Wycherley* was going thro' *Pall-mall* toward St *James's* in his
Chariot, he met the foresaid Lady [Castlemaine] in hers, who,
thrusting half her Body out of the Chariot, cry'd out aloud to him,
You, Wycherley, *you are a Son of a Whore*, at the same time laughing
aloud and heartily.

(John Dennis)

> I'll tell of Whores attack'd, their Lords at home,
> Bauds Quarters beaten up, and Fortress won:
> Windows demolish'd, Watches overcome;
> And handsome Ills, by my contrivance, done.

(Rochester)

'Riot' continues to oscillate between carnivalesque 'frolic' and political
protest, and between the disorderly lower stratum and the aristocratic
Sons of Belial, for the remainder of Charles II's reign. This chapter will
explore the emulation of riot and 'popular Libertinism' in some of the
most prominent *literati* of the 1670s, adherents of the Court and transgressors of the law. It begins by tracing the aftermath of the bawdy-house
riots and the whore-petition in the playwright William Wycherley, whose
adoption of tavern drinking rituals gave us the 'Filtre' as a paradigm
for simultaneous sexualizing and distancing (chapter 4, section 4 above).
Later sections deal with the Earl of Rochester and (more briefly) with contemporaries like Sir George Etherege, John Dryden, the Earl of Dorset –
already famous in the 1660s for manslaughter, incitement to riot, and
cultural patronage – Aphra Behn, and other women authors who criti-
cize libertine debauch even as they register its allure. (They include Jane
Barker, trenchant critic of 'the Deluge of Libertinism', and Elizabeth
Polwhele, recently discovered author of *The Frolicks*.) The subject remains 'whoring' in the larger sense, and in particular the contradictory
abject/sublime effects generated by the Great Whore and emulated by
her courtiers and assailants. Moving into the 1670s, I maintain my focus

197

on festive violence and the performative core of text and behaviour, as it is now manifested in the drinking rituals and 'frolics' of the newly confident Sons of Belial, the lampoons that reenact them, and the comedies that stage them for a theatre audience itself composed of fashionable or aspiring 'Wits'.

The disorderly and treasonable *évènements* of 1668 marked the psychic topography of London for generations afterwards. Similar pornotropic insurgencies broke out intermittently during the 1670s and crested in 1682; when the travellers Time and Death visit 'Erotopolis' in 1684, to investigate a new 'Rebellion' against their authority, they encounter the same difficulty getting into Moorfields that Pepys had found in 1668 – turning back 'for fear of the Prentices'.[1] As in 1668, lampoons and whore-pamphlets repeatedly associate the crisis of the day with the grievances of the prostitute, insulating national fears in bawdy pseudo-complaint or detached amusement. *The Poor Whores Complaint to the Apprentices of London, . . . Printed in the Year of our Great Affliction* (1672) bemoans the violence of stone-throwing crowds and the ravages of the new Dutch War, and makes a peace-offering to the '*Brave London-'Prentices*'; the whores will admit them at special discount prices, and will accept payment in kind from what they can smuggle out of their masters' workshops. The Dutch had distributed insulting images of royal extravagance and lechery during the previous war, so this might come from the same source.[2] Charles's 'womanizing' provided abundant opportunities for rituals of sexual mockery on an international scale.

Internal campaigns against sedition ran into the same riotous genital humour, at once representing and trivializing rebellion. Charles's high-handed attempts to close down the coffee-houses, for example, produces a series of comic petitions, ostensibly supporting the suppression but giving outrageously sexual reasons for doing so. *The Wandring-Whores Complaint* of 1663 asserts that 'the *Coffee-houses* have dry'd up all our Customers like Spunges; Lust and Leachery were never in lesse repute than since that liquor came up' (4). *The Women's Petition against Coffee . . . Presented to the Right Honorable the Keepers of the Liberty of Venus* (1674) draws out the political corollary by demanding 'Just Rights' and 'Antient Privileges', demands that despite their powerful sound refer exclusively to the sexual potency of their men, now '*Frenchified*', '*Eunucht*', and as feeble as 'a *shotten Herring*' in bed (6, 1, 2); by implication coffee-houses *cannot* breed sedition, as Charles had asserted. (The men reply that they have 'spent the best of our Blood and Spirits in your Service', 'condiscended to all the Methods of Debauchery', and 'Invented more Postures than *Aretine* ever Dreamed of'.) The pre-Restoration equation of rebellion with virility can thus be subsumed into the satire on female insatiability. Once again, sexualization generates an ambiguous politics. Do these pamphlets confirm or deny the original thesis, that coffee-houses breed dangerous sedition (or vigorous independence)? They certainly undermine the seriousness of Charles's campaign by lewd associations, and they do sound like in-house jests, breathing the smoke-filled satirical atmosphere of the coffee-house itself; as we know from secret police reports, such bawdy irreverence was seen as seditious in its own right. On the other hand, dissident politicking could be disarmed by equating it with low-grade sexuality and the lewd 'chatter' of the gossips' feast. (One pamphlet calls the coffee-house a '*refin'd Baudy-House*, where *Illegitimate Reports* are got in close *Adultery* between *Lying lips* and *Itching Ears*'.)[3] By setting *The Women's Petition against Coffee* in 'the *Utopian* Territories' (6), and associating it with the courtesans who rule the liberties of Venus, this pamphlet identifies alternative politics as a red-light district. Rather than valuing those locales where reality can be suspended and new constitutions devised in an atmosphere of freedom, it equates them with loose talk and whorishness; the public sphere is brought under the skirts of the public woman.

Libertine Wits tended to burlesque the consternation provoked by bawdy uprisings and to savour the absurdities of aligning state power with the prostitute subculture. The Earl of Dorset – an expert in making light of riots that seemed deadly serious to less privileged observers – mocked hysterical militarism in a poem on the 'Drums' that called out the guard against the apprentices in 1668. Capt. Alexander Radcliffe elaborates this theme in 'A Call to the Guard by a Drum', published among his *Carnal Ejaculations* in 1682 but probably dating from the earlier bawdy-house riots. In the grotesque bodies of the soldiers summoned to defend the Court, images of sex, diet, and excretion combine to form a social map of London:

> Though their Mouths are poor Pimps (Whore and Bacon being all
> Their chief Food) yet their Bums we true Courtiers may call,
> For what they eat in the Suburbs, they sh--- at *Whitehall*.

'Whore and Bacon Lane', we recall, was the address of the prostitute-character 'Bonny Besse' (p. 133 above), and it invokes the entire milieu of the *Wandring Whore* pamphlets. Radcliffe's verse allies itself to the whore-literature at several points, for example in a 'Poor Whore's Song' larded with insider references to the bawds 'Mother *Bennet*' (celebrated by Wycherley) and Mrs Cresswell (a constant presence in *pornographia* from 1660 on). In 'A Call to the Guard', a kind of 'Poor Whoremongers' Song', the contradictory status of the royal soldiers – their heads crammed with plebeian 'Whore and Bacon' but their arses 'true Courtiers' – mirrors the inversion of extremes brought about when they defend the palace that the rioters themselves had labelled a 'great bawdy-house'.[4]

The spark that ignited the bawdy-house riots, as we have just seen in chapter 5, was the suppression of liberty of conscience while Whitehall enjoyed a libertine or 'pornographic' freedom from restraint. Warren Chernaik has thoroughly explored the contradictory ideology of sexual liberation in Rochester and his contemporaries, male and female: attempting to base personal liberation on a deterministic and materialist philosophy, and further pulled apart by the split between Hobbesian pursuit of power and Epicurean pursuit of pleasure, 'the ideology of libertinism can justify oppression in the name of freedom, liberating the will to possess and destroy' (4–5). Rochester himself (speaking through the persona of Artemiza) complains that women of her time, though 'borne like Monarchs free, / Turne Gipsyes for a meaner liberty, / And hate restraint, though but from Infamy' (65). Artemiza reminds us that each brand of freedom carries a class-label, some 'meaner' and some nobler, and that Restoration sexual indulgence simulated the abject liberty of the 'gypsy'. (Her words apply to adventurers of both sexes, even though 'infamy' had less dangerous consequences for males under the double standard.) Specifically, Court Wits claim the freedom to act like a denizen of the *Wandring Whore* underworld without surrendering upper-class identity. What the mock-petition calls 'the Liberty of Venus' – a circumscribed brothel-area whose lawlessness permits violent 'tricks' and festive-punitive assaults – relates only obliquely to the constitutional liberty demanded by the bawdy-house protesters. Some versions of Rochester's infamous 'sceptre lampoon' add lines that capture the queasy ambiguity that erupted in those riots: when the speaker wishes long life for the sex-mad Charles II, 'For Wee shall never have such liberty to swive' (87), does he mean *never again*, or *never at all*? Does this celebrate a common sensuality or express bitterness at exclusion? Are 'we' male only, or does the lampoon speak for what Margaret Cavendish called 'Wanton and Free Women'? Are 'we' sharers in this 'liberty to swive', or are we perpetually shut out, enslaved to the pleasures of an absolutist monarch himself enslaved to his sex, dominated by the all-powerful mistress or Whore of State?

We saw in chapter 5 that the most intense focus of the 1668 riots – to judge by the satirical petitions as well as by the oral threats against bawdy 'greatness' – was neither the Guards nor the local 'grievance' of prostitution but the ascendency of the Countess of Castlemaine, the 'prerogative Queane' whose influence and extravagance emblematized tyranny. Her sexuality makes her simultaneously abject and omnipotent, 'humbled' to a groom in Marvell's *Last Instructions* (lines 91–2) but endowed with ferocious powers in Court lampoons, in scandalous rumour, and in the 'Answers' to *The Poor Whores Petition*. Lady Castlemaine (or the Duchess of Cleveland as she became) ravages the constitution like the 'teeth of time', devours 'Bishopricks' and royal sceptres, and dictates terrible penalties for opponents deemed unworthy to wear their 'Testicles' (chapter 5 above); she is both the presiding judge and the 'great Goddess' whose anger against the apprentices must be appeased by a burnt offering. Satires against the 'Whore of State' shifted during the 1670s to the French Duchess of Portsmouth, whose impeachment for treason brings full circle the 1668 prosecution of anti-Castlemaine protesters for the same offence. But Cleveland continued to trigger violent lampoons and occasional riots, like those that destroyed enclosures she had made in the Forest of Dean (1671).[5] In her sphere the personal remained the political, as we learn from several incidents in the life and writings of Wycherley. If the bawdy-house riots were a collective version of the stone-throwing that disturbed Pepys's attempt at public lechery, scaled up to match the enormity of Charles's affair with Castlemaine, then individual encounters with the ex-mistress could be interpreted as instances of that enormity and occasions for a miniature 'riot' of contradictory impulses – prurience, indignation, 'desire to see', and fear of emasculation.

Wycherley's brief affair with the Duchess of Cleveland grew directly from his début as a dramatist and his self-production as the new wit of the Town. The obvious dangers of cuckolding the sovereign led both parties to adopt disguises, maintaining the self-conscious theatricality that had initiated their union. In his first comedy *Love in a Wood*, generally known by its subtitle *St James's Park*, Wycherley had caught the duchess's attention by representing the carnivalesque social mingling of that zone of fashionable recreation, reflecting the ambiguities of the park back to an audience excited by her conspicuous attendance and encouragement of the play. Echoing (or anticipating) Rochester's notoriously obscene poem *A Ramble in Saint James's Parke*, Ranger proposes 'a Ramble' to the park in search of sexual 'Game', finding there a twilight zone where 'no woman's modest', where (by a double paradox) a man 'may bring his bashful Wench, and not have her put out of countenance by the impudent honest women of the Town' (I.ii.24, II.i.32). The park thus becomes a dizzying realm of misrule where *honestas* and courtesan-values are thoroughly intermingled. On a later visit the predatory widow Lady Flippant, herself an amphibious Horner-in-reverse who pretends to be a libertine in order to snare a husband, peers through the 'mungril light' to discern figures from the lower depths – a 'Satyr', a 'drunken Scourer', a knight, 'Rag-women, and Synder-women' – picking over this great human refuse-heap for the scraps of pleasure she cannot find (v.i.101); she too is a 'scourer' in the double meaning of that word, a scavenger and a seeker of rough sex or festive-violent excitement. As in Rochester's poem, where rag-pickers and heiresses 'promiscuously swive' with lords and apprentices (chapter 4 above), the prowlers in the park typify the unstable mix of social castes in the Restoration culture of priapism. (Etherege, too, celebrates the polymorphous perversity of St James's Park when he shows the Rochester-style élite rubbing shoulders with distinctly lower-class gossip-mongers, who use whore-pamphlet slang like 'oylie Buttock' but who nevertheless seem intimately conversant with the celebrity affairs that constitute Etherege's plot.)[6] Wycherley's first play lays claim to a libertine space that uncannily mirrors the contemporary scene, and that immediately becomes the setting for a pornotopian episode in his own life.

One song from Wycherley's play in particular stuck in the Duchess of Cleveland's mind, and prompted the scenario for her seduction of the author. As she prepares to visit the park that gave the play its name, the pseudo-libertine Lady Flippant condemns marriage and asserts the superiority of bastardy – linking 'greatness' and bawdiness as the 1668 rioters had done, though to opposite effect:

> Great Wits and great Braves
> Have always a Punk to their Mother. (I.ii.31)

This gave Cleveland her cue to compliment and expropriate the dazzling new author by pretending to apply Lady Flippant's principle. In the very park where his comedy is set, she drives up to him and 'thrusting half her Body out of the Chariot, cry'd out aloud to him, *You*, Wycherley, *you are a Son of a Whore*, at the same time laughing aloud and heartily'. John Dennis, who records Wycherley's own narration of the seduction scene, brings out the paradox of inverted civility when he remarks 'you may be surpris'd at so strange a Greeting from one of the most beautiful and best bred Ladies in the World'. Count Lorenzo Magalotti, visiting England in 1668, could afford to be more direct about her body language. All English ladies carry themselves badly, but the duchess turns this to her 'advantage': 'not only in her carriage, but in every gesture of the arms and hands, in every expression of her face, in every glance, in every movement of her mouth, in every word, one recognizes shamelessness and whoredom' – *il puttanesimo*.[7]

The Duchess of Cleveland's inversionary gambit – acting the *grande dame* by simulating the railing bawd or wandering whore – led rapidly to a deeper involvement, which Wycherley surreptitiously acknowledged in his dedication when *St James's Park* was published (a venture encouraged by her evident approval). Like the park itself, however, this dedication turns out to be a zone of ambiguity between lewd insult and gallant compliment. The *double entendre* is finely balanced: the repeated 'Favours' *could* refer only to her literary patronage; 'Generosity in your Actions' does not *necessarily* evoke her ability to perform the 'tricks of Aretin' that Pepys dreamed he enjoyed with her; 'obliging all the world' *might* just be an innocent tribute, if one suppresses all memory of the lampoons passed around in the circles that Wycherley was now entering. (The Court ballad 'Signor Dildo' attacks Cleveland as a Messalina-figure who 'Has Swallow'd more Pricks than the Ocean has Sand'.) Eroticizing the patronage relation need not dissolve it into sexual slur or libertine boasting, but may simply acknowledge in gallant-courtly language the power that puts the royal mistress in a position to receive dedications. Dryden's address 'To the Lady Castlemaine, upon her Incouraging his First Play', as James Winn points out, plays on the conventions of gender and the erotic imagery appropriate when addressing Court ladies: his Muse is cast upon her 'Hospitable Coast' and finds 'favour' there; Dryden will live 'more happy' because of her 'Pity'.[8] But in the *St James's Park* dedication Wycherley tips the balance decisively towards insult, dangerously rupturing the gallant pretence. After boasting of her ambiguous 'favours' he aligns himself with the vigilante apprentices and satirists, equating his address with the mock-petitions that first identified Castlemaine as the head of the common prostitutes: 'your Grace will be hereafter as much pester'd with such scurvy Offerings as this, Poems, Panegyricks, and the like, as you are now with Petitions' (7).

When he published *The Plain-Dealer* six years later, Wycherley chose to intensify his identification with the whore-petition and advertise his break with female patronage. His dramatic oeuvre, which opens with the double-dealing dedication to the royal mistress that articulates his sexual and dramaturgic apprenticeship, closes with the plain-dealing and patently scurrilous dedication of his fourth and last play, to the procuress 'Lady' Bennett. Casting himself as the poor whoremonger, if not actually the prostitute-author, he develops a full-blown 'Libertine Libell' from his earlier allusion to the mock-deferential 'Petition'; like that petition, he juxtaposes two extremes – the working bawd and the powerful upper-class voluptuary – to suggest their affinity and to invert the hierarchy of value that separates them. Mrs Bennett – given the familiar title 'Mother' by Radcliffe but promoted to greatness by Wycherley – had already been identified as 'a famous Strumpet' in 1660 (when Pepys is shocked to learn that she has procured a shop-girl whom he himself had fancied), and she supplies a burlesque rhyme in Butler's tribute to the sexual drive:

> [Love] mounted *Synod-men* and rode 'em
> To *Durty-lane*, and *little-Sodom*;
> Made 'em Corvet, like *Spanish* Jenets
> And take the Ring at Madam ------.

By 1668 she had become a focus of erotic and literary improvisation among the Wits. Pepys indulged in painfully exciting gossip about the 'Ballum Rankum' or nude dancing that she supposedly organized for the Court, inventing a new kind of 'mad trick' or erotic entertainment that would soon enter the vocabulary of masculine expertise. The Earl of Dorset devoted a full-length poetic narrative to Mrs Bennett and her service to the aristocracy: his mock-heroic *Battle of the Crabs* is set in the enchanted forest between her legs, where 'all the youth of England did repair / To take their pleasure and to ease their care'.[9]

This, then, is the august patroness whom Wycherley addresses in his last dedication, signing himself 'The Plain Dealer' and thereby confirm-ing the identity of character and authorial persona. In this savage attack on the hypocritical prudishness and sexual rapacity of great ladies, which repeats almost verbatim the snarling misogyny of Horner in *The Country-Wife* and Manly's attacks on Olivia in *The Plain-Dealer* itself, Wycherley openly adopts the prurient-aggressive unmasking vigilantism he con-cealed before. His version of *pornographia* uses wit, irony and literary allusion rather than rotten eggs or penknives, but it still 'marks' the common whore to convey a larger disgust at feminized authority. By retrospective parallelism, the newly promoted 'Lady' Bennett is associated with the indecently elevated duchess, branded as the sovereign whore ever since Damaris Page and Madam Cresswell claimed her protection in the petitions of 1668.

Wycherley's bawd-dedication gathers together the various threads of pornotropic discourse, both Continental and English, and weaves them into a noose for his ex-mistress. Like the bawdy-house rioters of 1668, he transfers his arousal and resentment from the Aretinesque substratum to the newly emergent sexual agency of upper-class women. Editors have noted extensive borrowing from Montaigne's 'Sur des Vers de Virgile', without identifying this as Montaigne's most licentious essay, in which not only the content but the author's self-presentation becomes intimately sexual; his other essays only reached the ladies' public rooms, but 'ce chapitre me fera du cabinet'. Wycherley transposes this topos to the milieu of prostitution, substituting Lady Bennett's procuring skill (already attested by Pepys) for the penetrative action of his own writing: 'lest the Chambermaid and the Page . . . cou'd gain no further admittance for [this Play], than to their Ladies Lobbies or outward Rooms, take it into your care and protection; for, by your recommendation and procurement, it may have the honour to get into their Closets'. This pun on 'procurement' allows him to belittle the experience of depending on a powerful lady to launch his literary career. When he promises to blazon Bennett's achievements in 'the Annals of our British Love', he alludes not just to the 1672 *Annals of Love* but to the far more scandalous *Histoire Amoureuse des Gaules*, 'the Loves of *France*' (as Harriet calls it in Etherege's *Man of Mode*) in which Bussy-Rabutin catalogues the sexual adventures of fellow-aristocrats like the comtesse d'Olonne; again the bawd, raised to the status of a national institution, stands in for the excesses of the great lady.[10] His mock-praise derives of course from the 1668 *Poor-Whores Petition* to Lady Castlemaine – whose irony and anti-Whitehall polemic Wycherley continues in poems like the heroic epistle 'To the Honour of Pimps and Pimping, dedicated to the Court' (*Works*, III.50–3) – and his proposal that poets should gain free admission to the brothel echoes the 1672 whore-petition's offer of reduced prices for the apprentices.

Wycherley's most (im)pertinent source, however, is Pallavicino's *La retorica delle puttane*, reissued as recently as 1673. That work was likewise dedicated in mock-respect to 'the most famous Courtesans', begins with a triple parallel of text, painting, and sexual career, praises the honour of a profession officially permitted 'in the best governed and most Catholic cities', and rises to an impudent proposal tinged with blackmail: in exchange for favourable literary treatment, the author should be admitted to the choicest morsels of pleasure. (In Wycherley's metatheatrical version, Pallavicino's request to 'have free entry to [your] pleasures without charge' becomes the principle that 'a Poet ought to be as free of your Houses, as of the Play-houses'.)[11] Each of these borrowings imparts a distinctive Wycherleyan twist, absolving the real courtesan and intensifying the focus on upper-class transgression. A superficially similar mock-dedication, that of *Holborn-Drollery* (1672), addresses the respectable women who take the air in Gray's Inn Walks, breaks off to vituperate the whores, and then returns to the fine ladies with elaborate protests that the digression had nothing to do with them (f. A5); Wycherley does exactly the reverse.

Apart from signalling his own expertise in the libertine subculture, Wycherley's adaptation of the whore-petition serves to attack the 'lewd Quality' in general and the royal mistress in particular. Certainly he targets the false honour of ladies less flamboyant (and less protected) than the Duchess of Cleveland, in the mocking tone already used by Horner to denounce the faux-respectable wives who hurry to enjoy his favours once his reputation as a eunuch has been established: 'By that Mask of modesty which Women wear promiscuously in publick, they are all alike, and you can no more know a kept Wench from a Woman of Honour by her looks than by her Dress; [Women of Quality have] their false Modesty, as well as their false Jewels, and you must no more suspect their Countenances for counterfeit than their Pendants.'[12] Wycherley's genteel charivari breaks down their façades and hoists up their underwear, dragging into the light secret vices that he himself (and his horn-waving *alter ego*) seems proud to share. But his bitter drollery also encompasses those like the duchess herself who avow their desire openly, who disturb the clear hierarchy of active-male and passive-female by taking the initiative. In the treason trial that followed the 1668 bawdy-house riots, we recall, one apprentice-defendant won a sympathetic discharge by telling how 'a Whore clapped hands on me, and I wrung my self from her' (chapter 5, n. 24 above). In his dedications Wycherley 'wrings himself' away from dependency, from the peculiar anxieties of being defined as a male sexual toy, from the taxing power-figure who patronized his masculinity as well as his career as a dramatist.

The sexual subject of the royal mistress had been described as a eunuch, a stallion, a jumped-up footman, a well-muscled but headless statue (as in Marvell's *Last Instructions*). Later critics cite Wycherley as the quintessence of secure male identity ('every Syllable, every Thought is masculine'), but at the time of his conquest by the Duchess of Cleveland his 'masculinity' was seen as undermining the aspiring writer's class status and free agency. One lampoon describes how Cleveland, bored by her current lover John Churchill, trudged down to the Temple 'Where brawny Wycherley lay, / Who performed the part of a drudge'. 'Brawny' has sometimes been taken as a compliment, the equivalent of Dryden's 'Manly Wycherley', but Rochester allows us to see its true connotation; in *Tunbridge Wells* it is the bullies Cuffe and Kick who display 'brawny back, and leggs, and Potent Prick', and in *A Ramble in Saint James's Parke* Corinna draws gallons of sperm 'from *Porters Backs* and *Foot-mens Brawn*'. (Mary Knight, who advised Cleveland in another Rochester lampoon to buy porters' pricks by the dozen rather than waste her money on Churchill, evidently played the role of go-between in the affair with Wycherley.) Wycherley's musculature allies him with those hefty working-class studs who crowd the sexual lampoons, particularly those directed against the supposedly insatiable duchess. From the point of view of Rochester, the virile but unknown poet would be only one of 'a dozen of Pricks', detachable, collectable, but essentially disposable. Satire casts Wycherley as a 'brawny' menial, valued only as meat, and even as a 'he-whore'.[13] By taking liberties in his dedications he tries to regain his own freedom of self-definition, though his brooding and petulant tone reveals him still obsessed with the betraying, consuming, all-powerful 'Jilt'.

Female erotic predation runs as a leitmotif throughout Wycherley's work, presented sometimes in a carnivalesque world-upside-down spirit, sometimes in the more strained and violent tone associated with Horner. In the burlesque *Hero and Leander*, for example, the heroine declares that

> When Men are turn'd to Women, Women then
> May without shame (I take it) turn to Men ...
> Alas when I'm on fire, I must cry out
> For quenching Engine of the largest spoute,

and then assaults Leander 'like a *Bully*' – though she still pleads with him to be careful of 'her Honour's Secret'.[14] In *The Country-Wife*, though Horner maintains his eunuch-disguise to pursue fresh sexual game, he seems equally concerned to escape the attentions of 'bullying' women who take the active role, like Hero: his new reputation for impotence will 'rid' him of 'the most insatiable sorts of Duns, that invade our Lodgings in a morning', and he is clearly still 'afraid' of visits by 'unbelieving Sisters of my former acquaintance, who' (not trusting to the carefully-engineered rumour) 'expect their sense shou'd be satisfy'd of the falsity of the report' (I.i.250, 253). (Horner makes these admissions, not in the company of those he wishes to dupe, but alone with his accomplice the quack-doctor.) In Wycherley's earlier comedy *The Gentleman Dancing-Master* two wandering whores or 'midnight Ramblers' terrorize the West End, striking more fear into the men than 'Bailiffs, Pursevants, or a City-Constable'; now 'the Women hunt out the men', and it is the trembling Monsieur who begs *them* to protect his 'honour'. Flounce and Flirt burst into private lodgings and fashionable restaurants, expertly identifying the worn-out lechers ('the hot Service you have been in formerly, makes you unfit for ours now') and wolfing down new customers with the same fresh appetite that they bring to the menu: 'Some young Rabits, I love Rabits.'[15] These are presumably the kind of 'Sisters' that Horner wants to be rid of, but his venture into high society exposes him to a more cannibalistic version of their appetite; when Lady Fidget declares that 'we think wildness in a man, as desirable a quality, as in a Duck, or Rabbet', she means in the soup. When Lady Fidget was maintaining her virtuous front earlier in the play she expressed contempt for great ladies who buy the services of a lower-class male lover, like lords 'keeping little Play-house Crea-tures' – a category that by implication includes the budding dramatist in need of 'favours' – but now she reveals her expertise as consumer and connoisseur (II.i.275, V.iv.343).

In Wycherley's *Plain-Dealer* this predatory theme takes on a darker tone. Olivia's Amazonian aggression in the bedroom-scene with Fidelia is obviously meant to be repulsive: Manly breaks out with the inelegant and even childish exclamation 'Wuh, she makes Love like a Devil in a Play', and Fidelia recoils so strongly that Olivia asks 'what, are you afraid of the fierceness of my Love?' (IV.ii.475). The dedication to Lady Bennett brings to a head these diatribes against imperious, devouring, castrating *femmes fortes*. Fine ladies now hate the penetrating wit of 'a Man that knows 'em' – that is, a man who strips them bare like Aretino and snarls at them like Horner – and instead 'must have a blind easie Fool' (370). Like 'the *Scythian* Women of old', Manly/Wycherley rages on, they 'must baffle a Man, and put out his Eyes, ere they will lye with him, and then too, like Thieves, when they have plunder'd and stript a Man, leave him'.

This melodramatic portrayal of female initiative – shared by Horner and Wycherley – evidently reenacts the author's own impressions of the senior mistress of England. The Duchess of Cleveland evokes the 'Scythian women of old' because she comes already marked as a devourer and dismemberer, depriving apprentices of their testicles and reducing the reverend bishop to 'a Turkish eunuch'. The cutting-off of Wycherley's affair may well have been as abrupt as its beginning, to judge by the final self-pitying 'leave him' of the *Plain-Dealer* dedication (conspicuously added to his source in Montaigne). If we look for parallels in his only other dedication, to the duchess herself, there too he may hint at her over-masculine sexual demeanour, praising her – in a context that encourages us to look for *double entendre* – for 'Spirit, Wit, and Judgment, and all other qualifications which fit Hero's to command' (7). (A similar moment in Dryden's address to Cleveland may allude to her taking the husband's role in the pseudo-lesbian wedding-ceremony she performed with Frances Stuart.)[16] Her first attack, 'thrusting half her Body out of the Chariot' and bawling out her insulting praise, confounded the young wit by confounding the features of a great lady and a London bully or 'dismembring' whore. Such role-reversal could be taken as a piquant variation in the game of sex, as it is in *L'Escole des filles*, but to the aristocratic libertine it could also inspire disgust and dread. When women become 'bullies', as Wycherley's Hero explains only half-jokingly, 'men are turned to women'. As that arch-rioter the Earl of Dorset put it, revealing the transgressor's deep commitment to traditional sexual politics, 'Nature's turned when women woo; / We hate in them what we should do' (*Poems*, 34). Incongruous as it may seem, the lord and the apprentice – the two extremes of riot culture – share a common concern, to discipline what they perceive as the inordinate powers of the 'new Whore of State'.

But if Wycherley's affair with the 'State' courtesan made him a whore himself – as the contemporary lampoon cruelly hinted – it also served to lubricate access to the homosocial world of the Court Wits. The Duchess of Cleveland was both a direct source of 'favours' and a gateway to élite male society, albeit a dangerous one since inner circles are frequently vicious and since the homosocial often boiled over into avowed passion. (When Sedley and Dorset staged their nudist performance on the balcony of the Cock Tavern, Pepys reports them 'acting all the postures of lust and buggery that could be imagined', adding 'that buggery is now almost grown as common among our gallants as in Italy, and that the very pages of the town begin to complain of their masters for it'.)[17]

When the powerful but unstable Duke of Buckingham, sexually obsessed with his cousin Cleveland and perpetually frustrated by her rejection of him, flew into a jealous fit and threatened to 'ruine' the young poet, Wycherley saved his own skin by gaining admission to the duke's company (through the intercession of Rochester and Sedley) and seducing him with a display of physical and mental talent. Buckingham 'was as much in love with Wit, as he was with his Kinswoman' Cleveland, who had evidently recommended her literary and erotic protégé; 'after Supper Mr *Wycherley*, who was then in the Height of his Vigor both of Body and Mind, thought himself oblig'd to exert himself, and the Duke was charm'd to that degree, that he cry'd out in a Transport, *By G----- my Cousin is in the right of it.*' The duchess's taste in men is rapturously confirmed. What exactly is this 'Vigor of Body' that brought Buckingham to his moment of 'Transport'? John Dennis (who narrates the episode in a letter to a gentleman friend) frequently uses the word to mean sexual potency, and Buckingham's reputation for heterosexual and homosexual sodomy not only circulated in lampoons, but was presented as evidence in a legal indictment – an astonishing proceeding against such a senior aristocrat, and an indignity that his father, James I's favourite, never had to undergo.[18] (Buckingham's lover was reputedly Edward Kynaston, last of the boy actors and for Pepys 'the loveliest lady that ever I saw in my life', who 'touched the audience more sensibly' than any actress and who grew up to play Harcourt in *The Country-Wife* and Freeman in *The Plain-Dealer*.) Buckingham's climactic exclamation, we should recall, endorsed the judgement not of the men who had recommended Wycherley but of 'my cousin' Cleveland, who had certainly tasted his physical charms. This metamorphic, theatrical milieu transforms the budding playwright's petition for acceptance into an act of seduction.

2 . 'LIKE A RUDE ROARING HECTOR IN THE STREETS':
WYCHERLEY, ROCHESTER, AND THE AESTHETICS
OF LIBERTINE AGGRESSION

In a dream that reveals how far libertinism worked its way through the 'pales and partitions' of respectable culture, Swift once dreamed of being forced to attend a secular sermon in his own cathedral; the usurping preacher was Viscount Bolingbroke, the most rakish of Swift's personal friends, and the words of the sermon came from 'the plays of Mr Wycherley'.[19] Swift's subconscious chose this ambiguous placing well, because Wycherley does indeed straddle the line that separates high from low discourse, canonical wit from scandalous 'bawdery and drollery'. Among the official institutions of Restoration London, the theatre is the most contaminated with 'vagabond lust', and among the Wits who wrote for the theatre in the 1670s, Wycherley's pen does the most to adulterate it. (It is Wycherley's Horner who first mentions *L'Escole des filles* on stage, propagating in mixed company the name of the book that Pepys was ashamed to read, and his subsequent seduction of the respectable ladies he taunts confirms everything that the French pornographic text says about married women.) To borrow the terms of the drinking ritual that Wycherley himself recorded for posterity, he infuses the 'Zesto' of illicit sexuality through the 'Filtre' of public decorum.

Wycherley's power derives from the controlled eruption of the disreputable. (Interestingly, he had in fact received the politest education of any Restoration author, sent at fourteen to be polished in the very heart of *préciosité* and refined breeding, where Julie de Montausier continued the tradition of the *salon* created by her mother Mme de Rambouillet.)[20] As we saw in section 1, the dedication of his first play *St James's Park* shatters the ostensibly respectful surface of the address to Lady Castlemaine by evoking the mock-petitions that so infuriated her, aligning his own polite discourse with the abject genre of the whore-pamphlet and the violent insurrection of the apprentices; the dedication of his last play turns plain dealing into pure *pornographia*, as he 'infiltrates' the *Retorica delle puttane* into his eulogy of the great London bawd. The prologue to *The Country-Wife* makes these 'low' allegiances playfully explicit, comparing the resilient poet to a 'Bully' or street fighter, to Kastril the Jonsonian 'roaring boy', and to the modern upper-class hooligan who dares to 'Hector with the Age' (245). And from the first scene, the satirical-priapic Horner assumes the 'barking' posture of the dog-perversion, prime exhibit of *The Wandring Whore*, *Erotopolis*, and *Venice Preserved* (chapter 4 above); assuming a misogynist pose for strategic purposes, he snarls at his lady visitors like the sexually damaged client nipping at whores from below the table.

Horner adopts this aggressive, hypermasculine manner to convince bystanders that he really has lost his virility in a surgical accident – no normal Don Juan would abandon *politesse* and 'ruin himself' with the ladies – but Wycherley clearly identified with it and developed it still further in the Plain-Dealer persona Manly, increasingly inseparable from himself. It is as Manly that he signs the dedication to Lady Bennett, and this apparently all-pervasive stance led Dryden to compliment 'The Satire, Wit, and Strength of Manly *Witcherly*' and Lord Lansdowne to remark that in his writing 'every Syllable, every Thought is masculine'. Wycherley would remain locked in the snarling posture for the rest of his life, attacking 'mercenary' women and 'the worst sort of Jilts, Wives' with the tenacity of a mastiff or an enraged apprentice.[21] Horner's simulation of overdone masculine aggression, fundamentally at odds with polite society and the stylized gallantry that Wycherley himself learned in the French *salon*, rapidly becomes a touchstone of 'plain-dealing' realism. Far from criticizing the solitary snarler, the comic dénouement of *The Country-Wife* rewards him as a phallic hero, all the female characters (even the virtuous Alithea) joining in a ring to perjure themselves on his behalf, confirming his false eunuch façade and thus protecting his sexual game. If the first scene of the play corresponds to the 'barking' perversion in *The Wandring Whore*, then this last scene resembles another tableau from the whore-pamphlets, in which the master of the Prick Office 'lyes naked upon his bed' and the 'females do every one of them buss the end of his Trapstick'. And Horner's response recalls yet a third scene of low bawdy transposed to a high place. To celebrate his triumph, Wycherley's bachelor-rake does exactly what his monarch did at the first New Year's ball after his marriage: in the presence of various husbands and mistresses, he calls for the violins to strike up the dance tune 'Cuckolds all a-row'.[22]

Throughout *The Country-Wife*, in fact, Wycherley enjoys experimenting with the boundaries and partitions of decorum, mingling discursive levels and conjuring up the scandalous association of words and places. The miniature drama of the 'Filtre' is reenacted in these covert evocations of the lower stratum. So when Horner announces his scheme to discover those women who are sexually 'right' beneath the façade of 'civil' sexiness, he picks up the kind of vagabond slang that appears in *Holborn-Drollery* or the joke-books of Richard Head ('as right as my Leg, and as good as ever twang'd'). His assumption of the sexual–medical role suggests the aphrodisiacs, universal solvents, and venereal cures promoted by back-street pharmacy, already a topic of upper-class wit when Sedley, drunk and naked on the balcony of the Cock Tavern, pretended to be a mountebank selling 'a pouder that should make all the cunts in town run after him'.[23] Horner in effect announces he has that powder, when he assures the quack-doctor and the audience that his eunuch-trick will make him the sexual passe-partout of the Town.

Other characters likewise act as conduits for clandestine *pornographia*. When the ugly cuckold Pinchwife compares marriage to whoring, reducing both to the simplest cash-for-sex transaction, he echoes the crude but effective reductionism of the whore-pamphlets: ''tis customary here to receive mony with wives . . . but give mony for wenches, . . . what? must *matrimony* be made a *matter* of *mony* where there's a *dainty Cunny?*' (*Wandring Whore* V.3); 'I must give *Sparkish* to morrow five thousand pound to lye with my Sister . . . we have as much a doe to get people to lye with our Sisters, as to keep 'em from lying with our Wives' (*CW* I.i.260, V.i.334). The raw exchanges between Pinchwife and Horner, as the deluded husband hands over his wife in disguise –

MR PIN.   I will not be a Cuckold I say, there will be danger in making me a Cuckold.
HOR.   Why, wert thou not well cur'd of thy last clap? (IV.iii.325)

remind us of the transfer of diseased sexual partners between the Earl of Southesk and the Duke of York, a silent pun made explicit in the last act, when Pinchwife grimly jests about what his wife might have 'communicated' (V.iv.349). Even Harcourt, the most honourable young man in the play, borrows from filthy texts like *L'Escole des filles* and *Newes from the New Exchange*, to shame the 'commonwealth of ladies'. In a scene that takes place in the fashionably sexy New Exchange, he remarks of Alithea (the most honourable woman in the comedy, only to be won on strict matrimonial terms) that 'all Women are like these of the *Exchange*', lying to 'their fond Customers' in order to 'enhance the price of their commodities' (III.ii.289). This coarse allusion exploits the ambiguity of the place in the same vein as those quasi-pornographic pamphlets (printed in the same year as *The Country-Wife*) that expound the 'character of the Exchange-wench'; as we know from *The Wandring Whore* and from Wycherley's own lewd verse, the fancy word 'commodity' served as slang for the vagina.[24] Harcourt here breaks down, not only the status-barrier between the highest and the lowest form of retail, but also the conceptual barrier between the virtuous Alithea and the prostitute. At the climax of the play, Harcourt will turn away from this rakish misogyny, and win Alithea, when he refuses to believe the evidence of her apparent whoredom (V.iv.347). In this scene of worldly seduction, however, he remains loyal to the cynicism of the Wits, and to the secret sexual language passed round in illegal pamphlets and unprintable lampoons.

  Throughout the play, Alithea tries to disprove the paranoia of her brother Pinchwife by combining worldly urbanity and innocence, love of the 'Exchange' and refusal to compromise her rectitude. But though she aspired to move freely in this world of masculine 'Wit' while remaining untainted by its destructive view of women, her protestations of purity themselves depend on her expertise in the literature of scandal. In her first conversation with Harcourt, for example, she asks rhetorically 'who boasts of any intrigue with me? what Lampoon has made my name notorious?' (II.i.267). Nobody has yet launched on her the violent abuse that bespattered the royal mistress, the powerful courtesan, or the 'Exchange-wench'. Alithea must feel particularly vulnerable, then, when Harcourt sadistically reminds her that her 'reputation', and thus her survival, depends not on her own integrity but on the estimation of men who think as he does; if she married the foolish Sparkish to honour a contractual obligation, she 'wou'd be thought in necessity for a cloak' (272). Public opinion would proclaim her marriage a mere cover-up for an unwanted pregnancy, sharing the cynicism of the most obscene verses and the most malicious gossip-pamphlets. The New Exchange prompts Harcourt to reiterate and generalize these sentiments, citing directly from the scandalous text that Horner had previously mentioned as a brutal affront to the ladies: *L'Escole des filles* arranges a 'cloak' marriage for the lascivious heroine, philosophizing that unmarried girls live in constant fear of pregnancy and ruin but a husband 'sert de couverture à tout'.[25] Though Alithea (whose name means 'Truth') survives these accusations against her, Harcourt's generalization about the New Exchange holds true for the rest of the world depicted within the comedy. His declaration that 'all Women' seek only to enhance their commodities foreshadows the more brutal maxim that Horner will draw from his encounter with Lady Fidget and her friends: mocking rather than celebrating their sexual acquiescence, he observes to their faces 'that great Ladies, like great Merchants, set but the higher prices upon what they have' (V.iv.344).

We must of course recognize Wycherley's ironic distance, dramatic irony, and playful metatheatricality: Harcourt's generosity eventually redeems the idea of Romance from the deluge of libertinism that he himself had augmented; Pinchwife's brutish clarity is muddied by his idiocy; prologues and dedications require a certain tongue-in-cheek performativity. When the *Country-Wife* prologue equates the poet with the young street bully ('trembling' with stage-fright so all the readier to draw his sword), his facetious exaggeration expresses the love–hate relationship between the playwright and the rowdy, critical first-night audience, while his pose as aggressive-lecherous apprentice whoremonger in the *Plain-Dealer* dedication plays a similar game between the author and his reader. Immediately after the bully image in the prologue to *The Country-Wife* the actor pretends to set the hectoring author aside and 'submits' the entire project – cast, text, and playwright – to the judgement and to the erotic invasion of the Pit; in the auditorium as in the dressing-room,

> We patiently, you see, give up to you
> Our Poets, Virgins, nay our Matrons too. (246)

The Sons of Belial are offered 'Matrons', as in *Paradise Lost*, but they are also given the chance for 'worse rape'; the poet as 'Brawny' street fighter gives way to the poet as public catamite, just as available as the actresses.

It may be true that Wycherley repudiates the more obvious resemblances between wit and hypermasculine hooliganism by association with absurd characters such as Pinchwife or Dapperwit. Nevertheless, his plain-dealing postures suggest a covert sympathy with the violence of libertine extremism. He may ridicule the identification of window-smashing and wit by putting it into the mouth of fops like Novel or Dapperwit, but elsewhere he seems more indulgent towards this punitive form of masculine play. The strongest attacks on it are given to discredited female characters, turning condemnation into sly celebration: it is the City bawd Mrs Joyner who exclaims 'what are Wits? but contemners of Matrons, Seducers or Defamers of married Women, and Deflourers of helpless Virgins, even in the Streets, upon the very Bulks; Affronters of midnight Magistracy, and Breakers of Windows in a word.' *The Gentleman Dancing-Master*, which starts with a lightly menacing reminder of the proximity of Bridewell, ends with the whore/actress Flirt welcoming the unfashionable cits of Lombard Street as lovers because 'You ne're will break our Windows.'[26] Again, we can assume that anything the City abjures would be cheered on by the modish Town audience.

Manly's excessive roughness in *The Plain-Dealer* (closely related to Molière's *Misanthrope*) is explicitly compared to the 'Hectoring' of a riotous debauchee and to threatening the 'Windows' of a suburban mistress, but the person who makes this observation is the prudish and vicious Olivia. (Manly himself, interestingly, fears that his bitter outbursts might make him sound like 'a bilk'd Whore' railing at her cheating customer (II.i.420).) Even more than Horner's aggressive unmasking, the Plain-Dealer's 'manliness' is endorsed by the play's conclusion, which rewards him with a true love (Fidelia) and a true friend (Freeman) to replace the hypocritical Olivia and Vernish. Manly expresses himself with unusual tenderness to the man he thinks is true – 'Nay, here is a Friend indeed; and he that has him in his arms, can know no wants. [*Embraces* Vernish]' – though by the end of the play he has transferred this trusting affection from Vernish to Freeman, played by the glamorous transgendered actor Edward Kynaston. Significantly this 'free man', who becomes the true moral touchstone of the drama, describes himself as 'an old Scowrer' – upper-class slang for the violent rake – who 'can naturally beat up a Wenches quarters that won't be civil'. Freeman enjoys, and polices, the circumscribed 'Liberty of Venus' defined in the anti-coffee petitions. A woman's refusal to be 'civil' in the sexual sense gives the élite male the 'freedom' to assault her uncivilly, and following this logic he 'naturally' asks his friend Manly, when Olivia jilts him, 'Shan't we break her Windows too?' He does gently rebuke Manly in his final 'plain-dealing' diagnosis: 'most of our quarrels to the World, are just such as we have to a handsome Woman – only because we cannot enjoy her, as we wou'd do.'[27] But his behaviour, his observations, and his comradely 'we' clearly sympathize with this release of masculine frustration through violence, provided it is channelled within the festive-aggressive rituals of aristocratic 'Scowring'.

Even direct physical assaults like nose-slitting and face-slashing, the most violent and least festive of the 'Liberties of Venus', seem to be treated ambivalently in Wycherley's comedies. Manly in *The Plain-Dealer* feels the urge to kiss his betrayer's lips 'and then tear off with my teeth, grind 'em into mammocks, and spit 'em into her Cuckolds face' (IV.i.460), a powerful echo of *Othello* with the significant difference that the object is the flagrant Olivia rather than the innocent Desdemona. In *The Country-Wife* such impulses are confined to the impotent bullying of Pinchwife, whose jealous outbursts fuse together the associations of pen, sword, pen-knife, and penis: when he forces Margery to write Horner a rejection-letter, he snarls 'Write as I bid you, or I will write Whore with this Penknife in your Face', and repeats his threat to 'spoil thy writing with this [*Holds up the penknife*]'; in his final torment, outplotted by Margery and the pro-Horner confederacy of women, he exclaims 'I will never hear woman again, but make 'em all silent, thus— *Offers to draw upon his Wife.*'[28] Here Wycherley continues a Jonsonian tradition – the sword-wielding husband in *Volpone* threatens to proclaim his wife a 'strumpet' and 'slit thy nose, / Like a raw rotchet' (III.vii.80), ironically because she *refuses* to prostitute herself to Volpone – and at the same time touches upon contemporary affairs of state. Horrifying as it seems, the threat to mutilate the alleged whore or her male accomplice, to deface the defamer of one's honour and 'mark' the sexual transgressor, was still relatively common in the domestic and political arena. Elizabeth Pepys twice promises to slit the nose of Deborah Willet, the hired companion fondled by her husband, and immediately invents the verbal equivalent of this gesture, enacting her anger on her ex-employee's social body rather than in the flesh: she forces the craven Pepys to write 'Deb' a letter in which he calls her 'whore'. Sir William Coventry, offended at Buckingham for mocking him in a scene of *The Country Gentleman*, passed on a message to the actor (not to the noble author) 'that he would cause his nose to be cut', as if public picturing demanded an equally visible retribution.[29]

By far the most dramatic of these aggressive moments involved – unsurprisingly – the royal mistresses, the fear of absolutism, the ambiguity of the theatre, the violence of the festive season, and the limits of Restoration (in)decorum. When Sir John Coventry proposed a tax on playhouses, the king's spokesmen asserted that 'the players were the king's servants, and a part of his pleasure', consequently exempt from jurisdiction and taxation; when Coventry then asked in the Commons 'whether did the king's pleasure lie among the men or the women that acted', the king (already the father of ten acknowledged bastards by five different mothers) grew furious at this evidence that gossip about his Court amours had once again entered oppositional discourse. (This was Christmas 1670, after a decade in which his private parts had been in everybody's mouth, an open secret at once obvious and unmentionable.) At Nell Gwyn's instigation (according to the inevitable lampoon) the unruly member was properly defaced: following the king's orders, twenty-five armed men from Monmouth's guard ambushed him outside his lodgings, 'threw him down, and with a Knife cut off almost all the End of his Nose'.[30] The anointed sovereign, already commander of a judicial system that could discipline his subjects by branding the cheek and mutilating the nose and ears, here chooses to mark his mistress's enemy the way bullies mark the faces of *puttane errante*; one lampoonist appropriately labels his guards 'bravos' and another calls them 'Hectors', pouring scorn on soldiers who would 'brandish your knives at the word of a strumpet' and allow Charles to 'prostitute' them to Nell's 'commands'. (As we saw in Mitelli's etching (fig. 3 above), the shaming knife-attack also humiliates the assailant, who muffles himself like a common thief.) Pinchwife – a former whoremaster and now a certified cuckold, as Wycherley knew Charles II to be – 'brandishes his knife' against the wife he imagines to be a whore, but in so doing he replicates those threats in miniature that might have been performed on the author himself, whose affair with the duchess made him both a 'horner' and a 'he-whore'.

Critics have noted the image of frustrated authorship in these moments of violent *pornographia*, the travesty of Othello's 'fair paper . . . to write Whore upon' (though Pinchwife's threat to write 'in' the face suggests the more disturbing image of inscription-carving). Margery is learning town wit, switching letters and writing her own sexual plot over his, and he responds in this blundering fashion, entirely lacking in 'genteel gaity of humour' or the *politesse* that Wycherley himself grew up in. Clumsy and gauche as they are, however, these gestures essentially resemble and cohere with those of the protagonist and the author, who rewrite the country wife as 'right' for adultery and rip away the mask of virtue from the City ladies. Pinchwife's violence combines two specific forms of libertine re-scripting, in fact. He offers to do to Margery what Charles II did to Sir John Coventry, using the aggression of a London bully or inflamed apprentice to achieve the same graphic results as the judicial process, which slit the nostrils of forgers and, quite literally, inscribed the initials of the crime on the face of the criminal. And he proposes a twisted version of the seductive beauty celebrated at Court, whose 'credentials' are clearly 'written in her face'. By writing *Whore* he would do in the flesh what another elder does to his daughter in words, in a play acted in the same year as *The Country-Wife* and on the same stage: he labels her 'wandering Whore!' or rewrites her as *La puttana errante*.[31] How is this different, finally, from Horner's successful endeavour to rewrite Lady Fidget and her circle as *L'Escole des filles*, or Wycherley's own redefinition of female virtue and female patronage as a *retorica delle puttane?*

Wycherley's friend and patron the Earl of Rochester embodied all the parts in the drama of fleshly insurrection, carnivalesque 'riot', inverted civility, and coercive freedom. In his actions, in his carefully crafted but seemingly improvised poetry, and in anecdotal representations, Rochester becomes the Sir Frederick Frolick of the 1670s, the true child of the Restoration. Gilbert Burnet concluded from long conversations that, even at the age of thirteen, the 'unregulated' euphoria of 1660 'produced some of its ill effects on him: he began to love these disorders too much' (*RCH*, 48). Offspring of a devout mother and an absentee father, one of Charles's closest aides who went into exile and died in 1658, Rochester was in effect adopted by the king (who generally acted as a rakish companion rather than as the patriarchal authority he craved). According to the neoclassical critic Thomas Rymer, he was 'loose from all Discipline' in a Court that only valued poetry if it was 'notably flourish'd with Ribaldry and Debauch', and 'he found no Body of Quality or Severity so much above him, to challenge a Deference' – a phrase that applies equally to his unrevised drafts and his intemperate behaviour (*RCH*, 166–7). Dryden's *Essay of Dramatick Poesie* had coupled 'wilde debaucheries and quickness of wit in reparties' as the quintessential marks of 'the conversation of Gentlemen', in drama as in life (xvii.56), and Rochester exploited this combination of talents to the maximum. But if Rochester's 'extravagance' (as Burnet put it) leads him to perform the role of the bawdy-house rioter – inventing violent 'Frollicks' (*RCH*, 51), attacking the royal mistresses and their fumbling master in the lewdest possible lampoons – he also identifies with the whore herself, giving a new twist to *pornographia*.

Rochester compares authors to courtesans quite sympathetically, in first-person satire and in speeches made for agreeable female personae who express much of his own mind. In the *Satyr against Mankind* his protests that 'Witts are treated just like common Whores, / First they're enjoy'd and then kickt out of doors', reflect upon his own relation to Charles II, who alternately encouraged and banished him from Court because of his outrageous sexual-political lampoons. In a prologue written for a private performance in the Whitehall theatre, Lady Elizabeth Howard – speaking for the Court Beauties with the temporary freedom of an actress – declares that 'Poets share the Fate by which we fall, / When kindly we attempt to please you all'; even more directly, Rochester's character Artemiza acknowledges that 'Whore is scarce a more reproachfull name / Than Poetesse', but this recognition makes her all the more eager to write, like her author 'Pleas'd with the Contradiction and the Sin'.[32]

The 'contradictions' central to Rochester's life-as-work include the violent contrast between the 'lacy precision' of the verse and the obscenity of its content, and the 'disproportion' (as he called it in a famous letter) ''twixt our desires and what [Fate] has ordained to content them', between the quasi-sublime grandeur of erotic ambition and the gross anatomy of sex, which in effect replicates the disorderly lower stratum within the body itself.[33] The most 'extravagant' of his verbal frolics unsettle the élite reader by equating Court amours with what Milton had called 'vagabond lust without pale or partition'. The notorious portrait of Charles's sexuality in the 'sceptre lampoon', for example, actually provoked enough wrath in its subject – or at least in his French mistress the Duchess of Portsmouth – to guarantee the poet's temporary banishment. The opening lines seek to bond with the reader in jovial obscenity, using the alliterative catch-phrase common in drinking-rituals and whore-pamphlets: the phallic king, whose 'Scepter and his Prick are of a length', rules over an island famous 'For breeding the best Cunts in Christendome'. But celebration soon gives way to contempt, as in other seditious tavern conversations. These verses were 'by mistake' slipped into the monarch's pocket, only inches from the organ personified as 'the prowdest, peremptory Prick alive', a single-minded creature who will 'break through' all religion and law 'to make its way to Cunt', but who can dominate only in a world of carnivalesque misrule:

> For Princes Pricks like to Buffoones at Court
> Doe governe Us, because they make Us Sport.

Illogically, this all-governing organ is also so 'disobedient' that poor Nell Gwyn has to use 'Fingers, Mouth and Thighes' to raise it, while even in its regnant state the 'graceless Ballocks' weigh it down and render it ridiculous.[34]

In his 'pornographic' representation of the genitals, as in his satire against fools and false wits, Rochester identifies with the 'peremptory prick' but opposes 'ballocks' in every sense. The royal testicles, the locus of authority in a hereditary monarchy, become uncultured plebeians who destroy any pretension to the stylish eroticism and absolutist grandeur of Louis XIV – much as Charles's boyish participation in the violent 'Frolicks' of his courtiers precluded the aloof disapproval that Louis adopted towards outbreaks of sexual vandalism at the French court. Yet at the same time the gross lower stratum provides an image of the whole régime, a synecdoche of monarchic rule on both sides of the Channel: the warmongering Louis becomes 'the Hector of France' and the pacific whoremonger Charles 'the Cully of Britain'. Since *cully* in brothel slang means both the whore's bamboozled customer and her hired thug, Rochester has effectively assembled the entire cast of *The Wandring Whore* in a single insult.[35]

The festive-violent identification of sexuality with the buffoon and the bully seems endemic to the Court lampoon. The ballad 'Signior Dildo', variously attributed to Rochester, Dorset, and Sedley and evidently a collective improvisation, represents both the phallus and its rival simulacrum as swaggering Italian visitors who come to grief in the streets of London. Whoever wrote it clearly knew the Italian tradition of visualizing life-sized running phalluses in disreputable company, most vividly shown in fig. 5 above. In the English poem, however, the obscene parade turns Signior Dildo and Count Cazzo into victims rather than conquerors. Principally, of course, they are brought low by the insatiability of the Court ladies paraded in this verse charivari, most of them (not coincidentally) Catholic and associated with the new Italian Duchess of York, who would produce an heir to the throne. But these foreign noblemen are also waylaid by the popular libertinism of Whitehall and Pall Mall – where 'a Rabble of Pricks' fall upon the Signior, just as Monmouth's guard had attacked Coventry and hired ruffians would beat Dryden – and by the intrinsic absurdity of the genital mechanism itself. Despite the masculine associations of 'balls', from the imagined female point of view they create a ludicrous spectacle, as they do in Rochester's vision of King Charles; 'my good Lady Sandys', patroness of drinking rituals and inventor of the smock 'Filtre', burst out laughing 'When she saw how the Ballocks came wabling after', how they 'retard' or 'overload' the infuriated Count Cazzo as he rushes to vindicate his honour.[36]

Rochester and his fellow Sons of Belial manage to make Court amours at once phallocentric and anti-phallic, rapidly modulating from priapism to impotence, and splitting off the genitalia into autonomous creatures who perform in the low carnivalesque mode. The same half-achieved separation occurs in the first-person narrative poems *A Ramble in St James's Parke* and *The Imperfect Enjoyment*, dramatic monologues in which a somewhat unstable persona goes through the crisis of jealous rage and impotence respectively. In *A Ramble* – Rochester's contribution to the portrayal of St James's Park as a 'mongrel' zone of promiscuity and social mingling, contemporary with park-scenes by his frolic-companions Etherege and Wycherley – the errant ex-mistress Corinna is polarized into '*Head*' and '*Tail*', and then reduced to a 'lewd *Cunt*' that 'came spewing home, / Drencht with the Seed of half the *Town*'. The jealous speaker pretends to accept the mistress's 'juicy' promiscuity as long as it follows the principle of pure hedonism – 'Such naturall freedoms are but just, / There's something gen'rous in meer Lust' – and maintains a resolutely pert and witty style that belies any disturbance in the content. Even the most vicious lines of *A Ramble* are mediated through outrageous Hudibrastic rhymes that draw attention to the comedic performance, identifying it as the kind of 'Burlesque or Drolling Poem' that Richard Flecknoe had associated with the rise of social and literary refinement: however vulgar the subject-matter, 'the very intention of it' sets it 'beyond the access of vulgar wits'. Nevertheless, the scene witnessed in the park does arouse considerable fury and release a flood of perversely inventive vituperation. When Corinna lets herself be won by foppish and pretentious pseudo-courtiers, products of 'Abortive imitation' rather than genuine wit or desire, she betrays the contract between mind and sex and becomes 'a *Whore* in understanding', her '*Cunt*' speaking at her mouth in a grotesque inversion of bodily hierarchy.[37]

In *The Imperfect Enjoyment*, Rochester's reworking of the Ovidian elegy in which a confident priapist suddenly loses his ability, Corinna becomes the sympathetic and willing partner in what begins as an encounter of erotic equals. Now it is the failed penis that serves first as a synecdoche for the entire person ('Trembling, Confus'd, Dispairing, limber, dry, / A wishing, weak, unmoving lump I ly') and then as a dissociated object, an 'it' or 'thou' with a glorious past and an ignominious future. Up to the moment of collapse it could be viewed heroically, as the agent of sublime dissolution, the 'all dissolving Thunderbolt' or the 'Dart of Love' which

> Stiffly resolv'd, wou'd carelessly *invade*
> *Woman* or *Boy*, nor aught its Fury stayed;
> Where e're it pierc'd, a *C--t* it found or made.[38]

By the end of the poem, when exaggerated anger takes over from over-acted shame, this former prowess has retrospectively been demoted; his confident erection becomes 'a Common Fucking Post' for whores to rub against, or 'a rude Roareing Hector in the streets', a blustering but shiftless representative of the festive-violent plebs, responsive to 'Lewdness' but incapable of 'Love'.

In other Restoration treatments of impotence, like the pornographic poems attached to the Rochester canon or the taunts that Wycherley's Horner receives when he pretends to have lost his virility, erection is equated with honour and flaccidity with 'base metal'.[39] Rochester's variation on this common theme inverts this inversion with a 'stiffly resolved' diatribe against the failing member that *includes* erection among its basest qualities. Like Horner in *The Country-Wife* or Marlow in *She Stoops to Conquer*, the 'Rochester' of *The Imperfect Enjoyment* articulates what Freud would later call 'the most prevalent form of degradation in erotic life': if he can perform priapically with the oyster- and cinder-wench but goes limp with a real lover, then the dichotomy of his head and tail must recapitulate the divisions of society. But is it class-hatred or solidarity-between-extremes that prompts him to denounce his erect penis as a roaring boy or street Hector, with implications of rude comic energy, 'pleasing contradiction' and the 'variety' of 'mean amours'? Transcribing the social hierarchy into the libertine body upsets it in the process, since the text that assigns this low 'street' status to the rabble-rousing organ shares exactly the obscenity and verbal violence of the discourse that epitomizes that status. The more he distances the phallus by loading it with lower-class attributes (crude rigidity, cowardice when called to higher service), the more it resembles the Rochester-figure itself, 'carelessly invading' every orifice, sex, and class. The abuse is so extreme as to sound jocular, and we should note that Rochester (like his stage-shadow Dorimant) was famous for railing violently at his own servants, who took it as a mark of affectionate familiarity. Most significantly, Rochester chooses for his distancing insult the very word, 'Hector', that only one generation earlier denoted a gang of upper-class debauchees – inseparable from the Ranters in their devotion to 'Carnelevation' – who affected lumpen manners in order to 'style themselves' apart from the prevailing seriousness.

Representing himself in conversation with Gilbert Burnet as an Enlightenment sage free from Christian superstitions, Rochester asserted that he lived a deliberate, principled life according to lofty neoclassical or Utopian values:

> the two *Maxims* of his *Morality* then were, that he should do nothing to the hurt of any other, or that might prejudice his own health: And he thought that all pleasure, when it did not interfere with these, was to be indulged as the gratification of our natural Appetites.[40]

But his own practice belies this rational and benevolent epicureanism. Pleasure derives precisely from the violent and often self-destructive transgression of norms that were considered natural, from the 'glory' that comes in Court circles from 'owning' some particularly extravagant encounter with disease and promiscuity (to cite Pepys's observation on the Earl of Southesk). Rochester and his cohort enjoyed simultaneously confusing and reinforcing the stratification of high and low culture, expropriating and reviling the unbridled gestures they associated with the whores and bullies of the underworld. Like his creature Artemiza, he delights in 'the Contradiction and the Sin'. Milton described the Sons of Belial as 'flown with insolence and wine'; Rochester (who told Burnet that 'for five years together he was continually Drunk') expressed the desire to 'make my wishes insolent, /And force some image of a false content', harnessing both insolence and wine for the creative process, raising the heat of fancy by any means necessary.[41]

In persona-poems like *The Imperfect Enjoyment*, closely related to perceptions of himself however dissociated by irony and performative bravado, Rochester identifies the wayward penis as 'a rude roaring Hector' or street hooligan and flaunts his sexual exploits in the social and material substratum of London – with the 'Oyster, Cynder, Beggar, Common whore', the same cast of abject women that had been assembled to discredit the womens' petitions thirty years earlier (chapter 3 above). Burnet recorded that Rochester 'took pleasure to disguise himself as a *Porter*, or as a *Beggar*, sometimes to follow some mean Amours, which, for the variety of them, he affected'. *The Imperfect Enjoyment* half-mockingly confirms his own reputation for acting out these debauched fantasies in 'affected' beggar's dress – the model for James Boswell a century later, who dressed in foul clothes and assaulted women in the street, not to pass as an authentic 'blackguard', but in hopes of being taken for a gentleman in disguise. With Rochester as with Boswell, the point is to revel in the performance itself, to define the common people as spectators, to use mean amours as a 'Filtre'. Rochester's nonchalant flaunting of inversion in immaculate couplets expresses pure *sprezzatura*, in the literal sense of embracing something valueless and 'mean' as well as in Castiglione's sense (the graceful dissociation from earnest endeavour that only the courtier can achieve). The flamboyant mobility that Rochester ascribes to the phallus – 'Stiffly resolved, 'twould carelessly invade / Woman or Boy' – exactly captures his attitude, a 'careless invasion', not an assimilation or identification with the popular culture. The leader of the 'Mob of Gentlemen' (in Pope's memorable phrase) must act as well as write with 'Ease', to disengage him from the actual mob and its 'vulgar wits'.[42] Even the most gratuitous displays of 'low' behaviour have as their purpose a distancing effect quite opposed to the solidarity and community they seem to evoke.

These gestures of cultivated anti-civility were intended precisely to *distinguish* the Wits from the lower orders they simulate. As the historian Anna Bryson puts it, ritualized violence or scouring 'had its own norms, and a definite rationale: that of humiliating the outsider and asserting group solidarity and superiority'. The 'Extravagancies' of the 'Town-Gallant', according to one pamphlet, serve to mark him off from the plebs, to '*Signalize* himself above Common Mortals'. Rituals of outrageous mingling actually reinforce gender and class barriers. The smock-drinking described by Wycherley sets up a 'Filtre' between physical sexuality and the subject of desire; by a similar mechanism, obscene toasts embarrass and expel the female they ostensibly celebrate, as Rochester's

Timon makes clear: in response to his wife's *précieuse* complaint that modern poetry is 'Unfit for Modest Eares' because young people care only about 'small Whores and Players',

> Mine Host drinks to the best in Christendome,
> And decently my Lady quits the Roome.[43]

The situation is further complicated by the 'low' status of the publican, who pretentiously imitates an aristocratic gesture itself imitated from the tavern and the brothel. Rochester sometimes roars out the alliterative catch-phrases of the Bartholomew Fair whore – praising Britain in his sceptre lampoon for 'breeding the best cunts in Christendome' – and thereby confirms two of his cherished principles: that the sexual body contains within itself the extremes of society, the genitals (and the discourse they inspire) corresponding to the drunken 'Hector' at home in the lower depths; and that Wits have much in common with prostitutes, unpacking their hearts with the rudest words. Here, however, his faux-genteel host merely drinks to 'the best', suppressing the 'dear Monosyllable' to create a conspiratorial bond with those who know the full formula. Dorset followed the same stratagem of suppression-to-display in his blason of an imaginary mistress: 'Her belly is soft, not a word of the rest, / But I know what I think when I drink to the best.'[44]

The migration of lower-stratum disorder describes not a random zig-zag but a dialectic of emulation and expropriation: the 'mad tricks' and drinking rituals of whore and rogue circulate through an economy of representation from plebeian disorder (simulating rakish excess) to aristocratic condescension (simulating the abject with a lofty contempt for common humanity). Upper-class riot attempts a kind of *Aufhebung*, a lifting and subsumption of contradictory extremes – the same unstable, oxymoronic synthesis that (as we shall see) Rochester discovers in the most seductive lyrics, naming it the 'mannerly Obscene'. The violence of the Sons of Belial in their 'Courts and Palaces' likewise asserts an aristocratic disdain for bourgeois restraints, and adopts the street-hooligan guise only to further their dissociation from 'low' obligations. Knowing how to 'make oneself into a beast', as Bruno declared in defining the qualities that guaranteed the survival of the pagan gods, is the essence of 'keeping oneself superior'. Rochester's desire to 'Raise pleasure to the topp' means overmatching rivals and winning the prize, as well as heightening sensation.[45]

The repertoire of 'Town-Gallant' behaviour is dramatized, in a tone hovering between satire and indulgent empathy, in another of Rochester's persona-poems, 'The Disabled Debauchee' or 'The Lord Rochester upon himself' (cited as the second epigraph to this chapter). Like Wycherley's Horner – perceived by his friend Harcourt as 'an old maim'd General, . . . unfit for action' but still able to advise soldiers on active service – Rochester imagines the libertine in a future state of syphilitic decay, urging the younger generation to heroic emulation by recalling his own triumphs in the stately pentameter stanza of Davenant's epic *Gondibert*:

> I'll tell of Whores attack'd, their Lords at home,
> Bauds Quarters beaten up, and Fortress won:
> Windows demolish'd, Watches overcome;
> And handsome Ills, by my contrivance, done.[46]

These raids on the 'homes' of supposed 'whores' correspond to the disorderly shaming rituals of the French *confréries de jeunesse* and the attacks on prostitutes in Italian cities (analysed in chapter 1 above), but they have been transformed into the 'handsome' gestures of aristocratic excess, an outpouring of enterprise like the 'Volleys of Wit' discharged during the drinking-party that precedes them. As in the comedies of Etherege and Wycherley, they have been *reclassé* rather than *déclassé*. The 'handsome ills by my contrivance done' include reckless bisexual debauches with Cloris and a link-boy brought in from the street (competing over 'Whether the Boy Fuck'd you, or I the Boy'), recalling the phallus that 'carelessly invades woman and boy' and reminding us that sodomy still enjoyed its Renaissance association with aristocracy; in a Roman lawsuit, we recall, a commoner who asked the courtesan for anal intercourse was accused of being a mere scrap-paper replica of a gentleman (chapter 1, n. 32 above).

Courtly simulations of urban hooliganism, experiments with the boundaries of tolerance, extended to other locations. On country weekends, Rochester and his followers would expropriate the kind of disorderly behaviour which, interestingly enough, the Church courts were now prosecuting less and less. In 1623 village bachelors were presented for dancing 'stark naked', and in a 1640 revel a woman 'was set upon her head and was bishoped'; Rochester's gang now supposedly indulge in games like flinging a dairywoman on her head and smearing her groin with the butter she intended to market, or running naked in Woodstock Park, 'expecting that several of the female sex would have been spectators but not one appear'd'. (Rochester had been officially appointed Keeper of Woodstock Park, but he interpreted this role as if he were Jonson's 'Ranger of Turnbull' or Ranger in Wycherley's *St James's Park*.) The confessional self-exposure, verbal obscenity, and sexual aggression of *A Ramble in St James's Parke* – directed against the 'abortive Imitation' of the false wits and the inversion of head and tail in Corinna – could be seen as the literary equivalent of actions like these, dancing naked and humiliating women by flinging them upside down. According to another gossip-chronicle, on a jaunt to Newmarket Rochester played a pimp-trickster role that seems to come straight from *The Wandring Whore*, arranging a brothel-visit for the disguised king but training the prostitute to pick the royal pocket during the act; again, his Court duties as Gentleman of the Bedchamber are reenacted in the ironic lower stratum, the 'Liberty of Venus'.[47]

Other rustic rambles improvised by Rochester broke down into open violence, and reveal active opposition to his 'careless invasion' rather than amused compliance. In the most notorious of these episodes, Rochester and Etherege severely beat a constable whose home they had stormed in search of 'the handsomest woman in Epsom', attempted to run him through with a sword, then fled when the watch intervened, leaving one of their company mortally wounded. Plebeian *pornographia* outwits both the local authority-figure and the visiting aristocrat, the raid on the constable having been contrived by a wily barber who avoided a similar fate by misinforming the upper-class gang that the policeman's house was the best brothel. Perhaps Rochester escalated the violence in revenge for this *lèse-majesté*, though he soon abandoned the pose of Cavalier warrior; since one member of their party was 'piked' to death, the frolickers seem to have encountered a former Cromwellian trooper rather than the rustic Dogberry they expected. Though Rochester went into hiding for some months, no legal proceedings followed this real-life version of the 'bloody war' that Etherege depicted so lightly in Sir Frederick Frolick. He himself refers to this ignominious Epsom brawl, but obliquely and ironically: in the *Satyr against Mankind* he converts it into the Wildean maxim 'all men would be Cowards if they durst', and in the spoof doctor's brochure – part of the disguise he adopted in hiding – he slips a sincere reference to the truth of courage '(which like false Metal one only trial can discover)' into a dazzling encomium of the counterfeit.[48] Evidently the libertine 'Morality' that Rochester explained to Burnet – all pleasure is legitimate except what hurts another – concealed the true source of his delight, delivering pain to others and running free, carelessly invading and evading, winging his way out of trouble with the 'inimitable' wit that turns vandalism and murder into 'odd Adventures and *Frollicks*' (*RCH*, 51).

The oxymoronic phrasing of the disabled debauchee's self-heroization – 'important mischief', 'handsome ills by my contrivance done' – exactly captures the paradoxical effect that Rochester strives for, and that earned him such applause in fashionable literary circles. The 'extravagance' of the wit and the 'handsomeness' of the contrivance are supposed to outweigh the 'ill', to heighten the abject gesture and transform it into the *je ne sais quoi*, the charming and inimitable artefact. Similar terms recur endlessly in the tributes paid by Rochester's acquaintances after his early death, when even critics who strongly disapprove of his morals endow his 'disorders' with an aura of seductive glamour. The Reverend Burnet, however severe on his 'excesses' and 'irregular appetites', links them directly to the heated brilliance and individuality of his imagination: 'He had a strange Vivacity of thought and vigour of expression; his Wit had a subtilty and sublimity both, that were scarce imitable' (*RCH*, 49).

The aristocratic rioter expropriates 'low' priapic culture and glamorizes the association of violence and sexuality in order to '*Signalize* himself above Common Mortals', to raise pleasure and status 'to the top' and claim a special prerogative; Rochester became the quintessential confirmation of this claim, 'fam'd for high Extreams', 'one of the *greatest of Sinners*', utterly 'singular', raised 'above the reach and thought of other men' by 'the heightening and amazing circumstances of his sins'. This kind of praise lifts him beyond Sir Frederick Frolick, promoting him from knight of misrule to lord of erotic-poetic sublimity. Women poets like Aphra Behn and Anne Wharton (his niece, adopted sister, and reputed lover) explicitly celebrate Rochester for embodying, and fusing together, 'all the charms of Poetry and Love'. Robert Wolseley explicitly defends Rochester's 'Obscenity' as 'the chief power, the main weight and stamp of the Poet's Expression', the baseness of the material being transfigured by 'Wit', 'Genius', or 'poetical Daemonianism'; Wolseley freely admits that Rochester's loose poems might 'offend Age and corrupt Youth' (while dismissing the issue as irrelevant to artistic quality), but then justifies them as effusions of youthful 'free spirit' appropriate for that season of life and as expressions of aristocratic style, diametrically opposed to what they resemble – '*Jack Pudding's* Buffon'ry', the 'witlesse Scurrility' of those 'Bully-Writers' and 'modern

Sparks' who think they achieve glory by slandering women and assaulting the watch, 'obscene Words thrown out at random like Bullies' Oaths, without Design, Order, or Application'. Even Thomas Rymer undermines his stern William-and-Mary moralism by treating 'The Disabled Debauchee' with complicit amusement, offering it (to the chaste female reader) as a prime example of how Rochester's 'Mercury dissolves all into Gaity and Diversion'. 'His own Stamp and Expression', his flights of fancy that 'no Imitation cou'd bound or prescribe', are most fully expressed in that mock-heroic moment when 'his *Gondibert* he sends forth . . . to *demolish Windows*, or do some the like *Important Mischief*'.[49]

3 . 'MANNERLY OBSCENITY' AND FEMALE TRANSGRESSION

Rymer's indulgent treatment of Rochester's 'handsome ills' typifies the mixture of feeble condemnation and fawning, celebrity-dazzled affection that runs through most male-authored depictions of the upper-class Sons of Belial. When Elizabeth Thomas creates a satirical portrait of a 'libertine' husband, any temptation to view his nocturnal 'scourings' with amusement vanishes when she shifts to the perspective of the sleepless, abused, and syphilitic wife, trapped in 'an evil worse than death'. But in most of her contemporaries – Milton being the obvious exception – disapproval is compromised by complicit humour and evaporated in the warmth of male bonding. We have seen Etherege initiate this comic treatment of violence in the character of Sir Frederick Frolick (1664), and pamphleteers frequently borrow the mock-heroic terms of Etherege's comedy, teasing the town-gallant for his 'glorious dreams' of having 'attacqu'd a Troop of Glass-windows' or 'beat up the Quarters of some Bawd, who commanded a Squadron of Wenches'. (A pamphlet countering these 'Remarques', probably concocted by the same author to maintain the comic debate, 'vindicates' the new manners on the grounds that to attack them is to revive the Rebellion of 1640.) Another tongue-in-cheek moralist, dissipating criticism through exaggeration, taxes the rake for the 'Heroic humours' that impel him to attack the police, threaten passers-by with murder, 'set all the *Women* on their Heads', and turn the neighbourhood into an image of hell, echoing with shrieks, oaths, and the sound of breaking glass; the indulgent tone dominates, though the details suggest the traumatic memory of large-scale urban riots like those of 1668.[50]

A consensus developed that festive violence expressed the 'vigour' of youthful sexuality and the sparkle of 'Wit' – or at least the *aspiration* to that highly valued aesthetic effect. In a provocative prologue, Dryden equates the progress of his own first play with the social advancement of the boy who first learns to masturbate, then to sleep with the dairy-maid, then to visit the whores of Whetstones Park, and finally to reach the *ne plus ultra* of fashion: 'He grows to break Glass-Windows in the end.' As in so many allusions to aristocratic riot, the tone hovers between satire and indulgence, establishing the playwright as an insider even while treating his younger self with *sprezzatura*. Thomas Shadwell, writing jauntily to Wycherley for news of the Town, asks whether 'the Brisk, the Gay, the Witty' still 'break Windows when they're Drunk'. Shadwell appears to take the issue more seriously in his 1669 Preface to *The Royal Shepherdess*, where he complains that 'Whoring, breaking Windows, beating Constables, *etc*' – or more precisely the ostentatious 'open profession' of these related activities – are 'esteem'd, among us, a Gentile [*sic*] gayety of Humour'; nevertheless, the letter to Wycherley (and the complacent first person plural in this Preface) suggests again that the criticism is made from *within* the social group that favours such an indulgence. That group extended into the highest echelons. Rochester himself broke not mere windows but an expensive glass sundial owned by the king, ostensibly to prevent it from 'fucking Time'. The running conceit of Whitehall as a 'great bawdy-house' becomes almost literal when a young royal visitor, made roaring drunk by the king himself, grew 'more frolick and merry than the rest of the company' and smashed the windows of the Maids of Honour during an attempt to raid their bedrooms; the narrator of this anecdote, far from disapproving, remarks that his 'mistress' the princess liked him all the better 'for that vigour'.[51] This foreign princeling later returned to rule over a supposedly more sober and progressive England, as King William III.

Contemporaries ironically recognized the violent frolic as 'polite' and 'courtly', paying attention to the status of the actor and not the act, even when they took a more critical stance. This is well illustrated in the stories that circulated around the most savage members of the nobility, such as the royal bastard Duke of Monmouth or the sons of Lord Wharton, younger kinsfolk of Rochester's apparently inspired to go beyond him into a second generation of 'extravagance'. (Thomas, later Marquis of Wharton, married Anne, the poet's niece–sister and guardian of his daughter, and according to one lampoon seduced and diseased the child in order to destroy her marriage prospects and keep the dowry in the family.) The transgressive anecdotes told-as-true about the brothers Thomas and Henry include stabbing to death one of Nell Gwyn's coach horses – an extreme reaction to the status-confounding spectacle of the common whore ensconced in a luxurious carriage – and defecating on the altar of Burford church, a reenactment of the Dorset–Sedley Cock Tavern show in a setting famous for the defeat of the Levellers. In a more conventional urban riot a Wharton-led group of revellers attacked the house of of the prosperous courtesan Susan Willis, breaking her windows and knocking down two gate-posts surmounted by stone globes (her 'balls', symbols of sexual power as well as architectural respectability); on this occasion the police were 'so civil as not to secure them' – an icily paradoxical reminder of the freedom of the polite classes.[52] Violent transgression did not, apparently, hinder success at the highest level of 'civil' society, since Thomas Wharton later became Viceroy of Ireland – much to Swift's disgust, who attempted to discredit him by publishing the story of his excremental frolic. (His success parallels that of another devotee of 'shiting' and manslaughter, the Earl of Dorset, who became Lord Chamberlain of England.) Indeed, if ritualized aggression were not a common form of aristocratic diversion, Swift's satiric equation of priapism, brothel-storming, and military ambition – itself a calculated affront to modesty in its Latin vocabulary – would lose much of its effect: 'The very same Principle that influences a *Bully* to break the Windows of a Whore who has jilted him, naturally stirs up a Great Prince to raise mighty Armies, and dream of nothing but Sieges, Battles, and Victories. *Cunnus teterrima belli / Causa*—.'[53] It is 'natural' for the out-of-control aristocracy to simulate the kind of riots that were now prosecuted as high treason when perpetrated by the lower orders, just as it is 'civil' for the authorities to connive at such demolition parties and polite for the scholarly satirist to flaunt the *cunnus* in the face of the public.

In representing other cases of what Milton called 'injury and outrage', the discourse of mitigation is strained but not abandoned; the proportions of blame and excuse may be reversed but the concept of 'careless invasion' or 'handsome ill' remains intact. In one incident three dukes, including Monmouth, attacked the watch and killed a beadle – 'on his knees', according to the censorious Duke of Buckingham – but immediately received a royal pardon 'for *Monmouth's* sake'; Marvell's comment in a letter ('it is an Act of great Scandal') could refer equally to the murder and to its indulgent treatment, which Dryden would later evoke in *Absalom and Achitophel*. (Buckingham, who extracted pathos and indignation from Monmouth's murder of the beadle, had himself received the royal pardon for slaughtering his mistress's husband, as we saw in chapter 4.) The incident provoked another satirist to create an unforgettable image of insouciant and decorative violence; though 'the silly fellow's death' has temporally postponed the Ball,

> Yet shall White-Hall, the innocent, the good,
> See these men dance all daub'd with Lace and bloud.

This rare moment of *saeva indignatio* is immediately dissipated by the next poem in the anthology, however, which puts the aristocratic culture of priapism back into the carnivalesque mode inherited from village war-games, from the mock-siege of the virgin castle in *The Practical Part of Love* to Rochester's 'Bawds' Quarters beaten up and Fortress won'; in parodic high style, Monmouth and his cronies 'attempt by storme' a brothel where one of them caught the clap.[54]

Even in Dryden, a far more delicate case of ambiguating and excusing violence, the critique of mitigating language fades into complicity. Before the rebellion Monmouth/Absalom was 'Prais'd and Lov'd' despite his 'faults', which were explained away in terms that recall the posthumous eulogies of Rochester:

> Some warm excesses, which the Law forbore,
> Were constru'd Youth that purg'd by boyling o'r:
> And *Amnon's* Murther, by a specious Name,
> Was call'd a Just Revenge for injur'd Fame.

How does this differ from Dryden's own treatment of Charles II's bastard-making as an overflow of 'vigorous warmth', a genial, disarming version of the priapic absolutism more brutally satirized in Rochester's 'sceptre lampoon' and the obscene travesty *Sodom*? In Rochester the monarchic and the sexual instruments are 'of a length', in *Sodom* the king declares 'My laws shall Act more pleasures than Command / And with my Prick I'le governe all the land', while in *Absalom and Achitophel* King David 'wide as his Command / Scatter[s] his Maker's Image through the Land'.[55]

In Milton's terms, then, the stylized adoption of 'vagabond lust' by the upper classes, far from sweeping away 'pales and partitions', helped to reinforce them. As Stallybrass and White put it, 'the mixture of "frolic" and violent outrage on the part of the Wits seemed to both defy and seek some limit to transgression'.[56] It flourished in areas of ambiguity and doubtful authority, along the uncertain borderline between two value-systems that the anti-Puritan Restoration had thrown into confusion – ethical propriety and aristocratic licence. Would the heroic debauchees be punished by the authorities, as was Sedley (though not Dorset) for his obscene display on the Cock Tavern balcony, or would they be pardoned by an indulgent king or dazzled *beau monde*? Punishment would reassure the gentleman-libertine of a stable world of proprieties, statuses, and boundaries; impunity would reinforce his own power to soar above convention, gaining the kind of unequal freedom that infuriated the 1668 rioters. Would the police enforce the law and kill the upper-class 'invader' in self-defence, as happened in Rochester's frolic at Epsom, or would they sacrifice legality to social deference, as they did when Lord Wharton, the defecating viceroy, smashed up the house of the demimondaine Mrs Willis? The bad boys of the Restoration Court obviously enjoyed playing near the edge, but that edge could easily crumble. Impunity could never be absolutely guaranteed. The controlled provocation of the crowd easily boiled over into real fury, a lesson driven home in the great bawdy-house riots of 1668. An angry mob stormed the tavern where Sedley and Dorset performed their obscene display of scatology and 'buggery', while Rochester evidently felt inhibited in his exhibitionist pranks by a similar possibility; when he tells Burnet that 'in their Frollicks they would have chosen sometimes to go naked, if they had not feared the people', he sounds like Pepys on the borders of Moorfields or the time-travellers venturing into Erotopolis, holding back 'for fear of the apprentices'.[57]

'The people' might therefore see a performance-artist like Rochester quite differently from the way he was interpreted by most of his peers and associates, denying the ironic distance that his creative 'contrivance' placed between himself and the lower stratum. His 'frolicking' impersonations of *Wandring Whore* characters – and the poems which further exploit the persona they create – tap into the exhilaration of transgression, retrieving honour from the most abject adventures in the underworld, 'Pleased with the Contradiction and the Sin'. The process of dissociation becomes most visible, as we have seen, in *The Imperfect Enjoyment*, where the speaker denounces his unpredictable penis as 'a rude roaring Hector', valiant with the 'oyster-cinder-beggar-common whore' but useless in better company, placing it simultaneously within his own identity ('worst part of me') and out in the alien 'streets'; we saw, too, that the obscene language of what Wolseley calls the 'Bully-Writer' is adopted so convincingly that it throws doubt on the untainted, aristocratic self implicitly preserved behind the 'hectoring' smokescreen. An enemy like the Earl of Mulgrave (the critic refuted in Wolseley's defence of obscene genius) could easily deny the all-important element of 'Wit' and level Rochester with the coarse 'Bawdry barefaced' that he impersonates.

Closer to 'the people', the obscure schoolteacher-poet John Oldham gave Rochester the oxymoronic title 'Court-Hector', equally dazzled and repelled by the 'bawdy witty Peer' after reading his obscene lampoons and hearing about the 'frolick' in which he vandalized the Whitehall sundial. Uneasily placed on the margins of literary society, Oldham had been challenged by the Court Wits to 'vindicate his reputation' as a poet by writing against virtue. Though the resultant pindaric ode ascribes the most desperate crimes to Rochester, its lewd diction and exaggerated, frenetic manner gave it sufficient ambiguity to amuse him; as a result Oldham was invited into the charmed circle of the Wits and learned to write like a Court Hector himself. A less ambivalent critic of aristocratic excess uttered a similar phrase in earnest, apparently unmediated by wit or performative dissociation: one Bartlet Phillipps was hauled before the Sessions Court for telling a servant of Rochester's 'Thy Lord is a Hector and a Shabb, and you are a rogue for serving him'; though Phillipps was found Not Guilty of 'raising discord between the nobles and commonalty', his utterance had still been interpreted as a seditious attack on the hierarchical structure of society.[58] Accusations like these form the screen against which Rochester projects his libertine lifework. His exaggerated, blustering, hectic poses neutralize, by acting out *in extremis*, the complaints levelled against him in these less witty, more consequential texts. Violence, drunkenness, impotence, cowardice, 'Love rais'd to an extream', sodomy, debauches that leave him 'drenched with the seed of half the Town', link boys, cinder-whores can all be admitted, then turned off as 'handsome ills', subsumed into 'genteel gaity of Humour'.[59]

The gender-specificity of the soft-edged or 'genteel' representation of festive violence can be tested by asking what happens when either the subject or the author is a woman. Do the 'frolics' of Court ladies and royal mistresses strengthen, or break down, the walls of 'the Liberty of Venus', the prison-house of sex? It was evidently easier to accept the cockney Nell Gwyn's violations of polite behaviour than Lady Castlemaine dressing as an orange-woman or a bridegroom, or impersonating the predatory whore when she hurls complimentary insults at Wycherley from her coach. Gwyn did trigger fears that she would become the new 'prerogative whore' after the incident of Coventry's nose, and did provoke sword-fights over her ambiguous 'honour', as we saw in chapter 1.

But she violated less expectations and defused many of the suspicions awakened by the more ambitious mistresses, settling comfortably into the jester-like *Wandring Whore* role, apolitical except for her cheery self-identification as the Protestant Whore in times of anti-Catholic tension: Pepys clearly enjoyed the spectacle of this 'bold merry slut' in her theatre box, 'lying laughing there upon people' (7 Jan. 1669). Though her sons were ennobled she herself remained plain 'Mrs Nelly', and did not provoke the status-confusion caused by elevating other mistresses to the peerage. Nevertheless, Gwyn was installed in the queen's entourage (as a Lady of the Privy Chamber), which caused one imitator of Juvenal to protest that 'Mean prostrate bitches, for a Bridewell fit, / With England's wretched Queen must equal sit.'[60] Burnet remarked that Charles 'never treated her with the decencies of a mistress, but rather with the lewdness of a prostitute', his convoluted grammar transferring whorishness from the slut to her sovereign. Affection for the Nelly-persona mingled with the 'secret scorn and hatred' that (according to Mrs Cresswell in *The Whores Rhetorick*) underlies the Bartholomew Fair jollity. Gwyn was not exempt from cruel satire, but it focusses more on her abject origins and the chaotic social mixing within her circle.

Titled ladies whose 'frolics' broke the frame endured far worse abuse. One lampoon apparently about the Countess of Southesk – mistress of the Duke of York and vehicle of her husband's syphilitic revenge – shows her dissolving the barriers between mother and daughter, economics and physiology, childhood and adulthood, prostitution and Court advancement: masturbating already in the womb and infected by her own mother, she now 'scatters diseases' throughout the town; rather than bringing a dowry she drains her fopling husband to death ('Her fortune but narrow and her c--t very wide'), and now 'will f--k for a penny' like any other prostitute. (Specifically she is compared to a ubiquitous figure in these lampoons, the Susan Willis whose 'balls' were broken by the Marquis of Wharton.) It comes as no surprise, then, to hear that 'her darling delight', and the transgression that crowns the poem, is 'to scower the town . . . In breaking of windows to scratch and to fight / And to lay with her own brawny footmen at night.'[61]

The extrovert heroines of 1670s comedy might be considered an attempt to tame this disturbing figure of the female scourer and to create a plausible mate for the various Sir Frederick Frolicks of the 'sex-craze' decade. These are dashing and sympathetic figures, unlike the caricatured City wives in Wycherley who drink lewd toasts and compete to consume the gamiest male flesh – a mirror-image of male debauchery only slightly milder than the lampoon version of Lady Southesk. Several dramatists wrote breeches parts for impudent, contriving heroines (ideally played by Nell Gwyn) who capture the male lead by achieving what Dryden called 'quickness of wit in reparties' while moderating the 'wilde debaucheries' considered equally essential for the real gentleman. In the anonymous *Woman Turn'd Bully* (1675) for example, Betty Goodfield, dressed as a gallant, learns the behaviour appropriate for her new sex and class ('you must take occasion to beat two or three Watchmen, and break all the Windows that dare oppose ye'), but deflects this violent impulse by cleverly appealing to class prejudice: 'to break windows shews too much like Confederacie with the Glasiers; and for a Gentleman [to] correspond with Mechanicks is, I fancie, very odious' (8).

The equivalent character in Elizabeth Polwhele's surprisingly bawdy farce *The Frolicks* (1671), though she compares herself to an Amazon, chooses the transvestite role to begin the series of outwitting-games that constitutes the entire comedy. Clarabell's 'frolics' reduplicate the author-effect, since they are identified on-stage by the key-word that advertises the title of the play – which Polwhele describes in her dedication as the work of 'a woman' temporarily throwing aside her modesty 'with a boldness that does not become a virgin'. Contrary to convention, the discerning characters rapidly penetrate her male disguise, so that she 'passes' for a woman in drag; the dupes, in contrast, take her for a 'he-devil', 'cock-chicken', 'picaroon' or 'rogue' (the last being a more ambiguous term that works on both sides of the gender-line). Metatheatrical self-reference comes to a head when Clarabell-in-disguise orders the violins to strike up 'the new air call'd "The Frolics"' and proposes that the men dance to it disguised as women, at which the rake-hero Rightwit exclaims 'Twould be a handsome frolic and worth talking on' – a striking anticipation of Rochester's 'handsome Ills'. Yet this escalation of the 'frolic' does not lead to the predictable outburst of 'scouring' violence and *Wandring-Whore*-style sexual immodesty, despite the presence of a Puritan constable and the use of phrases like 'wicked hector' in a complimentary sense. Clarabell parries Rightwit's outright propositions with songs that acknowledge 'rogue' sexuality while technically refusing to yield ('Thou shalt not touch my lips / Nor anything else that is warm'), and always remains in the active role, mistress of the game rather than the seducer. Female agency generates not only the frolics of the plot but the legal settlement that concludes it; her lawyer father accidentally gives her away by counselling her suitor that, if the woman takes the lead, he cannot be prosecuted for the felony of bride-theft.

Conversely the inventive caprice that makes Rightwit a fit match is gen-dered female: 'I am as humourous as a Woman, and can change as often.'[62]

Women's 'humour' and initiative likewise generate the most striking 'Frolick' in Polwhele's comedy, which diminishes both the violence and the male prestige attached to the title-concept. Two or three ex-mistresses hunt Rightwit down, not to devour him like Wycherley's Flounce and Flirt, but to tie his bastard children onto his back: his feeble protests and slurs ('Ye she-goats, you will not ravish me? . . . who knows rightly who's the father of a whore's child?') only emphasize his powerlessness and the women's activity. Clarabell makes the most of the jest, applauding the talent of the tricksters, leaving Rightwit bound up for long periods, and turning him into a fairground raree-show: 'Thou lookst just like the monster with three heads.'[63]

Hellena in Aphra Behn's 1667 *The Rover or The Banish't Cavaliers*, an-other female 'wild gallant' who uses cross-dressing to capture the title-character, helps us appreciate the feminist edge to this 'mad trick'. As a carnival disguise, Hellena dresses as a gypsy – perhaps answering Rochester's Artemiza, who blamed society ladies who 'turn gypsies for a meaner liberty' (p. 200 above). When the 'rover' Willmore urges her to sleep with him without marriage, maintaining the character of vagabond lust that she used to seduce him in masquerade, she retorts that she has no illusions about the burdens of such freedom: 'what shall I get? a cradle full of noise and mischief, with a pack of repentance at my back?' (V.517). Then she would be a 'gypsy' in fact and not in fiction, a true inmate of the liberty of Venus.

Without seriously challenging the double standard or the Cavalier values she shares with her male libertine characters, Behn's *Rover* does considerably diminish their glamour in comparison to the play she adapts, Killigrew's *Thomaso, or the Wanderer*. Behn did not simply rescue the workable scenes from Killigrew's sprawling closet-drama, but reblocked it to give the female parts greater prominence. In Hellena she created a new female character to match the masculine rake, a virtuous heiress who is nevertheless 'very free and witty', and whose part includes lines that in Killigrew were confined to the underworld of prostitution. Behn also makes the courtesan Angellica stronger and more sympathetic – famously associating her own writing with the self-advertising 'sign' that Angellica hangs out – and provides new scenes of female initiative such as the Neapolitan carnival scene (I.ii), where the double standard is temporarily suspended. A sequence of strangely poetic masquerades establishes the carnival as a zone of 'Legal Authoriz'd Fornication, where the Men are not chid for't, nor the Women despis'd as amongst our dull English': women pretending to be courtesans advertise their rates with labels on their clothing that read 'Roses for every Month', men dressed entirely in horns display the motto 'Flowers of every Night'. The principal female characters then enter as 'another Crew' in this procession, the upper-class wits dressed as gypsies and the predatory whore as a fine lady. The Cavaliers respond distractedly. Even Willmore, who misreads the 'Roses' masquerade as a 'liberty of Venus' where he can carelessly invade any woman, is nonplussed by the ambiguity of this female 'Ramble'. The brilliant conversation of these carnival simulacra brings their sexual availability into doubt; he fears that the provocative gypsy-figure he chatted with might have been 'some damn'd honest Person of Quality', that since her style was 'so very free and witty' she could not possibly be free.[64]

Behn's rake-hero Willmore is allowed to capture both the glamorous courtesan and the dazzling heiress, but he is flanked by companions who help to define, and to limit, the achievements of libertinism. Killigrew treats the exiled Cavalier characters with equal respect (since they are thinly veiled portraits of himself and his friends), hiving off any criticism of their swaggering onto the oafish Edwardo, a would-be gentleman who pursues their wild debaucheries without the necessary quickness of wit, and who is consequently duped and robbed by the 'Female Picaroon' whom he mistakes for a *grande dame libertine*. In contrast, Behn makes the central Rover-figure somewhat more brutal and adds a more gallant and respectful man to the group, their commander Colonel Belvile. She inflates the foolish Edwardo/Edward Blunt even higher – in the carnival scene he 'struts and Cocks' with male vanity, convinced by the prostitute's masquerade costume that a 'Person of Quality' has fallen helplessly in love with him – and she takes evident pleasure in having him cheated and dropped in a common sewer, her addition to the original. Behn's scatology reverses the ubiquitous male equation of the prostitute with the 'common shore' or public sewer, obligingly spelled out in Wycherley's insistence that 'A Common Woman, like the Common Shore, / Should be repair'd upon the Common Score.' She also suppresses the hideous revenge that Killigrew shows at length, when Edwardo has the trickster-whore's face slashed and threatens to cut off her nose with his sword. In Killigrew all violence is blamed on this dupe-character, including a coarse scene where he attempts to rape the virtuous heroine as she waits in her garden for her fiancé; Behn transfers this scene almost verbatim to her hero Willmore, without mitigating its ugliness.[65]

The nobler colonel frequently curbs his rakish friend's more questionable attitudes: when he appeals for help in freeing his beloved from captivity, for example, Willmore suggests that such 'obligations' could only be repaid by her sleeping with the whole group – 'thou know'st there is but one way for a Woman to oblige me' – but Belvile rebukes this exclusively sexual definition of woman as 'prophane', and denounces his attempted rape as the product of the same 'debaucht opinion', the work of 'a Brute, a Senseless Swine' (I.ii.464, III.ii.488). Yet even Behn's most sympathetic male reinforces the double standard and slips into a certain collusive familiarity with 'pornographic' violence, when he strips away the genteel appearance of the wealthier courtesans: 'Why yes Sir, they are Whores, tho' they'll neither entertain you with Drinking, Swearing, or Bawdry', and though they live 'where no Rogues in Office, Eclipsed Constables, dare give 'em Laws, nor the Wine-Inspir'd Bullies of the Town break their Windows; yet they are Whores' (II.i.467–8). When Willmore emerges from Angellica's mansion, Belvile even suggests breaking her windows (III.i.478). He may not be an 'old scourer' like Freeman in Wycherley's *Plain-Dealer*, but he shows the other side of his romantic idealism when he mocks the Constable and hurls the oppobrious word at the 'Whores' to shatter their upper-class façade.

We have seen that the poet Elizabeth Thomas took an unusually serious stance on the 'evil' of a riotous husband, and several of her feminist contemporaries attack the central idea that inversionary and violent behaviour denotes brilliance of 'Wit'. Margaret Cavendish rebukes the alienated aristocrat who adopts the low-picaresque life of Gusman but implies that if his wit were 'as good as Guzman's' this inversion would be more acceptable. One of her ventriloquized feminist voices even insists that women should manifest their 'Strength and Wit' just as men do, by exercise and conversation 'in Taverns, Brothels, and Gaming Houses' (chapter 3, section 4 above). The next generation of women writers recognizes, however, that the brothel culture generates a false conception of wit that threatens a return to old-fashioned misogyny – a possibility that we will see realized in Rochester's scouring attack on the free courtesan Susan Willis.

Even though she adores the memory of the arch-libertine Rochester, Aphra Behn herself pours scorn on fashionable rakes who think they show their 'design' and 'invention' by adopting 'Link-Boys Ribaldry' and 'battering half a dozen fair new Windows in a Morning after their debauch', impugning their aesthetic claim and thereby their right to condemn her plays because of her sex. Another feminist asserts that male poets depend entirely on 'an inspiring Bottle, Wench, or Vice', indeed 'Must be debauch'd and damn'd to get / The Reputation of a Wit'. The poet and novelist Jane Barker, who stood outside the circles of London self-promotion and male self-congratulation, likewise attacks libertine critics addicted to the idea that sexual violence and cultivated brutality express creativity: they 'think it wit' to harass 'a poor *Street-Whore*'. Elsewhere, surveying her reasons to remain committed to a single life, she lists among the pathologies of courtship the near-certainty of encountering 'some debauch'd pretender to lewd wit'.[66] Rather than flattering libertine anti-civility, condoning it by adopting an amused tone, or denouncing it in a voice that could be dismissed as Puritan earnestness, 'the ladies' reduce it to mere grossness, incompatible with polite society and the gallant manners that might seduce them.

Rochester himself adopts this position when he writes for a female persona. Lady Elizabeth Howard begins her Court prologue by attacking the unfortunate modern tendency for 'Wit' to grow 'Unmannerly'. This prologue exemplifies what it recommends, a conjunction of *politesse* and 'Wit' applied to the sexual realm. Putting erotically charged words into her mouth, Rochester makes Lady Elizabeth constitute herself simultaneously as courtier and courtesan. Even in this high-cultural register she is wholly sexualized; her seductive invitation to 'See my Credentials written in my Face' makes her a polite version of Corinna at the moment when 'at her *Mouth* her *Cunt* says yes', her *bijou indiscret* emanating from every visible part. Lady Elizabeth addresses her social equals from within the inner circle of those ladies whose 'Charms and Wit' conquer even the king himself, seated in the audience immediately in front of her and evidently prepared to be flattered rather than affronted by this unveiled allusion to his amours. But at the same time the analogies between dramatic and sexual performance, endemic in theatrical prologues of the mid-1670s, make her a public woman who strives to 'please you all', and who allows the audience to see her on the job. To illustrate the 'mannerly' mode of critical 'Wit' she points out (in the tone of her delivery as well as her words) that 'we' are never so rude as to laugh at male lovers while they are trying to do their best, and that 'we' can turn a statement like 'I hate you now' into a pouting, postcoital expression of 'kindness'.[67]

When Rochester impersonates female charm and sophistication he insists that erotic 'Wit' must be 'mannerly', and when he evaluates male poets he evokes the same ideal in the extreme form of a startling oxymoron. The 'handsome ills' contrived by Rochester's disabled debauchee express the same effect that he praises in the lyrics of his fellow-hooligans Dorset and Sedley, and emulates in his own verse: both riot and writing should be 'mannerly Obscene', as he puts it in *An Allusion to Horace*, and in this lies their seductive power. Herrick had listed 'cleanly-*Wantonnesse*' among the local effects of his verse, but Rochester transcribes this antinomy into the language of *politesse* and extends it to a whole genre, a whole programme for transmuting filth and aggression into poetic charm.[68] But does the 'mannerly' expunge the 'obscene' or accentuate it? 'Manners' in high-libertine culture *means* stylish aggression and exclusivity. The 'Ease' of the 'Mob of Gentlemen' depends on making the outsider *un*easy. As object of fascination and hostility, the courtesan functions alternately as the supreme insider, queen of the pleasure-world, and the quintessential outcast; as Rochester explains with typical lucidity – thinking of 'Wits' as well as 'Whores' – 'first they're enjoyed and then kicked out of doors'. If the Howard prologue defines the 'enjoyment' stage of this inevitable rhythm, then hostile misogynist lyrics like 'On Mrs Willis' form the equal but opposite 'kick'.

Rochester might appreciate 'handsome ills' and 'mannerly obscenity' in his fellow-poets, but in the Susan Willis poem (37) he associates the amphibious mix of attraction and repulsion with the female libertine and her power to enslave men – or more accurately, to arouse men so that their own 'Bollox' make them 'slaves' to her. Willis looks 'demurely Impudent, / Ungainly Beautifull'; 'Her modesty is insolent', making her a walking contradiction like Rochester himself, but not therefore pleasing. 'Ill natur'd though a Whore', she steps outside the 'Nelly' role of the good-natured plebeian strumpet who keeps the customer's class-position intact; 'She rails and scolds when she lyes down / And Curses when she spends', just as Rochester himself does (especially if he 'spends' prematurely). Willis becomes a nightmare conjunction of the two figures targeted by charivari, the railing scold and the sexually active termagant, and Rochester's verse adopts the filthy abuse of the shaming ritual. Butler's Skimmington riders shower turds onto the audience, the Renaissance courtesan and the Restoration actress lived in danger of hired ruffians smearing excrement into their faces, and Rochester's Willis suffers the verbal equivalent.

The first line of the Willis poem ('Against the Charms our *Bollox* have') serves almost as a title, an anti-charm to recite in case of need. There follows a mock-epic invocation of the 'Bawdy Powers', a self-conscious act of writing menstrual rather than poetic 'Flowers', in the psalm measure associated with the archaic solemnity of country churches. As with later literary vituperations (like Pope's Sporus) the counter-attack embodies much of the author; he does, after all, dip his own pen in the 'flowers' of this anti-Muse, and in a sense all his 'handsome ills' are written in that ink. The courtier Rochester expropriates the Billingsgate insults and the pathological endings of the whore-pamphlets to outperform all his predecessors in stylish execration, his sexual fury more deadly for being *composed*. Magdalena in the *Wandring Whore* calls a rival 'a tub of turds', and *The Character of a Town Misse* – one of the next generation of pamphlets, attacking the discreet mistress rather than the blatant street-walker – breaks off with an image of the decayed 'Miss' as stinking garbage, 'too foul to be *toucht* with any thing but a *Pen* or a Pair of *Tongs . . . Foh how she stinks.*'[69] Rochester concentrates these effects, with 'Augustan' balance and what a fellow-poet calls 'almost lacy precision', into a perfectly manicured explosion of disgust, a 'civil' plunge into abjection so complete that no continuation can be imagined. Dorset celebrates 'the best' vulva beneath the 'soft belly'; Rochester reverses that incantation and drinks to the worst. The poem concludes by summing Willis up as

> Bawdy in thoughts, precise in Words,
> Ill natur'd though a Whore;
> Her Belly is a Bagg of Turds,
> And her Cunt a Common shore.[70]

In these literary equivalents of the bawdy-house riot, writing itself becomes a tool of the 'blackguard' or scavenger. This poem is addressed, we must recall, to the same woman whose windows and 'balls' were broken up by the Wharton gang. Which is the more violent act?

4 . WHORING LITERATURE, OR THE ENDS OF FESTIVE VIOLENCE

If the term 'libertine' came to mean both a rule-free literary mode and an untrammelled form of sexuality, this is because Restoration critical discourse and literary practice encouraged their convergence. Both low and high culture glorified 'Wit', in its expanded sense of artistic originality, mental fertility, and performative brilliance – the kind of stylish confidence that turned outrage into amusement.[71] In the transgressive atmosphere emanating from the Court, many critics were prepared to find 'Volleys of Wit' in deviant behaviour spectacularly displayed; even the feminist counterblast, as we have seen, recognizes that loutish young males are driven by the desire to prove 'invention' and 'design' (as Behn put it), or in Jane Barker's words 'think it wit' to attack whores like Susan Willis and advertise their own fashionable lewdness. Following the same association, more reckless spirits identified 'extravagant' and forbidden eroticism as the fundamental source of literary creativity. In an exchange of deliberately outrageous burlesque letters, the future Lord Dorset teases Etherege for daring to turn his 'scurrilous wit' against 'prick and cunt, the source of it'; the genitalia drive every form of literary production,

> For what but prick and cunt does raise
> Our thoughts to songs and roundelays? . . .
> Then we write plays and so proceed
> To bays, the poet's sacred weed.[72]

Dryden plays with the same idea when he turns whoring and window-smashing into a mannerly obscene metaphor for the literary career, and reaffirms it late in life when he praises Eros in *Cymon and Iphegenia*: 'Love first invented Verse, and form'd the Rhime.'

Even antagonistic critics confirm the fusion of wit with libertinism and the intimate connection of sexual body and poetic gift. Anne Killigrew, praised by Dryden for her conspicuous chastity in a Court milieu where Maids of Honour like herself were considered fair game for window-smashing, promises to devote 'Soul and Body' to the Muse, even while observing that women, unlike men, could not achieve poetic success by publishing their erotic 'Flame'. Jane Barker criticizes 'the Deluge of Libertinism' and the lewdness of wit all the more trenchantly because her own conception of authorship, and her own commitment to the life of writing, entailed a vow of chastity – a stark polarization of sexuality and inspiration which links them in the very act of separation. Throughout the miscellany attached to her volume of poems, erotic praise of the woman writer coexists quite happily with the critique of 'debauched pretenders to lewd wit': the Muses have turned prostitute, poetry and illicit pleasure have become interchangeable, literature is dominated by those 'Who make their Verse *imbibe* the crimes, / And the lewd Follies too o'th'times' – in short, the poets of the culture of drink and violence 'think all Wit consists in Ranting'.[73] Dryden would make a similar connection in his famous funeral ode on Anne Killigrew; confronting another exemplary and pure woman poet, he confesses his own part in having 'made prostitute and profligate the Muse' – though his indecorously physical language ('steaming Ordures of the Stage'), and his adoption of a complacent first-person-plural 'We', undermines this confession and reinforces the solidarity of male writers against the chaste outsider (lines 58–65).

'Debauchery' was not only a *prerequisite* for wit but a literary procedure in its own right, a synonym for travesty: Thomas Duffett offered his burlesque version of the hit opera *Psyche* under the title *Psyche Debauch'd* (1678), and one prologue later added to *Sodom* announces it as 'the most debauch'd heroick Piece / That e're was wrote' (678). How did lyric and drama respond to the concerted effort of the Sons of Belial and their imitators to 'raise' the abject and to 'debauch' the heroic? The promiscuous switching of high and low extremes – performed in both the textual and social realm – intensifies what Lawrence Manley calls 'the appropriation upwards of popular seriocomic techniques and genres into a single, dominant literary system'. Carnivalesque inversion of hierarchy tends to strengthen it, and the principle of 'maintaining superiority by simulating the beast' applies to literary games like the 'Travesties' and burlesques of the classics that for Flecknoe reveal the 'nation growing more polite and witty'.[74]

As in the aggressive games of festive violence, this high-status refinement involves an 'uncrowning' or downward movement that drags down false nobility and confirms the class-position of the 'low' even as it expropriates lower-stratum gestures. When Rochester inserts obscenity into lyric forms previously used for romantic love, or forces an urgent 'Hectoring' tone into the stately heroic couplet, he clearly intends to degrade those forms as much as to 'raise pleasure to the top'. Court lampoons deliberately seek to de-class as well as defame their target, as we have seen: in Marvell's *Last Instructions*, which showed Rochester how to transfuse charivari and obscene lampoon into a high literary mode, Anne, Duchess of York, acquires an 'Oyster Lip' and a 'Wide Mouth that Sparagus may well proclaim' (lines 61–2), associating her with the scabrous oyster-women who deliver petitions and service the 'rude roaring Hector'; in verses perhaps transcribed by Aphra Behn, the Duchess of Mazarine is described as a kind of Ursula, presiding over a

Bartholomew Fair economy of meat and sperm, extracting sexual liquid from a whole 'Crew' of lovers and then 'treating' them 'with C--t-gravy'. The setting of this event – 'in Coffee houses' – links the bawdy *Petition against Coffee* to the politicized hatred of the king's French mistresses.[75]

The ignominy and lurid fascination of such attacks must have been increased by their resemblance to the shaming rituals of non-urbane and impolite society; as we have seen in chapter 2, obscene verses played an integral role in rural ceremonies of mockery, particularly against over-complaisant cuckolds among the men and over-assertive 'whores' among the women – the targets of village riots as well as insider satires against the sexual deviancy of the Court. It is ironic, then, that the verse lampoon should come to be seen as a form proper to the London élite, claimed as a preserve of the upper classes. Once glamorous insiders like Rochester 'carelessly invade' this popular form and 'Signalize' it with their distinctive style, their prestige adheres to it; Congreve's Mirabell even assumes that Lady Wishfort will be flattered and seduced by a lampoon (*Way of the World* i.i). This 'lifting' of the defamatory libel, like the enclosure of the commons, shut out its former participants – placing the cultivated vulgarity-effect (in Flecknoe's words) 'beyond the access of vulgar wits'.

To parallel this experiment in literary slumming, low-libertine elements work themselves upward into the most respectable genres. Tragedies on the Restoration stage were framed – or more accurately unframed – by wildly comic epilogues that emphasize the quasi-prostitutional status of the actress; Dryden's *Tyrannick Love*, for example, begins with a prologue that serves as a manifesto for libertine-aesthetic violence ('Poets, like Lovers, should be bold and dare') and closes with a striking example of that daring, when Nell Gwyn leaps up in the epilogue to explain in Hudibrastic rhyme that, though she died as a faithful attendant of the martyred queen 'Saint *Cathar'n*', in the flesh she lived the life of 'a Slattern'.[76] (Richardson's Pamela objected most strongly to the survival of this bawdy-epilogue convention, which seemed to her designed exclusively for the humiliation of women.) Cowley's 'Ode to the Royal Society' dwells at improbable length on the figure of Priapus and its wooden phallus, dragging the language of the bawdy catch into the most elevated poetic and scientific discourse: Rochester and Behn advertise the erect penis as 'that which I dare not name' when they adopt a prurient-modest female persona, and in Etherege's *Man of Mode* the coffee-house crowd in St James's Park titillate the audience with the lewd refrain 'there's something else to be done' (n. 6 above); with even greater effrontery considering the official publication where his ode appears, Cowley assures us that Priapus, emblem of the false authority that guarded the Garden of Knowledge until science threw it 'open and free', sports 'something else not worth a name'. Even here, intellectual freedom must be figured by 'free' sexual allusion. Dryden intrudes calculated violations of decorum, not just into the worldly-wise prologues of sex-comedy and illusion-breaking epilogues of she-tragedy, but into serious non-theatrical works designed to make his mark as a major voice of the 1660s. In his heroic poem on the splendours of the Dutch War, *à-la-mode* bachelor metaphors compare the prowess of the two navies to the relative sexual vigour of lovers and husbands. And in the essay *Of Dramatick Poesie*, simulating and idealizing the conversation of the Dorset–Sedley circle, he enforces a critical point by familiar allusion to the cries of women in orgasm, 'the fury of their kindness'.[77]

As part of this trickle-up effect, whole scenes and characters are transposed from the whore-dialogues to the prestigious public theatre. (However disreputable it seemed to the moralists, the stage still formed an extension of the Royal Household or King's Pleasure, and 'dramatick poesie' still held a high position in the literary hierarchy; performances in the Court theatre in Whitehall further enhanced the glamour and the playful courtesan-imagery, as we saw in Rochester's prologue for Lady Elizabeth Howard.) We have already seen Wycherley's 'infiltration' of perverse genres and postures into *The Country-Wife* and *The Plain-Dealer* (section 2 above). In Sir Francis Fane's *Love in the Dark* a father actually applies the phrase 'wandring Whore' to his own daughter, when she takes up with a 'hare-brain'd Gallant' (68), and Sedley had evoked it in *The Wandring Ladys*, a title that Pepys records only two days before he reveals his expertise with *La puttana errante* (6 Feb. 1668). The ubiquitous 'breeches' scene acts out the recommendation of Nanna to Pippa in Aretino's *Ragionamenti* (II.i.179 [186]), to captivate the aristocratic client by prancing around in his clothes (so looking like the boy he really prefers), and perhaps recalls the London customer who would rather have smooth-faced apprentices. The brothel scenes in Otway's *Venice Preserved* – when Antonio barks, crawls under the table, relishes Aquilina's toe-cheese, and ejaculates on stage – come as close as public decorum would allow to the 'mad tricks' described some twenty years earlier in *The Wandring Whore*. Other pervert-characters, like the flagellant Snarl in Shadwell's *Virtuoso*, might equally have stepped out of

Magdalena's list of customers. The 'proviso' scene, brought to a high
pitch by Congreve, had been rehearsed in the wandering whore's plans
to marry Francion (chapter 4, section 4 above), and Francion's own desire to climb in the world through low debauchery is in turn reenacted
in literary comedy.[78] The theme still flourishes in the 1690s in comedies
like Shadwell's *Scowrers*, where the 'City Wit' Whachum – living embodiment of what Flecknoe calls the 'vulgar wits' denied access to the
aesthetics of inversion – faithfully imitates 'the Sins of Gentlemen', the
violent 'Frolicks' of the title-characters.

The status-conflict over 'low debauchery' thus provides both the theme
and the method of drama, particularly in scenes where plebeian or apprentice characters try to emulate the disorderly behaviour that until
recently had been their own province. In the opening scene of Etherege's
Man of Mode, for example, the libertine hero Dorimant taunts his shoemaker for adopting 'Vices too genteel', and the shoemaker in turn pretends to lament that his journeymen 'instead of harmless Ballads sing
nothing but your damn'd Lampoons'. A female parallel arrives almost
immediately, in the form of a faux-genteel letter from a common whore,
complaining that she suffers from aristocratic 'Mallicoly' and asking
Dorimant for a guinea 'to see the Operies'. In response Dorimant –
Etherege's portrait of his friend Rochester – takes a subversive pleasure
in encouraging her to 'perk up i'the face of quality', to demonstrate the
identity of the whore and the countess (i.i.197–8, 204).

However much they borrow from the lower depths, such slumming
scenes still enforce rather than dissolve social hierarchy. However close
to its plebeian origins, the 'lampoon' carries an exclusively upper-class
connotation, unsuitable for the apprentices who insist on singing them.
The 'drolling' banter of Dorimant with his cobbler and his orange-
woman procuress – perhaps the same 'Orange Nan' listed in *The Wandring
Whore* – resonates with jovially menacing reminders of official punishments visited upon the lower orders. (Etherege is presumably influenced
by Plautus, where the witty slave is constantly threatened with cruci-
fixion and the whip by his friendly master.) Perhaps because the fat
orange-woman is also a respectable householder (chapter 1, section 2
above), the aristocratic wits call her 'Cart-load of Scandal' and 'Brandy
Bottle', mixing traditional Carnival-versus-Lent imagery with the official 'carting' prescribed for a convicted prostitute. This fleshy intruder
from the lower stratum defines popular culture in both its sensuous and
its punitive aspect, and irruptions of both recur throughout the play. The
sexual associations of fruit-selling, for example, migrate upwards through

the social classes: in Act I the orange-woman offers a ripe peach as she describes the heiress Harriet, and in Act V Belinda alludes to her fling with Dorimant as an expedition to find 'fresh Nectarines . . . the best I ever tasted' (I.i.191–2, V.i.266). Evoking darker kinds of female transgression, Dorimant's rejected lover wishes she had the power of a witch, and Dorimant himself, confronted by the hostile tongues of two cheated ladies and a waiting-maid, fears being 'scolded to death' (II.ii.218, V.i.273). These flippant, distancing allusions to crime and punishment likewise stem from that first orange-woman scene. Just as Wycherley assures the audience that Bridewell stands close to the theatre, ready to discipline any wandering whores who might disturb the play, so Etherege's Rochester-figure weaves into his affectionate abuse the pillory, the cropping of ears, denunciation to the Church courts, burning at the stake. For good measure, he also creates a kind of Skimmington ride for the shoemaker, picturing him with a termagant wife who beats his whore and leads him home in triumph.

The 'mannerly Obscene' lyric poetry of the Restoration Wits attempts to reenact, in finely polished rhyme and meter, the deliberate conjunction of festivity and violence, high and low behaviour, punitive and seductive gesture, that we have traced in Rochester and the ritualized transgressions of sex-comedy. Literary 'scouring', like its behavioural counterpart, borrows actions and phrases from the lower stratum in order to repudiate it – a calculated expropriation, consciously histrionic and therefore ironically disengaged. Just as the Earl of Rochester transformed *Wandring Whore* scatological insults into his verses 'against the charms' of Susan Willis, so the Duke of Buckingham takes the fancy slang of the low-life pamphlets – '*Julietta an Exquisite Whore*' – and works it into an epigram of superlative lewdness, besmirching his cousin Cleveland with a mélange of rage, prurience, and incest-fantasy. Henry Killigrew had been punished for ascribing sexual feelings to her in childhood, but this insolently laconic lampoon ('She was such an exquisite whore') takes obscenity to the limit: the female 'scourer' had been accused of masturbating before she was born, but Buckingham imagines the royal mistress even worse, copulating in the womb with her own father.[79] The 'extravagant' effect of Buckingham's and Rochester's verse-attacks – 'polite' epigrammatic form contrasting with Bartholomew Fair content, elevation of rank (in author or victim) jarring with *Wandring Whore* coarseness – helps to 'Signalize' their authors, keeping them superior by simulating the beast.

But if mannerly obscenity elevates the Wit, it denigrates the Whore and takes back all the ambiguous glamour that the courtesan and mistress had accumulated. To this extent the 'freedom' of libertine festive violence never disengaged from the social issues of class-privilege and the political campaign against the absolute mistresses who ruled the 'great bawdy-house' of Whitehall. Dorset's politely vicious lyrics against Dorinda continue this tradition literally into the next generation, since their subject is Catherine Sedley, Countess of Dorchester, mistress to the new king James II, and daughter of Dorset's old companion in 'lewdness and buggery' Sir Charles Sedley. Dorset combines a detached elegance of form with an imagery of street violence and filth, turning the link-boy from Rochester's 'Disabled Debauchee' into a violent anti-Eros:

> Her Cupid is a blackguard boy
> That runs his link into your face. (*Poems*, 44)

Behn had included 'a little Link-Boys Ribaldry' among the equipment of the fashionable gentleman rioter, and the earl now shows how to use it. 'Blackguard' street dirt seems to have been concentrated, rather than strained out, by the 'Filtre' of libertine wit. The shock ending of this disturbing lyric acts out its own content, thrusting a grimy insult into the reader's face, pillorying (and reproducing) the assertiveness and wit of a woman who claimed the same freedoms as men.

The gross, lower-stratum realism of Dorset's *pornographia* serves to counteract one effect of the 'urban revolution' that was spreading élite behaviour throughout London – the semiotic convergence or collapse of clear boundaries between the wicked prostitute and the fine lady. Polite society imposed on Alitheas and courtesans alike 'the double bind of demanding that women be both seductive and chaste'. 'Propriety and fashion sometimes worked against each other', Alice Browne points out in a memorable understatement; as Elizabeth Montagu would later put it, 'the *bon ton*' is often '*un peu équivoque*'. In one of the 1670s 'Town Miss' pamphlets, the prostitute attributes her success to this equivocal style – 'Brisk and Airy (which our dull Grandmothers would have call'd Wanton and Impudent) is long since become the Character of a Well-bred woman' – though after falling into the hands of a procuress she finds herself 'in a worse Servitude than the most wretched Gally-Slaves'.[80] Grim or low-comical descriptions of economic hardship tear off the 'Brisk and Airy' vizard, the stylish non-deferential self-presentation which could conceal either the well-bred woman of quality or the thriving adventuress. Wycherley's Horner invents his eunuch-trick to solve the same problem, which he diagnoses at the heart of 'civility' itself: how can he perform his binary classification, sorting all women into sex-objects or Alitheas, now that 'Women of Quality are so civil, you can hardly distinguish love from good breeding' (I.i.253)?

The spectacular advances of royal mistresses like Lady Castlemaine, the Duchess of Portsmouth, or Catherine Sedley confounded any attempt to separate sexual and social 'civility', or to impose a strict hierarchy on the illicit. This mingling of whores and duchesses inevitably provoked economic, sumptuary satire, dragging the *cortegiana honesta* down to the material level of what Rochester calls the 'oyster-cinder-beggar-common-whore'. Slanderous allusions to the most successful concubines often proletarianize them, as if to restore some classifying power over female sexuality: thus Gwyn (the only real plebeian among them) becomes 'laborious Nelly' toiling like a peasant to raise the royal penis, Mrs Monck (the general's former mistress) is derided as a New Exchange stallkeeper, Anne Hyde (married to the Duke of York in advanced pregnancy) as a strolling vendor of oysters or asparagus, Philipa Temple (an aspiring Maid of Honour) as a 'cheap, wholesome whore' content to be paid in ale and cheese.[81] The entire female Court is effectively moved to Whore and Bacon Lane, locked into the Liberties of Venus. Rochester's Susan Willis represents the ultimate stage in this economy of degradation, the open sewer.

In Dorset's 'Dorinda' lyrics Catherine Sedley – elevated to the peerage by her lover James II, and granted a pension that enabled her to marry within her own class – is figured as a squalid link-boy, thrusting his torch into your face, and as a rotting loin of veal, giving off the phosphorescent light of decadence. (Sedley herself preempted defamation with the same endearing frankness that the Duchess of Cleveland had applied to Wycherley, telling her children that 'if any body call either of you the son of a whore, you must bear it for you are so, but if they call you bastards, fight till you die'.)[82] Dorset intends the 'lucid loin' of bad veal to represent Sedley's repulsively brilliant wit, but it equally well describes his own stylishly lucid smut. Like Dorinda herself, these versified assaults 'At once both stink and shine'. Like the inversionary high-libertine culture that Dorset embodies to the full, they attain a kind of transient sublimity as they approach the abject, simultaneously rotting and glistening. Generations earlier, Ralegh had told the Court that it 'shines like rotten wood'; the Restoration courtier transfers this disquieting luminescence to the sexual body he pursues and dreads, violates and distances. This metaphoric transference from Court to courtesan is made thinkable by the 'mannerly Obscene' synthesis defined in this final chapter: aristocratic 'formalized "anti-civility"' meets the low-libertine, Bartholomew-Fair-style equation of sex with flesh for consumption and disposal.[83]

EPILOGUE

'In Bathsheba's Embraces old': pornographia
rediviva *at the close of Charles II's reign*

In the 1680s, the last period in English history when the monarch ruled without Parliament, political *pornographia* entered its terminal condition. All the forms that we have been tracing throughout this book reappear dropsically enlarged, malignantly intensified, or eerily lengthened like the shadows that Dryden's Achitophel uses to figure the declining years of Charles's reign. Absalom presents this ending scene more tenderly when he describes his father 'grown in *Bathsheba*'s Embraces old' (line 710), but he still places King David's adultery at the centre of the case for his removal. The lampoons and seditious oral comments recorded by secret agents showed less mercy to 'Bathsheba', the French Louise de Kéroualle, Duchess of Portsmouth: this ultimate 'Whore of State' is attacked in terms more virulent than anything written against the Duchess of Cleveland or Nell Gwyn, who finds herself transformed from absolutist nose-slitting termagant to loyal Protestant Whore.

The lapse of the Licensing Act in 1679, amidst the continuous hysteria of Popish Plot and Exclusion Crisis, revived the entire range of 'pornographic' text and gesture, in popular as well as élite culture. The Earl of Shaftesbury finds himself in Otway's *Venice Preserved* figured as the aristocratic rebel Renault and as the grotesque pervert Antonio, who seems to have migrated straight from *The Wandring Whore* (chapter 4 above). Antonio's brothel-antics explicitly recall Mrs Cresswell, who became a mainstay of Tory satire (including the second part of *Absalom and Achitophel*) when her trial in 1681 supposedly revealed Presbyterian City leaders among her regulars; fame in the political sphere in turn influences pornography, when the 1683 *Whores Rhetorick* gives Cresswell the main role and amplifies the Italian original with topical allusions. Monmouth embodies sexual excess in *The Whores Rhetorick* and in Behn's *Love-Letters between a Nobleman and His Sister*; his would-be regal attempts at faith healing provoke satires about 'the touching of naked flesh', and his West-Country insurrection reawakened what David Underdown calls the 'expressive violence' of the villages, where Skimmington-like riots 'reignited local divisions whose roots lay in the 1640s'. Seditious murmuring focussed quite logically on the king's sexuality, since the entire crisis derived from the lack of a legitimate son and the competing claim of the bastard Monmouth; one of the Nonconformists who denounces Charles's promiscuity links it directly to anxiety about the Protestant succession, asserting (like many others) that 'he ought to be divorced from the Queen that there might be an heir to the Crown'. Stephen College, executed for high treason after allegedly planning to capture the king during the Oxford Parliament debacle of 1681, reportedly declared in the coffee-houses that Charles 'came from a race of buggerers, for his grandfather king James buggered the old duke of Buckingham'.[1]

Militant opposition once again took a carnivalesque form. Abusive anti-government ballads were disseminated at rural fairs as well as in the festive-violent setting of Oxford during Charles's high-handed attempt to move and then to dissolve Parliament. The lampoon and engraved cartoon fatally attributed to Stephen College on that occasion take as their title-theme the fairground 'raree-show', depicting Charles as a two-faced monster, dressed in a Leviathan-like coat made up of female heads, who transports the Parliament in a back-pack like a travelling freak-show. The cryptic ballad sums up the points of grievance: the '*Cut-nose Guard*', the mistresses flaunted as 'Badges of Power', the 'Lecherous Loyns' that collapse under stress, the '*French*-Lap' where he goes to sleep.[2] The angry demonstration that threatened Nell Gwyn's coach at Oxford, at a time when the whole future of parliamentary rule hung in the balance, was later remembered for her quick-witted reading of the situation and deflection of the anger from sexual to religious-political targets ('I am the *Protestant* whore!'); but the mob had both points in view, effectively redefining her high-status procession in a royal coach as the shameful riding or 'carting' that traditionally punished the whore. As we have seen, satires like John Lacy's *Upon Nell Gwynne's and the Duchess of Portsmouth's Naked Pictures* describe (and provoke?) a very similar crowd, 'aloud in public streets', seething with punitive revulsion and prurient fascination at the spectacle of this 'monster' or raree-show. If Gwyn really did make that oft-quoted remark, she engaged in two witticisms at once: according to where the stress falls, she compares herself to the much-hated *Catholic* whore Portsmouth and to the popular agitator College, universally known by his nickname 'the Protestant *Joiner*'.[3]

The ultra-Protestant agitation of Monmouth, Shaftesbury, and their supposed agents inspired sexually inflected mock-processions and shaming rituals, constituting a kind of Grand Skimmington against the king. In the anti-Catholic demonstrations on Queen Elizabeth's Coronation Day (17 November 1680), illustrated and expounded in broadsides like *The Solemn Mock Procession of the Pope... through the Citty of London* (1680), the midwife Elizabeth Cellier is exposed on a floating platform with her Meal Tub and the 'Abhorrer of Petitions and Parliaments' is paraded backwards on a horse (or in another version an ass, the carnivalesque humiliation once reserved for the most blasphemous radical). Peter Burke uses this Skimmingtonian image to locate 'the politicisation of folklore', but parading sexual offenders always had a political point: *La puttana errante* figured the Sack of Rome as a genital triumph (chapter 1 above), the pageantry of Yard and Hole protested the emergence of a Puritan élite (chapter 2), and this cuckoldy riding remonstrates against 'the ill posture of things' – particularly the old and new grievances of London, the Fire and the Plot. The revival of ritual abuse on the 'Protestant' side provoked a vivid response in Jane Barker, a fervent Jacobite who went into exile with the Catholic Court after 1688, becoming in her own word a 'vagabon'. The heroic couplets of 'Fidelia weeping for the King's departure at the Revolution' are interrupted when 'the Rabble comes by in a mock procession carrying before them a cat crucified' – another shaming ritual devised by the Protestant crowd. This anti-papal cat massacre envigorates Barker as well as shocking her. Her verse monologue becomes a drama, complete with stage directions, and she herself turns into a ribald counter-protester of the kind we have seen so often at the edge of riots and rallies; the shamer's 'disgrace' turns back on itself, Fidelia retorts, like a shrew 'calling cuckold to her husband's face'. Barker's Jacobite sexual jeering redefines the Protestants' triumphal procession as a Skimmington *against* them.[4]

Legal actions participate in, and bring to a lurid climax, the repertoire of festive-violent rituals that associated sexual transgression with tyranny or sedition. Bawdy-house rioters must be 'deprived of their Testicles' at Castlemaine's urging (chapter 5 above), and Stephen College's mocking representation of the lecherous king-as-monster must likewise suffer the penalties of high treason, which included 'his *pudenda* cut off, which shews that his Issues are disinherited and their blood corrupted'. Following this logic, it seems inevitable that the 'most absolute' of the royal mistresses should be attained for treason herself. Lampoons and satires castigate the Duchess of Portsmouth as a French, diseased, Catholic, anal, avaricious secret agent, administering absolutism by contagion. Guildenstern may joke with Hamlet about his humble relation to the secret parts of Fortune ('her privates we') but in later Stuart England – when Portsmouth made pornocracy quite literal – the entire nation felt engulfed by the 'prerogative Queane'. As the most public of women her genitalia loom large in political discourse: Shaftesbury explains that through her 'the severest of [Louis's] commands may be more softly conveyed to us', and even the sober John Evelyn blames Charles's failure on 'abandoned and prophane wretches, who corrupted his otherwise sufficient parts'. Diplomatic correspondence reveals that in fact the duchess *was* the conduit for Charles's negotiated dependence on French money and French policies, while at the same time controlling access to the king by his own subjects, the key to power in Court culture. Like Cleveland, who was also threatened with a treason indictment, she aimed to influence and profit from all senior promotions in Church and state.[5]

Reversing the dynamics of the 1668 riots, when the outraged mistress added her real and fictional voice to the prosecution of popular insurgency, the 'Articles of High Treason' constitute a kind of mock-petition or cat-crucifixion transposed in deadly earnest to the realm of high politics. Shaftesbury – himself depicted by his enemies as a leaky and disordered body gripped by disastrous perversions – enumerated twenty-two counts of treason, covering the entire range of political, financial, and religious grievances, which begin and end with her corporeal power to corrupt. As in the lampoons, Portsmouth is imagined as a homogenous body of obscene liquid, 'a harlot all made up of French' (as Lacy puts it in his satire on her 'Naked Picture'). If tyranny is an 'imperial oil' which 'taints the blood' with incurable leprosy, the invasive mistress is a contagious substance identified by the single word *French*, which 'runs through the Princes Veins' and 'creeps into Royal Bed'; though it remains (deliberately) unclear whether this French blood derives from his mistress or his mother, the result is the same – ruling by French laws and 'swiving' for Monsieur's approval. The first accusation in the treason articles adopts the same paradigm of venereal contamination and ominous progeny:

the said Dutchess hath and still doth cohabit and keep Company with the King, having had foul, nauseous, and contagious Distempers; which once possessing her blood, can never admit of a perfect cure; to the manifest danger and hazard of the Kings person, in whose preservation is bound up the weal and happiness of the *Protestant Religion*, our Lives, Liberties, and Properties, and those of our Posterity for ever.

Like Cleopatra in *All for Love*, the illicit female 'marks' her hero fatally, dyeing him (and through him the entire nation) with an infamy all the more virulent because invisible. The high–low courtesan-duchess wields 'high and dishonourable absolute Dominion and power over the Kings Heart', which gives her an almost vampiric ability 'to draw from him the secrets of his Government', and ennobling her transfers this oxymoronic 'high Dishonour' to God. In return, she infuses her royal benefactor-victim with 'Poyson', artfully concealed in French 'Sweet-meats' and 'Broath'.[6]

It would be naive to assume that the plebeian and 'Protestant' Nell Gwyn escaped this murderous porno-political critique, although anti-Portsmouth polemic sometimes cast her in the role of loyal innocent. One brief lampoon declared in 1669 that Gwyn 'hath got a trick to handle' the king's 'p----,/ But never lays hands on his sceptre'; we have seen, however, that she was blamed for the brutal attack on Coventry in 1670, and thereafter she represents a shameful tyranny differing in degree but not in kind from that of the other 'Jilts' who 'ruled the State' (in Pope's words). Gwyn offered a source of protection (sheltering Monmouth when he was out of favour) and patronage (for Behn), and wielded enough power to instigate violent assaults on those who maligned her; Narcissus Luttrell records the theatre brawl that 'vindicated' her honour in his 'Relation of State Affairs', as we saw in chapter 1. Her very presence in the king's entourage caused a political scandal, since she rose illegitimately from the lowest stratum (though satirists certainly exaggerated her abject origins in the cellar and the ash-pit). She too is imagined as damaging the monarchy by an exchange of bodily fluids, 'soaking the Royall Bawble' in foul juices (and 'dwindling' it) while he 'anoints' her in an obscene travesty of coronation.[7] It would be more accurate to say that Gwyn and Portsmouth formed an indispensable pair, defining the two kinds of contaminating Other. Louise de Kéroualle, the French and courtly high courtesan, siphons in disease and absolutism while draining the royal coffers and forcing dependence on Louis XIV's pension; 'Mrs Nelly', the filthy cinder-woman, drags Charles down to her level as he pokes in her dust.

The symmetrical pairing of the two whores is inscribed in many anecdotes and lampoons. The 'Pleasant Dialogue betwixt Two Wanton Ladies of Pleasure' features in texts as various as a song by Rochester, a letter by Mme de Sévigné, and several broadside ballads sold in the street. Even their dogs engage in ritual combat and self-defining opposition. Before their actual fight, cheered on by both owners and predictably won by the stout English Tutty, each creature belabours the other with inappropriately canine insults (bitch, lap-dog) while rehearsing the standard boasts and accusations: the French Snap-short imagines Nell selling oranges, threatens to cry 'Treason', and brags that his mistress is 'a Whore of the greater Magnitude' because she has taken £40,000 out of the country and will soon let in a French invasion; Tutty defends Gwyn as 'a good Common-wealths woman . . . a Protestant, who shall be protected when your French Romish Bitch shall be pull'd Limb from Limb'.[8]

This ventriloquistic union of high and low courtesan revives the 'petition' subgenre, which as in 1668 and 1672 works unpredictably to belittle grievances or to magnify them. In the post-riot petitioning Damarose Page and Mrs Cresswell had appealed across class-barriers to their supreme leader in Whitehall, who replies in the haughtiest tones from the opposite end of town; in contrast, the 1679 'Humble Address of the Ladyes of Pleasure' is jointly presented by Nell Gwyn and the Duchess of Portsmouth on behalf of all the prostitutes of 'Moor Fields, Whetstons Park, Lukeners Lane, Dog and Bitch Yard'. This new sarcasm inverts the normal 'whores' complaint' trope by expressing gratitude for their prosperity, 'being daily sensible of the great Advantages we have reaped under Your Majesty's easy Government from the Play-Houses, Masks, Balls, Serenades, Hide-Park, and Saint James's Night Revells' – apparently an echo of Milton's 'wanton Mask, or Midnight Ball, / Or Serenate' (*PL* IV. 778–9). The new sexual régime, based upon the principle that 'those Foolish Things called Wives are grown Unfashionable, and Keeping of a Miss the principall Charecter of a Well Bred Modish Gentleman', grants even greater power and glory to the prostitute than she enjoys in Rome and Venice, some of us (in the collusive first person plural that levels royal mistresses and street whores) 'being Promoted not only to Great Titles, but to the Premier Direction of Publick Affairs'. Thus what Halifax called the 'Ministry' of Gwyn and Portsmouth could be named 'Premier' even before the office of Prime Minister had been recognized in fact. This satire particularly thanks Charles for his sudden and frequent dissolutions of Parliament, on the grounds that it exhausts those 'sober Country Clowns' who bring their wives to town, propose laws for 'Retrieving the Ancient Vertue of the Nation', and so threaten to drive the whores out of business. This must have seemed even more timely when retranscribed in a poisonous 'Garland' for the duchess in 1682, one year after Charles had dissolved Parliament forever and resumed his attempted absolutism.[9]

The neat separation of Portsmouth-as-political and Nell-as-apolitical frequently threatened to collapse, therefore. Even in the more affectionate lampoons that absolve her from direct involvement in state affairs, political language floods back in and undoes that separation. In a dramatic monologue addressed to Charles himself, Gwyn cedes all the pomp of public recognition to her rival, but on certain conditions:

> In her white hand lett thy Gold Sceptre shine,
> And what I must not name, bee put in mine,

so that every night she can 'unking' him again in bed.[10] Thus the 'free' sexual gestures of the prostitute can be applied at once to two different and indeed opposing political initiatives, the indulgence and crypto-Catholicism of the Court, and the smouldering embers of the Good Old Cause – the original impulse to 'unking' the Stuart dynasty.

Throughout libertine satire Charles is 'unkinged' by reducing him to a mere point in a triangle defined by the two kinds of whore. Since the goal is to dishonour royalism by subtracting agency from the king, he is inconsistently presented both as an out-of-control priapist and as an impotent fumbler; all 'rule' and initiative must be transferred to the sexual being who corrupts him. He is governed by the 'regnant whores', by his Page of the Back Stairs and procurer William Chiffinch (whose 'Tool' he kissed, according to the expert witness Titus Oates), and by the disembodying force of sexuality itself. He surrenders equally to his own 'Prick' – which 'Flyes out for the Royall Cause' quite independently, 'foams and swears he will be absolute' – and to the insatiable vulva that seems to exist simultaneously in the whores and in himself. Lacy's 'Naked Picture' satire addresses the king as a strange parasite upon female flesh, part carnivore and part reptile, drawn inexorably to 'ev'ry craving hole, / Which wolf-like in your breast raw flesh devours'. The monarch is imagined actually dwelling inside the 'C--t', fixed there 'as tortoise is to shell' and only 'peep[ing] out a little now and then'; but *it* also dwells inside *him*, like a cancer of desire. As Rachel Weil observes, 'the syntax and imagery make it difficult to tell what is devouring or engulfing what'.[11]

Though nobody but Stephen College literally accuses Charles of buggery, passive or active, he is still linked to that 'Italian' vice by rumours and by comparison to flamboyant pathic emperors like Heliogabalus, as well as to authors of orgiastic displays like Tiberius, David, Sardanapalus, and the King of Sodom. Like the mistresses, these ancient parallels allowed oblique criticisms that might lead to the scaffold if aimed directly at the monarch. In Oldham's mock-heroic ode *Sardanapalus*, for example, Charles clearly resembles the absolutist monarch driven exclusively by 'Cunt', who blithely exerts his 'Sovereign Pr--k's Prerogative' and ignores 'the Rabble's Mutinies' (the bawdy-house riots of 1668), the 'Railing Satyrs' who 'with leud Wit thy Sacred Pintle did Profane' (lampoons like Oldham's), the warnings of 'Oracles' (sermons and prophecies of the Annus Mirabilis), 'pretended Treachery' (the Popish Plot), and the 'Terror of Approaching Fate'. At the same time, Sardanapalus stands for a much longer tradition of *pornographia*, piling up his funeral pyre with triumphalist genital images that 'Show'd the choice Artist's Mastery and Design / And far surpast the Wit of modern *Aretine*', and initiating the final mass copulation with a ritual fanfare that echoes Aretino's jousting scene. To the extent that the satire on sexual absolutism is topical, moreover, it blurs the distinction between praise and attack. Oldham's mock-heroic merges with the courtly cult of sublime passion that he himself upheld, as we learn from a significant verbal resemblance between *Sardanapalus* and his serious ode on the marriage of Princess Mary to the future King William III: the demented priapic absolutist, embodiment of a doomed *ancien régime*, might attempt to 'F--k for Universal Monarchy', but the sober new leader is likewise invited to translate his Ambition into Love 'in her soft Arms . . . And fancy there an Universal Monarchy.'[12]

Charles is further tainted by associating the 'French' Portsmouth with the 'Italian' anus. Though the king boasts that 'I have a French arse / For my unruly tarse', more commonly that orifice proclaims the limits of his power rather than the extent of his pleasures; in the 'French blood' satire 'Female Buttocks dictate' all Charles's policies, and in other lampoons he is made an acquiescent cuckold by 'Vendosme's Buggring Tarse' in 'Portsmouths Arse', or so dominated that

> This French hag's pocky bum
> So powerful is of late,
> Although it is both blind and dumb,
> It rules both Church and State.[13]

This image of Portsmouth upheld the general analogy of sodomy, tyranny, and foreignness, even among satirists who seem vague about the anatomical details. (What does it mean when Charles 'buggers this Parliament much like the buggering of an old woman', or when the Gods in *Sodom*, 'buggered' by King Bolloxinian, cry out 'you've frig'd us out of imortallity'?) The political implications of that adolescent burlesque are never consistently worked out, but fragmentary motifs from contemporary satire are embedded in it: the priapic tyrant who governs with his 'Prick', the compliant courtier eager to bend over, incest and masturbation among the Court ladies, impotence and dissatisfaction everywhere, 'Prerogative' as synonym for royal mistress, a neighbouring king who sends seductive boys just as Louis sent de Kéroualle. Scene 1 of *Sodom* clearly alludes to the controversy over Charles's unilateral Declaration of Indulgence, though the anus is typically stretched to accommodate several contradictory meanings. Bolloxinian dissolves the taboo against buggery by mere proclamation, as the Popes were reputed to have done, but his phrasing suggests a sarcastic jab at the Puritans ('Let Conscience have itts force of liberty').[14] Homosexual sodomy has to signify both Dissent and everything the Dissenters opposed – arbitrary power, Catholicism, a standing army who please only themselves. Its metaphorical force is further limited by the lack of fit between sign and referent, since it hardly featured at all in the long list of Charles's sexual crimes. Ironically, *Sodom* would have been more effective as a satire against Buckingham or, two decades later, against William III, both men directly portrayed as sodomites.

After Charles's death and the ouster of his brother James, all this anti-Stuart *pornographia* emerged in print under the generic title 'Secret History', parading righteous Whiggish indignation against the slavery induced by priapism while indulging in its own phallic triumph. The verse *Poems on Affairs of State* (from which, the 1697 editor promises, 'we may collect *a just and secret History* of the former times') boasts on its title-page that it publishes 'without any Castration'. In a prose narrative attributed to Milton's ubiquitous nephew John Phillips – who had attacked female 'prerogative' as early as 1653 in his lewd anthology *Sportive Wit* – the entire tradition of libertine satire against the mistresses gathers to a ripe head. The dominant perversion is now incest, woven into every episode with an equally perverse ingenuity. Charles's affair with Castlemaine, begun on the first night of his return to London, is branded incestuous by calling her the bastard daughter of Queen Henrietta Maria (as we have seen in chapter 5 above), and he continues this transgression into the next generation by marrying a son by her to one of his own daughters. Moral and physical disease, which flows from the mistresses to the monarch in earlier satires and in the treason articles, now runs from the king into the body politic:

from the first Hour of his Arrival ... he set himself by his own Perswasion and Influence to withdraw both Men and Women from the Laws of Nature and

Modesty, and to pollute and infect the People with all manner of Debauchery and Wickedness ... Fornications and Adulteries [were] the Principle Tests of the Peoples Loyalty and Obedience.

Next, Louis XIV sends over Charles's sister Henriette, Duchess of Orleans, 'whose Charms and Dexterity, joyn'd with her other Advantages, would give her such an ascendant over him as could not fail of Success'; the secret Treaty of Dover emerges from their 'Incestuous Embraces', which 'so charmed his most Sacred Majesty, that he quite and clean forgot his Tripple League, and entred into a new and stricter Alliance with *France* than ever'. (Marvell planted the seed of this interpretation when he speculates that Henriette, who died immediately after returning to France, must have carried 'some State philter ... in her bowels', released during the autopsy.) Even Portsmouth, who prolonged this sexual–political 'strict Alliance' with French interests, is branded an 'Incestuous Punk' (citing a poem attributed to Marvell) and given the same extraordinary powers over Charles that the lampoons lament and reenact. To remove 'the Scandal of being a Whore' he made her his bigamous wife – for if the law allows men one wife, 'therefore a King, who is above Law, may surely have two' – and to please her he destroyed the British constitution, proving that he 'preferr'd the Caresses of the expanded nakedness of a *French* Harlot, before the preservation of three Nations'. When she recreates the Judgement of Paris with herself and two other 'Great Ladies' as the nude goddesses, he is irrevocably 'bound to her Charms' and powerless to refuse her request that he abolish Parliament.[15]

Satiric and Utopian commonwealths of women, like 'secret histories', petitions, and lampoons, blossomed in this period when (according to the ultra-royalist Dryden) 'the Good Old Cause revived'. The theatre was fascinated by Amazons and 'roaring girls' throughout the 1670s, and when Aphra Behn updated Tatham's crudely anti-Cromwellian *Rump* in 1682 she actually made Lady Lambert a sympathetic character, mitigating the misogyny of the Council of Women. Though feminist implications were generally obliterated by the dénouement, works like Shadwell's *Woman-Captain* (1679) could be taken as sympathetic thought-experiments rather than libertine mockeries, revealing the moment when 'the hero turns into a heroine' and 'power, as one might expect at the end of the early modern period, is shifting away from the will of the sovereign to the desire of the subject'.[16] The 'parliament of ladies' theme had rumbled on throughout the Restoration (even becoming a ballad tune and a chapbook), and

Henry Neville's satire of that name remained in circulation alongside more recent insider scandals savoured by MPs. But it expands, like most of the pornographic subgenres studied in this book, when constitutional anxiety rises and state censorship declines. Around the close of Charles II's reign, Utopian fiction invents an all-female kingdom, Thomas Durfey devotes a whole comedy to a 'commonwealth of women', Mrs Cresswell in *The Whores Rhetorick* trains her protégée in Amazonian values, and 'Sylvia' replies to Robert Gould's misogynist diatribe in a convincing replica of feminist anger, its satirical purpose only given away when 'she' proposes a separatist régime exclusively devoted to complaints against the oppressions of men.[17] The 1680 *School of Venus*, translating *L'Escole des filles*, conjures up a situation where 'Women govern the World and the Church', and 'leachery' is no longer considered a crime (chapter 1, section 2 above). These possibilities are realized in the satire to be discussed in the final pages below, the feverishly overwrought, book-length *Parliament of Women* of 1684.

It would be particularly hard to distinguish satiric from Utopian impulses in those pornographic texts that build upon the conceit of sex as an imaginary kingdom or city-state. *Hollands Leaguer* and *The Women's Petition against Coffee* explicitly link pornotopia with Utopia. *Erotopolis* (the 'City of Sex') bears the subtitle *The Present State of Bettyland* and takes the form of a geographical survey, presenting an undiscovered country which signifies at once the female servant class, the sexual body, and the London brothel-world (racked by 'Rebellion' and apprentice riots). *The Whores Rhetorick* encourages the young courtesan to transform her house into 'an amorous Republick', where every known porno-political joke can find shelter: the ambitious *cortegiana* resembles the 'cringing, fawning, supplanting, and undermining' courtier (chapter 1 above), establishes a meretricious 'credit' based on 'external appearances of pomp and grandeur', turns her mirrors into 'privy Counsellours', gives special favours to Whigs and Puritans, but should not be associated with sedition since in fact she 'quell[s] all insurrections'; in short, she 'moves in a higher sphere than the rest of Women, and her actions ought to seem publick-spirited, though Statesman-like she should contrive them all to meet in the centre of her own particular advantage'.[18]

We have seen that, already in the 1650s, a concern with tyranny could express itself as the sarcastic proposal 'that women ought to govern states rather than men' (chapter 3 above). John Hall, who dedicated one of his *Paradoxes* to this theme, denounced monarchy as rule by erotic bondage, enslaving the people in 'magic chains' – though he also brands the various radical-Utopian alternatives as emotional and delusive 'resveries', leaving little room for the rational republican centre that he recommends by implication. Oppositional thinking in the early 1680s develops this critique of sensual dependency, adjusting it for the new era of mistress-rule. Only an independent Parliament can prevent the subject 'from being given up as a prey, not only to the will of a Prince, but (which is ten times worse) to the unreasonable passions and lusts of favorites, chief ministers, and women' – three persons that the Duchess of Portsmouth combined in one; in this respect England resembles the Turkish Empire, where the 'prevailing concubine' or her 'she-slave' allegedly hold the real power. Rachel Weil finds here a convincing motive for sexual satire against Charles II. Algernon Sidney, the most distinguished victim of Charles's passion for treason trials, extends this analysis to the entire Court culture. Tyranny necessarily depends on desire in absolute monarchies, and the courtiers, whose 'servile natures are guided by sense rather than reason', are obliged to 'foment [the ruler's] passions, and by advancing his worst designs, to create an opinion in him that they love his person and are entirely addicted to his will'. Specifically, 'sensual pleasures' replace glory as the reward for service, and the old chivalric ideal collapses because honours can only be acquired by 'purchasing them from whores'.[19]

John Hall's critique became timely once again during the last and longest phase of Charles's rule without Parliament, 'in Bathsheba's Embraces old'. It reappears almost verbatim, though anonymously, in the pseudo-feminist *Fifteen Real Comforts of Matrimony* by 'a Person of Quality of the Female Sex' (1683, reissued as *The Womans Advocate* in the same year). Now the warning label ('*Paradoxes*') has been suppressed and the most obvious anti-monarchical passages deleted. To maintain the book's 'female' persona, the plagiarist now amplifies the political critique of gender – men have held power 'by violence and Usurpation for so many thousand years' – and adds specific examples of women's valour in siege warfare. What then happens to the argumentative core in this transference to a wider discursive frame and a more thorough impersonation of the feminist voice? The inverted arguments remain intact, with an additional streak of sexual mockery: those who argue for female inferiority adopt a philosophy 'as feeble and stupid as their limber and useless Limbs'. This brings the paradoxical appendix into line with the rest of the book, a pretended refutation of masculine excess even more obscene than the 'debauchery' it attacks. The ostensible 'woman's advocate' becomes the railing bawd from Aretino or *The Wandring Whore*, expert in the perversions of her clients but voluble only in the illicit realm. Women's rights consist only in voluminous sexual fulfilment; women's criticism dissolves into comic banter against the impotent husband. The 'advocate' defines (and confines) her entire discourse when she defends the festive licence of the gossip's feast, 'a time of freedom, when women, like Parliament-men, have a privilege to talk Petty Treason'.[20]

The reiteration of Hall's paradox suggests a persistent desire to halt speculation about alternative forms of government, Utopian 'resveries' to which women themselves contributed. Projects for new constitutions and imaginary states – what the 1684 *Parliament of Women* calls 'Female Piles of Man-modelling' – included proposals for colleges by Bathsua Makin and Mary Astell, and Elizabeth Cellier's detailed plan for a self-governing corporation of midwives; Cellier's professional institution-building surely made her more vulnerable to accusations of interference in the body politic, a satirical trope made grimly real in the furore over the Meal Tub Plot allegedly hatched at her house.[21] Feminists (and their imitators) increasingly adopt the language of high politics, with a Whiggish rather than an absolutist tone. The flaming Tory Aphra Behn – impersonating a male seducer – defines the 'Golden Age' as an era of uninhibited sexual licence 'which freeborn we by right of Nature claim our own', and the pert heroines of Shadwell's comedies declare 'We are born free and we'll preserve that freedom', or 'I am a free Heiress of *England*, where Arbitrary Power is at an end.' Explicitly Utopian writing takes three divergent forms – the Amazonian kingdom or female-separatist institution, the asexual *terra incognita* where normal biological reproduction is replaced by plant-like propagation, and the rational application of political economy to human breeding in a freshly colonized land. Judith Drake's *Defence of the Female Sex* affirms the historical existence of the Amazons, as Hobbes had done; William Petty drew up proposals to boost population by 'Californian marriages' of one 'Hero' and multiple wives; Henry Neville shifted from the satiric parliaments of ladies to the novelistic *Isle of Pines*, where a single shipwrecked patriarch generates an entire island society by systematic mating with four female castaways – a little phallocentric kingdom implicitly contrasted to the pornocratic state of England. Mary Astell, insisting that women should 'obtain Empires', will soon expropriate for serious ends what had been thinkable only as 'paradox'; though initially she refers only to 'Empire' over the secluded self, the logic of her argument soon leads her to question women's exclusion from 'Power and Authority' in the nation. Within a half-century the identical critique of sexual hierarchy appears in the clownish charivaresque verse of the *Rump* ballad –

> We will not be Wives
> And tye up our Lives
> To Villanous slavery –

and in the piercing, elegant question formulated by Astell: 'If all men are born free, how is it that all women are born slaves?'[22]

All these topics recombine in the longest of these texts, the 1684 *Parliament of Women, or A Compleat History of the Proceedings and Debates of a Particular Junto of Ladies and Gentlewomen, with a Design to Alter the Government of the World*, which brings to a sticky end a long tradition of imagining such female gatherings. Throughout this book we have explored representations that throw into doubt whether sexuality or political authority is the principal theme, confusing these issues so thoroughly that they cannot be separated into tenor and vehicle. *Newes from the New Exchange, or the Commonwealth of Ladies* remarks of one MP that 't'is a very hard matter to know whether she be a Lady or Leviathan' (chapter 3, section 3 above), and this question hangs over later excrescences of the genre. The 'Parliament' satire becomes an exchange or clearing-house for sexual, economic, and constitutional humour, a *cour de miracles* where even the lamest jokes walk again. One ballad mixes *The Gossips Meeting* with *The Merry Market-women of Taunton*, and sings them 'to the Tune of The Parliament of Women' (1674). Another broadside, *A List of the Parliament of Women* (1679), combines the mock-official 'complaint' with the mapping and cataloguing effects of *The Wandring Whore*: protesting against the 'tyrannical' exclusion of women from the professions, inspired by the historical precedent of the Amazons, and scornful of men's incompetence as rulers, MPs from all the disreputable 'Liberties' of England gather at London Bridge, 'whose roaring Noise was most agreeable to the Harmony of their Tongues'. ('A Writ of Queen *Mabs*' provides their ancient precedent, found in 'the Records of *Utopia*'.) Similar 'parliament of women' ephemera did appear as late as 1710, and Pope still finds it a useful emasculating device; when he presents Addison giving laws to his 'little Senate' (*Epistle to Arbuthnot*, line 209) he invokes the all-female 'senaculum' of the decadent emperor Heliogabalus, a classic example of gender-inversion. But the book-length 1684 *Parliament* is the most encyclopaedic of these counter-institutions, and most fully displays the spectacle of an increasingly broad sexual humour struggling to contain an unintended Utopian articulation of women's autonomy.

The ancient and Renaissance sources of the 'parliament of women' continue to work their way to the surface. Erasmus's *Senatulus* (chapter 3 above) reminded generations of readers that the original founder of the 'Ladies' Senate' was Heliogabalus, whose scandalous life was pointedly evoked in satires against Charles II, his pleasures just as far-fetched, multiplex, all-absorbing, and inappropriate for a ruler. The emperor who took female parts in the theatre and transferred legislative power to women also supposedly searched for the best-endowed lower-class men and promoted them to high office in exchange for sexual performance, putting pressure on courtiers to join in these debauches as a sign of their loyalty. Charles likewise insists that his courtiers take mistresses, makes 'Fornications and Adulteries the Principle Tests of the Peoples Loyalty and Obedience', culls out the finest genitals, and promotes them to autonomous agency, though the favoured organ is now the 'C--t' rather than the 'donkey-sized penises' preferred by Heliogabalus.[23] Even this convention is broken in *Sodom*, which combines the literary theme of the depraved emperor with the oral tradition of complaint about the king who 'buggers Parliament'.

Erasmus's own colloquy, which highlights the women's petty conflicts over rank and misguided admiration for Heliogabalus, was translated in the seventeenth century into English, French, Dutch, and Irish, and imitated in numerous other texts. John Wilson steals a scene of his comedy *The Projectors* from Erasmus, augmented by a populist comparison to 'Fumblers' Hall' and a faux-feminist outburst lifted from Margaret Cavendish ('if the reins were in our hands, if we did not manage them better, I am sure it could not be worse!'); but this 'commonwealth of women' scene barely relates to the rest of the play, and evidently stirred no topical passion or grievance in 1665. In France, Samuel Chappuzeau's two dramatizations *Le Cercle des femmes* (1656) and *L'Académie des femmes* (1661) play down the bawdy element and amplify the teasing of 'feminine' fashions and precedence-squabbles, now joined to topical satire against the *femme savante*. Nevertheless, the expanding discursive frame and the increased need for verisimilitude leads Chappuzeau to fabricate a more eloquent feminist voice – the same process that we saw in the 1683 expansion of Hall's paradox. In the *Académie*, especially, the assembly is urged to 'waken from sleep', cast off 'tyranny', gain the upper position, establish economic independence, 'emancipate' all women over twenty by granting them widow's privileges, and gather their demands into a 'manifesto'. Of course satiric exaggeration and inversion still dominate these scenes, which Chappuzeau closes (and contains) by having the father burst in, impatient with all this 'caquet'. But the 'parliament of women' trope could evolve beyond facetiousness altogether: the Irish translation of Erasmus is supplemented by speeches on increasingly serious subjects, from women's education to the theology of prayer, and François Poullain de La Barre cites a classical female senate in his (half-)serious argument for 'The Equality of the Two Sexes'. Meanwhile, a pornographic counter-tradition developed, vastly amplifying the worldly acceptance and free discussion of sexuality hinted at moments in Erasmus's original colloquy. In Nicolas Chorier's *Aloisiae Sigeae Satyra Sotadica*, itself a Latin dialogue resembling Erasmus's in form, the learned Tullia reconstructs an older and lewder 'senatulus' of matrons, which supposedly advised Messalina during the reign of Claudius. In this version they pronounce neither on affairs of state nor on social niceties but on sexual performance, 'the office of the loins, the variety of figures, and the arousal of inert and vegetative desire'; their grave official proclamation caps the number of bouts a wife can legitimately demand (seven per night), but sets no limit whatsoever on the invention of postures, provided they express 'mutual Love'.[24] In the same vein but in the English charivari/lampoon tradition, the elderly cuckold Sir John Denham is disciplined by a 'new parliament' of London ladies who reward 'hee that Fuckes best' (chapter 4, section 4 above), ribald ancestors of modern sex-counsellors and columnists.

The 1684 version of *The Parliament of Women* borrows so heavily from the satiric tradition that it becomes the textual equivalent of the institution it travesties, a representative assembly of the topos. The framework and the debates over admissibility and precedence come from Erasmus, perhaps via Chappuzeau. But passing hints in Erasmus now expand into pages of debate. Rather than Heliogabalus, Messalina now becomes the Classical figure turned from a scandal into a shining example – prompted by the lampoon-tradition of comparing the royal mistresses to Messalina, and by the *senatulus* passage in Chorier's *Aloisia Sigea* (explicitly discussed in the text and recommended for the official curriculum). The religious irreverence of Erasmus's younger speakers (who pose tricky questions about 'the wives of monks') becomes fullblown anti-Puritan satire, a revival typical in the aftermath of the Exclusion Crisis. Fanatic MPs want to abolish school-learning and 'reduce our Language to its primitive plainness', like Quakers or the pioneers of the Royal Society; frequent use of pseudo-godly speech suggests a strong desire to apply 1640s anti-radical humour to the new feminist rhetoric (anger 'has pierced to my very Bowels, when I have lain stretched forth under the Pressure of Male-insurrection'). They reject Catholicism despite its lax régime, because female Cardinals would have to become lesbians, and settle for Antinomianism after hearing how the Ranters 'meet together Male and Female, Higgledy Piggledy, put out the Candle, put off their Cloaths and play at catch-that-catch-can bravely without fear'. These words are lifted from Burton's *Anatomy of Melancholy*, while Rabelais is plundered for the synonym 'Thelemites' (on the same page the speaker demands the abolition of clocks, a theme explicit in the original Abbey of Thélème and in Rochester's *Satyr against Mankind*). In the long pseudo-learned debate over the various forms of government (monarchy, republic, anarchy), one of the aristocrats describes a commonwealth as the inverted Hell of *Pantagruel* II.xxx, where great princes empty latrines and sell mustard.[25]

The Erasmian debate over whether to include prostitutes in the women's parliament becomes a mock-epic confrontation, reenacting the petitioners' march on Westminster and the corporate complaints of the Whores and Bawds. A disreputable army under Betty Mackerel and Orange Moll bursts in, propelled by demands for their 'equal Right to have their shares in Counsel', their 'undeniable Liberties and Properties' – slogans that echo the Whiggish heroines of comedy and the declaration of 'Liberty' in *Sodom*. (Sodomy itself is resolutely condemned, however, for expressing 'great Scorn, Contempt, Neglect, and Reproach of the Whole Commonweal of Women'.) Eventually they resolve this status-conflict by comic treaty: the prostitutes (including the procuress Lady Bennett, dedicatee of Wycherley's *Plain-Dealer*) inscribe their names in the roll-call of members, and the ladies (including 'Lady Squeamish') abolish the 'difference between them and Us; they are Daughters of Joy and so are We, Only we have the best of the Market.' This motif is lifted directly from *The Country-Wife*, where (as we saw in chapter 6) 'great Ladies, like great Merchants, set but the higher prices upon what they have'. Before this Horneresque resolution, however, the female class-war had erupted in a Rabelaisian battle of grotesque body-parts – literally a *farce*, since the severed noses and 'pieces of Buttocks' strewn on the floor resemble 'a mixture for *Lombardy* Pies'. This reduction of the common whore to butcher's meat (with an equally common pun on 'Buttocks') continues when the bullies who came to their assistance 'had their Chitterlings so stretched that they quite lost the use of 'em'.[26]

The Duke of Lenox exclaimed when confronted by militant women's petitions 'Away with these women, wee were best to have a parliament of Women' (chapter 3 above), but the reader of this monstrous assemblage seems prompted to cry 'Away with this bauble, 'tis but a parliament of Whores', or perhaps a Kitchen Cabinet. In this Rabelaisian battle between the ladies and the whores representation is literally prostituted, and as they unpack their hearts with words *pornoglossia* (as I called it in chapter 1) becomes a heteroglossia so extreme that it disintegrates into inhuman cackle. As in so many earlier 'parliaments', 'petitions', and 'commonwealths', sexual satire becomes a loose cannon that fires in several directions at once. To the extent that *The Parliament of Women* concerns women at all, it proposes that the only community they can sustain is orgiastic anarchy, the only political cause 'Nature's Good Old Cause'. But it also discredits and 'comedifies' democracy *per se*. Representative government, diverted to Oxford in 1681 and then suspended altogether, must be associated with scattered bodies and gabbling voices, 'unanimous confusion' (40) rather than purposeful convocation and incorporation.

Nevertheless, the very profusion of this chaos-effect undermines its reductive intention. The double goal of the satire pulls it in opposite directions: to encompass both misogyny and anti-Whiggery, it appeals from legitimate male institutions to a 'female' anarchy which then throws doubt upon those institutions posited as the original standard. The swarming multiplicity of voices, compared to the 'Cackling' of hens and the eruption of farts, obviously implies a contrast with the authoritative single voice of royal power, but it still seems strangely effective: mockery of tongues that 'never ceas'd till they had *talk'd* themselves into a numerous Society' anticipates – as it tries to discredit – a new conception of political culture, which would indeed (after 1688) be constituted by discussion of grievances in the public sphere. To mirror the real Parliament (prorogued as a direct result of Portsmouth's erotic influence), these 'Publick Ladies' invent a carnivalesque heraldry of distaffs, horns, and inverted chamber-pots, with a phallus instead of the all-important mace that Cromwell had reduced to a bawble. The ambiguity of these symbols – do they parade women's humiliation or proclaim their triumph? – extends from the parliamentary discussions in the text to the publisher's forematter, since distaffs and horns are explicitly rejected by the ladies, yet appear in the engraved frontispiece. In Humphrey Mill's punishing *Nights Search* a bawd is 'crowned' with carrot-tops and chamber-pots (chapter 1, section 3 above), but the gesture becomes more ambivalent when it is adopted as a deliberately outrageous costume; one of the commonwealth ladies in the 1650 *Newes from the New Exchange*, for example, enters 'with a *piss-pot* on her head, a *pipe* in her mouth, and a *pintle* in her Tail' (18). When the Speaker of the 1684 *Parliament* dons a chamber-pot as ceremonial headgear (and puts a pipe in her mouth), the reader must recall the '*Amazonian*' speech at the opening of the session, which complains that women are 'tied to our Distaffs' and used by men as mere 'Bed-pans and Close-stools'.[27]

It might please male readers to see 'women' so ready to gather under the sign of the phallus, and to define their 'freedoms' purely in terms of unlimited access to adulterous partners, but the reasons for this symbolism could be less reassuring. As the 'Poetess' Lady Polyhimne explains, the phallic mace is modelled on the thyrsis carried by the independent and unrestrained Bacchantes, and in any case this 'Utensil' is the only part of a man that women value; when it is brought in to the Chamber, the entire assembly laughs at the thought that this is the first time it has served for anything other than 'Ornament'. Which is the tenor and which the vehicle here? Which is the bawble and which the real locus of power, and why does it take a 'female' speaker to raise the question? The French proverb quoted in a later speech ('Contre le vit Estendu non est pas aucun Remede') might suggest more respect for the erection, but the point is to show how men are powerless to refuse any request when their 'prick' is 'extended'; they too are 'stretched forth under the Pressure of Male-insurrection'. Once again, the satire slashes in several directions. Mockery of effeminacy begins as early as the first debate, when the junta decides on the dress-code for the upcoming Parliament: apart from hat and breeches little change need be made, since men have already adopted smooth chins and curly periwigs. The lightweight treatment of the phallus suggests the Whigs' lack of respect for divine kingship and succession through the blood-line, but it recalls even more strongly the feeble absolutism of Charles II, who lets 'Female Buttocks dictate' and thereby becomes 'a lascivious *Dildoe K[ing]*'. As Weil remarks of this and all attempts to equate royal authority with male sexuality, 'a Priapus was a giant dildo, [and] a dildo is also a woman's tool'.[28]

Expanding on the pornographic 'Offices' of the *Wandring Whore* and mock-petition pamphlets, the speakers' complaints and proposals reveal, by reversing, a conspiratorial state that harnesses all its resources to the subjugation of women. Education, religion, technology, the printed word, the market economy – all serve this goal and must all be destroyed together. Throughout the text, telling demonstrations of these linkages snag the attention and break the lubric flow into nonsense. Men's historical and physiological claim to the 'Birth-right' is traced to Esau's mess of pottage, a dubious concoction 'of Balls and Cocks Combes, ... the main Structure upon which they build their Superiority over us'. (The original 'Porridge' adds a Puritan note, since this was their usual term of hatred for the Book of Common Prayer.) Hostility to this 'Structure' combines Levelling, castrating, and demolishing impulses: 'Let us down with it, my Lady Speaker, down with it to the ground; and level it as smooth as a Bowling Alley' (47). Squabbles over rank and precedence, the main theme of Erasmus's *Senatulus*, are candidly explained as 'bones thrown in by the Men to distract [our] Counsels, well knowing that nothing could serve them in their Dominions but our own Divisions' (92). Since men have only now acknowledged women's equality – a reference to Poullain de La Barre's *De l'Egalité des deux sexes* – they must be hiding a greater secret, women's superiority (42–3). Male power can be arrested by sabotaging the military-industrial complex, blocking the mines, cutting out the drum-heads, 'and then for their Guns, ... stop 'em up and fill 'em with melted lead, and hide 'em in the Garret under the Maids Beds' (75); the final bathos attempts to neutralize a point actually made during the Civil Wars, that women can pull down the defences they helped to build. If 'Private Families are but the Epitomes of Great Commonwealths', as Filmer argued, then seizing the state should be as easy as ruling the roost, 'and if the Enemy be stubborn, and won't yield, take a knife and disable him for good an all' (76).

In some cases, these 'dark passages' of bodily violence deflect the political argument into a simple dichotomy, with women standing for 'natural' physicality and 'common' sexuality, men for private property, education, enclosure, and chastity, enforced with a brutal technology of locks and forceps (one husband starves his wife and 'bound her up with an *Italian* Padlock, to secure his *Liberty* and *Property* as he call'd it'). Elsewhere, however, members propose a more complex counter-culture, constructing a women's history, a women's law, and a women's canon of educational texts. All these themes had been initiated more crudely in the mock-petitions and whore-pamphlets. Like Magdalena legitimizing prostitution, they research and publish ancient precedents for female rule; like Lady Castlemaine answering the whores' petition or the 1679 'Parliament' citing Queen Mab, they date documents by the female reigns of 'Pope Joan' and 'Empress Maud'. Aspiring literacy is mocked throughout the *Parliament of Women*, in passing references to popular, rude, or female-authored texts: ballads, *Aristotle's Problems*, 'the Queen of *Navars*

Novels', Margaret Cavendish's *World's Olio*, reviving the memory of the writer mad enough to suggest that

> we are shut out of all power and Authority by reason we are never imployed either in civil nor marshall affaires; our counsels are despised and laught at, the best of our actions are trodden down with scorn, by the over-weaning conceit men have of themselves. (Cited as epigraph to chapter 3 above)

When Priss Fotheringham set up her quasi-governmental brothel, we recall from chapter 4, she suppressed all anti-pornographic books and endorsed *The Crafty Whore* and *The Nights Search*. Taking this trope one step further, *The Parliament of Women* describes three books at length and promotes them to the exclusive national curriculum, entrusted with the entire task of subject-formation: they are precisely the texts that form the core curriculum of libertine literature, Aretino's *Ragionamenti*, Chorier's *Aloisia Sigea*, and *L'Escole des filles* – the work that posed the question answered here, what would happen if women ruled the world but remained exclusively focussed on sex? Book-learning is simultaneously rejected and converted into counter-technology, as in the modest proposal to wipe out the male population by sexual exhaustion, at a rate of fifteen deaths per woman-month 'according to a true Arithmetical Calculation'. Other speakers combine the old demands of the 'ladies' parliament' with the new scientific approach to breeding: men are kept in protective livestock enclosures for stud work and biologically modified so that they breast-feed.[29]

This 'Female Pile of Man-modelling' (125) thus articulates a powerful truth, generated from the disparity between its satirical purpose and the rhetoric of institutional and economic liberty it unleashes. Even its broadest and most time-worn jokes rehearse some unsettling principle. When the new Parliament alters the rules of market-trading by revising all weights and measures – the three-foot yard being too sad a reminder of better days – it suggests that other yardsticks might shrink in the winds of historical change, that apparently stable entities rest upon negotiable interests and conventions (137–8). Sexual morality will likewise change once 'no Property can be claimed' in women, and – as in Hobbes's reconstruction of the state of Nature – single mothers own their children irrespective of the father (132). Since marriage has become no more than a wholesale meat-market, with husbands in effect saying 'this Chump of Beef is mine because I have put a Scewer into it', every woman will now be able to take men at board wages, and swap them with their neighbours according to 'fair Exchange, as the Change goes' (126, 129). Behind the veil of female impersonation, the lewd satirist confronts-and-trivializes the same problem of commodification that concerned serious moralists. Jane Barker, in the poem that articulates her fear (or faith) that a writer's career must entail celibacy (chapter 6, section 4 above), likewise exposes the hard reality that makes the marriage market like any other; aristocrats hope in vain to attract City heiresses, who know that titles mean nothing without landed wealth attached – 'For now a days, few value *Ladyship*, / Since in th'Exchange it is so very cheap.'[30]

Since a prostitute is someone who sells what should never have become a commodity, it seems quite logical that an undertow of economic degradation should run through all the *pornographia* we have studied, from the charivari and 1640s 'parliament' satires to the violent evictions of working women in the bawdy-house riots and the 'mannerly obscene' lyrics that attack the ambitious courtesan. Many of the real and parodic women's petitions addressed (or belittled) economic concerns like the destruction of the luxury industries by Civil War or the 'slavery' of wives – concerns mocked in frequent 'Complaints for Want of Trading' by fictitious prostitutes and midwives. It is no accident that hostility to women preachers focussed on an independent lace-woman or that female petitioners were repeatedly told to 'go home and spin' as well as being branded as whores. The pornotropic treatment of women's work provided a universal figure for larger anxieties about political and economic instability: 'floating' negotiable prices, detached from any traditional standard of intrinsic value, correspond to the 'loose' woman or the 'wandering' whore.[31] The grotesque games of the 'Chuck-Office' flourish just as London was conceiving itself as a dazzling international emporium. Bawdy-house rioters are prosecuted for crimes against property in general. Objections to the royal mistresses would have been less intense had Charles II not been 'spending' the nation's substance on 'embezzling Cunt, that widemouthed greedy monster' (Wilson, 63). The most militant speaker in *The Parliament of Women* grasps the economic substructure of sexual satire and converts it into a simulacrum of materialist feminism. Since fluctuating market values prevail, women must

beware how ye expose your selves; for women, like all sorts of Commodities, lose their intrinsick value by being too often exposed; we are not therefore to expose our selves, but to oppose our selves; we are to oppose our selves against the Crafts, wiles, Subtilties and Polices of those that have for so many hundred years enslav'd us. (8)

It goes without saying that these masculine 'Crafts' and 'Polices' (*sic*) include the very text that gives voice to this parodic call for freedom.

In the 1684 *Parliament of Women*, as in all inversionary pornographic satires, women's agency becomes one of the 'liberties of Venus', a trivial zone of sex and carnival, unthinkable as a serious alternative. The simulated rhetoric of female anger forces us to link the verbs *expose* and *oppose*, and invites us to reverse the direction of the polemic; we are meant to replace these oppositional voices with satiric exposée, equating all political innovation with the exposure of flesh for sale. But the weight and momentum of the rhetoric reverse that reversal. Sexual subordination stands revealed as 'policy' rather than nature. In all early modern *pornographia*, and most fully in those mocking 'petitions' and 'parliaments' that voice a feminist politics in an attempt to embalm it in absurdity, history reverses the famous aphorism that Karl Marx wielded against Louis Napoleon: world-changing ideas make their first appearance as farce.

Notes

In all references the place of publication has been omitted if it is (or includes) London. Old spelling has been preserved (except for long s, u/v, i/j, thorn 'y', and 'then' for 'than'), but punctuation has been silently modernized when the original would mislead even the experienced reader. For reference, I have retained an electronic copy with full transcriptions of primary texts and fuller documentation of the critical literature.

PREFACE

1. Introduction to *Exilius, or the Banish'd Roman* (1725), ff. A2-v, and see Carol Barash, *English Women's Poetry, 1649–1714: Politics, Community, and Linguistic Authority* (Oxford, 1996), 196.
2. Bodleian MS Firth c. 16, p. 111; *The London Jilt* (1683), 2; for *The London Bully* see ch. 4, section 4 below.
3. James Wright (1694), cited in Maximillian E. Novak, *William Congreve* (New York, 1971), 45; cf. my 'The Properties of Libertinism', in Robert Purks Maccubbin (ed.), *'Tis Nature's Fault: Unauthorized Sexuality during the Enlightenment* (Cambridge, 1988), 75–87.
4. Furetière's *Dictionnaire*, s.v. 'Carême-prenant'; for the soldiers, cf. Michèle Fogel, 'L'Amour de la guerre ou la confiscation', *Nouvelle Revue de Psychanalyse* 33 (1986), 272, and for literary usage see my 'Lovelace and the Paradoxes of Libertinism', in Margaret Anne Doody and Peter Sabor (eds.), *Samuel Richardson: Tercentenary Essays* (Cambridge, 1989), 70–88.
5. *A Character of England, As It Was Lately Presented in a Letter to a Noble Man of France*, '3rd edn' (1659), 9, and for details see ch. 4, section 4 below.
6. Cf. Lena Cowen Orlin (ed.), *Material London, ca. 1600* (Philadelphia, 2000), in the series 'The New Cultural Studies'; more relevant to the current book is Lawrence Manley's *Literature and Culture in Early Modern London* (Cambridge and New York, 1995).
7. John Bender, 'A New History of the Enlightenment', *Eighteenth-Century Life* 16 (1992), 4; cf. Hunt (ed.), *The Invention of Pornography: Obscenity and the Origins of Modernity, 1500–1800* (New York, 1993), esp. Rachel Weil's chapter on

'Pornography and Politics in Restoration England', Susan Wiseman on the 'porno-political' (ch. 3, n. 43 below), and Bridget Orr, 'The Feminine in Restoration Erotica', in Clare Brant and Diane Purkiss (eds.), *Women, Texts and Histories, 1575–1760* (1992), 195–216.

8. *Newes from the New Exchange, or the Commonwealth of Ladies* (1650), 10 (ch. 3, section 3 below); *The Parliament of Women* (1684), 41 (discussed further in my Epilogue).

9. *The Poetics and Politics of Transgression* (Ithaca, NY, 1986), 19, 25.

10. *One Flesh: Paradisal Marriage and Sexual Relations in the Age of Milton* (Oxford, 1987), 2nd edn (Oxford, 1993), 25, citing 1 Cor. 6:16 (in the original *pornē*, the root word in 'pornography').

11. For the fatal attraction of liberationism even in ostensibly Foucauldian studies like Harold Weber's *Restoration Rake-Hero* and Peter Wagner's *Eros Revived*, see my review-essays 'The Culture of Priapism', *Review* 10 (1988), 1–34, and 'Sex and Consequence', *Review* 11 (1989), 41–85; for the problem of following Foucault blindly, see my review of *The Journal of the History of Sexuality* in *Modern Philology* 91 (1993–4), 405–12. My dependence on the archival research of historians – notably Elizabeth Cohen, Martin Ingram, Susan Amussen, David Underdown, Tim Harris, Ann Hughes, Ian Archer, Laura Gowing, Anna Bryson, Peter Earle, and Randolph Trumbach – raises further hermeneutic questions endemic to 'historicist' and 'cultural' projects. How can we know if 'operations' had an effect? In other words, are we trapped within textuality or can we construct a historical *pragmatics* of sexuality?

12. *Pouvoirs de l'horreur: essai sur l'abjection* (Paris, 1980), 12; *Powers of Horror: an Essay on Abjection*, transl. Leon S. Roudiez (New York, 1982), 4; *Histoires d'amour*, Folio Essais (Paris, 1983), 105.

1 *PORNOGRAPHIA* AND THE MARKINGS OF PROSTITUTION: AN INTRODUCTION

1. *A Brief Historical Relation of State Affairs, from September 1678 to April 1714* (Oxford, 1857), entry for 26 Feb. 1680.

2. Jonson I.140 (conversation with Drummond), IV.322–3 (*Poetaster*, 'To the Reader'), V.298 (*Alchemist* I.i); Rochester, 118. The Plautus passage (*Pseudolus* 519, 544–5) is analysed in William Fitzgerald, *Catullan Provocations: Lyric Poetry and the Drama of Position* (Berkeley, 1995), 56–7.

3. 'In the Fields of Lincoln's Inn', Rochester, 275 (posthumous ascription of a poem perhaps by Sir Charles Sedley); for the Sack of Rome see n. 49 below, and for the sexual 'Good Old Cause', ch. 4, section 1.

4. Caspar von Barth, *Pornodidascalus, sive colloquium muliebre Petri Aretini . . . addita expugnato urbis Romae* (Frankfurt, 1623); *Rare Verities, the Cabinet of Venus Unlocked and Her Secrets Laid Open* (1658), f. A6 ('*Pornodidascalians*'). Note that Barth chooses to couple his version of *Ragionamenti* I.iii with an account of the 1527 Sack of Rome.

5. *Letters Written from New-England, A.D. 1686*, ed. W. H. Whitmore (Boston, 1867), 112–13 (she asked for 'the *School of Venus*'); cf. Proverbs 5:5 and 6:13.

6. Laura Gowing, 'Gender and the Language of Insult in Early Modern London', *History Workshop* 35 (Spring 1993), 12, a case in Bridewell where a witness calls her neighbour 'a notorious whore' to dissuade two men from bailing her *on a charge of theft* (and see ch. 4, n. 66 below for similar discreditings); cf. Gowing, *Domestic Dangers: Women, Words, and Sex in Early Modern London* (Oxford, 1996), 85 and 203.

7. *The Pursuit of Stability: Social Relations in Elizabethan London* (Cambridge, 1991), 213.

8. Ed. Bruno Lavagnini (Catania, 1935), 196.

9. *Œuvres libertins*, ed. Frédéric Lachèvre, Le Libertinage au XVIIe siècle, 5 (Paris, 1918), 108. For the precarious category '*cortegiana honesta*', see Margaret F. Rosenthal in *The Honest Courtesan: Veronica Franco, Citizen and Writer in Sixteenth-Century Venice* (1992), *passim* (and 274–5, n. 89 for the degrading *Catalogo*) and Bette Talvacchia, *Taking Positions: On the Erotic in Renaissance Culture* (Princeton, 1999), 106–8.

10. Archer, *Pursuit of Stability*, 238; Fiora A. Bassanese, 'Private Lives and Public Lies: Texts by Courtesans of the Italian Renaissance', *Texas Studies in Literature and Language* 30 (1988), 299 ('Fasseli gratia per poetessa'), 312; Rosenthal, *Honest Courtesan*, 66–72, 186–9; Franco, *Poems and Selected Letters*, ed. and transl. Ann Rosalind Jones and Margaret F. Rosenthal (1998), 62, 166–70 (her reply to Maffio Venier's 'puttana' attack, paraphrasing it as 'meretrice' and pretending to be flattered because that word is related to 'merit'); Antonio Cavallino?, *Tariffa* (1535), ed. Guillaume Apollinaire (Paris, 1911), 54, 86; *Le Zoppino, Dialogue de la vie et généalogie de toutes les Courtisanes de Rome (XVIe siècle), littéralement traduit, texte Italien en regard* (Paris, 1883), 10. For a successful defence *against* levelling legislation, by a woman who 'did not consider herself a *meretrice* but rather a *cortesana*', see Rosenthal, *Honest Courtesan*, 72, 291 n. 33.

11. Pietro Aretino, letter 293 to Angela del Moro known as 'La Zaffetta', 25 Dec. 1537, and letter 139 to Sperone Speroni, 6 June 1537 ('l'impudicizia sua, per sì fatto onore, può meritamente essere invidiata e da le più pudiche e da le più fortunate'); for Speroni's later *Orazione contra le cortegiane*, see Rosenthal, *Honest Courtesan*, 27. The gang-rape is celebrated in Lorenzo Venier's poem *La Zaffetta*, also known as *Il trentuno della Zaffetta*, which acknowledges Aretino as its inspiration, and the *trentuno* or assault by (at least) thirty-one men is a frequent theme in Aretino himself, e.g. *Ragionamenti* I.ii.78–83 [84–7], II.ii.256–7 [267].

12. Gowing, 'Gender and the Language of Insult', 14, 11 (text partly restored from Gowing, *Domestic Dangers*, 84), 17; Rosenthal, *Honest Courtesan*, 188 (Venier's bad address and elaborate description of Veronica Franco as 'monster' made of urban salvage). Turnbull or Turnmill Street in Clerkenwell combined prostitution and butchery; *A List of the Parliament*

of Women (1679) gives the MPs for 'Turmill-street' as Mrs Knock-Ox, Mrs Impudent, Mrs Tripe-wash, and Mrs Lye-apace.

13. The cart, pillory, and ducking-stool were used interchangeably for crimes of sex and speech; Archer's *Pursuit of Stability*, for example, records a brothel-keeper sentenced to the pillory by 'a sessions for bawds and scolds' (232) and prostitutes ducked in the Thames (250, and see n. 30 below and ch. 2, nn. 21, 34 for further examples including 'whores' being associated with the 'bridle' and male whoremongers being ducked). Lynda Boose, 'Scolding Brides and Bridling Scolds: Taming the Woman's Unruly Member', *Shakespeare Quarterly* 42 (1991), 179–213, asserts that the cucking-stool and pillory were strictly differentiated according to sex (195, 186).

14. Ch. 4, section 2 below. For slang usage, see Gordon Williams, *A Dictionary of Sexual Language and Imagery in Shakespearean and Stuart Literature* (1994), s.v. 'buttock', and Wycherley, *Works* III.170 (the 'Juicy, Salt Commodity' of the oyster-seller).

15. Nottingham University Library, Portland MS PwV 42, pp. 318, 322 (Charles is 'so Gracious / To poak for Princes in thy Dust and Ashes'); *POAS* I.169 ('A Ballad Called the Haymarket Hectors', 1671), 426.

16. See my '*The Whores Rhetorick*: Narrative, Pornography and the Origins of the Novel', *Studies in Eighteenth-Century Culture* 24 (1995), 304, and Aretino, *Ragionamenti* I.iii.127 [135].

17. Archer, *Pursuit of Stability*, 231–2.

18. Wycherley, *CW* I.i.253–4; Edward Ravenscroft, epilogue to *The Citizen Turn'd Gentleman* (1672), and Hannah Wooley(?), *The Gentlewomans Companion* (1675), both cited in William J. Pritchard, 'Outward Appearances: the Display of Women in Restoration London', PhD dissertation, University of Chicago (1998), 128, 254; author unknown, *The Night-Walkers Declaration, or the Distressed Whores Advice to all their Sisters* (1676), 5.

19. I have found no evidence for this story before 1752, though Defoe might be alluding to it when Roxana remarks of her own unwillingness to embrace Catholicism 'tho' I was a Whore, yet I was a Protestant Whore' (an episode contextualized in an article by Alison Conway, forthcoming in *Eighteenth-Century Studies*). James Granger, *A Biographical History of England*, 2nd edn (1775), IV.189, retails the anecdote as a 'known fact', without giving any source, and every writer on Behn since then has likewise repeated it without reference. Better-documented stories show her accepting the title 'whore' (e.g. Pepys, 26 Oct. 1667) and colluding with Monmouth, so the conjunction 'Protestant Whore' is at least plausible; cf. Wilson, 58 ('The Ladies' March', 1681), where the aging Nelly is called 'A saint to be admired the more/Because a Church of England's whore'.

20. *Letters*, 63, 75–6, 117–18; for more detailed studies of Cavendish (including her failed attempts to petition for her exiled husband's estate), see ch. 2, section 3, ch. 3, section 3, and ch. 5, section 3 below.

21. Pallavicino, *La retorica delle puttane* (1642; 'Villafranca', 1673), 102; author unknown, *The Practical Part of Love* (1660), 73; Behn, *Love-Letters*, in *Works* II.18; the anti-mercenary declaration is used so frequently in *The*

London-Bawd that one tricked customer warns 'have a care of them that would pretend they were not mercenary, for they'll be trebly paid for what they do ('4th edn', 138–9). Philander's conditional praise of his unfaithful wife, if only she had pursued her desire 'generously', echoes Rochester's *Ramble in Saint James's Parke* (ch. 6, section 2 below).

22. 'The Soft Wanton God: Rochester's Obscenities, Acerbity and his Surprising Geniality', *TLS*, 17 Sept. 1999, 4.
23. See Milton, *CPW* III.167 ch. 5, n. 32 below, and cf. Hamon L'Estrange, *The Reign of King Charles* (1655), 9 ('the coition of a Representative').
24. Thompson, 141–2, citing anti-papal slanders by Gregorio Leti; for Lucy Hutchinson on the catamites in James I's Court, see ch. 5, n. 2 below. Frequent ribald assertions of Charles II's bastardy (e.g. ch. 5, n. 32 below) derive from insider rumours about Henrietta Maria's intimacy with Lord St Albans, supposedly witnessed by Thomas Carew; cf. Anthony Low, *The Reinvention of Love: Poetry, Politics and Culture from Sidney to Milton* (Cambridge, 1993), 144–5.
25. Diary entries for 16 July 1662, 15 May 1663 (and cf. 13 Jan., 9 Feb. 1668 for his encounter with pornography); cf. 'The Haymarket Hectors' (n. 15 above), which imagines Charles II 'consulting his cazzo' when he takes up with Nell Gwyn. For Pepys, see ch. 5, sections 1–2 below, my 'Pepys and the Private Parts of Monarchy', in Gerald MacLean (ed.), *Culture and Society in the Stuart Restoration: Literature, Drama, History* (Cambridge, 1995), 95–110, and Harold Weber, *Paper Bullets: Print and Kingship under Charles II* (Lexington, KY, 1996), 92–6.
26. Chorier, *Satyra Sotadica*, 276–7; Greater London Record Office, Middlesex Sessions Rolls, MJ/SR 1582.1, translating *L'Escole des filles, ou la philosophie des dames* (1655), ed. Pascal Pia (Paris, 1969), 29; Cavendish, *The Unnatural Tragedy*, cited in Chernaik, 200.
27. For *ribaldi* as a social group, see Richard C. Trexler, *Dependence in Context in Renaissance Florence* (Binghamton, NY, 1994), 116–26; for Milton's *CPW* II.225 see ch. 2, n. 18 below.
28. Evelyn, *A Character of England, As It Was Lately Presented in a Letter to a Noble Man of France*, '3rd edn' (1659), 9; Susan D. Amussen, '"The Part of a Christian Man": the Cultural Politics of Manhood in Early Modern England', in Amussen and Mark A. Kishlansky (eds.), *Political Culture and Cultural Politics in Early Modern England: Essays Presented to David Underdown* (Manchester and New York, 1995), 218, 219 (Amussen exaggerates when she asserts that 'extra-marital sexual activity was not a part of [men's] presentation of themselves *to the world*' [218, my emphasis], though they were clearly unwilling to present it to the *magistrate*); for Restoration hooliganism, see ch. 6 below, and for sporadic attempts to charge male customers found in London brothels, see Archer, *Pursuit of Stability*, 211, 250–1. Otway is cited from Williams, *Dictionary of Sexual Language*, *s.v.* 'buttock'.
29. Milton, *SA*, lines 410–11, 416–18, 537, *CPW* II.258; one of Milton's sources must have been the *Regno femineo* in Ariosto's *Orlando furioso* (ch. 3, n. 37 below), esp. XX.lxii and lxiii. *Drudgery* as a contemptuous word for intercourse

is ubiquitous in, e.g., Behn's *Love-Letters* (II.95), Rochester (38), Wycherley (*Works* III.154, IV.192), and Dryden (*Works* IV.151, 179, V.213, XIII.111); the heroic king in *Sodom* explains that he abandoned heterosexuality because 'the Drudgery has worn out my desire' (304).

30. Coryate cited in Rosenthal, *Honest Courtesan*, 73; deposition cited in Archer, *Pursuit of Stability*, 207; Sir George Etherege, *Poems*, ed. James Thorpe (Princeton, NJ, 1963), 43 (the exchange of verse letters with the future Earl of Dorset cited ch. 6, section 4 below); defamatory diatribe cited n. 12 above from Gowing. Another form of linguistic agency given to the illicit woman was the naming of her child's father, often during labour-pains and witnessed by the midwife, and sometimes in a public meeting (e.g. Gowing, *Domestic Dangers*, 72–4).

31. Donne, *Satire* I, line 108 (a ref. I owe to Karen Newman); Behn II.94, I.67, 68; Chorier, *Satyra Sotadica*, 189–90, 183 ('Redde [mentulam] commodatam, proterva. Quam reddis, mea non est: non agnosco'); Amerigo Vespucci alleged that the women of the New World 'being very lustful, *make* their husbands' members swell to such thickness that they look ugly and misshapen', according to Raymond Waddington, 'Rewriting the World, Rewriting the Body', in Arthur F. Kinney (ed.), *The Cambridge Companion to English Literature 1500–1600* (Cambridge, 2000), 295 (my emphasis).

32. Elizabeth S. Cohen, 'Honor and Gender in the Streets of Early Modern Rome', *Journal of Interdisciplinary History* 32 (1991–92), 614–15 (original text kindly supplied by Dr Cohen). For menstrual blood in magic designed to create sexual love in another person, see (for fiction) Aretino, *Ragionamenti* I.iii.121–2 [129] (whores exult in their ability to make men devour their 'scabs and *marchese*'), and (for legal depositions in Venice) Guido Ruggiero, *Binding Passions: Tales of Magic, Marriage, and Power at the End of the Renaissance* (New York and Oxford, 1993), 92, 244 n. 15, 255 n. 22, 247 n. 45; for sexual magic in England cf. Gowing, *Domestic Dangers*, 228.

33. *Works* XIII, II.i.46, III.i.55, and cf. I.i.32 ('the Conqu'ring Soldier, red with unfelt wounds'). For the shifting relation of 'Prostitute' and 'wife' see IV.i.85, III.i.69, II.i.42, IV.i.75, V.i.106.

34. 'Gender and the Language of Insult', 10; *Domestic Dangers*, 80, 103 (citing similar work on 'losing face' in the Middle Ages).

35. The sheet from which fig. 3 is taken, a wall calendar, is illustrated in Hilde Kurz, 'Italian Models of Hogarth's Picture Stories', *Journal of the Warburg and Courtauld Institutes* 15 (1952), pl. 30d, and in David Kunzle, *History of the Comic Strip* (Berkeley, 1973), 292.

36. Aretino, *Ragionamenti* II.i.197 [205]; Francis Kirkman, *The English Rogue and Other Extravagants*, Part 3 (1671), 63–4 (a continuation of the work begun by Richard Head). For facial mutilation in different classes and cultures, see Rosenthal, *Honest Courtesan*, 237, G. R. Quaife, *Wanton Wenches and Wayward Wives: Peasants and Illicit Sex in Early Seventeenth Century England* (New Brunswick, NJ, 1979), 26, Pepys, 19 and 20 Nov. 1668, Grace Hart Seely, *Diane the Huntress: the Life and Times of Diane de Poitiers* (1936), 181; Alan Nelson informs me that in 1548 the mistress of the sixteenth Earl of

Oxford had her nose mutilated by several members of his family, perhaps at his own instigation, and cites the broadside 'balade of a preist that loste his nose' ('to be without nose was the marke of an whore').

37. Cohen, 'Honor and Gender', 623 (and cf. 607 n. 15 for the crime of 'deturpatio facieis curialis stercore humano' or 'filthying courtesan's faces with human dung'); Hans Jakob Christoffel von Grimmelshausen, *Lebensbeschreibung der Ertzbetrügerin und Landstörtzerin Courasche*, ed. Wolfgang Bender (Tübingen, 1967), 89 ('die berühmteste Putana'), 91; State Papers transcribed in John Harold Wilson, *All the King's Ladies: Actresses of the Restoration* (Chicago, 1958), 27–8.

38. Cohen, 'Honor and Gender', 607, 613, 615 (the assailant had been accused of having a 'big mouth' and 'opening to everyone', and appropriately her voice gave her away when she joined the men she had hired to storm her insulter's house).

39. Poem xxxvii, lines 9–10; cf. Fitzgerald, *Catullan Provocations*, 66–7.

40. Elizabeth Cohen, 'Camilla la Magra, prostituta romana', in Ottavia Niccoli (ed.), *Rinascimento al femminile* (Bari, 1991), 189–90 (an assault also involving lewd verses), and 'Honor and Gender', 597–625, esp. 603 (graffiti of phalluses and horns), 604–5, 606 (legal codes specifying penalties and offences, including horn-throwing); Rossiaud summarizes his *Annales* and *Cahiers d'histoire* articles in 'Prostitution, Sex and Society in French Towns in the Fifteenth Century', in Phillipe Ariès and André Béjin (eds.), *Western Sexuality*, transl. Anthony Forster (Oxford and New York, 1985), 75–94, esp. 84–7; Gowing, *Domestic Dangers*, 72, 96, 97, 104. Quaife, *Wanton Wenches*, 157, records a woman using excrement to defile a neighbour's house in Somerset. For the larger context of *bachelleries* and 'abbeys of misrule', see Natalie Zemon Davis, 'The Reasons of Misrule', in *Society and Culture in Early Modern France* (Stanford, CA, 1975), 97–123.

41. 'Honor and Gender', 607, 621 (explicit associations between attacks on the house and on the face), 618.

42. Rossiaud, 'Prostitution', 85; Cohen, 'Honor and Gender', 604.

43. Marvell, letter to William Popple, 14 Apr. 1670, *Letters* 317; for Donne see ch. 2, n. 33 below, and for 'A Rapture', *The Poems of Thomas Carew, with His Masque Coelum Britannicum*, ed. Rhodes Dunlap (Oxford, 1949), 49–53.

44. Ladurie, *Carnival in Romans*, transl. Mary Feeney (New York, 1979), esp. 95–6, 223–4. For Evil May Day see *The Booke of Sir Thomas Moore*, ed. W. W. Greg (Oxford, 1911), and Simon Hunt, '"Leaving Out the Insurrection": Carnival Rebellion, English History Plays, and a Hermeneutics of Advocacy', in Patricia Fumerton and Hunt (eds.), *Renaissance Culture and the Everyday* (Philadelphia, 1999), 299–314; for the bawdy-house riots and the high treason trial that followed them, see ch. 5 below, and for Udine, Edward Muir, *Mad Blood Stirring: Vendetta and Factions in Friuli During the Renaissance* (1993).

45. Edward Ward, *The London-Spy Compleat, in Eighteen Parts*, '4th edn' (1709), 141–3 (the Spy protests that flogging the 'tender Back and tempting Bubbies'

of prostitutes in Bridewell 'was design'd rather to Feast the Eyes of the Spectators, or Stir up the Beastly Appetites of Lascivious Persons, than to Correct Vice or Reform Manners'), 153; *Good Sir W------ Knock: The Whores Lamentation for the Death of Sir W[illiam] T[urner]*, 'Printed for the Assigns of Posture-Moll' (1693), 1–2 ('Poor Whores are Whip'd, whilst Rich Ones Ride in Coaches'); Shakespeare, *King Lear* IV.vi.160–3; Wycherley, Prologue to *The Gentleman Dancing-Master*, 125, *Works* IV.192; Gowing, *Domestic Dangers*, 105 (and cf. 192). The charivaresque punishment of James Nayler is discussed in ch. 2, section 2 below.

46. James Harrington, cited ch. 5, n. 26 below; Eco, 'The Frames of Comic "Freedom"', in Thomas A. Sebeok and Marcia E. Erickson (eds.), *Carnival!* (Berlin, New York, and Amsterdam, 1984), 1–9 (the English carnivalesque is less starkly inversionary than the Italian, and resembles more what Eco here calls 'humor'); Gowing, *Domestic Dangers*, 215; Leah S. Marcus, 'Justice for Margery Evans: a "Local" Reading of *Comus*', in Julia M. Walker (ed.), *Milton and the Idea of Woman* (Urbana and Chicago, 1988), 77; for Shrove Tuesday attacks, see chs. 2 and 5 below, and for the ambiguity of Shakespeare's phrase 'chartered libertine' (*Henry V* I.i.48) see my Preface.

47. *Erotopolis, or a New Description of Bettyland* (1684), sometimes attributed to Charles Cotton; *Mundus Foppensis* (1691), cited in Michael McKeon, 'Historicizing Patriarchy: the Emergence of Gender Difference in England, 1660–1760', *Eighteenth-Century Studies* 28 (1995), 307; Ward, *Rambling Rakes* (1700), 8–9, *London-Spy*, 153. The 'separate' area ('but Three Yards from the street') is in fact the criminal sanctuary in Whitefriars known as 'Alsatia' – a kind of mock-manor with its own aristocracy, immortalized in Shadwell's *The Squire of Alsatia* and in Laroon's *Cryes* – not, as McKeon asserts, a sodomite subculture.

48. Jonson, *Volpone* IV.ii.96; for 'Carnelevation' among the Ranters and the Hectors, see ch. 2, n. 2 below, and for the iron bridle see Boose, 'Scolding Brides'. The concept of the '*anti*-processional' is formulated in E. P. Thompson, '"Rough Music": le Charivari anglais', *Annales ESC* 27 (1972), 289.

49. Aretino, *Ragionamenti* I.i.25–7 [31–2], II.ii.233 [243], 256–7 [267]; Bette Talvacchia, 'Professional Advancement and the Use of the Erotic in the Art of Francesco Xanto', *Sixteenth-Century Journal* 25 (1994), 142–9, fig. 12; the single-leaf *Hue and Cry* is undated, but Luttrell's copy, Newberry Library, Chicago, Case 6A 158(72) is inscribed 30 Mar. 1680. See ch. 4, n. 17, below for jousting imagery, and p. 140 for the 'hue and cry' title.

50. Gowing, *Domestic Dangers*, 247, notes an adulterous couple overheard on Christmas Eve saying 'I hope I have skoured you now, I hope so quoth she . . . and laughed at it' (cf. ch. 6, section 3 below for aristocratic 'scouring', and ch. 4, section 2 for pig-roasting); Milton, Columbia edition IX.95 ('Fescennina' for sexual adventures in the woodshed); Chorier, *Satyra Sotadica*, title of Colloquium VII (*Fescennini*); Lorenzo Venier, *La Puttana errante, poème en quatre chants de Lorenzo Veniero . . . littéralement traduit, text italien en regard* (Paris, 1883), 22, 28, and final canto *passim*.

51. A version of this very large drawing was sold on the Paris art market with a full-scale engraving (PIASA, 9 Apr. 1999, lot 3); fig. 4 shows the reduced outline etching, probably eighteenth-century, in the BnF, Paris, Estampes (Rés. Ae 33).

52. Etherege, *Poems*, 46; Butler, *Hudibras* II.ii.640–6, 702; Rochester, 254 (attribution questionable).

53. Ruth Mellinkoff gathers many instances from earlier history and from ethnography, including instances of tail-lifting and relishing of the despised role, in 'Riding Backwards: Theme of Humiliation and Symbol of Evil', *Viator* 4 (1973), 153–76; see ch. 2, n. 35 below for its use in punishing dissidents and Epilogue, n. 4 for the 'Abhorrer of Petitions', and cf. Claude Noirot, *L'Origine des masques, mommeries, bernez et revuennez es jours gras de Caresmeprenant, menez sur l'asne a rebours et charivari* (Paris, 1608).

54. Ingram, 'Rhymes', 176; Marvell, *The Rehearsal Transpros'd*, ed. D. I. B. Smith (Oxford, 1971), 72–3 (expanding on an anecdote in Montaigne, *Essais* II.xxxii, by adding the cuckoldry theme); Robert Plot, cited in Boose, 'Scolding Brides', 207.

55. Ed[ward] S[ta]cy, *The Country Gentleman's Vade Mecum, or His Companion for the Town* (1699), 10; Butler, *Characters*, ed. Charles W. Daves (Cleveland, OH, 1970), 246; William Cecil, Lord Burghley, *Precepts* (1637), cited in Patricia Meyer Spacks, *Gossip* (1986), 123; Burghley's copy of Aretino's *Ragionamenti* is illustrated in David Foxon, *Libertine Literature in England, 1660–1745* (New Hyde Park, NY, 1965), plate V.

56. Montaigne, *Journal de voyage en Italie*, *Œuvres complètes*, ed. Albert Thibaudet and Maurice Rat, Bibliothèque de la Pléiade (Paris, 1962), 1235; *Biographie universelle*, 'Ferrante Pallavicino'; Herbert, 'The Forerunners'; Jonson, dedication of *Volpone*, V.21 (a point I owe to Wendy Roth). For suspicions of rhetoric's prostitutional aspect, see Milton *PR* IV.343–64 and Jacqueline Lichtenstein, 'Making Up Representation: the Risks of Femininity', *Representations* 20 (Fall 1987), 78–9.

57. Ruggiero, *Binding Passions*, 43–5, 91, 93–4, 100–2, 105; Rosenthal, *Honest Courtesan*, 73; Feldman, 'The Courtesan's Voice', paper delivered at UCLA conference, The World of the Courtesan, 1995, 1–7. For a largely unenthusiastic account of courtesans as poets see Bassanese, 'Private Lives'.

58. *Works* III.155–6, and for the 'he-whore' lampoon see ch. 6, section 1 below. Behn's own publicity encouraged this kind of humour; the epilogue to *The Dutch Lover* (1673) uses the same 'half a crown' joke.

59. Shakespeare, *2 Henry IV* I.ii; Rochester, 259, 37, 78–9 (for Dorset see ch. 6, section 4 below); *The Town-Misses Declaration and Apology* (1675), 7.

60. Brown, *A Continuation or Second Part of the Letters from the Dead to the Living*, '2nd edn' (1707), 171, and cf. Williams, *Dictionary of Sexual Language*, s.v. 'buttered bun'; Doody, *The True Story of the Novel* (New Brunswick, NJ, 1996), 268–9 (includes Ingelo quotation).

61. Gould, *A Satyrical Epistle to the Female Author of a Poem, Call'd Silvia's Revenge* (1691), 5, 19; Fyge, *The Female Advocate, or an Answer to a Late Satyr against the Pride, Lust and Inconstancy of Woman* (1687), 4.

62. 'Courtesan Curiosities', paper given at MLA Annual Convention, Chicago 1999, 7–8.
63. *The London-Bawd*, 3rd edn (1705), 26–34, repeats the facial mutilation story in *Decameron* VII.viii; Grimmelshausen, *Courasche*, 84, *Tariffa*, 64–8, Wilson, 211, 219, 222 n. 51; Princess Michael of Kent, *Cupid and the King* (1991), 46–7 (anecdote about a Spanish husband's revenge on François I), and cf. Lorenzo, conte Magalotti, *Relazioni d'Inghilterra, 1668 e 1688*, ed. Anna Maria Crinò (Florence, 1972), 78. For the 'St Antholin's' story and its later permutations, see my 'Pictorial Prostitution: Visual Culture, Vigilantism, and "Pornography" in Dunton's *Night-Walker*', *Studies in Eighteenth-Century Culture* 28 (1999), 55–84.
64. Terms used in prosecutions of *L'Escole des filles* in France and England, cited from Pia (ed.), *L'Escole*, 177 ('contre l'honneur de Dieu, de l'Eglise et fort contraire aux bonnes moeurs et dissipline chrestienne') and MJ/SR 1582.1 (n. 26 above).
65. Ames, *Catalogue* (1691), 2 (authorship suggested by Hugh Amory, cited in Thompson 93); for the other Fair pamphlets mentioned here, see ch. 4, n. 30 below, and for market discourse cf. *The Womans Brawl, or Billingsgate against Turn-Mill-Street* (1680).
66. (1640), ff. A3, B1-v, B6v,):(7, pp. 1–10, 75, 99, 273–6; for puns on Mill's name and the constable's round, see ff. A3, B5v, V7. Both parts of the *Nights Search* were reissued in 1652, and evidently remained in circulation.
67. *Bentivolo and Urania* (1660), 2nd edn (1669), f. b3; for Barker, see Preface above.
68. *Dialoghi italiani: dialoghi metafisici e dialoghi morali*, ed. Giovanni Gentile, 3rd edn, ed. Giovanni Aquilecchia (Florence, 1958), 602, 673–4.
69. Nicholas Goodman, *Hollands Leaguer* (1632), f. F4v; Carew, *Poems*, ed. Dunlap, 157–8. Momus's commentary (163–8) manages to contaminate the Caroline masque by mentioning 'riotous Assembly', overcrowded jails and mass escapes from them, epidemics, venereal disease, transportation to New England, free elections, and the abolition of Star Chamber.

2 CEREMONIES OF ABJECTION: SEX, POLITICS, AND THE DISORDERLY SUBCULTURE

1. 291; Ingram presents several cases of gentry approval, including the (fictional) speech by Margaret Cavendish discussed in section 3 below, to undermine the argument that popular and élite culture were totally separate ('Ridings', 100, 104–8).
2. Edmund Gayton, *Pleasant Notes upon Don Quixote* (1654), quoted in Nigel Smith, *Literature and Revolution in England, 1640–1660* (1994), 46; linking the sexual excesses of the Ranters and the Hectors, Gayton cites '*Carnelevation*' as a familiar term used by that street gang.
3. *The Daring Muse: Augustan Poetry Reconsidered* (Cambridge, 1985), 123.

4. For *abbayes* and *abbesses* in France, see Rossiaud, 'Prostitution' (ch. 1, n. 40 above); for English usage, cf. 'Lucy Negro, Abbess de Clerkenwell' in the Gray's Inn Christmas revels *Gesta Grayorum* (1594) (a reference I owe to Bruce Smith) and Richard Ames, *The Folly of Love* (1691), 13 (the notorious Posture Moll as '*Lady Abbess*').

5. G. R. Quaife, *Wanton Wenches and Wayward Wives* (New Brunswick, NJ, 1979), 166, 168; Underdown, 71, 95; for mock-sermons see further Ingram 'Rhymes', 166, 'Ridings', 95, and ch. 4, n. 71 below. The homophobic 'Groaning' took place in Westonbirt, Gloucs., as late as 1716; it is analysed in David Rollison, 'Property, Ideology and Popular Culture in a Gloucestershire Village 1660–1740', *Past and Present* 93 (Nov. 1981), 70–97, esp. 73 and 90–1. Ingram's 'Ridings' article is a riposte to Rollison's interpretation; neither historian makes the connection to the supposed ceremonies of the 'Molly houses' (nor so far as I know has any discussion of texts like Edward Ward's 'Of the Mollies Club' interpreted them as a charivaresque mockery).

6. Quaife, *Wanton Wenches*, 149, 170, 173; see ch. 1, section 2 above for sexual 'jousting', Rabelais II.xxii for Panurge's (literally) smearing the Lady of Paris, and Underdown, 258, for the 1645 mock-battle on Blackheath. For model castles cf. *Annalia Dubrensis* (1636), ff. E2–3v, F3v, H1, and the Naples carnival that set off the rebellion of Masaniello (n. 37 below).

7. Underdown, 101; Ingram, 'Ridings', *passim*, esp. 100 ('sodomy' in 1661, perhaps referring to the parodic embraces of two men, with one dressed as the 'wife'); Butler, *Hudibras* II.ii.565–844 (pp. 142–9, discussed further in section 3 below); Susan Dwyer Amussen, *An Ordered Society: Gender and Class in Early Modern England* (Oxford and New York, 1988), 118 n. 57 (for the copulation staged in one such Skimmington). The mount in these 'ridings' was sometimes an ass and in many regions of England a 'stang' or pole, a word that in Northern dialects and Scots could also refer to the erect penis, as in Dunbar.

8. Paul Hair, *Before the Bawdy Court: Selections from Church Court and Other Records Relating to the Correction of Moral Offences in England, Scotland and New England, 1300–1800* (1972), 137–8, 190, 215; Ingram, *Courts*, 164. For a general ethnography, see Jacques Le Goff and Jean-Claude Schmitt (eds.), *Le Charivari: actes de la table ronde organisée à Paris (25–27 avril 1977) par l'Ecole des Hautes Etudes en Sciences Sociales et le Centre National de la Recherche Scientifique* (Paris, 1981), and for an earlier synthesis (based largely on nineteenth-century sources including Hardy's *Mayor of Casterbridge*), E. P. Thompson, '"Rough Music": le Charivari anglais', *Annales ESC* 27 (1972), 285–312.

9. Underdown, 55, supplementing the account of the 'Wells May Game' in C. J. Sisson, *Lost Plays of Shakespeare's Age* (Cambridge, 1936), 162–85, with further material from Star Chamber archives; John Hole had in fact been accused before the bishop of adultery with Mrs Yard (Sisson, *Lost Plays* 165). Ronald Hutton, *The Rise and Fall of Merry England: the Ritual Year, 1400–1700* (Oxford and New York, 1994), 159, refers to the victim as John *Hale*.

10. Ingram, 'Ridings', 105 and 'Rhymes', 166 (I have added an *accent grave* to the hunting-cry 'à whore' as a reminder that 'a' is not the indefinite article but the Anglo-Norman preposition); Underdown, 100–1; Quaife, *Wanton Wenches*, 168–9, 201; Amussen, *Ordered Society*, 97, 99–103 (on defamation suits, increasing to a female majority after 1660). For London see Laura Gowing, *Domestic Dangers: Women, Words, and Sex in Early Modern London* (Oxford, 1996), esp. ch. 3, and for the West Country (in the earlier seventeenth century) Ingram, *Courts*, ch. 10 *passim*, esp. 301–13.

11. Ingram, 'Rhymes', 166, 178–86, 'Ridings', 86, 87, 95, *Courts*, 117, 164–5, 293; Underdown, 101, 280; Sisson, *Lost Plays*, 174, 176. For the numerous London sites where libels and epigrams might be posted, see Manley, *London*, 418.

12. Sisson, *Lost Plays*, 176. For the readership of such verses, see Joy Wiltenburg, *Disorderly Women and Female Power in the Street Literature of Early Modern England and Germany* (1992), ch. 3, and Bernard Capp, 'Popular Literature', in Barry Reay (ed.), *Popular Culture in Seventeenth-Century England* (1985), 198–243.

13. Ingram, 'Rhymes', 180; letter of Rev. Chantrell (1621), cited in Thomas Cogswell, 'Underground Verse and the Transformation of Early Stuart Political Culture', in Susan D. Amussen and Mark A. Kishlansky (eds.), *Political Culture and Cultural Politics in Early Modern England: Essays Presented to David Underdown* (Manchester and New York, 1995), 284; Ingram, *Courts*, 313; Underdown, 127. 'The Westminster Whore' is transcribed from Bodleian MS Rawl. Poet. B. 35, f. 36 rev., and dated '*c.* 1610', in E. J. Burford (ed.), *Bawdy Verse: a Pleasant Collection* (Harmondsworth, 1982), 63; cf. 73–5, 'Panders, Come Awaye'.

14. Gowing, *Domestic Dangers*, 72; diary of Henry Machyn, cited in Douglas Bruster, 'The Horn of Plenty: Cuckoldry and Capital in the Drama of the Age of Shakespeare', *SEL* 20 (1990), 195 (a reference I owe to Wendy Roth); pp. 195–7 cite more extensive allusions to the place, including a 1623 lament by John Taylor the Water-Poet that the 'monumental memorable Horn' has disappeared (numerous Restoration references show, however, that 'Horn Fair' remained imprinted on London geography). Ingram, 'Rhymes', 169 records a Skimmington-like mockery in Charing Cross, 1563, perhaps the earliest 'riding' known. For the festive-aggressive rivalry of fishmongers and butchers, see Michael D. Bristol, *Carnival and Theater: Plebeian Culture and the Structure of Authority in Renaissance England* (1985), ch. 5 (and esp. 76, where Taylor cheers on the 'friendly, frolic, frank, free-hearted, famous flourishing Fishmongers, and brave, bold, battering, beef-braining butchers' in a flashy alliterative style that emulates their carnival exuberance).

15. *Bartholomew Fair* IV.v.105; see ch. 4, section 2 below for Bartholomew Fair as a site of promiscuous mingling.

16. Ingram, 'Ridings', 84–5 (Montacute), 106–7 (literary references to ridings).

17. Jonson, *Bartholomew Fair*, Induction, 14; Henry Morley, *Memoirs of Bartholomew Fair*, 'New Edition' (1880), 181–4. For the Countess of Castlemaine's

visit to the Fair, see ch. 5, n. 11 below, and for Henri IV's see Pierre
de L'Estoile, *Journeaux-Mémoires* VIII (Paris, 1880), 14 (entry for February
1602).

18. *CPW* II.225, a passage added in the second edition of *The Doctrine and Dis-*
cipline of Divorce.

19. *Select City Quaeries, Discovering . . . City Bawds, Whores and Trepanners* (1660),
III.13. The sonnet 'I did but prompt the age to quit their clogs' anticipates
the 'clog' lampoon cited in Thompson, 120. In *Colasterion*, Milton threatens
to write 'a rough *Sotadic*' against his adversary (*CPW* II.757), but in many
ways this violent and sometimes obscene polemic already is one; for the
genre of the *Satyra Sotadica* see Chorier, cited ch. 1, n. 8 above.

20. Underdown, 101 ('credits'), 102; Ingram, 'Ridings', 96, 'Rhymes', 175.

21. *Bartholomew Fair*, Induction, 13 and 14 ('would not a fine Pumpe upon the
Stage ha'done well, for a property now?'); this is clearly a distinct usage of the
noun *pump*, although *OED* only records the verb in this punitive sense (4a,
1632, by Brome, who was present behind the arras during the performance
of *Bartholomew Fair*, according to the stage-keeper). Florio's definition is cited
in David O. Frantz, 'Florio's Use of Contemporary Italian Literature in
A Worlde of Wordes', *Dictionaries* 1 (1979), 50. See Gowing, *Domestic Dangers*,
100, for pumping as the washing of 'actual dirt' and symbolic pollution in
London, and Quaife, *Wanton Wenches*, 198, 201 for ducking as a punishment
for fornication.

22. Henry Oxinden cited in Ingram, 'Ridings', 105 (and cf. 93); Underdown,
102. The 1618 expulsion of an extramarital couple in Burton-on-Trent,
to cries of 'à whore', was led by the constable, who claimed the authority
of 'ancient usage and custom' ('Ridings', 105) and the justices' approval (a
line of argument still being used to justify a festive Skimmington in 1653,
as cited in Underdown, 264).

23. *Courts*, 165; 'Ridings', 100. The Skimmington should perhaps be viewed as
an extension of the licentious festivities that accompanied *all* weddings.

24. Rossiaud, 'Prostitution' (ch. 1, n. 40 above), 84-5. I am not here trying to
conflate shaming rituals and organized adolescent subcultures (and I accept
Ingram's warning in 'Ridings', 104, n. 72); though adolescents and 'rude
boys' invariably joined in, the main instigators could come from a wide
range of social positions, even the squire's wife (n. 26 below). Nevertheless,
charivari clearly resembles bachelor and apprentice rioting, and can be
interpreted as a temporary, elective bachelorhood. Keith Thomas links
'rough music' to the unruliness of youth, especially apprentices, even though
it does enforce community norms; 'Age and Authority in Early Modern
England', *Proceedings of the British Academy* 62 (1976), 219.

25. Ingram, 'Rhymes', 176 (also cited in ch. 1, section 2 above).

26. Ingram, 'Rhymes', 187, 'Ridings', 105, 109; Quaife, *Wanton Wenches*, 199;
Star Chamber proceedings cited in Peter Stallybrass, '"Drunk with the Cup
of Liberty": Robin Hood, the Carnivalesque, and the Rhetoric of Violence
in Early Moden England', in Nancy Armstrong and Leonard Tennenhouse

(eds.), *The Violence of Representation: Literature and the History of Violence* (1989), 56. For youth 'abbeys', see Davis and Rossiaud, ch. 1, n. 40 above.

27. 'A quiet Life, and a good Name' (1719), *Poems*, ed. Harold Williams (Oxford, 1937), I.221; Ingram, 'Rhymes', 176 (including contemporary remarks about inadequacy and citation from Swift's poem).

28. *A Bawd, a Vertuous Bawd, a Modest Bawd* (1635), 31–2. For the association between down-filled bedding and sexual penetration, cf. Quaife, *Wanton Wenches*, 168, a defendant cited for saying 'Mary Pittard's thing is as soft as a feather pillow.'

29. Ingram, 'Rhymes', 176, 'Ridings', 90, 101; *A Proclamation against Excesse of Lavish and Licentious Speech of Matters of State* (1620), appropriately promulgated on Christmas Eve (a reference I owe to Fritz Levy).

30. Ingram, 'Ridings', 108, 'Rhymes', 184–5, 186. Ingram notes that *exclusively* political charivaris were rare until later in the seventeenth century, but recognizes that the domestic variety was often political in a broad sense. In addition to examples already noted, see 'Ridings', 93, 95, 103, 108, 'Rhymes', 171, 173, 183–6; for the West-Country Skimmingtons against enclosers and 'projectors' see also Underdown, 106, 110–11 (cf. 216, anti-excise riots). For verses against Buckingham see Alastair Bellany, '"Raylinge Rymes and Vaunting Verse": Libellous Politics in Early Stuart England, 1603–1628', in Kevin Sharpe and Peter Lake (eds.), *Culture and Politics in Early Stuart England* (1994), 285–310; for charivaresque elements in conflicts among the Jacobean gentry and their local officials see Richard Cust, 'Honour and Politics in Early Stuart England: the Case of Beaumont Versus Hastings', *Past and Present* 149 (Nov. 1995), 57–94.

31. Bernardo Prosperi, letter of 21 Sept. 1496, cited in Deanna Shemek, *Ladies Errant: Wayward Women and Social Order in Early Modern Italy* (1998), 37.

32. Underdown, 106, 110–11 (for pillorying transvestite rioters see also 111 n. 20 and Stallybrass, 'Robin Hood', 56). This form of cross-dressing may have been intended as an effective disguise, in contrast to the festive-burlesque kind common in May Games, which chose the most incongruous men for their beards, heavy frame, or 'general inability to make convincing transvestites' (Hutton, *Merry England*, 118).

33. Ingram, *Courts*, 54, 236, 249, 257, 338; though this full penance was rarely enjoined, it was still effective as a deterrent for anyone dependent on 'credit' for a living (for some cheerfully vulgar female exceptions, see p. 337 and Quaife, *Wanton Wenches*, 194). Amussen, 'Manhood' (ch. 1, n. 28 above), 226 cites a *man* terrified that public penance 'a great hindrance to his preferment in marriage'. The entire issue of punishment was keenly debated in Parliament, as Keith Thomas shows in 'The Puritans and Adultery: the Act of 1650 Reconsidered', in Donald Pennington and Keith Thomas (eds.), *Puritans and Revolutionaries: Essays in Seventeenth-Century History Presented to Christopher Hill* (Oxford, 1978), 257–82.

34. Underdown, 243; Ingram, 'Ridings', 92–3, 'Rhymes', 172–4 (includes earlier parallels from France); Stallybrass, 'Robin Hood', 50. For riding backwards, see also Stallybrass's source Ruth Mellinkoff, ch. 1 n. 53 above.

35. *A Complete Collection of State-Trials* (1742), II.272; Rosemary Kegl, 'Women's Preaching, Absolute Property, and the *Cruel Sufferings (For the Truths Sake) of Katharine Evans & Sarah Chevers*', *Women's Studies* 24, special issue *Gender, Literature, and the English Revolution*, ed. Sharon Achinstein (1994), 57 (Kegl also notes anxieties *within* Quakerism about Nayler's inability to control his female followers (56, 67)).

36. Underdown, 273 (and 274); John Ogilby, *The Entertainment of His Most Excellent Majestie Charles II, in His Passage through the City of London to His Coronation* (1662), 28; Tim Harris, *London Crowds in the Reign of Charles II: Propaganda and Politics from the Restoration until the Exclusion Crisis* (Cambridge, 1987), 63; Greaves, *Deliver Us*, 224; Morley, *Bartholomew Fair*, 187; Pepys, *Diary*, VIII.360, n. 1 and entry for 9 Jan. 1666; letter of 8 Mar. 1666 cited in Steven C. A. Pincus, *Protestantism and Patriotism: Ideologies and the Making of English Foreign Policy, 1650–1668* (Cambridge, 1996), 364. The identity between the St Bartholomew's Massacre and the 1662 ejection of dissident clergy is articulated by the grotesque figure of the Duchess of Albemarle in *The Third Advice to a Painter* (1667), line 244 (sometimes attributed to Marvell).

37. Ingram, 'Ridings', 109; Milton, *Eikonoklastes*, *CPW* III.345, 348 (a reference I owe to David Loewenstein); Peter Burke, 'The Virgin of the Carmine and the Revolt of Masaniello', *Past and Present* 99 (May 1983), 3–21 (suggesting that many carnivalesque details, esp. the kitchen army of women, are myths imposed by the upper-class commentator); Underdown, 'Language', 119–22; Lois Potter, *Secret Rites and Secret Writing: Royalist Literature, 1641–1660* (Cambridge, 1989), 35. Lucy Hutchinson concurs with the royalists that Fairfax was 'pertinacious in obeying his wife' (*Memoirs of the Life of Colonel Hutchinson, with a Fragment of Autobiography*, ed. N. H. Keeble (1995), 241). On polarized stereotypes of Cavalier and Puritan, see Underdown, 142–3, 164, and his figs. 8A-B for Skimmington imagery in political caricatures.

38. Cogswell, 'Underground Verse', 288; Conway, letter of 20 May 1640, *HMC Portland* III.64, noted in Underdown, 'Language', 109; Valerie Pearl, 'London's Counter-Revolution', in G. E. Aylmer (ed.), *The Interregnum: the Quest for Settlement, 1646–1660* (1972), 50–1.

39. Underdown, 177, 178, 253–4 (horns thrown into a Quaker meeting in 1656, and see ch. 1, n. 40 above for earlier Italian proscription of this gesture), 240 (Ranters 'closer to the festive culture of the disorderly poor'), 249–50; Gerrard Winstanley, *Works*, ed. George Sabine (New York, 1965), 295, 330. For 'Rant' still used to mean a radical Protestant cell after the Restoration, see Greaves, *Enemies*, 197. The testimony of the Quaker Dorothy Waugh, led through the streets of Carlisle in the scold's iron bridle, is discussed in many histories including Lynda E. Boose, 'Scolding Brides and Bridling Scolds: Taming the Woman's Unruly Member', *Shakespeare Quarterly* 42 (1991), 205–6, and Kegl, 'Women's Preaching', 58.

40. John Lilburne, *Englands Birth-Right Justified* (1645), 42; Richard Overton et al., *The Picture of the Councel of State Held forth to the Free People of England* (1649), 25–8; Richard Overton, *The Commoners Complaint, or a Dreadful Warning from Newgate, to the Commons of England* (1647), 17–20; Mary Overton, *The Humble*

Appeal and Petition of Mary Overton, Prisoner in Bridewell (1647), 6–7. These episodes are discussed in Ann Hughes, 'Gender and Politics in Leveller Literature', in Amussen and Kishlansky, *Political Culture*, 162–88, esp. 164, 174, 179, 188 n. 71.

41. Anne Locke, *The Markes of the Children of God* (1609), cited in Merry E. Wiesner, 'Women's Defense of Their Public Role', in Mary Beth Rose (ed.), *Women in the Middle Ages and the Renaissance: Literary and Historical Perspectives* (Syracuse, NY, 1986), 20. For a useful review of women's part in Civil War sieges, see Higgins, 219–21.

42. Taylor, *St Hillaries Tears* (1642), 6; Butler, *Hudibras* II.ii.806, p. 148 (see section 3 below for Butler's bawdy elaboration, and ch, 3, n. 26 for angry reminders of their efforts by women themselves); Strong, *Joanereidos* (1645), ff. A2v, A3, C4v, E1-4v, esp. E3-v, (1674), ff. a2, b1v-2v, b3-v (and for explicit association with charivari and popular women's festival, cf. b3v, where his immortal name will 'still ring / Whil'st Wives wear Breeches, and whilst Milk-maids sing'); Strong's poem, *Feminine Valour Eminently Discovered in Westerne Women*, compared the women of Lyme to heroines of the Old Testament like Jael.

43. Higgins, 183, 190; *Hudibras*, II. ii. 801–4; Underdown, 271, 273, and cf. 283 ('400 maidens in white and green' led by the mayor's wife and carrying crowns and wreaths, Bath, 1661). Note that in the Maldon grain riots of 1629 the militant leader, Ann Carter, gave herself the rank of 'Captain' (Stallybrass, 'Robin Hood', 55).

44. *Orations* f. a4, pp. 221–2 ('An Oration against a Foolish Custom'), 222–3, 225–6. For Newcastle's recommendation, see Stallybrass, 'Robin Hood', 69.

45. Lines 620–80, 701–2 (also cited in my epigraph); Doody, *Daring Muse*, 121, 122; for the distaff, apparently used as a weapon, see also Marvell, *Last Instructions*, line 385. For Griselda plays at the Fair, see ch. 5, n. 11 below, and for women who take an active role in sexual disorder see Quaife, *Wanton Wenches*, 149, 156–8, 167.

46. Lines 655–706; for a sampling of puzzled reactions see Quaife, *Wanton Wenches*, 200. For ancient triumphs, see Onofrio Panvinio, *De Ludis Circensibus. De Triumphis* (Padua, 1642), a ref. I owe to Martha Pollak, and note that bawdy shaming-rituals actually did accompany the triumph (Suetonius, *Julius Caesar*, 49.4); *Hudibras* also equates egg-throwing with the Roman 'Ovation' and the cucking-stool with the Venetian ceremony of marrying the Adriatic (lines 731–46).

47. *Characters*, ed. Charles W. Daves (Cleveland, OH, 1970), 81–2; *Hudibras* II.ii.655.

48. Following Wilders's notes, I have conflated this passage (II.ii.771–4, p. 148) with I.i.810–11, p. 25, where Ralpho defines bear-baiting, another popular merriment that he finds idolatrous, as 'when men run a-whoring thus / With their Inventions'; both passages cite Psalm 106:39.

49. Lines 791–814; Hudibras is silenced by a shower of excrement and eggs, and then taken to the stocks in the classic posture, forced to ride facing the

'Arse' (964). For donations of silver plate see ch. 3, n. 12 below and Pepys, 3 April 1663.

50. *The Politics of Mirth: Jonson, Herrick, Milton, Marvell, and the Defense of Old Holiday Pastimes* (1986), 263; Marcus touches on the concerns and materials of this chapter at several points, e.g. 38–63, 214, 303 n. 2, 309 n. 34.

51. Lines 389–91 (373–96 for the whole episode, which ends with Holland 'riding' the 'next neighbours' of England), *Poems* 157. For an earlier version of this discussion, see my 'The Libertine Abject: the "Postures" of *Last Instructions to a Painter*', in Warren Chernaik and Martin Dzelzainis (eds.), *Marvell and Liberty* (1999), 217–48.

3 'THE POSTURE OF A FREE STATE': POLITICAL PORNOGRAPHY AND THE 'COMMONWEALTH OF WOMEN', 1640–1660

1. *Memoirs of the Life of Colonel Hutchinson, with a Fragment of Autobiography*, ed. N. H. Keeble (1995), 70; for Cavendish see ch. 2, section 3 above (her parody of masculine fear of women's 'liberty') and n. 66 below (also cited as an epigraph to this chapter).

2. Underdown, 'Language', 121, citing John Crouch's *Man in the Moon*; ironically, the ultra-royalist here develops Milton's radical attack on those who 'cry liberty' when they mean 'license'.

3. *Mercurius Militaris, or Time's Only Truth-teller* (22–29 May 1649), 2; Underdown identifies this 'unrelenting sexual invective' as a pirated version ('Language', 126), and I will cite it below as 'pseudo-*Militaris*'.

4. *True Copie of the Petition of the Gentlewomen and Tradesmens-Wives, in and about the City of London* (1641/2), cited in Brian Patton, 'The Women Are Revolting? Women's Activism and Popular Satire in the English Revolution', *Journal of Medieval and Renaissance Studies* 23 (1993), 74; Cavendish, *Letters*, 360.

5. Underdown, 211. The literalist position, which I share, is set out lucidly in Achinstein, 131–63, and restated in her introduction to *Gender*.

6. Brathwaite cited in Herford and the Simpsons, *Ben Jonson* X.170; Harrison T. Meserole (ed.), *Seventeenth-Century American Poetry* (New York, 1968), 441, 446–7, 449. For the imprecise or polymorphous meaning of the 'Sodomite' in anti-Roundhead polemic, cf. Humphrey Mill's *The Second Part of the Nights Search* (1646), 128 ('He must commit Incest, / Or else a Rape, or bugger any beast . . . He's for the Subjects Liberty . . . He'l only kill / The Kings ill wishers'), and contrast Laura Gowing, *Domestic Dangers* (Oxford, 1996), 55.

7. 4; for a modern edition and commentary see Lois Potter (ed.), 'The *Mistris Parliament* Political Dialogues', *Analytical and Enumerative Bibliography* NS 1 (1987), 100–77. Potter identifies the eunuch to whom Parliament (illogically) prostituted herself as the Earl of Essex, divorced on grounds of impotence (113); for Cromwell as town bull, cf. *DNB*, *s.v.* Marchamont Nedham, and n. 12 below for Cromwell goring Anna Trapnel. For the pseudo-obstetric 'Groaning', see ch. 2, n. 5 above.

8. Potter, *Secret Rites and Secret Writing: Royalist Literature, 1641–1660* (Cambridge, 1989), 35 (and 145); Potter (ed.), '*Mistris Parliament* Dialogues', 120, 114–15 (citing a sermon by John Hackluyt, plausibly identified as the author of the first pamphlet). *Mercurius Pragmaticus, Communicating Intelligence from All Parts*, Thomason E.552(12) (23–30 April, 1649), f. A4, presents a particularly clear connection between an actual 'Monster' (conjunct twins) and 'the many headed Monsters at *Westminster*'.

9. Susan Dwyer Amussen, *An Ordered Society* (Oxford and New York, 1988), 1 (and cf. 2 for family and state order 'intertwined'); Augustine discussed in my *One Flesh* (Oxford, 1987, 1993), 43–5; Samuel Purchas, *Microcosmus*, cited in Clive Hart and Kay Gilliland Stevenson, *Heaven and the Flesh: Imagery of Desire from the Renaissance to the Rococo* (Cambridge, 1995), 97; Milton, *CPW* II.278–9 (their '*fanatick* dreams' are caused by the same blockage as in 'menstruous bodies'); for attacks on Milton see Christopher Hill, *Milton and the English Revolution* (1977; New York, 1979), 109, 130–2, 451–3.

10. *Gangraena*, reissued in facsimile by The Rota (Exeter, 1977), III.24; this is of course the same Presbyterian divorce-hater that Milton called 'shallow Edwards'. For other marital experiments, see Keith Thomas, 'Women in the Civil War Tracts', *Past and Present* 13 (April 1958), 49–50, and for Mrs Attaway, n. 16 below.

11. My *One Flesh*, 84–94; Edmund Gayton, passage cited ch. 2, n. 2 above (classifying 'the late Ranters' with street gangs like the Tityre-Tues and Hectors); *Her Own Life: Autobiographical Writings by Seventeenth-Century Englishwomen*, ed. Elspeth Graham, Hilary Hinds, Elaine Hobby, and Helen Wilcox (1989), 125; Humphrey Ellis, *Pseudochristus* (1650), 51, and cf. 50 ('so might any whore say the like'); Richard L. Greaves and Robert Zaller (eds.), *A Biographical Dictionary of British Radicals in the Seventeenth Century* (Brighton, 1982–84), entries for individuals named here. For Antinomian obstetrics and divine pregnancy, see Ephraim Pagitt, *Heresiography*, 2nd edn (1645), 106–7, *The Ranters Monster* (1653), Phyllis Mack, *Visionary Women: Ecstatic Prophecy in Seventeenth-Century England* (Berkeley, Los Angeles, and Oxford, 1992), 117 n. 87; Mitchell Robert Breitwieser, *Cotton Mather and Benjamin Franklin: the Price of Representative Personality* (1984), 70–3; Susan Howe, *The Birth Mark: Unsettling the Wilderness in American Literary History* (1993), 104–7. The second volume of Edwards's *Gangraena* whipped up sales by announcing, on its very titlepage, 'A Relation of a Monster lately born at *Colchester*, of Parents who are Sectaries' (described II.4–5, with special attention to its deformed hand, and a printer's hand in the margin to draw our attention).

12. Mack, *Visionary Women*, 1, 106–7, 110 (for women's donations to the Parliamentary cause, see ch. 2, section 3 above), 112 n. 71, 120–1; Peter Toon (ed.), *The Correspondence of John Owen (1618–1683)* (1970), 47. For Poole, see also Rachel Trubowitz, 'Female Preachers and Male Wives: Gender and Authority in Civil War England', in James Holstun (ed.), *Pamphlet Wars: Prose in the English Revolution* (1992), 112–13, and Brian Patton, 'Revolution, Regicide, and Divorce: Elizabeth Poole's Advice to the Army', in Alvin Vos (ed.),

Place and Displacement in the Renaissance: Essays from the 25th Annual CEMERS Conference (Binghamton, 1995), 133–45.

13. John Vicars, *The Schismatick Sifted* (1646), 34; J. D., *The Knave in Graine* (1640), Malone Society Reprints (Oxford, 1960), f. B1v; *Discoverie*, 2–3, 4, 6 (for Poole, see n. 12 above); Thomas Cogswell, 'Underground Verse' (ch. 2, n. 13 above), 282, 296–7 n. 22, citing Folger MS V.a. 345; *A Dialogue betweene Sacke and Six* (1641), f. A4, a ref. I owe to Achinstein (147).

14. *Letters*, 29, 103–5, 157–60. The 'pure Lady, or Lady Puritan' of the first letter, the 'Mrs P. I.' of the second, and the 'Mrs P. N.' who now 'is, as I did believe she would be, *viz.* a Preaching Sister', seem to be the same person, and the difference in initials is probably a printing error.

15. M. M. Goldsmith and Ivan Roots, introduction to Rota facsimile of *Gangraena*, i; Mack, *Visionary Women*, 87, 111–12; Trubowitz, 'Female Preachers', 115–16.

16. Fairfax's officer is denounced on *Gangraena* III.22, Mrs Attaway on I.84–9, II.10–11, and III.26–7. For the uncertain source of the reporters' 'horror', see Achinstein, 152–3; for the bawdy reworking see *Tub-Preachers Overturned* (1647), 15.

17. Illustrated in Tamsyn Williams, '"Magnetic Figures": Polemical Prints of the English Revolution', in Lucy Gent and Nigel Llewellyn (eds.), *Renaissance Bodies: the Human Figure in English Culture, c. 1540–1660* (1990), 87, 104.

18. *The Naked Woman, or a Rare Epistle Sent to Mr Peter Sterry, Minister at Whitehall* (1652), f. A2v, pp. 1, 7–11, 17. Achinstein's valuable discussion (149–51) polarizes the two discutants more than the text warrants.

19. *Rump, or an Exact Collection of the Choycest Poems and Songs Relating to the Late Times* (1662), II.196; *Newes from the New Exchange* (Thomason E.590[10], 30 Jan. 1649/1650), 2, 6, 7, 10, 20 (this pamphlet, usually attributed to Henry Neville, is cited more fully in section 3 below); *Now or Never*, 4; Phillips, *Sportive Wit, the Muses Merriment: a New Spring of Lusty Drollery, Jovial Fancies, and Alamode Lampoons* (1653), first part, f. C6, and see Hill, *Milton and the English Revolution*, 489, and Thompson, 211.

20. Andrew Willet (1614), cited in Keith Thomas, 'the Puritans and Adultery: the Act of 1650 Reconsidered', in Donald Pennington and Keith Thomas (eds.), *Puritans and Revolutionaries: Essays in Seventeenth-Century History Presented to Christopher Hill* (Oxford, 1978), 262; for earlier New England legislation making adultery a capital crime see Mary Beth Norton, *Founding Mothers and Fathers: Gendered Power and the Forming of American Society* (New York, 1996), 342–3. Ann Hughes, 'Gender and Politics' (ch. 2, n. 40 above), 181, cites a growing consensus among historians including Amussen and Gowing that at each social level the household was clearly 'embedded in a public world'.

21. Constance Jordan, 'Renaissance Women and the Question of Class', in James Grantham Turner (ed.), *Sexuality and Gender in Early Modern Europe: Institutions, Texts, Images* (Cambridge, 1993), 96, 99–100; Thomas Jordan, 'The Rebellion', cited and analysed in Achinstein, 134–5.

22. *Leviathan*, ed. C. B. Macpherson (1968; repr. Harmondsworth, 1985), 13:183–7, 14:190, 196, and cf. also 6:123–4, 15:211 (for ease of location I have prefixed the chapter number).

23. *Leviathan* 20:254; *Elements of Law*, cited in Teresa Brennan and Carole Pateman, '"Mere Auxiliaries to the Commonwealth": Women and the Origins of Liberalism', *Political Studies* 27 (1979), 189; key elements of this argument, like the equality in strength of the sexes and the dominion of the mother, are stated even more unequivocally in *De Cive* (cited in Brennan and Pateman, 188). In practice Hobbes spent little time pondering the implications of his important theoretical deconstruction of male suprematism, to judge from passing remarks about men stealing each other's 'wives' in the state of nature (13:185) and the 'naturall timorousnesse' of women and 'men of feminine courage' that exempts them from military service (21:270).

24. Sir Charles Sedley, *Bellamira*, cited in Chernaik, 214; I am here reapplying to Hobbes a statement originally meant to suggest that women are mere objects to be plundered freely by men (as in a similar theatrical instance cited by Chernaik, 42, 'I am for reducing Love to the state of Nature: I am for no propriety, but every man get what he can').

25. Samuel Rawson Gardiner (ed.), *The Constitutional Documents of the Puritan Revolution, 1625–1660*, 3rd edn (Oxford, 1906), 142; *Representative of . . . the City of London* (6 Feb. 1649), cited in Thomas, 'Puritans and Adultery', 277 (and see 263); Achinstein, 132–3 (Whitelocke complaining that the petitioners were 'almost scolding'), 136–41 (full discussion based on detailed reading of newsbooks). In 1653 Katharine Chidley presented a petition for the release of Lilburne signed by 6,000 women (Mack, *Visionary Women*, 123, and cf. 104, where she suggests Chidley as author of the pro-Leveller and anti-military 'Petition of Women' of 5 May 1649); for Fell, see Greaves and Zaller, *Dictionary*, *s.v.*. For contrasting interpretations, compare Ann Marie McEntee, '"The [Un]Civill-Sisterhood of Oranges and Lemons": Female Petitioners and Demonstrators, 1642–53', in Holstun (ed.), *Pamphlet Wars*, 92–111, with Hughes, 'Gender and Politics'.

26. *The Kingdomes Weekly Intelligencer, Sent Abroad to Prevent Mis-information* (1643), 229–30; Higgins, 194–6, with details added from Walter Yonge's diary.

27. Higgins, 180, 181, 184–5 (Milton mentions respectfully in *Apology for Smectymnuus*), 190–91, 192, 197 (Clarendon); Agostini translated in *Calendar of State Papers, Venice, 1642–1643*, ed. Allen B. Hinds (1925), 225, *Venice, 1643–1647* (1926), 8 (conflating two separate days according to Higgins 191); *Kingdomes Weekly Intelligencer*, 229.

28. Patton, 'Revolting?', 73–4 (*True Copie*), 76; Higgins, 188 (1642 *Petition of many Thousands of Courtiers, Citizens, Gentlemens and Tradesmens-wives*), 196, 197, 198; *Mercurius Civicus, London's Intelligencer* (1643), 88. For Lord Holland see further n. 43 below.

29. *Mercurius Pragmaticus, Communicating Intelligence from All Parts*, Thomason E.552(12) (23–30 April, 1649), f. A1v; *Mercurius Pragmaticus (For King Charls II)*, Thomason E.554(12) (1–8 May, 1649), f. C3v (one of at least

three distinct pamphlet-series with the same title, variously attributed to
Marchamont Nedham and John Cleveland), and recall that the Skimmington derived its name from the skimming-ladle; Higgins, 180, 199–200, 205,
212; McEntee, 'Oranges and Lemons', 99, 104, 105 (fails to recognize the
quotation from Isaiah 38:14–15); *Continued Heads, or Perfect Passages in Parliament* (20–27 April 1649), 12; John Crouch, *The Man in the Moon, Discovering a
World of Knavery under the Sunne* (16–23 April 1649), 11; for the account of the
Welsh women added to Holinshed in 1587, see J. L. Simmons, 'Masculine
Negotiations in Shakespeare's History Plays: Hal, Hotspur, and "the Foolish Mortimer"', *Shakespeare Quarterly* 44 (1993), 446. Leveller attacks on the
whoredom of their enemies made use of 'the rhetoric of sexual slander used
by London women' (as Hughes recognizes, 'Gender and Politics', 177).

30. *Mercurius Pragmaticus* (E.552[12]), f. A2 (amplifying the 'Civill-Sisterhood of
Oranges and *Lemmons*'); *Mercurius Pragmaticus (For King Charles II)*, Thomason
E.555(13) (8–15 May 1649), ff. D2v-3; *Mercurius Pragmaticus (For King
Charles. II.)* (24 April–1 May 1649), 10 (Thomason E.552[15]); *Mercurius
Pragmaticus, Communicating Intelligence from all Parts*, Thomason E.552(16)
(24 April–1 May 1649), ff. Qqq2v, 3 (probably by Nedham, this version
complains bitterly about the two piracies with the 'Charles II' subtitle
[f. Qqq1v]); Higgins, 203; for the *puttana's* arms, see ch. 1, n. 50 above.

31. *Mercurius Pragmaticus (For King Charles II)* (8–15 May 1649), f. D3; pseudo-
Militaris (n. 3 above), 2–3 (the spelling 'untrust' is presumably a misprint
rather than a pun). For Marten, constantly cited in these pamphlets, see
Hughes, 'Gender and Politics', 176; C. M. Williams, 'The Anatomy of a
Radical Gentleman: Henry Marten', in Pennington and Thomas (eds.),
Puritans and Revolutionaries, 119 (ironic barbs re the suitability of Marten's father as head of the chief 'bawdy court' in England, the Court of Arches); Underdown, 'Language', 117 (virtually every mention of Marten in Crouch's
Man in the Moon involves a sexual double entendre); Higgins, 187 n. 47,
records Valerie Pearl's finding that already in 1642 Marten had helped
women petitioners get a reading by the Commons. For a particularly dense
phallic portrait of Marten, see Samuel Butler, *Mercurius Menippeus*, in *Satires
and Miscellaneous Poetry and Prose*, ed. René Lamar (Cambridge, 1928), 357–8;
for Butler's joke on 'stand', see ch. 2, section 3 above.

32. Patton, 'Revolting?', 76, 75.

33. *Virgins Complaint* (1642/3), 3–5, 6, 8 (Thomason dates the 1646 reprint
'Aug. 24', which suggests a link with Bartholomew Fair); *Humble Petition of
Many Thousands of Wives* (1643), 4, 7 (cf. 6); *Mid-Wives Just Petition* (1643),
ff. A4-v; *Widowes Lamentation* (Thomason E.88[26], 6 Feb. 1644), 7, 8. For
comment see Patton, 'Revolting?', 77–80; Higgins, 189; Thompson, 103
('Sexual potency is the last refuge of the defeated'), 109. For bawdy female
pseudonyms see Diane Purkiss, 'Material Girls: the Seventeenth-Century
Woman Debate', in Clare Brant and Diane Purkiss (eds.), *Women, Texts and
Histories, 1575–1760* (1992), 82–3, and Crouch, *Man in the Moon* (16–23
April, 1649), 11 ('*Ruth Turn up, Doll Burn-it*, and sister *Wag-tayle*').

34. Thompson, 59; *Declaration of the Maids*, broadside. For a satirical verse 'Players Petition to the Parliament' see *Rump* I.32ff, and for an authentic petition by the suppressed actors, from 1650, see C. H. Wilkinson (ed.), *Theatre Miscellany: Six Pieces Connected with the Seventeenth-Century Stage*, Luttrell Society Reprints 14 (Oxford, 1953), 119–22; for the events of 1659 see Tim Harris, *London Crowds in the Reign of Charles II* (Cambridge, 1987), 42–4, John Tatham, *The Rump* (1661), 63 (and 39–40), and cf. *The Practical Part of Love* (1660), 76.

35. *The Cuckoo's Nest at Westminster* (1648), 7–8.; Gardiner (ed.), *Constitutional Documents*, 139 (cited in Thompson, 9); Hutchinson, *Memoirs*, 256; Underdown, 211; Higgins, 185–6 (cf. remarks on women petitioners who 'teach the Parliament how to make Lawes', p. 92 above). Earlier uses of the trope tend to refer to cabals and intrigues rather than public demonstrations; cf. a letter from the Earl of Worcester to the Earl of Shrewsbury, 2 Feb. 1604, describing the Court ladies as 'the feminine comon welthe', cited in John Nichols, *The Progresses of James I* (1828), 1.318.

36. 'Aelius Lampridius', *Antonii Heliogabali Vita*, in *Scriptores Historiae Augustae*, ed. and tr. David Magie (1924; repr. 1980), II.112 (for earlier imperial 'postures' see Suetonius, *Tiberius* 43); *Senatulus sive Gynaikosynedrion* (1529), in Desiderius Erasmus, *Opera Omnia*, Part I, vol. III, *Colloquia*, ed. L.-E. Halkin et al. (Amsterdam, 1972), 627, 631–2, 633.

37. Ariosto, *Orlando furioso*, XIX.liv-XX.xcv, esp. XIX.lvii; Hall, *Mundus Alter et Idem* ('A World Different and the Same'), Book II, in *Works*, ed. Josiah Pratt, X (1808), 171–8. This romance is translated (and expanded with much Rabelaisian diction) by John Healey as *The Discovery of a New World* (c. 1609), ed. Huntington Brown (Cambridge, MA, 1937); for a modern translation and commentary, see John Millar Wands, *Another World and Yet the Same: Bishop Joseph Hall's Mundus Alter et Idem* (1981). All of these versions reproduce the map of Viraginia from the 'Frankfurt' (really London) edition, 1605 or 1606. For an ingenious reading of both Artus and Hall see Ann Rosalind Jones and Peter Stallybrass, 'Fetishizing Gender: Constructing the Hermaphrodite in Renaissance Europe', in Julia Epstein and Kristina Straub (eds.), *Body Guards: Cultural Politics of Gender Ambiguity* (1992), 92–4.

38. *Mundus* 173, 67 (this babble 'would have amazed our Desiderius had he been alive today'), 175, 70; the sexual habits of the males of 'Loçania', 172, were not translated. For similar passages in Hall's verse satires, see Wands, *Another World*, 158.

39. *Mundus*, 178; cf. *Discoverie*, 75, 'My habite was manlike, my face womanlike (for I had yet no beard).'

40. *Apology for Smectymnuus*, *CPW* I.881, 887, 914; for an earlier use of the *Mundus* in Milton's anti-Hall polemic, see I.697.

41. *The Parlament of Women, with the Merry Lawes by Them Newly Enacted* (1640, reissued 1646, 1647, and 1656 with the spelling *Parliament*), esp. ff. A2v, B4v. For a full discussion of the genre, including the 1646 version of this pamphlet, see Achinstein, 141–3; Patton, 'Revolting?', 81–3, perceptively

links it to the mock-petition, but mistakenly discusses the 1647 reprint of the *Parliament of Women* (ostensibly set in Rome) as if it were Neville's *Parliament of Ladies* (whose title it imitates by changing 'Women' to 'Ladies').

42. Bodleian Wood 654A(9), *The Parliament of Ladies* (1647), 11, 13, 14–15; *The Parliament of Ladies . . . The second Edition corrected by the originall, unto which is added a Supplement of some further proceedings in the said Parliament* (Thomason E.388[4], 18 May 1647), 13–14 (the 'Supplement' containing the dildo-story, ff. B3–4, appropriately printed in two fonts different from the main text); *The Ladies Parliament* (Thomason E.1143[1], 15 July 1647), f. C2 (a version with variants throughout and an obscene lampoon in place of the dildo-episode); *The Ladies a Second Time Assembled in Parliament* (Thomason E.406[23], 13 Sept. 1647), 2, 11; *Newes from the New Exchange*, 16–17. An earlier version with slightly different title, dated 26 March 1647, appears in Bodleian MS Don. b. 8, pp. 129 – 32, alongside comparable lewd satires on Parliament dating from the Restoration (cf. Epilogue, n. 17 below); a minor offshoot of the genre can be found in *An Exact Diurnall of the Parliament of Ladyes* (Thomason E.386[4], 6 May 1647), where a female gathering in Oxford (including Moll Cut-Purse, who reappears in the dildo Supplement) sentences defeated royalist leaders to various Rabelaisian punishments. Though these Parliament satires form a tight group, milking the same jokes, I am not convinced that they come from the same author, and I use 'Neville' only for the first one. They do, however, claim an affinity with the parallel mock-petition genre: cf. *Second Time*, 7, 10, and Patton, 'Revolting?', 81, citing *Hey Hoe for a Husband, or, The Parliament of Maids, Their Desires, Decrees, and Determinations* (1647).

43. *Newes from the New Exchange*, 3; *Parliament of Ladies*, 14–15; *Second Time*, 5. Cf. *DNB*, 'Henry Rich, first Earl of Holland' (beheaded 1649), and 'Lucy Hay, Countess of Carlisle'; both Holland and she had been erotic cynosures of the Court, Holland inspiring 'unpleasing caresses' from James I and Carlisle lewd verses by Carew and Suckling. For Neville's other projects see Susan Wiseman, '"Adam, the Father of All Flesh": Porno-Political Rhetoric and Political Theory in and after the English Civil War', in Holstun (ed.), *Pamphlet Wars*, 149–53, and Greaves, *Deliver Us*, 198; ironically enough, Neville demolished patriarchalist theory in his later treatise *Plato Redivivus*, according to Gordon J. Schochet, *Patriarchalism in Political Thought: the Authoritarian Family and Political Speculation and Attitudes Especially in Seventeenth-Century England* (Oxford, 1975), 204.

44. *Newes from the New Exchange*, 10, and cf. 11, 'he that will please [Lady Middlesex] (which she abundantly loves) must convert a *Weavers beam* into a *dildo*'.

45. Wiseman, 'Porno-Political Rhetoric', 147; Nigel Smith, *Literature and Revolution in England, 1640–1660* (1994), 48, cast Neville as a defender of the Commons, but a contemporary witness like *Match Me These Two, or the Conviciton (sic) and Arraignment of Britannicus and Lilburne, with an Answer to the Pamphlet Entituled The Parliament of Ladies* (Thomason E.400[9], 29 July 1647), 13, sees the satire as an attack on the whole institution of Parliament.

46. F. A2, pp. 4, 6, 7–8. The publisher George Horton constructs an elaborate title-page to appeal to the apprentices (the presumed buyers?), almost entirely unrelated to the actual contents – a trick also played in his *Pray Be Not Angry, or the Women's New Law, with Their Several Votes, Orders, Rules, and Precepts, to the London-Prentices* (1656), a compilation of irrelevant misogynist commonplaces.

47. Domna Stanton analyses the *Caquets* pamphlets in 'Recuperating Women and the Man behind the Screen', in Turner (ed.), *Sexuality and Gender*, 247–65. *Mistress Parliament Presented in Her Bed* (1648) imitates the general situation of the *Caquets*, the melancholy narrator who hides behind a curtain to listen, and perhaps their squabbles over precedence (Potter (ed.), '*Mistris Parliament* Dialogues', 139); as an English analogue Potter cites *The Gossips Feast, or Morall Tales* (1647) (144).

48. Ian Maclean, *Woman Triumphant: Feminism in French Literature, 1610–1652* (Oxford, 1977), 192–3, citing François-Hédelin, abbé d'Aubignac, *Zenobie*, 1647 and Gillet de la Tessonerie, *Sigismond*, 1646. For Le Moyne, see Maclean, Woman Triumphant, ch. 8 *passim*, and Joan DeJean, *Tender Geographies: Women and the Origins of the Novel in France* (New York, 1991), 29–32, 41–2.

49. 1642 version, Brendan O Hehir, *Expans'd Hieroglyphicks: a Study of Sir John Denham's 'Cooper's Hill' with a Critical Edition of the Poem* (Berkeley and Los Angeles, 1969), 113–14.

50. Peter R. Newman, *A Companion to the English Civil Wars* (New York, 1990), s.v. 'Queen's Pocket Pistol'; for Queen Henrietta's playful self-titling (in a letter to Charles I), and her heroic rescue of a lapdog under cannon-fire, see Françoise Bertaud de Motteville, 'A Short History of the Troubles in England, as It Was Related by the Queen of England, Henrietta Maria', *Memoirs for the History of Anne of Austria* (1726), I.220, and Sophie Tomlinson, '"My Brain the Stage": Margaret Cavendish and the Fantasy of Female Performance', in Brant and Purkiss (eds.), *Women, Texts and Histories*, 148–9 (and 142 for Flecknoe). The sexual militancy of the complaining midwives was inspired by Henrietta Maria's military initiative (p. 94 above).

51. John Paulet, Marquis of Winchester, transl., *The Gallery of Heroick Women* (1652), cited in Carol Barash, *English Women's Poetry, 1649–1714: Politics, Community, and Linguistic Authority* (Oxford, 1996), 58; see 36–7 for the English influence of Le Moyne's project, 85 for Cowley, and 57 for Philips's own celebration of Boadicea as *femme forte*. DeJean provides details of de Saint-Baslemont's biography and writings, and reproduces a version of Deruet's painting from the Musée Carnavelet, Paris, in *Tender Geographies*, 24–8; for the *frondeuses* see 37–8 and ch. 1 *passim*.

52. 'J. De la Salle', *Paradoxes*, ed. J. Davies (1653), ff. *8, *12 (the commender 'Fear God Full Flesh' links Hall's paradox to women's preaching), pp. 104, 107–8; neither the 'govern States' paradox nor the forematter appears in the first (1650) edition.

53. *Paradoxes* (1650), 54–77, esp. 61, 64–5, 67. This was in fact composed when Hall was an undergraduate.

54. Pope cited in Mack, *Visionary Women*, 108 ('we should not obey them ... farther than is according to God's commission', though Pope also condemned women's religious independence); *Mercurius Pragmaticus (For King Charles. II.)* (24 April–1 May 1649), 10–11 (Thomason E.552[15]). For Hall's serious contributions to radical thought, see David Norbrook, *Writing the English Republic: Poetry, Rhetoric and Politics, 1627–1660* (Cambridge, 1999), 219, and *An Humble Motion to the Parliament of England Concerning the Advancement of Learning and Reformation of the Universities* (1649).

55. *Twelve Humble Proposals* (1653), 5, 9, 11, 12; these concrete demands are linked to the *New Jerusalem* treatise by marginal cross-reference (11), and thus make specific the political implications of the larger exegetical work. The *Mappe* must have appeared late in 1651 or 1651/2, since Cary (who uses the name Rande in the forematter but not on the title-page) refers to finishing it only in August of 'this present year 1651' (f. A7); Thomason's date 'Aprill 17' must already be in 1652.

56. Cf. Susan Wiseman, 'Unsilent Instruments and the Devil's Cushions: Authority in Seventeenth-Century Women's Prophetic Discourse', in Isobel Armstrong (ed.), *New Feminist Discourses* (1992), 183. Cary's *Mappe* (sometimes wrongly identified by the title of a shorter work prefaced to it, *The Little Horns Doom and Downfall*) is more accurately summarized in Kate Lilley, 'Blazing Worlds: Seventeenth-Century Women's Utopian Writing', in Brant and Purkiss (eds.), *Women, Texts and Histories*, 107–11.

57. Maclean, *Woman Triumphant*, 115–17; DeJean, *Tender Geographies*, 48–50, 61–4, and *passim*; Susanna Åkerman, *Queen Christina of Sweden and Her Circle: the Transformation of a Seventeenth-Century Philosophical Libertine* (Leiden, etc., 1991), 241 (and 303–4 for de Motteville's comments on Christina).

58. *The Worlds Olio* (1655), 74; *Natures Pictures Drawn by Fancies Pencil to the Life* (1656), 235. The two passages are connected, since the Lacedemonians (Spartans) are also mentioned in the fictional passage. For the casual mention of an outrageous sexual arrangement, see also *Blazing World*, ch. 5, section 3 below.

59. *The Blazing World and Other Writings*, ed. Kate Lilley (1994), 53, 95–100, 213–14; *Bell in Campo*, Part II, in *Playes* (1662), esp. 608; Tomlinson, 'Cavendish and Performance', 147–50. For details of Montpensier's siege tactics, see DeJean, *Tender Geographies*, 37–8.

60. Crouch, cited in Hughes, 'Gender and Politics', 175; for Lady Fairfax, see ch. 2, n. 37 above; Tomlinson, 'Cavendish and Performance', 146 (an article that begins with Cavendish and the Italian comedians in Antwerp, *Letters*, 405–8). For petitions for separation, see Amussen, *Ordered Society*, 127, and for a serving-woman's attempt to petition against her oppressive mistress, and counter-efforts to frame her as a pregnant whore, see Thomas Ivie, *Alimony Arraigned* (1654), 24–7.

61. The 'Inventory' (205–12) is followed by the prescriptive essay 'Noble Minds in Strong Bodies' and by a poem on the qualifications of the 'Judge' who must rule this imaginary commonwealth; for the avowed self-contradiction of the

Olio, see the 'Epistle' to Book III (135). Cavendish protests in *Philosophical and Physical Opinions* (1655), f. A3v, that the printer scrambled her MS and placed the 'Strong Bodies' essay wrongly in the Commonwealth section, but its themes do cohere with its accidental neighbours.

62. *Olio*, 210–12 (with anticipation of Millamant).

63. Åkerman, *Christina*, 288, cites a number of such deprecations, including a maxim in which she characterizes 'le sexe feminin' as a 'defaut de la nature', but then crosses out the last three words; for her attack on marriage as 'esclavage', see p. 109 above. For eyewitness accounts of Christina's sexually 'daunting' behaviour, and specific parallels with Cavendish (who met her in 1654) see Tomlinson, 'Cavendish and Performance', 158.

64. *Letters*, 107, and see 69, 319–321, 332; *Poems and Fancies* (1653), preface 'To all Writing Ladies'.

65. Hobbes, *Leviathan* 13:186; Cavendish, *Olio*, ff. A4v–5v ('The Preface to the Reader'). Similar arguments from men's technology appear in other writings, but in the mouths of discredited speakers; see *Orations*, 227 and *The Female Academy* in *Playes* (1662), 664–5. John Rogers shows that changes in Cavendish's theory of matter between 1655 and 1663 diminish the importance of mechanical (and masculine) brute force, in atoms as in 'Work-men'; *The Matter of Revolution: Science, Poetry, and Politics in the Age of Milton* (1996), 202.

66. *The Philosophical and Physical Opinions* (1655), f. B2v; this passionate demand for education and responsibility (often cited by twentieth-century feminists) was omitted in the 2nd edition of 1663. For a similar assumption of women's positive exclusion, see *Natures Pictures*, f. C1 (a reference I owe to Amy Greenstadt).

67. Cavendish, *Letters*, 27 (she does qualify this statement by continuing 'unless to our Husbands', but this in turn is undermined by the Hobbesian 'and not always to them'), 28, *Olio*, 71 (essay 'Men ought not to strive for Superiority with Women'); Gallagher, 'Embracing the Absolute: the Politics of the Female Subject in Seventeenth-Century England', *Genders* 1 (1988), 28.

68. *Letters*, 63, 117–18 (and 52 for Cavendish's admiration for the ready eloquence that she herself lacked), 76 (and cf. 83, 'Mr. *A. B.* hath Married a Common Courtesan, if she had been Particular, it had been more Excusable'); *Orations*, 228; Tomlinson, 'Cavendish and Performance', 143, 159; Pepys, 11 April 1667.

4 THE WANDERING WHORE'S RETURN: THE CARNIVALIZATION OF SEXUALITY IN THE EARLY RESTORATION

1. *Rump, or an Exact Collection of the Choycest Poems and Songs Relating to the Late Times* (1662), 1.31; *An Exact Narrative of His Most Sacred Majesties Escape from Worcester* (1660), cited in Harold Weber, *Paper Bullets: Print and Kingship under Charles II* (Lexington, KY, 1996), 35; Samuel Butler, *Characters*, ed. Charles W. Daves (Cleveland, OH, 1970), 61.

2. Hutchinson, *Memoirs*, ed. N. H. Keeble (1995), 278; Carol Barash, *English Women's Poetry, 1649–1714* (Oxford, 1996), 43 (citing Jevon and similar imagery in other poems on the Restoration); Hall, ch. 3, section 3 above; Butler, *Satires and Miscellaneous Poetry and Prose*, ed. René Lamar (Cambridge, 1928), 41–2. Butler's critique of Restoration libertinism mirrors the sexual satire against religious dissidents scattered throughout *Hudibras* (ch. 2, section 3 above) and the *Characters*, e.g. 106 ('A Ranter is a *Fanatic Hector*, . . . for he believes all Religion consists in Looseness, and that Sin and Vice is *the whole Duty of Man*'), 320–1.

3. Cavendish, *Letters*, 105–6, 7; Burnet, *Some Passages of the Life and Death of John Earl of Rochester, RCH*, 49–51.

4. *Bartholomew Faire, or Variety of Fancies* (1641), 1; Rochester, *A Ramble in Saint James's Parke*, 77 (for Wycherley, see ch. 6, section 1 below).

5. James Newton, 'An Account of some Effects of *Papaver Corniculatum luteum*, etc.', *Philosophical Transactions* 20 (1699), 263–4 (a reference I owe to Christopher Bond).

6. (1650), title-page; the dialogue between whore, pimp, pandar, bawd, and prodigal had already been used in Humphrey Mill, *A Nights Search, Discovering the Nature and Condition of All Sorts of Night-Walkers* (1640), 20–5, 47–52 (and the scolopendra, a poisonous centipede or mythical vomiting fish, was used as a tavern-insult to women in a Shirley play of 1633 (*OED*, 3)).

7. Keith Thomas, 'Puritans and Adultery' (ch. 3, n. 20 above), 279, 275; *Alimony Arraign'd, or the Remonstrance and Humble Appeal of Thomas Ivie, Esquire* (1654), *passim*; and cf. Hughes, 'Gender and Politics' (ch. 2, n. 40 above), 178.

8. Edmund Goldsmid, *Explanatory Notes of a Pack of Cavalier Playing Cards, Temp. Charles II* (Edinburgh, 1886), plate opposite p. 21; Tatham, *The Rump* (1661), 24–8, 43; Paula R. Backscheider, *Spectacular Politics: Theatrical Power and Mass Culture in Early Modern England* (Baltimore, 1992), 25, 28. For more *Rump* titles, see Wing, STC, R2270–9, and for Behn's revision of Tatham's play see Epilogue, n. 16 below.

9. *The Qualifications of Persons Declared Capable by the Rump Parliament* (1660), 5–6; *Perfect Diurnall, or the Daily Proceedings in the Conventicle of the Phanatiques* (Thomason E.1017[21], 19 March 1659/60), 7; *The Remonstrance or Declaration of Mr Henry Mart[e]n* (1648), 3; Phillips, *Montelion, or the Prophetical Almanack* (1660), f. A5 (and numerous references in the 1661 edition, e.g. f. A5v); *Wandring Whore* v.6; 'Mercurius Philalethes', *Select City Quaeries, Discovering Several Cheats, Abuses and Subtilties of the City Bawds, Whores, and Trapanners* (1660), 1.4; for sexual slurs on Marten, see also Susan Wiseman, 'Porno-Political Rhetoric' (ch. 3, n. 43 above), 139–44, 155–6 n. 17. Marten was also conspicuous for his opposition to the Adultery Bill (Thomas, 'Puritans and Adultery', 278).

10. (1632), title-page, ff. A3, F2v.

11. By 'Eugenius Theodidactus', i.e. John Heydon (Thomason's copy dated 13 Dec. 1660); for a medical attestation in print, see Lennard J. Davis,

Factual Fictions: the Origins of the English Novel (New York, 1983), 53 (and cf. Shakespeare's *Winter's Tale* IV.iv). Meg Spenser had already featured in Humphrey Mill, *The Second Part of the Nights Search* (1646), where her dying speech boasts 'My Girles were free' (49).

12. Pepys, 1, 2, 4, 6, 22, and 30 Aug. 1660. The passages cited for the last two months are (in order of mention) 20 Nov.; 10 Dec.; 17 Nov.; 19 Nov., 4 Dec.; 27 Nov.; 30 Nov., 3–4 Dec.; 10 Dec.; 3 Dec.; 10, 16, 21 Dec.; 16 Dec.

13. 24 ('Ventricia'), 25, 55, 85; 'Mother Cunny' is listed in *The Wandring Whore*, e.g. III.13.

14. Aretino, *Ragionamenti* I.i.14 [20] ('la leggenda della Puttana errante di Vinegia'), I.i.19 [24], I.i.46–7 [52], II.i.185 [192] (*Tariffa*); *Practical Part*, 39–40; cf. Thompson, 57, 72, and Marsh's catalogue in *The Wits, or Sport upon Sport* (1662), following p. 186 (it also includes the *Rump* anthology and Tatham's play of that name); see ch. 1, n. 4 above for *Rare Verities*, the translation of Sinibaldi's sexological treatise reissued as *Venus Her Cabinet* (identifiable by its subtitle). The *Catalogue* idea was put into practice in the *Wandring Whore* series (section 3 below).

15. *The Wandring Whore: a Dialogue between Magdalena a Crafty Bawd, Julietta an Exquisite Whore, Francion a Lascivious Gallant, and Gusman a Pimping Hector* (with no indication on the title-page that it will be continued) is dated by Thompson 28 Nov. 1660, without evidence (66), and parts II–V are dated by Thomason between Dec. 1660 and March 1661. (Each 'number', like the individual dialogues that make up Aretino's *Ragionamenti*, represents one day's discussion.). The 'sixth' in 1663 is clearly a different enterprise from a different publisher, purporting to tell Garfield's own, respectable version of events and exonerating him from the fifth issue. For Garfield see William Riley Parker, *Milton: a Biography* (Oxford, 1968), 568, 571, and David Foxon, *Libertine Literature in England, 1660–1745* (New Hyde Park, NY, 1965), 9, 28, 30.

16. II.12, and cf. the 'Prefatory Note' to a facsimile edition by The Rota of *The Wandring Whore, Numbers 1–5* (Exeter, 1977); Marsh's book is explicitly named in *Strange and True Newes from Jack-a-Newberries Six Windmills* (1660), 5.

17. *Wandring Whore* V.6, VI.4, V.4; Aretino, *Ragionamenti* II.i.180 [187]; for sexual 'jousting' see ch. 1, n. 49 above, and for the Wells game against the Puritan Hole, ch. 2, n. 9. Garfield's trade sign, conspicuously displayed on the title-page of e.g. *Daphnis and Chloe, a Most Sweet and Pleasant Pastorall Romance for Young Ladies* (1657), was the rolling press used to print engravings, so it would be plausible to associate him with illicit production of 'Aretino's postures'.

18. *Wandring Whore* VI.7; Bodleian Vet. B3 f. 304, *La puttana errante, overo dialogo di Madalena e Giulia, di M. P. Aretino* ([Leiden, c. 1666]), 5; *Tariffa*, ed. Guillaume Apollinaire (Paris, 1911), 6, 122. The translation begins on p. 5 of the *Sixth Part* with the opening sentence of the Italian (cleverly translating 'la Tortera' as 'the Pye-woman') and runs almost verbatim to the obviously hasty end of the pamphlet.

19. *Six Windmills, passim; Wandring Whore* I.6–7 (and cf. 5–6, a historical document showing the earlier toleration of brothels); Cowley, cited in Manley, *London*, 523. In Henry Marten's brothel, according to John Crouch's *Man in the Moon* (1649), 172, the prostitute would 'fling' gold crowns into her own vagina.

20. *A Strange and True Conference between Two Notorious Bawds, Damarose Page and Pris. Fotheringham* (1660), 7; *Wandring Whore* III.14, II.13; *Six Windmills*, 5 (the beauties are to be 'hanged in order one after another'); cf. Pepys, 20 Dec. 1660 (though the musician's name is John Singleton and not George, both Pepys and Dryden in *MacFlecknoe* use the surname only). For the 1662 order to reprint Richard Mocket's *God and the King* (1615), see Susan Dwyer Amussen, *An Ordered Society* (Oxford and New York, 1988), 55–6, 63, and Underdown, 287; for the idea of a libertine canon, cf. *The Practical Part of Love* (section 1 above).

21. Head, *Rogue*, 3rd pagination, 39 (f. Ccc4); for the criminal haunt as a 'separate' London, see ch. 1, n. 47 above.

22. *London*, 341, 344, 346, 347, 352, 414.

23. Cited in Mikhail Bakhtin, *Rabelais and His World*, transl. Hélène Iswolsky (1968; Bloomington, IN, 1984), 107–8.

24. *Wandring Whore* III.3, V.8; *Wandring Whore* III.4 cites Martial (as does the 1650 *Newes from the New Exchange*), and *Sixth Part* title-page quotes lines 4–6 of Claudian's *Carmina Minora* 22 (kindly identified by Gordon Braden).

25. *Wandring Whore* I.10 (Cresswell's gallery), I.15, II.5, II.11, III.13, IV.12; *Select City Quaeries*, III.19; *Tariffa*, 58–60 (Elena Ballerina); 'Merc[urius] Dem[ocritus]', *The Wandring-Whores Complaint for Want of Trading . . . in a Merry Discourse between Jezabel the Crafty Bawd, Ruth the Buttock, Two Noble Culls, Isbel the Wandring-Whore, Gusmond a Valiant Hector*, etc. (1663); and cf. *Six Windmills*, 3 (membership extended to several named 'wandring whores'). A named list of (male) vagrants and criminals had appeared as early as 1566 in Thomas Harman's *Caveat for Common Cursitors*.

26. *Wandring Whore* IV.5, I.6 (and for the Dutch wench, section 3 below), II.6, 8, 11, III.6 (another example of Francion's implausible Cockney expertise); 'Philo-Puttanus', *The Whores Rhetorick, Calculated to the Meridian of London, and Conformed to the Rules of Art* (1683), 171. The 'Italian Padlock' (I.4 and 9, where the Venetian Julietta describes it) was a running joke in London, e.g. in Phillips, *Montelion* (1660), f. A5; for the 'scotch spur' (I.4), some kind of aphrodisiac device, see James T. Henke, *Gutter Life and Language in the Early 'Street' Literature of England* (West Cornwall, CT, 1988), 'Scotch-spur'.

27. *Strange and True Conference*, 5 (allegedly by 'Megg Spenser'); Jonson, *Bartholomew Fair* IV.v.106 (and cf. n. 29 below for Knockhum as 'the Ranger of Turnbull'; Manley, *London*, 419 (and cf. 413–14 on actual proverbs and epigrams with London placenames); Laura Gowing, cited ch. 1, n. 12 above (for a similar topographical insult made by Mrs Pepys, suggesting that Samuel might look for Deb Willet in Whetstones Park, see diary for 16 Nov. 1668); Margaret F. Rosenthal, *The Honest Courtesan* (1992), 188;

Dryden, *MacFlecknoe*, line 72; *Wandring Whore* VI.4, and note an even fuller list of recommended cruising streets, already given to Francion in II.9–10.

28. *Wandring Whore* I.7 (I infer a sexual meaning for this bridge only a thumb's breadth wide, where '1500 pike-men' were recently defeated [8], since 'toss his Pike' [9] is Magdalena's phrase for what Julietta does to Francion), IV.9, I.9, 12, 13; *Tariffa*, 38; Phillips, *Sportive Wit* (1653), first part (*Jovial Drollery*), 43, second part (*Lusty Drollery*), 14–15.; *Whores Rhetorick*, 122–3; Edward Ward, *The London-Spy Compleat*, 4th edn (1709), 140.

29. *Bartholomew Fair* II.v.51 (and for Alice's complaint, IV. v. 105); Knockhum's 'Ranger' nickname makes a Royal Forest out of the notorious Turnbull or Turnmill Street (ch. 1, n. 12 above). For London as year-long fair, already proverbial in 1611, see Manley, *London*, 418.

30. *Bartholomew Fairing*, 2; *Bartholomew Faire, or Variety of Fancies* (1641), '5' (mis-numbered for 3). (A Victorian reprint, Charles Hindley (ed.), *The Old Book Collector's Miscellany*, III (1873), item 13, p. 3, reads 'sucking Exchange', but the letter is indisputably 'f'.) For examples of pornographic 'fairings' from later in the century, see ch. 1, n. 65 above.

31. *Wandring Whore* II.12 (cf. I.15 for a listing of 'Ursula' among the whores, further specified as 'Ursula Higgins' in the next instalment, II.5); Phillips, *Sportive Wit* II.117. For comic traditions around butchers, linked to their role as suppliers of horns, see ch. 2, n. 14 above. The sexual use of 'pie' and 'pieman' in these whore-dialogues predates the earliest record of 'Simple Simon' in Iona and Peter Opie's *Oxford Dictionary of Nursery Rhymes* (Oxford, 1952).

32. For blackguard mock-arms see ch. 2, n. 37, ch. 3, n. 29 above (and con-trast the 'pastoral' dairy-ladles used in the Skimmington, the source of that name); for fireplace soot in (literally) smutty literature see *Erotopolis, or a New Description of Bettyland* (1684), 97–9, and for libertine love as 'blackguard boy' in Dorset's poetry, ch. 6, section 4 below.

33. *Rabelais and His World*, ch. 2 *passim*; interestingly, the translator uses the London place-name 'billingsgate' to render a phrase that literally means 'familiar public-square speech' (I am grateful to Gary Saul Morson for advice on the Russian text). For a judicious reading of Bakhtin see the Introduction to Peter Stallybrass and Allon White, *The Poetics and Politics of Transgression* (Ithaca, NY, 1986).

34. *Journal*, ed. E. Kanceff (Turin, 1976), I.143–4; Tarczylo, 'From Lascivious Erudition to the History of Mentalities', in G. S. Rousseau and Roy Porter (eds.), *Sexual Underworlds of the Enlightenment* (Chapel Hill, NC, 1988), 35.

35. *Six Windmills*, 1, 4, 6; Thompson, 65; 'Eugenius Theodidactus', *Ladies Cham-pion*, 5 (Aretino was not in fact burned at the stake for publishing his sixteen sonnets on the *Modi*, and the idea of 'six and thirty' postures comes from the prose *Puttana errante* spuriously published as his, most recently in 1660).

36. III.15 (the only place where the name 'Eubulus' appears in the apparently authentic numbers, the other disclaimers being anonymous); *OED*, 'pub-lication', 1 and 3 (Taylor's equation of 'prostitution and publication'). For

'obliterated' names, compare III.16 and V.16. Garfield's boast echoes Robert Greene's claim that his coney-catching pamphlets had caused the numbers of whores and thieves to dwindle (A. V. Judges (ed.), *The Elizabethan Underworld* (New York, 1930), 226).

37. II.9, 11, III.10 (for further use of this list of place-names, see II. 10, discussed below).

38. Manley, *London*, 343, 344.

39. Ingram, 'Rhymes', 179, *Courts*, 165 and cf. 182 (a rhymed list of names which did indeed lead to action against its previously undetected victims); Laura Gowing, 'Gender and the Language of Insult in Early Modern London', *History Workshop* 35 (Spring 1993), 5; Thomas, 'Puritans and Adultery', 274; Mill, *Nights Search*, 99 (section 25); Peter Burke, *Historical Anthropology of Early Modern Italy: Essays on Perception and Communication* (Cambridge, 1987), 38 ('PUTTANA SCORTESE', 'PUTTANA RIFATTA LIQUIDA E STREGA', capitals original).

40. *Sixth Part*, 5 (cf. topical jokes on 'Syringes' in Phillips, *Montelion* [1660], f. A5). *The Practical Part of Love* suggests that the wearing of condoms was already a common practice in the lower strata (the men's fencing team in 'Loves University' normally 'play at single Rapiers with a cap on' (37)). For neighbourly denunciations of deviant sexuality see Lawrence Stone, *Family, Sex, and Marriage in England, 1500–1800* (1977), 144–5, and Ingram, *Courts*, 244–5.

41. Aretino, *Ragionamenti* I.ii.92 [98–9], II.i.187–8 [195–6], II.ii.273 [284]; Evelyn, letter to John Evelyn, junior, endorsed by recipient 'From my Father 1680', British Library MS Evelyn, Correspondence, vol. 13, number 1526. Thomas Dekker had presented the London underworld as 'monsters that live in darkness' (Judges, *Elizabethan Underworld*, 312, 362–3), but his model is the allegorical romance, not the fairground raree-show.

42. *Wandring Whore* II.8; *Strange and True Conference, passim* (occasioned by Fotheringham's imprisonment in Newgate, presumably because of her scandalous performances); *Six Windmills*, 2; Marcus, *The Other Victorians: a Study of Sexuality and Pornography in Mid-Nineteenth-Century England* (New York, 1966), 159–60. This playful-aggressive game is still referred to familiarly in Charles Walker, *Authentick Memoirs [of] Sally Salisbury* (1723), 66–8.

43. *Six Windmills*, 3; for real-life cases of men and women arrested for 'enacting lewd postures', see Randolph Trumbach, *Sex and the Gender Revolution. I. Heterosexuality and the Third Gender in Enlightenment London* (1998), 158.

44. *Wandring Whore* I.6–7, 8–9 (see ch. 1, n. 32 above for ingesting body secretions in sex-magic and Nanna's boast that 'we make men eat our *marchese*'); *Practical Part*, 48; Evelyn, letter to his son. For supposedly genuine examples of the 'smock-straining' ritual, including Wycherley's account of the 'Zesto' imparted by soiled underwear, see section 4 below.

45. Jacques Rossiaud, 'Prostitution' (ch. 1, n. 40 above), 92; G. R. Quaife, *Wanton Wenches and Wayward Wives* (New Brunswick, NJ, 1979), 175, the case of Meredith Davy of Minehead further discussed in Alan Bray, *Homosexuality*

in Renaissance England (1982) 48, 76–7, and Stephen Orgel, *Impersonations: the Performance of Gender in Shakespeare's England* (Cambridge, 1996), 38–9.

46. Quaife, *Wanton Wenches*, 26, 134 (repeated 171–2), and for contraception and abortion, 55, 79, 118 (a *mother* beats the woman her son has made pregnant), 119–20, 148, 151; Amussen, 'Manhood' (ch. 1, n. 28 above), 213.

47. Trumbach, *Sex I*, 157, 161, 164, 165; *Select Trials at the Session-House in the Old-Bailey* (1742), I.109 (it is hard to know whether 'spit' is a misprint or euphemism for the 'trick' described in *Wandring Whore* III (p. 145 above)); Stone, *Broken Lives: Separation and Divorce in England, 1660–1857* (Oxford, 1993), 33–78; for similar assaults on pregnant wives in America, see Mary Beth Norton, *Founding Mothers and Fathers* (New York, 1996), 237–8.

48. Ivie, *Alimony Arraign'd*, 16–17, 19; Christine Phipps (ed.), *Buckingham, Public and Private Man: the Prose, Poems and Commonplace Book of George Villiers, Second Duke of Buckingham (1628–1687)* (1985), 31; Trumbach, *Sex I*, 157 (a mob protesting against a rumoured act of buggery); *Practical Part*, 83–4 (and see section 1 above). For Buckingham's response, see n. 70 below, and for other accusations of sodomy, this time homosexual, ch. 6, n. 18 below.

49. *A Hellish Murder Committed by a French Midwife on the Body of Her Husband* (1688), 33–4; for other examples of violent males simulating attack dogs, cf. ch. 2, n. 6 above and ch. 5, n. 16 below (like a 'Mastiff').

50. *Wandring Whore* V.7–8 (this assault resulted in a lawsuit); Aretino, letter 315 to Battista Zatti, 11 Dec. 1537 (defending the *Modi* and his sonnets upon them).

51. *Wandring Whore* IV.6–7. For the whore-murder connection, see *Remonstrance of Henry Mart[e]n* (n. 9 above); Lois Potter (ed.), 'The *Mistris Parliament* Political Dialogues', *Analytical and Enumerative Bibliography* NS 1 (1987), 150; Peter Lake, 'Deeds against Nature: Cheap Print, Protestantism and Murder in Early Seventeenth-Century England', in Kevin Sharpe and Peter Lake (eds.), *Culture and Politics in Early Stuart England* (1994), 259 (the use of 'whore' for a murderess who cuts a foetus out of the abdomen of her victim and thus becomes a 'tragical midwife'), 264.

52. *Wandring Whore* II.7. For 'acting the beast' as an expression of superiority, see ch. 1, section 4 above (Bruno) and cf. Blaise Pascal, *Pensées*, 317, 329, in the numbering established by Jacques Chevalier for the Pléiade edition.

53. *Wandring Whore* V.4–5; see ch. 6, section 4 below for links to the proviso-scene in comedy, and *Practical Part*, 73, for Helena's refusal to draw up a 'treaty'.

54. Pepys, 6 April 1668 (for the context, anti-Castlemaine satires being 'spread abroad', see ch. 5, section 3 below); the episode is proposed as a paradigm of homosocial exchange in Duane Coltharp, 'Rivall Fopps, Rambling Rakes, Wild Women: Homosocial Desire and Courtly Crisis in Rochester's Poetry', *The Eighteenth Century* 38 (1997), 23. For other versions of the disease-story see ch. 1, n. 63 above, Antoine Hamilton, *Mémoires de la vie du comte de Grammont*, ed. René de Planhol (Paris, 1926), 168, Gilbert Burnet, *A History of My Own*

Time, ed. Osmund Airy, I (Oxford, 1897), 406, and 'An Historicall Poem', in Marvell, *Poems*, 219.

55. *PL* IV.509–11, 765–70, I.497–505, VII.25–33; *PR* II.159, 183; *The Book of Common Prayer* (1662), liturgy for 'King Charles Martyr' (30 Jan.).

56. Pope, ch. 6, n. 12 below; *The Poor Whores Complaint to the Apprentices of London, . . . Printed in the Year of our Great Affliction* (1672), broadsheet. For 'middling' or higher-status apprentices, see Tim Harris, *London Crowds in the Reign of Charles II* (Cambridge, 1987), 17–18, and see ch. 5 below for apprentice riots of political motivation; for the lower echelon, see Patricia Fumerton, 'London's Vagrant Economy', in Lena Cowen Orlin (ed.), *Material London, ca. 1600* (Philadelphia, 2000), 211–12 (citing Paul Griffiths, *Youth and Authority*).

57. Gowing, *Domestic Dangers* (Oxford, 1996), 187, 190–1 (a case where the cuckolded husband published edifying conduct-books for wives); Barker, Magdalen College, Oxford, MS 343, ff. 74 and cf. 72v; the first passage can also be found in Carol Shiner Wilson (ed.), *The Galesia Trilogy and Selected Manuscript Poems of Jane Barker* (New York and Oxford, 1997), 322. For apprentices' sexuality and disorder, see Steven R. Smith, 'The London Apprentices as Seventeenth-Century Adolescents', *Past and Present* 41 (Nov. 1973), 150, Keith Thomas, 'Age and Authority in Early Modern England', *Proceedings of the British Academy* 62 (1976), 214–17, and Amussen, 'Manhood', 222; for girl apprentices, see K. D. M. Snell, *Annals of the Labouring Poor: Social Change and Agrarian England, 1660–1900* (1985), ch. 6 *passim*.

58. *The Ape-Gentle-Woman, or the Character of an Exchange-Wench* (1675), 5; Pepys, 12 Feb. 1660, 27 Dec. 1662, 1 Jan. 1668. For apprentice actions against the Cromwellian army, and bawdy reactions, see ch. 3, n. 34 above.

59. Robert Jordan, 'The Extravagant Rake in Restoration Comedy', in Harold Love (ed.), *Restoration Literature: Critical Approaches* (1972), esp. 87–8; *Wandring Whore* I.10; Head, *The English Rogue Described* (1665), 3rd pagination, 34–40 (ff. Ccci v–4v), f. A7. Earlier in his career as lewd apprentice the rogue visits 'Mother *Cr--* formerly famous for the Citizen's wives that frequented her house' (1st pagination, 76) See ch. 5, section 2 below for further discussion of Head's rogue.

60. *The London Bully, or the Prodigal Son* (1683), 5, 14, 19, 28–9, 73–5.

61. James Shirley, *The Gamester* (1633), cited in Anna Bryson, *From Courtesy to Civility: Changing Codes of Conduct in Early Modern England* (Oxford and New York, 1997), 249; Evelyn, *A Character of England, As It Was Lately Presented in a Letter to a Noble Man of France*, '3rd edn' (1659), 9, 31, 32, 37–8; Cavendish, *The Worlds Olio* (1656), 215 (for her critique of the knight who models himself on Guzman, see n. 4 above).

62. More ('Alazanomastix Philalethes'), *Free-Parliament Quaeres* (1660), 4; *Practical Part*, 71–2; *Wandring Whore* III.3; for the Nevillesque *Commonwealth*, which also describes the smock-ritual, see section 1 and ch. 3, section 3 above.

63. *Newes from the New Exchange*, 20 (cited in section 1 above); Ivie, *Alimony Arraign'd*, 24–7 (supposedly the wife's trick to render plausible her false accusation of pregnancy against the maid); Evelyn, letter to his son

(n. 41 above), *Diary*, ed. E. S. de Beer (Oxford, 1955), entry for 2 April 1668; Richardson Pack, 'Some Memoirs of William Wycherley Esq', 8–9, prefixed to Wycherley's *Posthumous Works*, ed. Lewis Theobald (1728). For literary uses of the toasting formula, evoking but not actually naming the obscene word, cf. ch. 6, section 2 below.

64. 'The Conyborough of Coopers Hill', in Bodleian MS Don. b. 8, p. 287; the threat to 'stone' Denham is recorded in Hamilton's fictionalized version (*Memoirs de Grammont*, 194).

65. 'London, hast thow accused me', *Poems*, ed. Emrys Jones (Oxford, 1964), 30–1, 127cf. Manley, *London*, 513.

66. The Earl of Bridgwater's agent so describes Elizabeth Evans, the aunt and chief supporter of a fourteen-year-old Breconshire servant-girl raped and robbed as she returned home; cited in Leah S. Marcus, 'Justice for Margery Evans: a "Local" Reading of *Comus*', in Julia M. Walker (ed.), *Milton and the Idea of Woman* (Urbana and Chicago, 1988), 70. The case of the acquitted window-breaker appears in the Old Bailey records, brought to light in Margaret Anne Doody, 'Women as Witnesses and Victims', paper delivered to the Midwest Conference on British Studies, University of Illinois at Chicago, October 1989.

67. Peter Earle, *The Making of the English Middle Class: Business, Society and Family Life in London, 1660–1730* (1989), 202. For defamation cases largely involving women, see ch. 2, n. 10 above; for threats against the windows of a woman who 'won't be civil', see Freeman in Wycherley's *Plain-Dealer*, ch. 6, section 1 below.

68. These phrases were added in the lost English translation of *L'Escole* (Greater London Record Office, Middlesex Sessions Rolls, MJ/SR 1582.1). Stephen Primate, *The City and Country Purchaser and Builder* (c. 1667), 101–2, estimates £5 7s to glaze a town house of 3 bays.

69. For Goring, see Wilson, 224 n. 140. The manslaughters, convictions and pardons of Philip, seventh Earl of Pembroke (whose brother started a sword-fight in the theatre to 'vindicate' Nell Gwyn, ch. 1, epigraph above) appear in *DNB* under Philip Herbert, fourth Earl; see also James Anderson Winn, *John Dryden and His World* (New Haven, 1987), 326. Pepys records Buckhurst's case on 22 and 25 Feb. 1662. For Rochester's 'violent' love of pleasure see *RCH*, 51 (cited p. 119 above).

70. Phipps, *Buckingham*, 15–16, 31, 50; Pepys, 17 Jan., 5–6 Feb., 15 May 1668, 19 May 1669 (and cf. 22 July 1667); John Harold Wilson, *A Rake and His Times: George Villiers, 2nd Duke of Buckingham* (New York, 1954), 237–41 (Commons), 231, 248 (Lords); Bryson, *From Courtesy to Civility*, 248.

71. Pepys, 1 July 1663 (and 1 Feb. 1669 for the later attack on Kynaston); Anthony à Wood, *Athenae Oxoniensis*, ed. Philip Bliss (1813–20; repr. New York, 1967), IV.731, and *Life and Times*, ed. Andrew Clark, I (Oxford, 1891), 476–7, II (1892), 335–6 (adding that 'phanaticks' spread the story with aggravated resentment); V. de Sola Pinto, *Sir Charles Sedley, 1639–1701: a Study in the Life and Literature of the Restoration* (1927), 61–7, 307–9. For

mock-sermons see ch. 2, n. 5 above (for rural examples) and Thompson, 52–3. For the Bow Street episode, cf. also my 'Properties of Libertinism' (Preface, n. 3 above), 79–80, and Bryson, *From Courtesy to Civility*, 254–5.

72. 23 and 26 Oct. 1668; for Sedley's trial, see Wood and Pinto, cited above. Robert Brink Shoemaker, *Prosecution and Punishment: Petty Crime and the Law in London and Rural Middlesex, c. 1660–1725* (Cambridge, 1991), 30, notes that Sedley's case was used thereafter as the basis for prosecutions of all 'open and scandalous lewdness', while private acts such as fornication and adultery remained unindictable.

5 MONSTROUS ASSEMBLIES: BAWDY-HOUSE RIOTS, 'LIBERTINE LIBELS', AND THE ROYAL MISTRESS

1. *PL* VII.26–7, 32; *A Mask*, line 550.
2. Thomas Hollis, letter cited in Francis Blackburne, *Memoirs of Thomas Hollis, Esq.* (1780) 93; Hutchinson, *Memoirs*, ed. N. H. Keeble (1995), 63, 67; for Henrician scandals see Jonathan Goldberg, *Sodometries: Renaissance Texts, Modern Sexualities* (Stanford, CA, 1992), 47 ('minions') and 55 (leaking news of the king's impotence).
3. *The Poetics and Politics of Transgression* (Ithaca, NY, 1986), 101–2; Cavendish, *Letters*, 106 (ch. 4 above).
4. *The Secret History of the Reigns of K. Charles II and K. James II* (1690), 22 (a reference I owe to Annabel Patterson): if Castlemaine really had been 'his Sister by the Mother's Side, as being begotten by the E. of St. A. upon the Queen's Body, after the Death of C. the First', she would have been ten years old in 1660. For Charles's own bastardy, see n. 32 below; for the mock-wedding told as a lesbian number from pornography, see Wilson, 3, and Herzog August Bibliothek, Wolfenbüttel, MS Cod. Guelf. 405 Novi, f. 286.
5. Charles II, letter to Clarendon, *c.* June 1662, cited in Godfrey Davies, 'Charles II in 1660', in *Essays on the Late Stuarts* (San Marino, CA, 1958), 29–30; Cavendish, *Letters*, 76–7 (for her other remarks on the rise of the courtesan, see ch. 1, n. 20, ch. 3, section 4 above).
6. 16 July 1662; 15 May 1663; 15 Aug. 1665; 30 May 1668, 1 Sept. 1666, both episodes involving Henry Killigrew junior (grievously wounded for spreading scandal about Buckingham's mistress, as we saw ch. 4, n. 70 above).
7. Pepys, 29 July 1667 and 14 June 1667 for his explicit connection of the Medway naval disaster to the Fire; *POAS* 1.146 ('The Fourth Advice to a Painter'), cited in Harold Weber, *Paper Bullets: Print and Kingship under Charles II* (Lexington, KY, 1996), 93. Though much of Pepys's gossip about ecclesiastical fornication is unsubstantiated, Castlemaine did in fact promote her dissolute uncle to bishop.

8. Marvell, letter 'To a Friend in Persia', 9 Aug. 1671, *Letters*, 325; 'Concerning Bishop Braybrook' (dated 10 Dec. 1675), in MS memoirs by Lord Coleraine, British Library Stowe MS 1055, f. 20 (by the time of transcription she was Duchess of Cleveland).

9. Cavendish, *Letters*, 117; *POAS* I.420 (dated as early as 1669); Pope, *Essay on Criticism*, lines 536–8; for the association of absolutism and erotic bondage cf. John Hall's 'magic chains' (ch. 3, section 3 above) and Milton's attack on the bishops as emasculators in his early polemic (e.g. *CPW* I.588–9). The rumours circulating about Castlemaine's threat to print the king's letters to her (Pepys, 10 June 1666) make her a figure of literal 'publication' as well as literary patronage, sexual anarchy, and political influence.

10. *The London Jilt, or the Politick Whore, . . . Interwoven with Several Pleasant Stories of the Misses Ingenious Performances* (1683), f. A5.

11. 31 Aug. 1661, 29 June 1663, 18 and 30 Aug. 1667. Pepys felt distinctly uncomfortable seeing Puritans mocked in the puppet-play in Jonson's *Bartholomew Fair*, e.g. on 7 Sept. 1661 (where he sat close to the future Lady Castlemaine) and 4 Sept. 1668.

12. Pepys, 23, 25, and 29 July 1664; *Strange and True Newes from Jack-a-Newberries Six Windmills* (1660), 5; *Wandring Whore* I.6 ('the Poulterers wives cryes, *No mony, no Cony*'); the whore that particularly interested Pepys, named 'Cocke', had already featured in Humphrey Mill, *The Second Part of the Nights Search* (1646), 44–5.

13. Pepys, 1 Sept. 1668; Wordsworth, *The Prelude* VII. 708.

14. Manley, *London*, 520 (various uses of 'drollery', including Nedham's), 353; Pepys, 24 May, 28 Sept. 1660, 7 May 1661; Chartier, *The Cultural Uses of Print in Early Modern France*, transl. Lydia G. Cochrane (Princeton, NJ, 1987), 332–3; *Rare Verities* (1660), ff. A5v, B1v. For a collection of lewd 'Drolls' extracted from other comedies, see John James Elson (ed.), *The Wits, or Sport upon Sport* (1932).

15. *The Daring Muse: Augustan Poetry Reconsidered* (Cambridge, 1985), 122; *Punch* only dropped the phallus after *Private Eye* spotted it and adopted it as their own emblem.

16. *The English Rogue Described, in the Life of Meriton Latroon* (1665), 1st pagination, pp. 76–86 (ff. F6v–G3v), 3rd pagination, p. 19 (f. Bbb2); one commendatory poem calls the picaresque characters '*Misrules*' (f. A7v). For eggs as a weapon in real carnival, see Bouchard, ch. 4, n. 34 above, and for the crowd trampling the wife in the mud in a real Skimmington, see Ingram, 'Ridings', 82; for the sewer as the ultimate ignominious end, cf. the fates of Heliogabalus and Masaniello (ch. 2, n. 37 above). For the apprentice riots see Gordon Williams, *A Dictionary of Sexual Language and Imagery in Shakespearean and Stuart Literature* (1994), 'Shrove Tuesday'; Peter Burke, 'Popular Culture in Seventeenth-Century London', *London Journal* 3 (1977), 145; Ronald Hutton, *The Rise and Fall of Merry England: the Ritual Year, 1400–1700* (Oxford and New York, 1994), 188 (citing the passage from John Taylor the Water-Poet that I discuss in ch. 2, section 2 above), 244 (asserting that Shrove

Tuesday riots did *not* revive in London after the Restoration). Tim Harris,
'The Bawdy-House Riots of 1668', *Historical Journal* 29 (1986), 539, suggests
that the custom had been unobserved for so long that Charles might never
have known about it, but in 1660 *Six Windmills*, 4, 6, refers familiarly to
Priss Fotheringham as a potential victim of 'the *Shrove-tuesday boyes*'.

17. *A Compleat Collection of State-Tryals* (1719), II.33, 36 ('if they meddle with
nothing but bawdy-houses, they do but the magistrates drudgery'), cited
hereafter by page number from this volume. For other apprentices' actions,
see Pepys, 3 and 12 Feb. 1660, 26 Mar. 1664, 26 July 1664; Max Beloff,
Public Order and Popular Disturbances, 1660–1714 (1938), 30–2, 37, 40, 146. A
number of printed apprentices' petitions survive from 1647, and cf. also *The
Apprentices Hue-and-Cry after Their Petition* (1660); for hostility to the poet, cf.
William Riley Parker, *Milton: a Biography* (Oxford, 1968), 569. For a bawdy
Declaration of the Maids of London in support of an apprentices' rising in 1659,
see ch. 3, n. 34 above.

18. *State-Tryals*, 31–40; in fact one of the defendants in this very trial was an
apprentice (36), and Harris finds that according to most accounts they
formed the bulk of the crowd ('Riots', 538). (None of those involved in legal
proceedings was a sailor, despite circumstantial evidence suggesting their
participation.) For Ke[e]ling see Pepys, 23 Oct. 1668, 12 Dec. 1667, and
Steven C. A. Pincus, *Protestantism and Patriotism: Ideologies and the Making of
English Foreign Policy, 1650–1668* (Cambridge, 1996), 424.

19. Pepys, 25 Mar. 1668; Harris, 'Riots', 540, produces documentary evidence
for this phrase independent of the ubiquitous Pepys. For Allon White's
concept of 'displaced abjection' applied to apprentice riots, see Michael D.
Bristol, *Carnival and Theater* (1985), 69.

20. *Wandring Whore* II.10; *State-Tryals*, 36; Harris, 'Riots', 541 (citing the original
'Petition') and 542, citing the MS version dated '1 April' (after the arrest
of the rioters for high treason, but before their trial). Greaves, *Enemies*, 197,
interprets a break-in at the palace, 28 Mar. 1668, as 'probably the last gasp
of the riot'.

21. 1st pagination, pp. 76–86 (ff. F6v–G3v).

22. *State-Tryals*, 33, 34, 38, 40 ('Curiosity to see'); Pepys, 24 Mar. (turmoil caused
by absurd-looking Guards) and 25 Mar. 1668 (Mrs Daniels in a coach
headed for Bishopsgate, then a festive trip to Islington with wife and Deb,
again skirting the riot area but in 'fear'). The defendant William Green
did not explicitly make the carnivalesque defence, but his hat-throwing and
whooping led to the inference.

23. Pepys, 24–25 Mar. 1668; *State-Tryals*, 32–5; some courtiers did maintain the
amused stance, like Dorset and Wycherley (ch. 6 below). For the Bridewell
riot of 1756, see Stallybrass and White, *Transgression*, 48; John Cleland and
Henry Fielding both wrote pamphlets on the arrest of Bosavern Penlez,
apprehended in a very similar riot in 1749.

24. *State-Tryals*, 33, 39 (Hale's dissent), 36. For Justice Foster's analytic denunciation of this case (the work of a 'violent Cavalier' and 'fit only for the

Star-chamber'), see *A Complete Collection of State Trials*, ed. T. B. Howell (1816), VI, cols. 908–11.

25. Greaves, *Enemies*, 197.

26. Ingram, 'Ridings', 98; MS additions to *Sir Thomas More* (transcription in *The Riverside Shakespeare*), lines 113–14; *Oceana*, ed. S. B. Liljegren (Heidelberg, 1924), 152; Harris, 'Riots', 537, gives the impression that Harrington endorsed this view.

27. Bodleian MS Don. b. 8, p. 347; this satire applies to the submissive male the idea of the sexual 'Good Old Cause' (*Practical Part of Love*, ch. 4, section 1 above, also used in *Six Windmills*, 4) and the image of the 'naked arse' as heroic armament (*Puttana errante*, ch. 1, n. 50 above). The sheer scale of anti-Puritan bawdy verse can be gathered from the anthology *Rump* (1662).

28. Dorothy P. Ludlow, 'Shaking Patriarchy's Foundations: Sectarian Women in England, 1641–1700', in Richard L. Greaves (ed.), *Triumph over Silence: Women in Protestant History* (Westport, CT, 1985), 110 and 122 n. 60, citing contemporary pamphlets and Champlin Burrage, 'The Fifth Monarchy Insurrections', *EHR* 25 (1910), 735–6, 743, 744 n. 61, 746; B. S. Capp, *The Fifth Monarchy Men: a Study in Seventeenth-Century English Millenarianism* (1972), 82, 116, 174, 199; Sir Francis Fane, 'Iter Occidentale, or the Wonders of Warm-Water, 1674', British Library Harl. MS 7319, ff. 12, 15. Phyllis Mack, *Visionary Women: Ecstatic Prophecy in Seventeenth-Century England* (Berkeley, 1992), 102, stresses that Trapnel actually condemned Venner's (earlier) attempt at armed rising. See Ch. 3, Section 1 above for a woman stripping to protest a sermon in Whitehall, though in fig. 9 the preacher is also female.

29. Richard L. Greaves and Robert Zaller (eds.), *A Biographical Dictionary of British Radicals in the Seventeenth Century* (Brighton, 1982–84), *s.v.*; *Invisible John* (1659), 1 (this title refers to Barkstead's possession of a 'Stone lent him by an Italian' [2] that made him invisible); *The Inchanted Tower, or Berkstead His Dreame, Interpreted by Squire Dun, with His Comments on Habeas Corpus Cum Causa* (1662), 3, 5 (an allusion to Macchiavelli's image of the New Prince sexually dominating Fortune); Pepys, 19 Apr. 1662; *Mercurius Publicus*, cited in White Kennett, *A Register and Chronicle, Ecclesiastical and Civil* (1728), 663. Barkstead had been accused of suspending habeas corpus arbitrarily (*Invisible John*, 2), so emphasis on his bodily mutilation may have been a grim pun. The martyrological *The Speeches, Discourses, and Prayers of Col. John Barkstead, Col. John Okey, and Mr. Miles Corbet* (1662) constantly emphasizes the cheerfulness of Barkstead and his fellow-prisoners.

30. *Mirabilis Annus Secundus, or the Second Part of the Second Years Prodigies* (1662), 36, confusingly cited by Greaves (*Deliver Us*, 215) as if from the first part of *Secundus*; the *Speeches, Discourses, and Prayers* (n. 29 above) were 'Faithfully and Impartially Collected, for a general Satisfaction' (according to the title-page).

31. Harris, *London Crowds in the Reign of Charles II: Propaganda and Politics from the Restoration until the Exclusion Crisis* (Cambridge, 1987), 22, 24 (where he coins

the term 'police crowds'); Hutton, *Merry England*, 30; *State-Tryals*, 35. For the 1680 *Solemn Mock Procession*, see Epilogue below.

32. Pepys, 23 Aug. 1660, 27 July 1667; Marvell, *Last Instructions*, lines 769–84; Greaves, *Deliver Us*, 22–3 (including the Jermyn genealogy), 111; *Enemies*, 234, 4; Hammond, 'The King's Two Bodies: Representations of Charles II', in Jeremy Black and Jeremy Gregory (eds.), *Culture, Politics and Society in Britain, 1660–1800* (Manchester, 1991), 23; Thompson, 128. For Milton on Charles I and his mother, see *CPW* III.167.

33. *Sodom*, 325; Marvell, *Last Instructions to a Painter*, lines 146, 132, 30–44, 49–102 (esp. 61–2 for the Duchess of York as asparagus vendor and 87ff for Lady Castlemaine's footman), 150; Underdown, 216 (Skimmington-like elements in the anti-Excise riots of 1647 and 1649); song ('That Beauty I adored before, / I now as much despise'), reprinted from *Westminster Drollery* (1671) in Montague Summers (ed.), *The Works of Aphra Behn* (1915), VI.364. For a more detailed analysis of Marvell's poem, see my 'The Libertine Abject: the "Postures" of *Last Instructions to a Painter*', in Warren Chernaik and Martin Dzelzainis (eds.), *Marvell and Liberty* (1999), 217–48, and for genital graffiti in a tavern (Marvell's ironic visual standard) cf. Etherege, ch. 1, n. 52 above.

34. 'To the Tune of the Jovyall Tinker', Bodleian MS Don. b. 8, p. 186; Wilson, 64; 'The Whore of Babylon', Dyce 43, ff. 31–4 (entitled 'On the Duchess of Portsmouth' in British Library MS Harl. 7317, ff. 67–68v); ; 'A Ballad', Bodleian MS Don. b. 8, p. 185 (Wilson, 10–12 transcribes an 'identical' version from a British Library MS); for the rude etymology from *lève le cul* (or 'Hitch-Buttock'), see *OED*, 'level-coil'.

35. Pepys, 14 June 1667; Edmund Ludlow cited in Pincus, *Protestantism*, 426; *Depositions in the Castle of York*, ed. James Raine, Surtees Society XL (1861), 83; John Cordy Jeaffreson (ed.), *Middlesex County Records* III (1888), 327; Greaves, *Deliver Us*, 213, 220–4, 225 (and cf. 22, 110, 207), *Enemies*, 168, 174–82, 228; Greaves and Zaller, *Dictionary*, 'Elizabeth Calvert'; Kegl, 'Women's Preaching' (see ch. 2, n. 35 above), 62; Sir Francis Bacon, 'Of Sedition and Troubles', *Essayes*, ed. Michael Kiernan (Cambridge, MA, 1985), 43.

36. Thomason E.1017(42) (24 March 1660), 7–8.

37. Bodleian MS Don. b. 8, pp. 190–3, the '1 April' version cited n. 20 above (the printed version, *The Gracious Answer*, signs off with a much later date, 24 April); as Harris shows ('Riots', 542) the two versions differ widely after the first paragraph.

38. Letter to Arlington, transcribed in George Kitchin, *Sir Roger L'Estrange: a Contribution to the History of the Press in the Seventeenth Century* (1913), 176; Greaves, *Enemies*, 168, 175, 176.

39. Evelyn, *Diary*, ed. E. S. de Beer (Oxford, 1955), entry for 2 April 1668; Pepys, 6 April 1668, finding the petition 'not very witty, but devilish severe against her and the king'; Harris, 'Riots', 541, *London Crowds*, 84.

40. *Poor-Whores Petition*, broadsheet (as are all the printed works in this 1668 'petition' group).

41. All citations from the *Whores Petition* unless otherwise indicated; the *Citizens Reply*, predictably, emphasizes the shame to London, the danger of 'sedition' and 'insurrection', and the need to keep the sword in '*Justice* hand'.

42. All citations from the printed *Gracious Answer* unless otherwise specified; for Castlemaine's theatricality in this passage, see David Roberts, *The Ladies: Female Patronage of Restoration Drama, 1660–1700* (Oxford, 1989), 77.

43. John Phillips, *Montelion, or the Prophetical Almanack* (1662), f. A5 (opposite a crude woodcut showing Peters with a woman on his knee, both almost naked); Bodleian MS Don. b. 8, p. 193; Rachel Weil, 'Sometimes a Scepter Is Only a Scepter: Pornography and Politics in Restoration England', in Lynn Hunt (ed.), *The Invention of Pornography: Obscenity and the Origins of Modernity, 1500–1800* (New York, 1993), 146–7, comments on the anti-Catholicism of this MS 'Answer'.

44. *The Blazing World and Other Writings*, ed. Kate Lilley (1994), 224, 183; *Letters*, 43.

45. *Blazing World*, ed. Lilley, 133. The passage about meddling women (135), in this gynocratic context (and coming immediately after unacceptable arguments for excluding women from religion), is 'silently ironized' – as Lilley argues in 'Utopian Writing' (ch. 3, n. 56 above), 121.

6 'MAKING YOURSELF A BEAST': UPPER-CLASS RIOT AND INVERSIONARY WIT IN THE AGE OF ROCHESTER

1. *Erotopolis, or a New Description of Bettyland* (1684), 177. Thompson, 91 records later brothel attacks in 1679 and 1682 in addition to 'the normal Shrove Tuesday assaults' (but see Ronald Hutton, *The Rise and Fall of Merry England* (Oxford and New York, 1994), 244).

2. George Kitchin, *Sir Roger L'Estrange* (1913), 170, 173; Annabel Patterson, *Marvell and the Civic Crown* (Princeton, 1978), 124–5, pl. 3 (showing the Dutch cartoons that provoked the renewed outbreak of hostilities in 1672).

3. *The Character of a Coffee-House, with the Symptomes of a Town-Wit* (1673), 1, 6 (cited in Patricia Meyer Spacks, *Gossip* (1986), 123); cf. *The Mens Answer to the Women's Petition against Coffee* (1674), 1, Tim Harris, *London Crowds in the Reign of Charles II* (Cambridge, 1987), 28–9, and Steve Pincus, '"Coffee Politicians Does Create": Coffeehouses and Restoration Political Culture', *Journal of Modern History* 67 (1995), 807–34 (note the gender-equality of the coffee-house as opposed to the masculinity of the tavern, 815, 823–5). In an early work, Jürgen Habermas makes the oft-cited but under-verified connection between the coffee-house and what was later translated as 'the public sphere': *Strukturwandel der Öffentlichkeit* (Darmstadt, 1962).

4. Charles Sackville, sixth Earl of Dorset, *Poems*, ed. Brice Harris (New York, 1979), 90–1; Radcliffe, *The Ramble, an Anti-Heroick Poem: Together with Some Terrestrial Hymns and Carnal Ejaculations* (1682), 70, 24–6.

5. Max Beloff, *Public Order and Popular Disturbances, 1660–1714* (1938), 78. For Articles of Treason against Portsmouth (and perhaps against Cleveland), see Epilogue below.
6. *Sir Fopling Flutter, or the Man of Mode* III.iii.240; these strollers reek of smoke from the coffee-house and sing a bawdy catch with the refrain 'there's something else to be done'. Cynthia Wall, *The Literary and Cultural Spaces of Restoration London* (Cambridge, 1998), 166, claims that St James's Park remained 'the sole province of sovereign and court' until Charles's death in 1685. For 'buttock' cf. ch. 4, section 2 and ch. 1, nn. 14, 28 above (the word identifies denizens of a criminal zone 'in *London*, separate from *London*'); for 'scour' see ch. 1, n. 50, Gordon Williams, *A Dictionary of Sexual Language and Imagery in Shakespearean and Stuart Literature* (1994), and Shadwell's comedy *The Scowrers*.
7. Dennis, 'To the Honourable Major Pack, Containing some remarkable Passages of Mr Wycherley's Life', reprinted in *Critical Works*, ed. Edward Niles Hooker, II (Baltimore, 1943), 409–10 (first epigraph above), cited also by Friedman, 5–6n; Magalotti, *Relazioni d'Inghilterra, 1668 e 1688*, ed. Anna Maria Crinò (Florence, 1972), 84, cited (in English translation only) in William J. Pritchard, 'Outward Appearances: the Display of Women in Restoration London', PhD dissertation, University of Chicago (1998), 68 and 186. Dennis's '*Pall-mall*' could refer to the street that Wycherley called 'the Old Pell Mell' (Friedman, 43n, 83) or to 'the new Pell-mell' i.e. the Mall flanking St James's Park.
8. Rochester, 254; Winn, *'When Beauty Fires the Blood': Love and the Arts in the Age of Dryden* (Ann Arbor, MI, 1992), 61–4; the 'delicately sexual' meaning of 'Pity' derives from an earlier draft shared by the author.
9. Pepys, 22 Sep. 1660, 30 May 1668; Butler, *Hudibras*, 110–11 (II.i.367–70); Dorset, *Poems*, 119; Radcliffe, n. 4 above; for 'Ballum Rancum' (variously printed *Raneum* or *Rancun*) as a euphemism for male genitalia or virility, see Ferrand Spence, *Lucian's Works Translated from the Greek* IV (1685), 305, a reference I owe to David Robinson. Wycherley's dedication appears in Friedman, 365–72. Gerald Weales, *The Complete Plays of William Wycherley* (New York, 1967), 519–20, suggests that Wycherley's 'Plain Dealer' signature implies no overlap between the persona and the author himself, even though Wycherley increasingly signed his own letters that way.
10. Montaigne, *Essais* III.v, *Œuvres complètes*, ed. Albert Thibaudet and Maurice Rat, Bibliothèque de la Pléiade (Paris, 1962), 825; Wycherley, *PD*, 366; Friedman, 371n; Etherege, *Man of Mode* IV.i.251.
11. Pallavicino, *La retorica delle puttane* (1642; 'Villafranca', 1673), 4; Wycherley, *PD*, 370. Friedman cites mock-dedications in *Scarron's City Romance* and *Holborn-Drollery*, but not this one.
12. 368, and cf. *CW* I.i.253 and V.iv.345. In one crucial respect this passage in the *PD* dedication is closer to *La retorica delle puttane*, which recommended an outward appearance of extreme modesty; Horner, on the other hand,

complained (at first) that for reasons of fashion all women now looked *willing*, though many were not in fact 'right'.

13. Wilson, 20–1 (cf. Bodleian MS Don. b. 8, p. 212, 'bragging Wicherly' changed to 'brawny'); Rochester, 53, 79, 90, 422 (satires and gossip-diaries that link Wycherley's and Knight's names). Wilson interprets the lines 'Cleveland was doubtless to blame / On such a he-whore to dote' in the 'brawn' lampoon to mean Churchill, who did receive large sums of money from Cleveland (20–1), but the focus of these stanzas is on Wycherley. *Brawny Wycherley* is the title of Willard Connely's 1930 biography; for earlier praise of his masculinity, see Dryden and Lord Lansdowne, cited n. 21 below.

14. *Works* IV.91, 92, 95 (with additional line supplied from Wycherley's MS completion of the censored first edition, *Hero and Leander in Burlesque* (1669), Victoria and Albert Museum, London, Dyce 17.P.55, p. 46).

15. I.ii.148–50, 152, 154; cf. *CW* I.i.254 ('the vizard Masques you know never pitty a Man when all's gone, though in their Service').

16. As Winn suggests in '*Beauty*', 64; for the rumour as recounted to Pepys by two different gossips, see 8 and 17 Feb. 1663.

17. 1 July 1663; Shadwell encouraged the belief that Dryden, trying vainly to blend in to the glamorous circle of Court Wits, yelled out 'Let's bugger one another, By G---!', cited in Winn, *John Dryden and His World* (New Haven, 1987), 225.

18. Dennis, *Critical Works* II.410; Christine Phipps (ed.), *Buckingham, Public and Private Man: the Prose, Poems and Commonplace Book of George Villiers, Second Duke of Buckingham (1628–1687)* (1985), 338, 341. For Buckingham's possible authorship of verses on his cousin as 'exquisite whore', see n. 79 below; for Kynaston see Pepys, 18 Aug. 1660, Katharine Eisaman Maus, 'Playhouse Flesh and Blood: Sexual Ideology and the Restoration Actress', *ELH* 46 (1979), 597 (and ch. 4, n. 71 above for Sedley's assault on him).

19. 'Holyhead Journal, 1727', in *Prose Works*, ed. Herbert Davis, V (Oxford, 1962), 205–6.

20. B. Eugene McCarthy, *William Wycherley: a Biography* (Athens, OH, 1979), 24 (drawing on records of Wycherley's conversations with Joseph Spence and John Dennis about his youth in Angoulême).

21. Dryden, 'To my Dear Friend, Mr Congreve, on his Comedy called *The Double Dealer*', line 30 (bulging to six feet in emulation of Wycherley's brawn); Lansdowne cited in McCarthy, *Wycherley*, 98; Wycherley, *PD*, 369.

22. *A Strange and True Conference between Two Notorious Bawds, Damarose Page and Pris. Fotheringham* (1660), 5; Pepys, 31 Dec. 1662. I accept Weales's conjecture that the 'Dance of Cuckolds' specified at *CW* V.iv.352 might have been identified by this tune (*Complete Plays*, 370–1). Intriguingly, Elizabeth Polwhele's unpublished 1671 comedy *The Frolicks, or The Lawyer Cheated* ends with a song about cuckolds (ed. Judith Milhous and Robert D. Hume (Ithaca, NY, 1977), 137); this obscure woman author anticipates many elements of Wycherley's drama, including the country-wife eager to see the city and the link between plain speaking and London bawdy.

23. I.i.254 (the catch-phrase 'Probatum est' identifies Horner himself as a mountebank, working in concert with the Quack); Head, *Nugae Venales* (1675), 25; Pepys, 1 July 1663 (for the Cock Tavern riot, see ch. 4, section 3 above). For the colloquial sexual use of 'right' (not in *OED*), cf. Abraham Cowley, *The Guardian* (1641), V.v, in *Essays, Plays and Sundry Verses*, ed. A. R. Waller (Cambridge, 1906), 228, Cosmo Manuche, *The Loyal Lovers* (1652), 5, and *Holborn-Drollery* (1672), 93.

24. *Wandring Whore* 1.6, II.8, VI.8 (all cited in ch. 4 above); Wycherley, *Works* III.170 (cited ch. 1, n. 14 above); cf. 'Philo-Puttanus', *The Whores Rhetorick* (1683), 114, 'let her Frenchifie her Commodities, or, (to avoid ribaldry), her Merchandize'. See further my '"News from the New Exchange": Commodity, Erotic Fantasy, and the Female Entrepreneur', in Ann Bermingham and John Brewer (eds.), *The Consumption of Culture, 1600–1800: Image, Object, Text* (1995), 419–39.

25. *L'Escole des filles, ou la philosophie des dames* (1655), ed. Pascal Pia (Paris, 1969), 169.

26. *PD* V.ii.494; *Love in a Wood, or St James's Park* I.ii.23 (where Friedman provides rich documentation for the window-smashing habit), III.i.55; *Gentleman Dancing-Master*, Prologue (125) and Epilogue (235), spoken by Flirt (cf. n. 15 above for her voracious hunt for men and rabbits); this epilogue is thus related to pamphlets like *The Wandring-Whores Complaint for Want of Trading* (1663) or the 1672 *Poor Whores Complaint*, which also refers to the depletion of customers by the Dutch war (p. 198 above).

27. *PD* II.i.418, V.ii.490, 497–8 (a scene set in the Cock Tavern), iii.507. Masculine friendship (false as well as true) is also conspicuously eroticized in *CW*: Horner addresses his old whoring-companion Pinchwife 'kiss me deare Rogue', a phrase that Wycherley's friend Shadwell had given to a dubious man-kissing coxcomb in *The Sullen Lovers* (IV.iii.324, cf. I.i.264 and n.); Harcourt/Kynaston complains that Sparkish 'will not let us enjoy one another', and Sparkish promises *him* that after marriage 'thou shalt enjoy me sometimes dear Rogue' (I.i.256, II.i.271). Horner seems inexplicably intimate with his 'Dear Mr Doctor' (the play begins with the two of them emerging from his bedroom in a pattern echoed only in the China scene), and responds most intensely to Margery when she adopts the breeches part of 'Little Sir James' (III.ii). Eve Sedgwick, in ch. 3 of *Between Men: English Literature and Male Homosocial Desire* (New York, 1985), analyses the homosocial dynamic in *CW* but misses hints of more direct contact between males.

28. IV.ii.312, 313, V.iv.349; note the covert allusion to Jonson's *Silent Woman*.

29. Pepys, 19 and 20 Nov. 1668, 6 Mar. 1669; for court cases involving a husband threatening his wife with 'naked sword', see Peter Earle, *The Making of the English Middle Class: Business, Society and Family Life in London, 1660–1730* (1989), 203, and Lawrence Stone, *Broken Lives: Separation and Divorce in England, 1660–1857* (Oxford, 1993), 34.

30. Marvell, *Letters*, 321 (see also 125, 135, 325); Gilbert Burnet, *A History of My Own Time*, ed. Osmund Airy, I (Oxford, 1897), 487–9; *POAS* I.159–62 ('The King's Vows'), 169–171 ('The Haymarket Hectors').

31. Sir Francis Fane, *Love in the Dark* (1675), 68 (and for the 'genteel gaity' of violence see Shadwell, *The Royal Shepherdess* (1669), f. A3); cf. Michael Neill, 'Horned Beasts and China Oranges: Reading the Signs in *The Country-Wife*', *Eighteenth-Century Life* 2.2 (May 1988), 10–11; W. Gerald Marshall, 'Wycherley's "Great Stage of Fools": Madness and Theatricality in *The Country Wife*', *SEL* 29 (1989), 416. Earlier critics psychoanalysed Pinchwife's aggression, which allowed them (within this narrow perspective) to see an affinity between the cuckold's sword and the rake's penis; cf. Anthony Kaufman, 'Wycherley's *The Country Wife* and the Don Juan Character', *Eighteenth-Century Studies* 9 (1975/76), 225.

32. 58, 118, 64; Chernaik, 63 cites a similar analogy from an early eighteenth-century preface to Rochester ('as a Beauty owes her Ruin to her own Charms, so did my Lord'). Courtesans themselves were often described as witty, at least in the invention of 'new lechery'; cf. *Newes from the New Exchange, or the Commonwealth of Ladies* (1650), 7.

33. *Letters*, 241–2 (fragment of a letter to his wife, probably echoing *Troilus and Cressida* III.ii).

34. 85–9 and notes (for the 'Liberty to swive' variant, see p. 200 above); *POAS* I.423; for critical comment, cf. Chernaik, 56–60 and Rachel Weil, 'Sometimes a Scepter Is Only a Scepter' (ch. 5, n. 43 above), 125, 143.

35. 87; for violent antics involving French courtiers and prostitutes, unpleasantly close to the 'mad tricks' of *The Wandring Whore*, see Maurice Lever, *Les Bûchers de Sodome: histoire des 'infâmes'* (Paris, 1985), 162–3, and Patrick Wald Lasowski, *Libertines* (Paris, 1980), 71–2.

36. Love places it among the disputed works (248–57), showing that the earlier version has little link with Rochester and that the better-known B text (used in earlier editions of Rochester) has clearly been revised at a date after his death. Numerous critics have commented on this poem as evidence for Rochester's derisory view of the genitals, e.g. Stephen Clark, '"Something Genrous in Meer Lust"?: Rochester and Misogyny', in Edward Burns (ed.), *Reading Rochester* (New York, 1995), 36 (expanding on Harold Weber's observation that 'from the female point of view the male body provides an essentially comic spectacle').

37. Flecknoe, *The Diarium or Journall* (1656), cited in Manley, *London*, 515; Rochester, 76–80 For another impersonation of jealous fury and misogyny, clearly given to the villain of the play, see Lycungus in the scene Rochester wrote for Sir Robert Howard's *Conquest of China* (128–30), and for the aristocrat's (pseudo-)praise of 'generous' lust, ch. 1, n. 21 above (Behn's *Love-Letters*).

38. Lines 41–3, modified from Keith Walker (ed.), *Poems* (Oxford, 1984), 31. In some MSS the phrase 'twou'd carelessly invade / Woman or Boy' reads 'Woman or Man'; a third group, which Love favours (353–4), reads 'Woman, nor Man', even though this renders meaningless the idea of 'making' a vulva where none existed. For the 'hector' directly associated with erection, cf. *The Maidens Complaint against Coffee* (1663), cited in Pincus, 'Coffeehouses', 824.

39. As in the widely disseminated poem 'Base mettell hanger by your Master's Thigh!' (Rochester, 264–5, included in Love's 'Appendix Roffensis' of works once attributed to Rochester but unlikely to be by him); the image of the limp penis disobedient to its 'Master' may derive from a sense that in the closing diatribe of *The Imperfect Enjoyment* Rochester indulges in a routine for which he was famous – the abusive but half-ironic dressing-down of a servant. The paradox of 'honour' (in both the phallic and the chivalric sense) is elaborated throughout Wycherley's *CW*; cf. II.i.281 for a particularly intricate example.

40. *RCH*, 57; cf. Thomas More, *Utopia*, ed. Edward Surtz and J. H. Hexter, *The Yale Edition of the Complete Works of St Thomas More* IV (1965), 144 (no kind of pleasure should be prohibited, providing nothing inconvenient results from it), 166 (appetites given by nature should not be feared).

41. 11 (but cf. 'Insolent' used with more negative connotation by Lucina in Rochester's adaptation of Fletcher's *Valentinian*, 171); for his confessed alcoholism see *RCH*, 50.

42. Rochester, 15; Burnet in *RCH*, 54; Boswell, *London Journal, 1762–1763*, ed. Frederick A. Pottle (1950), 272–3; Alexander Pope, *The First Epistle of the Second Book of Horace, Imitated*, line 108.

43. Bryson, *From Courtesy to Civility* (Oxford and New York, 1997), 250 (and cf. 269, citing the 1673 *Remarques*, 'the desire of glory and singularity among gentlemen is now as violent as ever'); *The Character of a Town-Gallant* (1675), 9; Rochester, 261 (among disputed works because possibly by Sedley); Walker (note to *Poems*, 81) compares the sceptre lampoon and *Wandring Whore* III.3 (ch. 4, section 2 above).

44. Dorset, *Poems*, 91, and cf. Wycherley, *Works* IV.98 ('a Brimmer to the Best'). The euphemistic version of the 'best cunt' toast can still be detected in Pope's early *Sappho to Phaon*, line 57 ('In all I pleas'd, but most in what was best'), and in Fielding's *Shamela*, Letter X.

45. 23, and cf. Duane Coltharp, 'Rivall Fopps, Rambling Rakes, Wild Women: Homosocial Desire and Courtly Crisis in Rochester's Poetry', *The Eighteenth Century: Theory and Interpretation* 38 (1997), 29. For Bruno see ch. 1, section 4 above.

46. Wycherley, *CW* III.ii.288; Rochester, 45 (alternative titles listed on p. 539 include 'Maimed Debauchee'). The heavy-handed turn to political satire at the end (comparing the impotent rouser of others' mischief to the 'Statesman') does not alter the overall attitude of amused indulgence toward earlier debauchery.

47. Underdown, 95; Vivian de Sola Pinto, *Enthusiast in Wit: a Portrait of John Wilmot Earl of Rochester, 1647–1680* (Lincoln, NE, 1962), 147, n. 5 and 167, n. 1, in both cases citing Hearne and warning against the reliability of this 'salacious old gossip'; Theophilus Cibber, cited in Graham Greene, *Lord Rochester's Monkey, Being the Life of John Wilmot, Second Earl of Rochester* (New York, 1974), 95–6. Rochester's own allusion to the Woodstock nude escapade (*Letters*, 159) turns female spectatorship into an irony against 'the strange decay of manly parts'.

48. Letter of Charles Hatton, 29 June 1676, cited in Bryson, *From Courtesy to Civility*, 250; Rochester, 61, 113, 367 (citing Marvell's letter on the incident). Walker (ed.), *Poems*, 292–3, gives a full account. For the paradox of counterfeit and real in the 'Alexander Bendo' medical spoof, see Anne Righter, 'John Wilmot, Earl of Rochester', *Proceedings of the British Academy* 53 (1967), 47–69.

49. *RCH*, 113, 46, 102 (and cf. 101–10, 132–3, 160 for Behn's and Wharton's passionate Rochester-cult), 146–57 (Wolseley's remark that ''tis thought as glorious a piece of Gallantry by some of our modern Sparks, to libel a Woman of Honour, as to kill a Constable who is doing his duty' (146) is particularly risky since Rochester had attempted precisely that), 169 (Rymer).

50. Thomas, 'Epistle to Clemena, Occasioned by an Argument She Had Maintained against the Author', in Roger Lonsdale (ed.), *Eighteenth-Century Women Poets* (Oxford, 1989), 34–6; *Remarques on the Humours and Conversations of the Town* (1673), 30; *Remarks upon Remarques, or a Vindication of the Conversations of the Town* (1673), ff. A4v–5v, 19, 50; *Character of a Town-Gallant*, 8.

51. Dryden, 'Prologue to *The Wild Gallant*, Revived', the play whose first run had been encouraged by the patronage of Lady Castlemaine (cf. Winn, *Dryden*, 183–4); Wycherley, *Works* II.244 (Shadwell's letter and its reply, and for his Preface see Jordan, 'Extravagant Rake' (ch. 4, n. 59 above), 80), and cf. Shadwell's *Woman-Captain* (1679) for window-breaking debauchees; Chernaik, 79; Sir John Reresby, *Memoirs*, ed. Andrew Browning (Glasgow, 1936), 82 (the incident occurred during the Prince of Orange's official visit to woo Lady Mary, in late 1670 or early 1671).

52. Wilson, 220–1, 224, 292–4, drawing upon evidence from HMC Reports and Swift's *Examiner*, numbers 23 and 25; the church-defiling scene (without the Burford location) is expanded in a 1683 satire with other details like getting into the pulpit with dirty bottoms and 'ma[king] their footmen frig in every pew' (123). (Though Swift claims the excremental prank earned Thomas Wharton a fine of £1000, Wilson has not been able to find evidence for the prosecution.) The group who attacked 'Mrs Willis's balls' includes the single name 'Wharton', which presumably refers to the oldest brother rather than to Henry (*pace* Wilson, 293).

53. *A Tale of a Tub*, ed. A. C. Guthkelch and D. Nichol Smith, 2nd edn (Oxford, 1958), 165 n. 1, recording the reading of Swift's first editions; the Horatian *cunnus* ('Cunt is the most frightful cause of war') was eventually dropped by Swift, but revived in some versions of *The Norton Anthology of English Literature*, where it is translated for the benefit of non-Latinists as 'woman'.

54. Marvell to William Popple, c. 1 May 1671, *Letters*, 323; Phipps, *Buckingham*, 152; Bodleian MS Don. b. 8, pp. 208, 209. For the pseudo-chivalric storming of 'Grimcunt Castle', and related episodes in pornography, see ch. 2, n. 6 above.

55. *Absalom and Achitophel*, lines 8–10, 37–40 (II.5–6); *Sodom*, 303. (The 'Command' of *Absalom* line 9 punningly combines the instruction of Gen. 1:28 to 'increase and multiply' and David's command over the realm of Israel.)

No satisfactory explanation has yet been produced for the '*Amnon's* Murther' lines (39–40), which hint at another killing by Monmouth, involving someone of social consequence.

56. *The Poetics and Politics of Transgression* (Ithaca, NY, 1986), 101; for a fuller treatment, see my 'Properties of Libertinism' (Preface, n. 3 above), 81.

57. *RCH*, 53 (and cf. ch. 4, section 4, ch. 5, n. 22 above); Marvell, *Letters*, 321, records that Monmouth's attack on Coventry's nose was aborted because 'Company coming made them fearful to finish it'.

58. Oldham, 'Suppos'd to be spoken by a Court-Hector at Breaking of the Dial in Privy-Garden', dated in his autograph manuscript 'Croydon July 1676', *Poems*, ed. Harold F. Brooks with the collaboration of Raman Selden (Oxford, 1987), 57, 400; Selden, 'Rochester and Oldham: "High Rants in Profaneness"', *The Seventeenth Century* 6 (1991), 89–103; John Cordy Jeaffreson (ed.), *Middlesex County Records* IV (1892), 29, cited (with incorrect reference) in Thompson, 129. Several of Oldham's mock-anti-libertine poems, including this one and the ultra-obscene 'Upon the Author of the Play Called *Sodom*', were published as Rochester's in his *Poems* ('Antwerp', 1680).

59. Cf. the Song 'An Age in her Embraces pas'd', 28 ('Love rais'd to an extream'), and 15, 45, 79, already cited above. It is even possible, though Rochester is so slippery that even the best scholars remain quite unable to decide the issue, that he himself wrote the fictional speech 'to the Post Boy' ('Frighted at my own Mischeifs I have fled / And bravely left my Lifes Defender dead; / Broke Houses to break Chastity and Dy'd / That floor with Murther which my Lust denyd'); Love includes this among the probable poems (42–3), despite the uncharacteristic and clumsy puns on the town of Rochester and the 'Peerless Peer', whereas Chernaik rejects it (71 and n. 55).

60. Cited (without clear attribution) in Greene, *Rochester's Monkey*, 103. Despite Burnet's comment – recorded, like other information here, in Philip H. Highfill et al., *A Biographical Dictionary of Actors . . . in London, 1660–1800* (Carbondale and Edwardsville, IL, 1973–93) – the insider Rochester still included 'nell' alongside Cleveland in his list of royal mistresses in whom 'a Heroick head is liker to be ballanc't with an humble taile', and 'whose honour was ever soe extensive in theire heads that they suffered a want of it in every other part' (*Letters*, 75). For satires against Gwyn see ch. 1, n. 15 above, Epilogue, nn. 7, 8 below, and 'On Several Women about Town' (1680), Wilson, 32–5.

61. 'Much has been said of strumpets of yore', reprinted from a Scots collection (which records the Southesk attribution) in *Merry Songs and Ballads Prior to the Year A.D. 1800*, ed. John S. Farmer (1897), V.21–3 (the countess is given a prominent part in 'Signor Dildo', so she was no stranger to the lampoon genre).

62. Hume and Milhous (eds.), 81, 57, 97–101 (cf. 106, 'Oh, how I love this Rightwit and his wicked wit! He has gone beyond me in this frolic'), 125, 80. The prototype for the 'Madcap' heroine is the Nell Gwyn vehicle Florimell in Dryden's *Secret Love*; in Dryden (and in Behn's *Rover*) she provides a comic

alternative to the high-style romance plot, but in Polwhele she dominates the entire play.

63. 110–11 (and 112–13, 115 for further variations). The bondage theme is reiterated when Rightwit and another friend are thrown into prison and depend on the ingenuity and wealth of Clarabell to release them; she exults in their captivity by pretending that they have come to visit her brothel ('What say you now to a score of wenches, or a fresh tavern frolic, ha?' 119).

64. I.i, *Works* V.458 (Hellena proposes 'let's Ramble'), I.ii.461–5; Todd's notes provide useful summaries of the changes Behn makes as she borrows from Thomas Killigrew, as does Chernaik, 259 (and for other *Rover* parallels 185, 193–4, and 204). Behn's invented carnival scene actually reverses a scene in Killigrew's original, when the Cavaliers behave respectfully towards a group of veiled 'Ladies' until Thomaso 'prove[s] them Whores'; *Thomaso*, in *Comedies and Tragedies* (1664), 317 (partially recycled in Belvile's exposé of 'Whores', discussed below). In her book of that title Todd raises Behn's postscript about '*the Sign of Angellica*' to an emblem of feminist writing, even though Behn only refers to having borrowed the character from Killigrew.

65. Wycherley, 'To a poor Whore, who would fain have father'd a Pox on him', *Works* IV.249; Behn, *Rover* I.ii.463, 468, III.ii.485–7, IV.i.506; Killigrew, *Thomaso*, 357–9. In Killigrew's play Blunt merely escapes through the window in his underwear, and (with the help of a book, 409) begins to plan the ponderous revenge that includes hiring 'Bravo's' to slash Lucetta's face (422–3) and threatening her nose (447). Cf. Anthony Kaufman, '"The Perils of Florinda": Aphra Behn, Rape, and the Subversion of Libertinism in *The Rover, Part I*', *Restoration and Eighteenth-Century Theatre Research*, 2nd ser. 11.2 (Winter, 1996), 1–21, and Chernaik, 207–8, for the attempted-rape scenes.

66. Behn, 'An Epistle to the Reader', *The Dutch Lover* (1673), *Works* V.161; *Triumphs of Female Wit, in Some Pindarick Odes, or, The Emulation* (1683), 5; Barker, *Poetical Recreations* (1688), I.5, I.115.

67. 118–19 ('Prologue'), 43 (a poem to the same lady after she became Lady Felton, urging her to abandon both the pen and the sword and to devote all her 'Charms and Wit' to 'dying' in his arms, as if the sexual encounter should express her entire being), 78; the best analysis of these poems is Edward Burns, 'Rochester, Lady Betty and the Post-Boy', in Burns (ed.), *Reading Rochester*, 74–81. The concrete sexual meaning of *kind* ('How kindly can we say – "I hate you now"') can be gauged from Behn's Willmore, who asks of the courtesan-masquers 'will they not be kind? quickly be kind?' and who tells Angellica (after she pulls a gun on him) that his blood runs so hot that he 'cou'd oblige thee with a kindness, had I but opportunity' (*Rover* I.ii.461, V.i.512).

68. Rochester, 72–73 ('songs and verses mannerly Obscene' which arouse even the chastest woman 'without forcing blushes'); Robert Herrick, 'The Argument of his Book'.

69. *Wandring Whore* IV.8; *The Character of a Town Misse* (1675), 8.

70. 37 (as in the Wycherley poem cited n. 65 above, 'shore' means 'sewer'); cf. Peter Porter, 'The Professional Amateur', in Jeremy Treglown (ed.), *Spirit of Wit: Reconsiderations of Rochester* (Oxford, 1982), 63. For criticism see Earl Miner, *The Restoration Mode from Milton to Dryden* (Princeton, 1974), 380, Ken Robinson, 'The Art of Violence in Rochester's Satire', in Claude Rawson and Jenny Mecziems (eds.), *English Satire and the Satiric Tradition* (Oxford, 1984), 106, and Chernaik, 10. For the pun on poetic and menstrual 'Monethly Flowers', see also the verse-epistle to Julian ('Thou Common shore of this Poetique Town'), attributed to Buckingham, in *The Gyldenstolpe Manuscript Miscellany*, ed. Bror Danielsson and David M. Vieth (Stockholm, 1967), p. 206. In Shadwell's verse-letter to Wycherley the subject of Sue Willis comes up a few lines after the jocular enquiry about window-smashing Wits (n. 51 above), and so constitutes a kind of incitement.

71. The capacity of 'wit' to turn insult into raillery and detach the speech-act from its content is vividly illustrated in Wycherley's Sparkish, the foppish fiancé of Alithea (*CW* II.i.272–3); when his rival Harcourt loads him with insults he delightedly explains them as flattering displays of ingenuity, typical between 'we wits', but explodes in fury when Harcourt impugns his 'parts' (i.e. the intelligence that underlies wit).

72. Etherege, *Poems*, ed. James Thorpe (Princeton, NJ, 1963), 40–45 (and 109 for date and authenticity). Cf. *The Letterbook of Sir George Etherege*, ed. Sybil Rosenfeld (1928), 240, for Etherege in his fifties still chortling to Dorset over their youthful exploits with whores.

73. *Exilius* (cited in Preface above); 'A Virgin life', in Germaine Greer et al. (eds.), *Kissing the Rod: an Anthology of 17th-Century Women's Verse* (1988), 360; Magdalen College, Oxford, MS 343, ff. 75v–76 (I am grateful to Alison Shell for sharing her transcripts of this MS); *Poetical Recreations* I.15, I, f. A5v, II.32, 95. For Killigrew, Barker, and other women writers' commitment to chastity as a condition for authorship, see Carol Barash, *English Women's Poetry, 1649–1714* (Oxford, 1996), 165, 172, 196–7.

74. Manley, *London*, 518–19, 515 (citing Flecknoe).

75. Bodleian MS Firth c. 16, p. 115 (see *Scriblerian* 25 (1992–3), 3–4, for caution about the identification of the handwriting as Behn's); cf. Mulgrave's insult about royal mistresses who appear in so many lampoons that they are 'as Common that way as the other' (*Gyldenstolpe MS*, ed. Danielsson and Vieth, p. 249).

76. Dryden X.114, 193 (cf. Winn, *Dryden*, 206); Pamela's criticism of Mrs Oldfield's obscene epilogue to *The Distressed Mother* occurs in Richardson's sequel, sometimes known as *Pamela II*.

77. Cowley, *Poems*, ed. A. R. Waller (Cambridge, 1905), 448–53 (first published in Sprat's *History of the Royal-Society*); Behn, song in *The Dutch Lover* V.185 (but cf. I.6 for a slightly earlier version in a male voice); Rochester, 'A Young Lady to her Antient Lover' (30); Dryden, *Annus Mirabilis*, lines 109–110 (cf. 881, the wind whipping up the Fire 'like crafty Courtezans'); *Essay*, in *Works* XVII.31.

78. Otway, *Venice Preserved* III.i (ch. 4, section 4 above) and v.i (Antonio's 'Oh-h-h yet more! nay then I die, I die'); proviso scenes predated the Restoration, e.g. Shakerley Marmion's *A Fine Companion* (1633), III.v, f. F4 (adapted as *The Rampant Alderman* in 1685), but the low-level version in *Wandring Whore* predates their reintroduction into dramatic writing. Congreve's Mirabell only half-ironically prohibits his future wife to lead the kind of life imagined in *The Wandring Whore* and the lampoon, drinking lewd toasts to 'fellows' and recruiting a bawd-confidante to serve her promiscuity.

79. Phipps, *Buckingham*, 154 (attribution uncertain but 'possible'); Pepys, 21 Oct. 1666; 'Southesk' lampoon, n. 6 above. The combination of anger and incest would be particularly appropriate if Buckingham were the author, since he and Cleveland were first cousins and this seems to have prevented her from yielding to his passionate sexual requests. For 'exquisite', cf. the subtitle of all the *Wandring Whore* series and *Six Windmills*, 5 (books that will 'make the older sort [of prostitute] more exquisite'); Elizabeth Polwhele displays her lower-stratum expertise in *The Frolicks* when the genteel French bawd Procreate is denounced by an abusive nobleman as 'an exquisite and honorable procuress' (81).

80. Browne, *The Eighteenth Century Feminist Mind* (Brighton, 1987), 34, 40; author unknown, *The Night-Walkers Declaration, or the Distressed Whores Advice to all their Sisters* (1676), 5.

81. Rochester, 86; Smith (ed.), *Letters of Osborne*, 249; 'An Essay of Scandal', Wilson, 64. See p. 244 above for Marvell's Duchess of York.

82. Antonia Fraser, *The Weaker Vessel: Woman's Lot in Seventeenth-Century England* (1984), 407; see *DNB*, 'Sedley, Catherine', for other witticisms by her.

83. Dorset, *Poems*, 45–6; 'The Lie', *The Poems of Sir Walter Ralegh*, ed. Agnes M. C. Latham (1929), 45; Bryson, *From Courtesy to Civility*, 266. Cf. Wilson, 64 (the aging Cleveland 'shines i'th'dark like rotten wood by night'), 58 (an obscene lampoon on Catherine Sedley's miscarriage).

EPILOGUE. 'IN BATHSHEBA'S EMBRACES OLD': *PORNOGRAPHIA REDIVIVA* AT THE CLOSE OF CHARLES II'S REIGN

1. Harold Weber, *Paper Bullets* (Lexington, KY, 1996), 79 (Monmouth's female relative 'touching'), 194 (testimony at College's trial, and cf. 187 for sexual satire against him); Underdown, 291; *Calendar of State Papers, Domestic, Charles II, 1683*, 77 (and see Marvell, letter to William Popple, 14 April 1670, *Letters*, 317, for Charles himself recognizing the divorce possibility, as his own grandfather had done). For other oral comments on royal sexuality (especially the Duchess of Portsmouth) see Richard Greaves, *Secrets of the Kingdom: British Radicals from the Popish Plot to the Revolution of 1688–1689* (Stanford, CA, 1992), 10, 49, 364 n. 57, and for anti-Puritan allusions to 'Mother Cresswell' see *POAS* II.433–4, III.295, 384–5, 441, and n. 18 below; Mrs Cresswell remarks that the sexual adventures of certain courtiers

(unnamed, but unmistakably referring to Charles II and his son Monmouth) might 'afford matter for a Novel' (*Whores Rhetorick*, 182), and Behn's *Love-Letters*, an *à clef* fantasia on the scandals of Monmouth and his co-conspirator Lord Grey, seems to fulfil this hint.

2. Thompson, 128; Stephen College (alleged author), 'A Raree Show', *POAS* II.429 (cited from facsimile of old-spelling text); B. J. Rahn, '*A Ra-ree Show* – a Rare Cartoon: Revolutionary Propaganda in the Treason Trial of Stephen College', in Paul J. Korshin (ed.), *Studies in Change and Revolution: Aspects of English Intellectual History, 1640–1800* (Menston, 1972), 78–98; the anamorphic costume of the 'Leviathan' character combines the famous frontispiece to Hobbes's work with the cloak of female heads engraved by Abraham Bosse and Wenceslaus Hollar, interpreted as portraits of Thomas Killigrew in the British Museum catalogue of Prints and Drawings, *Satirical and Personal Subjects* I (1870), numbers 1021 and 1022 (the series later retitled Political and Personal Satires). Though he devotes an entire chapter of *Paper Bullets* to College's trial and his function as a plebeian scapegoat for Shaftesbury, Weber analyses neither the poem nor the engraving, which he refers to as a woodcut, as does the otherwise reliable Paul Hammond in 'King's Two Bodies' (ch. 5, n. 32 above), 32.

3. *POAS* I.426, cited ch. 1, section 2 above (cf. 425 for the alternative title and the ascription to Lacy, an embittered former lover of Gwyn's); for the apocryphal 'Protestant Whore' story, the starting-point of many studies both trivial and scholarly, see ch. 1, n. 19 above.

4. British Museum, Political and Personal Satires, cat. nos 1084 (horse) and 1085 (ass); Burke, 'Popular Culture in London', in Barry Reay (ed.), *Popular Culture in Seventeenth-Century England* (1985), 157; *The Poems of Jane Barker: the Magdalen Manuscript*, ed. Kathryn R. King (Oxford, 1998), 21, 31.

5. Hammond, 'King's Two Bodies', 38; Evelyn, *Diary*, ed. E. S. de Beer (Oxford, 1955), entry for 6 Feb. 1685; Nancy Klein Maguire, 'The Duchess of Portsmouth: English Royal Consort and French Politician, 1670–85', in R. Malcolm Smuts (ed.), *The Stuart Court and Europe: Essays in Politics and Political Culture* (Cambridge and New York, 1996), 247–73, esp. 258, 261 (even Monmouth has to apply to her for a submissive interview with his father), 268–71 (French ambassador's perception of her power and *crédit* with Charles); Folger Library MS L. C. 888, 17 Jan. 1679, ''tis said Articles are Drawne up Against the dutchess of Cleveland in like manner as was Against the dutchesse of Portesmouth' (I am grateful to Philip Hines for his expertise in this source, the Newdigate Newsletters).

6. *POAS* I.427; Hammond, 'King's Two Bodies', 30 (and 29 for other images of contagion); 'On the Dissolution of the Club of Voters, Anno 1678', in *The Second Part of the Collection of Poems on Affairs of State* (1689), 12; *Articles of High-Treason, and Other High Crimes and Misdemeanours, against the Dutchesse of Portsmouth* (1680), r–v. For Dryden's Cleopatra, see ch. 1, section 2 above.

7. 'The Lady of Pleasure', Nottingham University Library, Portland MS PwV 42, pp. 317, 323 (and cf. 318 and 322 for her career as a

cinder-woman); *POAS* 1.171, 420, 426. Anticipating the fight over Gwyn's honour, on 19 Feb. 1680 brawls broke out in the same playhouse after some gentlemen insulted Portsmouth, prompting Charles to close the theatre completely (Maguire, 'Portsmouth', 252).

8. Rochester, 91 (using the voice of Nell, Rochester complicates the dialogue by reminding us that Portsmouth had yet another rival, the duchesse de Mazarin); Marie de Sévigné, letter to Mme de Grignan, 11 Sept. 1675 (inventing an anti-Kéroualle speech for Nell, whose eccentric character pleases her); *A Pleasant Battle between Two Lap Dogs of the Utopian Court* (1681), 2–4.

9. Portland MS PwV 42, pp. 53–6; for the 1682 version, see *The Duchess of Portsmouth's Garland, from a MS in the Library of the Faculty of Advocates* ([Edinburgh], 1837), xii–xiv; George Savile, Marquis of Halifax, *Complete Works*, ed. Walter Raleigh (Oxford, 1912), 193 ('the immediate Hours of her Ministry'); all the citations in *OED* 'Prime Minister', 3 (referring to a British rather than foreign leader) post-date *POAS* 1.187 ('sodomy is the Prime Minister's sport', 1672) and this satire. For the term 'absolutism' (which I use to refer to what Charles's critics feared, rather than what he actually established) see John Miller, 'The Potential for "Absolutism" in Later Stuart England', *History* 49 (1984), 187–207. The petition genre continued to veer between political satire, underworld *pornographia*, and mockery of women's frustration (in the 1690s, when the female population still significantly outnumbered the male): see *The Petition of the Ladies at Court* (1681); *The Bully Whig, or the Poor Whores Lamentation for the Apprehending of Sir Thomas Armstrong* (1684); *An Answer to the Poor Whore's Complaint, in a Letter from a Bully Spark of the Town to Mistress Nell* (n.d.), despite an allusion to 'The Parliament of Women' not a political satire and not about Gwyn; *The Petition of the Ladies of London and Westminster, to the Honourable House of Husbands* (1693), *The Petition of the Widows* (1693), *A Humble Remonstrance of the Batchelors*, and *A New Bill* in response to the previous three, reprinted in the *Harleian Miscellany*, ed. William Oldys and Thomas Park, IV (1809), 326–9, 400–3, 437–41, 504–7.

10. Bodleian MS Don. b. 8, p. 504 (I am assuming, in default of other plausible candidates, that the rival is Portsmouth rather than the Queen).

11. Hammond, 'King's Two Bodies', 27 and n. (cf. 28 for Charles kneeling to kiss Portsmouth's 'book', i.e. the two-leaved book (ch. 1, n. 69 above), and *POAS* II.110 for his letting Danby 'lie with' him, Hammond's other example of 'homosexual' allegation); 'On the Duchess of Portsmouth', British Library MS Harl. 7317, ff. 67–68v; Lacy, *POAS* 1.426; Weil, 'Sometimes a Scepter Is Only a Scepter' (ch. 5, n. 43 above), 148. Interestingly, Louis XIV was also depicted as impotent in French satire, as Kathryn A. Hoffmann observes in *Society of Pleasures: Interdisciplinary Readings of Pleasure and Power during the Reign of Louis XIV* (New York, 1997), 155–8 (reacting against *preciosité*, 'political erotica reinstated the phallus [but] only to show its weakness', 157).

12. Hammond, 'King's Two Bodies', 31 and nn; Lorenzo conte Magalotti, *Relazioni d'Inghilterra, 1668 e 1688*, ed. Anna Maria Crinò (Florence, 1972), 88

(Charles's frolics, which reenact David dancing before the ark, and his bedroom familiarity with a good-looking sixteen-year-old messenger called 'Booton', 'fornito in qualche parte più da gigante che da ragazzo'); John Oldham, *Poems*, ed. Harold F. Brooks with Raman Selden (Oxford, 1987), 280, 345–50.

13. *POAS* II.179, 'A New Ballad' (in the same form that College later used for 'A Raree Show'), 291; 'Portsmouth's Return', Portland MS PwV 42, p. 160 (alluding to her very public affair with Vendôme during a trip to France, where she also acquires fashionable new dildos and vaginal sponges); 'On the Dissolution' (n. 6 above). In many cases the sodomitic theme is brought in merely so that *arse* can rhyme with *tarse*.

14. 329, 303–6, 315–20, 325–6, 305 ('this indulgence shalbe issued forth'); for buggering Parliament, see ch. 5, n. 32 above. For lengthy explications of politics in the play, see Richard Elias, 'Political Satire in *Sodom*', *Studies in English Literature* 28 (1978), 423–38; Weber, *Paper Bullets*, 112–27; Cameron McFarlane, *The Sodomite in Fiction and Satire, 1660–1750* (New York, 1997), 50–1, 81–92. Harold Love, 'But Did Rochester *Really* Write *Sodom*?', *Papers of the Bibliographical Society of America* 87 (1993), 326–9, 332–3, shows more convincingly that *Sodom* is an outsider's satire against the generic passive courtier, with no trace of any recognizable individuals – to which I would add the remarkable absence of allusions to Portsmouth and her 'French Arse'.

15. Weil, 'scepter', fig. 3.1 (1697 title-page); Annabel Patterson, 'Marvell and Secret History', in Warren Chernaik and Martin Dzelzainis (eds.), *Marvell and Liberty* (1999), 34–5, 32 (the 'philter' from Marvell's *Account of the Growth of Popery*); *The Secret History of the Reigns of K. Charles II and K. James II* (1690), 22–5, 49–50, 85–7.

16. *Absalom and Achitophel*, line 82; John Tatham, *The Rump* (1661), ch. 4, section 1 above; Elizabeth Bennett Kubek, '"Night Mares of the Commonwealth": Royalist Passion and Female Ambition in Aphra Behn's *The Roundheads*', *Restoration* 17 (1993), 88–103, esp. 97; Susan Staves, *Players' Scepters: Fictions of Authority in the Restoration* (Lincoln, NE, 1979), 170 (and see 171, 293–4, for other plays involving female rule, including Edward Howard's 1671 *The Six Days Adventure, or the New Utopia*); John P. Zomchick, 'Force, Contract, and Power in *The Woman-Captain*', *Restoration* 20 (1996), 181. Chernaik cites Howard's *Womens Conquest* (also 1671) as a particularly vivid case of the Amazonian leader 'giv[ing] Men sole supremacy' in the last act (199).

17. For chapbook, see n. 25 below; Bodleian MS Don. b. 8, pp. 129–32, compiled by an MP (Weil, 'Scepter', 141, samples the contents including a list of MPs who pimp for their own daughters); J. S., *A Discovery of Fonseca* (1682); Durfey, *The Commonwealth of Women* (performed August 1685, published 1686), an Amazonian community ruled by man-haters who all convert when the hero arrives; *Sylvia's Revenge, or a Satyr against Man, in Answer to the Satyr against Woman* (1692), and cf. Chernaik, 121 ('the poem offers no alternative to a state it presents as intolerable'); *Whores Rhetorick*, 154–6.

18. *Whores Rhetorick*, 26, 42 (and cf. 59, 'the administration of my Republick', 124, 'her Government'), 110, 217. For allusions to Cresswell's Whig clientele, see 28–9, 61–2, 190; for other gibes at the Puritans, see 2–3 (to preserve fairness, Dorothea's father is ruined *both* by Cromwellian sequestrations *and* by Charles's false promises to the Old Cavaliers), 148, 151, 183, 187, 207; the 'Statesman' remark echoes the ending of Rochester's 'Disabled Debauchee' ('Thus, Statesman-like, I'll sawcily Impose, / And, safe from Action, valiantly Advise', 45).

19. Weil, 'Scepter', 149–151, citing an Orientalizing polemic of 1681 and Sidney's posthumous 1698 *Discourses on Government*.

20. 124, 129–30, 126, 24; for an actual execution for petty treason see the case of the French midwife Marie Hobry (ch. 4, n. 49 above), analysed in Frances E. Dolan, *Dangerous Familiars: Representations of Domestic Crime in England, 1550–1700* (1994), 34–5, 37. To help integrate the plagiarism from Hall into the book, the preface ('To the injur'd Ladies') repeats the gynocratic argument and launches into a list of *femmes fortes*.

21. For hostility against Cellier in *The Solemn Mock Procession*, see p. 254 above, and for her institutional proposal (presented to James II, but presumably the result of earlier planning), see *A Scheme for the Foundation of a Royal Hospital*, in *Harleian Miscellany*, ed. Oldys and Park, IV.142–7.

22. Chernaik, 138 (Behn 1.33), 121 (Shadwell); Shadwell's *Scowrers* cited in Staves, *Players' Sceptres*, 135 (the entire chapter on 'Sovereignty in the Family' being relevant); Drake cited in Richard A. Barney, *Plots of Enlightenment: Education and the Novel in Eighteenth-Century England* (Stanford, CA, 1999), 278 (and see ch. 3, section 3 above for Hobbes); *The Petty Papers: Some Unpublished Writings*, ed. the Marquis of Lansdowne (1927), II.52–4; Onofrio Nicastro, *Henry Neville e l'isola de Pines, con testo inglese e la traduzione italiana di The Isle of Pines* (Pisa, 1988); *Rump* (1662), II.196 (cited ch. 3, section 1 above); Catherine Gallagher, 'Embracing the Absolute: the Politics of the Female Subject in Seventeenth-Century England', *Genders* 1 (1988), 33, 35–6. For asexual reproduction see my *One Flesh* (Oxford, 1987), 162–4 (Browne, de Foigny, Milton's fallen Adam), and Weber, *Paper Bullets*, 123–4.

23. For Heliogabalus see Hammond, 'King's Two Bodies', 31 and the *Vita* ascribed to Aelius Lampridius, ch. 3, n. 36 above.

24. Wilson, *Dramatic Works* (Edinburgh, 1874), 243–9, esp. 244, 246; Chappuzeau, *Cercle* and *Académie*, ed. in one volume by Joan Crow (Exeter, 1983), 45, 92–5 (notes cite borrowings from Chappuzeau's own translation of Erasmus's *Senatulus*); Dómhnall O Colmáin, *Párliament na mBan [i.e. Parliament of Women]* (c. 1697), ed. Brian O Cuív (Dublin, 1977); James Stewart, 'Párliament na mBan', *Celtica* 7 (1966), 135–41 (also identifies English and Dutch translations); Poullain, *De l'Egalité des deux sexes* (1673), in *The Equality of the Two Sexes*, transl. A. Daniel Frankforter and Paul J. Morman (Lewiston, NY, Queenston, Ont., and Lampeter, 1989), 176 (an anecdote ascribed to Cato); Chorier, *Satyra*, ed. Bruno Lavagnini (Catania, 1935), 276–7 (though this sounds like an authentic quotation, it appears in none of the Classical

sources for the life of Messalina, and Chorier himself uses the non-classical *senatulus* to refer to the episode).

25. 38, 41, 104–5, 112, 86; motifs directly translated from Erasmus include seniority awarded according to the number of children (8) and debate over admitting virgins (28) and wives married to eunuchs (33). For the Burton plagiarism (104–5) see *Anatomy* III.iii.4.2; for other Rabelaisian borrowings see n. 26 below (penile chitterlings) and 127–8 (Hans Carvel's ring). Dated references to preachers of the Civil War era (101) suggest that more earlier passages have been stolen than I have identified here. For later piracies of this magpie text, see the manuscript extract in Bodleian MS Rawl. Poet. 84, ff. 9-v, and the chapbook imitation in *Samuel Pepys's Penny Merriments*, ed. Roger Thompson (New York, 1977), 253–9.

26. 120, 124, 116, and cf. *CW* v.iv.344 (originally 'prizes', which adds a hint of naval plunder); the heavy-handed repetition suggests the brain-damaged Wycherley as author as well as source. The method chosen to seal the compact between high and low transcribes it to the lowest possible stratum; the parties excrete into each others hands, then 'shake fists together' with the proverbial words 'Shitten come Shites is the beginning of Love' (122, cf. Pepys 17 April 1662).

27. 1, 10 ('cackling' corresponds to the literal meaning of *caquet*, which suggests a lost French original), 52, 14, 5–6; though horns are eventually rejected as insignia, some 'women' argue to retain them as their most effective weapon, and they later vote to compensate the proprietress of Horn Fair at Cuckold's Point (133).

28. *Parliament*, 15–16, 46 (another sign of a French original, though Romance-language proverbs about sexuality circulated in England as we know from Pepys on the *cazzo dritto*, ch. 1, n. 25 above), 2; 'On the Dissolution' (the 'French blood' satire, n. 6 above), 12; Weil, 'Scepter', 151.

29. 25 (the 'Italian Padlock' or chastity belt often mentioned in *The Wandring Whore*, e.g. ch. 4, n. 26 above), 49, 84–5, 43, 4, 22, 29, 80 (Cavendish), 102 (Marguerite of Navarre), 136–7, 71–2, 133, 140; an episode from Aretino's *Ragionamenti* is translated on pp. 130–1, and the other libertine texts were discussed in great detail earlier (30–2).

30. 'The Lovers Elesium, or Foolls Paradice: A Dream', Magdalen College, Oxford, MS 343, f. 74v (orig. 'vallew').

31. A point I owe to Joanna Picciotto.

Index